THE FIRST 100 YEARS OF THE
DONS

The Official History of
Aberdeen Football Club
1903–2003

Jack Webster

Hodder & Stoughton

Copyright © 2002 Jack Webster

First published in Great Britain in 2002 by Hodder and Stoughton
A division of Hodder Headline

The right of Jack Webster to be identified as the Author of the Work
has been asserted by him in accordance with the Copyright, Designs
and Patents Act 1988.

1 3 5 7 9 10 8 6 4 2

A CIP catalogue record for this title is available from the British Library

ISBN 0 340 82344 5

Typeset in Photina by Palimpsest Book Production Limited,
Polmont, Stirlingshire

Printed and bound in Great Britain by
Clays Ltd, St Ives plc

Hodder and Stoughton
A division of Hodder Headline
338 Euston Road
London NW1 3BH

Contents

The author explains . . .   ix
Happy centenary!   xi

THE MODERN TALE

1	Nightmare nineties	3
2	'Smith must go!'	8
3	Miller steps in	12
4	Dick Donald	14
5	Stewart Milne	17
6	Tough times for Willie	21
7	Aitken takes over	24
8	Hampden joy at last	28
9	Welcome, Mr Hansen!	32
10	Goodbye Pittodrie?	39
11	Ebbe's second season	45
12	Pressure group	50
13	Cummings – and goings?	53
14	Talk of a coup	55

THE EARLY YEARS

| 15 | The black and gold | 69 |
| 16 | Philip in charge | 77 |

17   Donald Colman   81

18   Madam boots the bobby   85

19   Enter the Dons   91

20   Blackwell's umbrella   99

21   Hutton's run of success   104

22   The Jackson four   109

23   'Stick to singing, son!'   116

24   Benny – the greatest?   120

25   McLaren's luck   124

26   The great mystery   128

27   Smith, Cooper and McGill   133

28   Mills and Armstrong   137

29   Sadness in the sun   141

30   Hitler's war   147

POST-WAR TO THE GOLDEN AGE

31   Hamilton–Williams–Baird   155

32   Silver and gold   160

33   Scottish Cup at last!   165

34   Allister–Young–Glen   172

35   Pearson's magic   177

36   Courage of Hather   185

37   We are the champions!   192

38   Call this a bonus?   198

39   Golden Harry   205

40   Time runs out for Tommy   210

41   Takeover battle   216

42   'Cup-tie' McKay   224

43   Calder & Co.   232

CONTENTS

44 Firemen save the Cup   238

45 Ally's magic   248

46 McNeill takes over   254

47 Anniversary night   261

48 Enter the Golden Age   263

49 Liverpool lesson   270

50 Robson on the run   272

51 Pittodrie's greatest night   276

52 The glory of Gothenburg   285

53 Dons – number one in Europe   295

54 Requiem for Chris   305

55 The end for Fergie   309

ON REFLECTION

56 Fergie remembers   317

57 Arise, Sir Alex!   324

58 Miller looks back   329

59 Where are they now?   334

60 Remains of the day   346

61 Teddy Scott   349

62 We'll support you evermore!   353

63 Towards a new century . . .   361

    Centenary facts and figures   365

    Index   389

Acknowledgements

My thanks to Mr Alan Scott, managing director, for access to the *Aberdeen Journals* library and for use of photographs; also to head librarian Duncan Smith and printer Bruce Irvine for their willing efforts. My thanks to *Evening Express* sports editor Jim Strachan and to sports journalists Charlie Allan, Andrew Moir and Neil White.

A special word for Alastair Macdonald, former sports editor of the *Press and Journal*, who provided so much of the facts-and-figures section, as helpful as he was for the first edition of this book twenty-five years ago.

Down Pittodrie way, my gratitude to Linda Macdonald and so many of the staff, not least Dave Macdermid, Andrew Shinie and Caroline Calder; and in Glasgow, to Bob Todd, the computer wizard who guided me through the minefield of a bewildering technology.

Final thanks to those scores of people who gave me so much of their time to help reshape this book – and who find their own way into the centenary story of Aberdeen Football Club.

J.W.

Photographic Acknowledgements

The author and publisher would like to thank the following for permission to reproduce photographs:

Colorsport, Empics, Offside Sports Photography/Mark Leech, Popperfoto.

All other photos are from private collections.

The author explains . . .

In mysterious circumstances, the records of Aberdeen Football Club had disappeared by the mid 1970s, and the few remaining people who could give witness to the early story were in danger of going the same way!

As an avid Dons fan who was also a writer, it struck me that somebody had better salvage the story before it was too late. But my suggestion to the directors that I might write a book was met with a distinct lack of enthusiasm. 'You should wait till the centenary in 2003,' said the letter from chairman Dick Donald, to which I responded that some of us might not be around at that major milestone.

So, entirely of my own volition, I set out to catch as many old players and supporters as I could before they died. In the course of the research, I spent months in the vaults of the Public Library at Woodside, reading every day's edition of local newspapers from the reign of Queen Victoria in an attempt to piece the story together. It was a sweated labour of love, culminating in the first-ever book about the Dons, which I hoped would suitably mark the seventy-fifth anniversary of the club in 1978.

On that memorable August night, 2,000 supporters crowded into the Capitol Cinema for a launching celebration, with old films of the Dons, music with Jack Sinclair and his band and a glittering array of Dons players through the century, all the way to the young Willie Miller and Gordon Strachan.

One man came quietly upon the scene and said very little. The new manager, Alex Ferguson, had just been in charge of his first game and modestly told a BBC reporter that he could only try to emulate the feats of the past. Feats of the past? How could we have guessed on that rain-sodden night of celebration that this former Rangers player and recently sacked manager of St Mirren was about to create the real history of Aberdeen Football Club? Within a few years he had rendered my book so out of date that I had to re-write it.

Such is the fascination of history. On the field of play, the Golden Age of Fergie may now have come and gone but the story rolls on regardless, with new dramas unfolding as we finally arrive at the centenary.

I have re-cast the whole tale of Pittodrie, bringing it up to date in time for the massive celebrations of 2003, rounding off one hundred years in the life of Aberdeen Football Club.

JACK WEBSTER

Happy centenary!

In the great momentum of change, we reach the centenary of Aberdeen Football Club at a time when the grand old game itself is in a state of revolution. More immediately, down the familiar routes around King Street, those faithful fans who have come to regard Pittodrie as the spiritual home of their beloved Dons face the prospect of heading in another direction altogether.

So we meet the dawn of a second century, in which our children and grandchildren may know only the girders and shimmering blue lights of a futuristic stadium, pausing to hear tales of the great names and great days and nights that linger in the heads and hearts of the elderly.

As we celebrate the biggest birthday in the history of Aberdeen Football Club, it is time to let the future take care of itself and look back on the story of Pittodrie, in all its pain and pleasure, when the click of the turnstile propelled us into another world, away from everyday cares, an emotional roller-coaster that left memories to last us a lifetime.

The story takes us back to 1903, the year when the Wright Brothers took flight in the very first aeroplane from a field at Kitty Hawk, North Carolina; the year when Henry Ford created his motor company in Detroit; the year of a new-born babe in the Eltham district of London who would grow to be the comedian we all know as Bob Hope.

For all its apparent distance, the beginnings of Aberdeen Football Club are just a human lifetime away. It was then that a group of our ancestors gathered one evening in the Aberdeen Trades Hall and agreed to bring together three local football clubs and form them into a limited liability company, with a capital of £1,500. It was the first and rather belated bid to bring the city of Aberdeen into the mainstream of Scottish football. The club went on to reach the top league in the land from which it has never been relegated, an achievement shared with Rangers and Celtic.

The crowds of North-east men (it was mainly men in those days) who trekked down Merkland Road East in the cloth-capped uniform of the early twentieth century were soon generating enthusiasm for the team that would later, but not yet, come to be known as the Dons. For all their passion, those early supporters would go through a lifetime of attending Pittodrie without having as much as a single trophy to celebrate. What a tribute to their loyalty that they kept coming through those turnstiles for forty-three years before the first glimmer of silver appeared on the Aberdeen sideboard.

The dominance of the Old Firm in modern times is farcical enough but it hardly compares with the situation in the first half of the twentieth century. Consider this depressing fact – in the forty-three years from 1904 until 1947 the Scottish league championship was won by Motherwell in 1931 and by either Rangers or Celtic on every other occasion.

Even when the Dons did lay hands on a trophy – the League Cup of 1946 – it was a restricted competition, before Scottish football had fully re-established itself after the Second World War. Nevertheless, the opponents in the final were the mighty Glasgow Rangers, back at full strength and facing an Aberdeen team which read: Johnstone; Cooper, McKenna; Cowie, Dunlop, Taylor; Kiddie, Hamilton, Williams, Baird, McCall.

With the last kick of the game, George Taylor gave the Dons a 3–2 victory, as well as a boost towards the following season, when they won the Scottish Cup for the very first time. The first league championship was won in 1955 but there was another fifteen-year gap before the Scottish Cup reached Aberdeen for the second time. (That League Cup victory, incidentally, took place on a significant date – 11 May.)

If the Pittodrie faithful had been soundly educated in the art of patience, their reward would come in the late 1970s with the arrival of Alex Ferguson as manager. Who could have foreseen that the thirty-five-year-old Ferguson, just sacked by St Mirren, would lead Aberdeen into the Golden Age of Pittodrie, an eight-year spell when the Cocks of the North were not only the undisputed champions of Scottish football but a force to be reckoned with in European terms as well?

Whereas it had once been a rare feat to bring home a piece of Scottish silverware, the Dandy Dons entered the arena of national cup winners, all the way from Scotland to Russia, from the Baltic to the Mediterranean. When all the eliminating had been completed, who would have bet a brass farthing that Real Madrid, the greatest club name in the world, would be left to face the virtual unknowns of Aberdeen?

And beyond that, what form of insanity would have induced a forecast that the home-grown bunch from Pittodrie would not only beat the legendary Real to carry home the European Cup Winners' Cup, but go on to win the European Super Cup as well and be declared the number one team in Europe in 1983?

It may have been the stuff of *Boys' Own* dreamland but the hard fact is that we woke up one morning and found that it was all true. Alex Ferguson had indeed led the greatest Aberdeen team of all time to the ultimate drama in Gothenburg's Ullevi Stadium and set the seal on the finest moment in the club's history. Such is the magical uncertainty of life.

The incomparable Fergie moved south to lead Manchester United to even greater heights and prove himself the most successful manager in the history of British football. Back in the North-east of Scotland, he left a memory that lingers in the hearts and minds of a lucky generation. It created a high-level benchmark against which all else was liable to pale into disappointment. But for those of us who grouse and grumble, would we prefer it if the fairytale had never happened? So let us savour the Golden Age, not as an albatross around our necks but as an inspiration to believe that all things are possible in this bewildering world.

The fans who pounded their way to Pittodrie through all those years of no reward still glowed with memories of great players and memorable performances. They would rave about Donald Colman and Alec Jackson, Benny Yorston, Willie Mills and Matt Armstrong, just as a later generation would remember Charlie Cooke, Jimmy Smith and Zoltan Varga. All these men had one thing in common – none of them won a single prize as a Dons player.

Although we may seldom think of it in these terms, football is an art form through which we crave perfection. In the North-east of Scotland during the past century, that search has been focused on Pittodrie. But as we celebrate the centenary in 2003 with a range of attractions including a grand marquee dinner on that hallowed turf, it may be appropriate to take a nostalgic look at the place we call our football home. Pittodrie, they say, has outlived its day and faces major problems of re-development, although try telling that to many a diehard supporter for whom it is an unthinkable depart-ure. But the board's ambition is to move Aberdeen Football Club to a greenfield site at Kingswells, a vast complex with all the space no longer available around Pittodrie. The scheme involves public authorities and includes a soccer academy, training grounds, swim-ming pool, hotel and car parks.

In the excitement of a new century, a new beginning, it may be time to rise in one last burst of applause for good old Pittodrie, down there between King Street and the great North Sea, as they make plans to bring down the final curtain on our very own theatre of dreams.

THE
MODERN TALE

1
NIGHTMARE NINETIES

Ask a modern audience to nominate the worst decade in the history of Aberdeen Football Club and they would very likely plump for the 1990s. Success on the field was certainly a pale shadow of the 1980s and the fact that five managers went out through a revolving door within seven years creates a hint of farce, compounded by the worst financial position the club has ever known. If alliterations are the fashion, it would be tempting to call that decade the nightmare nineties.

In terms of achievement, however, there is one surprising fact to be faced. Leaving aside the golden age of Alex Ferguson, the 1990s ranks among the more successful decades in the story of Pittodrie. In a world of impatient demand for instant success, we have just been recalling the fate of our forefathers, many of whom witnessed the foundation of the club in 1903 and had to wait another forty-three years before the very first prize arrived at Pittodrie.

After four barren decades, the 1940s produced two cups. The fifties brought the club's first league championship and one League Cup but nothing else, except three unsuccessful Scottish Cup finals.

For all Aberdeen's rich playing talents, including Bobby Clark, Charlie Cooke, Jimmy Smith, Martin Buchan, Dave Smith and Arthur Graham, the sixties brought no prizes at all. In 1970, Buchan became the youngest-ever captain to lift the Scottish Cup after the memorable 3–1 victory over Celtic, but the seventies produced little more – the League Cup of 1976, during Ally MacLeod's brief tenure as manager, and the lesser Drybrough Cup. The seventies did, however, bring us Alex Ferguson and all that that would entail in the 1980s. When his memorable feats were over, sights were set so high that Fergie's successors were on a hiding to nothing.

Ian Porterfield took on the immediate mantle and failed. By 1988, it was the turn of Alex Smith, with co-manager Jocky Scott, to show what he could do. In the light of more recent events, we need to remind ourselves of Smith's record. In four years leading into the nineties, he brought home the Scottish Cup and Skol League Cup in season 1989–90 and was runner-up to Rangers in the league championships of 1989, 1990 and 1991. What would we give for that kind of success today, beating Celtic to the second spot for three years in succession?

Ah, but the rub was Rangers. Playing second fiddle to the Ibrox club was, at that time, an unthinkable affront. The supporters had not yet adjusted to the new reality and, by the following season, their impatience and anger brought Alex Smith the sack. The biggest frustration of all had come on the very last day of season 1990–91 when the Dons were due to play Rangers in Glasgow.

That season had started with the disorientation of witnessing an Aberdeen side without the great Willie Miller, a fixture in the first team for seventeen years and now gone, his playing days over. Willie was badly injured in a Scotland–Norway game at Hampden in 1989. He made a brief return for the Dons in the spring of 1990, but after testing out his pre-season fitness during the summer, he decided to call a halt at the age of thirty-five.

Strangely, Willie's debut game in 1973 had coincided with the last appearance of another memorable player, Zoltan Varga, the Hungarian whose silken skills with a ball were among the most exquisite ever seen at Pittodrie. Another Gothenburg hero, Neil Simpson, had gone to Newcastle and Charlie Nicholas, having played his part in defeating his beloved Celtic in the 1990 Cup final, had followed his heart and returned to Parkhead.

Paul Mason remained a valued member of the team, Hans Gillhaus was still around and was joined by yet another Dutchman, Peter van de Ven. Against Rangers in a league game at Pittodrie, goalkeeper Theo Snelders had been carried off with a broken cheekbone after a horrendous collision with Ally McCoist, and the club sought a replacement in Andy Dibble from Manchester City. After a dramatic penalty shoot-out in the 1990 Scottish Cup final, the Dons were once more in the cup winners' competition of blessed memory but Dibble was not eligible for Europe. After beating Famagusta of Cyprus, the Dons went out to Legia of Warsaw, with Michael Watt in goal.

Through all this, the Dons had topped the league table at one stage of that 1990–91 season, with Eoin Jess emerging as the rising star. But they fell away and Rangers seemed *en route* to another league title – except that the Ibrox club, too, began to slip. Coincidentally, the Dons found a new lease of life and, with only two games to go, they were within two points and four goals of the leaders.

In their second-last game, they went behind to St Johnstone but fought back to win. On the same afternoon, Rangers were being trounced 3–0 at Motherwell. The Dons were now equal on points and had a two-goal advantage. How the fortunes of football can swing! Almost unbearably, the league title would be resolved in the last game of the season between Rangers and Aberdeen at Ibrox. Rangers had to win; the Dons needed only a draw.

In 1980, Fergie's team had come from far behind to pip Celtic at the post for the very first triumph of that new age. Could the Dons now repeat the dose for Rangers? The northern legion arrived at Ibrox full of quiet apprehension. Perhaps the lesser demand of a draw was not such a good incentive after all.

Theo Snelders was out through injury and Michael Watt was plunged into the maelstrom which is Ibrox Stadium on a day like this. He did not have long to wait to see the shape of things to come. Rangers went on the charge from the first whistle and Watt was so severely clobbered by Mark Hateley that he didn't fully recover for the rest of the game. At the other end, Jim Bett and Peter van de Ven had excellent chances to score but Mark Hateley gave Rangers victory with a goal either side of the interval and the title remained at Ibrox.

There was a keen sense that Aberdeen had been steam-rollered out of that championship, not just by the Rangers players but by the irresistible might of the Ibrox machine. Much has been written and said about the friction between Aberdeen and Rangers and at least some of it dates from that May day of 1991.

The match was surrounded by palpable aggression, and manager Alex Smith recalls that Brian McGinlay said it was the most hostile he had ever refereed. There were those who vowed they would never set foot inside that stadium again – and some never have.

Throughout the years of Alex Ferguson, the Rangers support had found that their right to victory was not so divine as they imagined. The lad from their own doorstep of Govan, himself a former Rangers player, had shown that the Old Firm could be tackled, tamed and beaten on a regular basis, not just at Pittodrie but right in the football heart of Glasgow. It went so badly against the grain that there would have to be retribution one day and now that Fergie was gone, the account was being squared.

There are supporters throughout Scotland, not just in Aberdeen, who will admit that they have been successfully intimidated out of visiting Ibrox Stadium. It is a sad reflection on the state of society, especially when you remember those days before segregation when Aberdeen and Rangers fans stood side by side on the terracing and cheered their respective teams without the venom that contorts the face of football today.

Alex Smith and the team had come so close to the victory that might well have set them on the road to a new age of success. But instead of being able to claim every one of the main honours in his first three years, guaranteeing him at least survival if not the mantle of a hero, Smith faced a new season with the simmering frustration of recent failure. It became the prelude to a dip in performance and his final exit from the portals of Pittodrie.

The Dons embarked on the new season with the early departure of popular full-back David Robertson who was on his way to Ibrox of all places. Smith signed Paul Kane from Oldham and Gary Smith from Falkirk but results were going so badly that his days at Pittodrie were clearly numbered. How he must have longed for those earlier times when manager Jimmy Philip survived the twenty-one years from 1903 to 1924 without having won a single trophy; nor did anyone think of sacking him. Under no cloud at all, he just resigned, to be followed by Paddy Travers who managed for fourteen years with no more to show for them than an unsuccessful appearance in the Scottish Cup final of 1937.

We live in different times. A section of the crowd was determined that Alex Smith must go, paying little heed to his considerable achievements and deep knowledge of the game. He had the backing of his number two, Jocky Scott, a great favourite in his playing days at Aberdeen. In all truth, while the crowd would claim their own Jocky, they had never quite taken to Smith and, chanting and demonstrating, they were in no doubt about who they wanted in his place.

2
'SMITH MUST GO!'

ALEX SMITH came from a coal-mining community near Stirling. He played for the local juveniles, as did his close friend Billy Bremner. When Bremner went to Leeds United, Smith went to Kilmarnock. Later, he played for Stirling Albion and Stenhousemuir where, in 1969, he became the first-ever manager before Bill Shankly's brother Bob invited him to manage Stirling Albion.

At Albion, Alex Smith nurtured such talents as John Colquhoun, Willie Irvine and Brian Grant, knowing that every year, for the club to survive, he had to bring on a player who could be sold for upwards of £60,000. In one such deal, he sold Brian Grant to Aberdeen for £35,000, with another £25,000 to come when he reached forty first-team appearances.

Stepping into the Premier arena in 1986, he led St Mirren to a famous victory over Dundee United in the 1987 Scottish Cup final, *en route* to the European Cup Winners' Cup competition. He brought in £400,000 for the sale of Steve Clark to Chelsea and £920,000 when Ian Ferguson joined Rangers, before running into some conflict at Love Street.

Just as Alex Ferguson was sacked by St Mirren in the spring of 1978, so was Alex Smith sacked by the same club in the spring of 1988. As a student of Fergie, he had hardly missed a European night at Pittodrie during the golden years and now he was being invited to take over from Ian Porterfield as manager of Aberdeen, arriving in time to conclude the transfer of Jim Leighton to Manchester United for £500,000. When offered the job, he invited two former

Dons, Jocky Scott and Drew Jarvie, to join him from their management roles with Dundee.

In view of both sackings, the board of St Mirren must have felt a little foolish one week in 1990 when Ferguson won the FA Cup with Manchester United at Wembley and Smith led Aberdeen to victory in the Scottish Cup final at Hampden. A sacking from Love Street began to look like a pre-requisite for success.

Having learned to delegate, Alex Smith left the immediate coaching to Jocky Scott and Drew Jarvie, and assessed the Pittodrie strengths, from Miller, McLeish, McKimmie and Bett to Connor, Grant, Nicholas and David Robertson. He went out to buy Theo Snelders, Paul Mason and Hans Gillhaus and introduced youngsters Eoin Jess, Stephen Wright, Greg Watson, Scott Booth, Andy Roddie and Michael Watt. It was an impressive array of talent, with Gillhaus in particular, signed from PSV Eindhoven for £650,000, stirring excitement.

Events caught up with Alex Smith, however, and he well remembered how it all unfolded: 'The trouble began at Pittodrie in September 1991 when we played BK Copenhagen in the UEFA Cup. I had appointed Willie Miller as coach and had the idea that I would manage for a few years until Willie was ready for the job. Alternatively, he could have gone to another club before returning to Pittodrie.

'Willie was in the dug-out that night when Copenhagen scored with just four minutes to go. Suddenly I heard a single voice shouting "There's only one Willie Miller!" and then the crowd took up the chant. It became "Smith must go!"'

He had also intended to bring Alex McLeish into the management team, reviving the Miller–McLeish partnership, which might eventually have done wonders for the Dons. But he was not to be given the time. Fan-power was on the rampage. By the turn of the year, allowing nothing for a mounting injury list, the chants were augmented by placards, spelling out the message.

The Pittodrie board more or less bowed to the pressure, glad to get the fans off their backs, and appointed the most important player in the entire history of the club. Willie Miller was the strong, silent type at that time, far removed from the more extrovert and loquacious character he would become in his radio incarnation of later years. Surely, the argument went, Willie was the man of destiny who would carry his proven strength of character from the field of play to the role of manager, a natural inheritor of the job once perfected by his fellow-Glaswegian and former mentor who was now rising to even greater heights at Old Trafford.

Theory does not always work in practice, however, and there were those with misgivings about exposing their greatest legend to the risks of subsequent failure and humiliation which come so regularly to football managers these days. But there was a belief that Willie Miller might just be the exception, a matter that time alone would judge.

Willie had his private thoughts: 'Before he was sacked, Alex Smith asked me to become coach to the first team. Then he was gone and I was called in to be offered his job. Of course you have doubts in a situation like that but it was a challenge I could not turn down. I thought Alex's sacking was an injustice but football can be an unjust business.'

Alex Smith still believes Willie had the same potential as a manager that he had as a player and could have matched the managerial career of Alex McLeish, who strode on from Motherwell to Hibs and then to Rangers.

Smith also believes there was enough talent in that unhappy period at Pittodrie to challenge their predecessors of the 1980s. You began to see his point when scanning the names – Theo Snelders, Alex McLeish, Jim Bett, Stewart McKimmie, Hans Gillhaus, Bobby Connor, Paul Mason, Willem van der Ark, David Robertson, Eoin Jess and Scott Booth, with Willie Miller trying to overcome injury.

But Smith was on his way, bitterly disappointed that the unsavoury business had ended as it did and annoyed that too many people had listened to the outside voice of what he knew to be an organised group. (He claimed photographic evidence of one surprising ring-leader.) He went on to manage Clyde and Dundee

United, and his memories remain warm: 'Aberdeen was an exceptionally good club to manage, with the best quality of players I had experienced. With their youth policies, I can see the New Firm of Aberdeen and Dundee United emerging again.'

With a fresh and popular face and a new beginning, there was a spirit of hope and optimism around Pittodrie. The board were now spared the wrath of the supporters, who had achieved what they wanted and could hardly, for a decent passage of time at least, pursue and pillory the directors for a lack of response and imagination.

3

MILLER STEPS IN

WILLIE MILLER settled into the manager's chair and made his first deal when he bought Mixu Paatelainen from Dundee United for £400,000. In the summer of 1992 he brought in his old sparring partner and Celtic hero Roy Aitken as a player and assistant manager, and signed two more players who would make a significant contribution to the Pittodrie fortunes.

Duncan Shearer and Lee Richardson both came from Blackburn Rovers. The Fort William-born Shearer had made his main impact with Swindon Town, where his scoring feats should have attracted Scottish attention sooner than they did. The Dons landed him for £300,000. The first player to leave in Willie Miller's time as manager was the mercurial Hans Gillhaus. With the skills of an artist, an in-form Gillhaus would always have found a place in the Aberdeen team but he had clearly made up his mind to go.

In his first full season as manager, Miller offered a serious challenge to Rangers, with Shearer scoring an impressive twenty-eight goals. The Dons reached the Skol League Cup final and at Hampden Shearer scored an equalising goal to put the match into extra time. Just six minutes from a penalty shoot-out, the Aberdonian defector to Ibrox, David Robertson, crossed a ball that was firmly mis-directed into his own net by the hapless Gary Smith. Having thus lost out in the Skol Cup, the Dons were destined once more to finish as runners-up to Rangers in the League – but the two clubs were due to meet yet again in the Scottish Cup final.

With Hampden in the midst of re-development, the final was held at Celtic Park on 29 May 1993. Rangers were in full flight and in the mood to complete their first treble in fifteen years. Murray and the inevitable Hateley put them ahead and although Lee Richardson pulled one back for the Dons, the Cup was off to Ibrox.

Because of Rangers' league championship, the consolation for Aberdeen was a place in the Cup Winners' Cup, always a name to stir northern hearts. In the event, after trouncing Valur of Iceland by an aggregate of 7–0, they failed at the second hurdle and went out to Torino of Italy on an aggregate of 5–3.

Aberdeen had been planning a gigantic new grandstand for the beach end of Pittodrie, and that end of the ground was out of use throughout 1992–93 as building work proceeded. Gradually the Richard Donald Stand took shape and was built in time for Dick to witness the final result. His health had been failing for some time and he died on Hogmanay Day 1993. The tribute became a memorial to the club's greatest-ever chairman. Ironically, for one whose shrewd business sense had kept Aberdeen Football Club out of debt for all those years, that stand bearing Dick Donald's name put the club into the red for the very first time. The cost of £3.5 million was partly offset by a grant but Dick Donald would still be turning in his grave if he had seen the way clubs including Aberdeen were flirting with debt.

The new stand was high and impressive, with a spectacular view of the pitch, albeit from behind a goal, yet there is little doubt that this mighty creation, for all its virtues, unbalanced the equilibrium of Pittodrie. The focal point of a football ground is best placed around the halfway line but now there was a lop-sided effect which came to symbolise some of what was happening at the club.

The main noise of the crowd was coming inevitably from behind the beach-end goal. The old grandstand on Pittodrie Street was taking on a second-rate appearance and the stadium itself began to exude a sense of its own discomfort.

4
DICK DONALD

DICK DONALD had laid the foundations of Aberdeen Football Club's rise to the heights of European glory, and his death brought to an end a sixty-five-year connection with Pittodrie which was without equal in length or significance.

His failing health included a stroke when he was eighty, before Alzheimer's set in. Sadly he was not well enough to attend the opening of the Richard Donald Stand. The ceremony was performed by the Princess Royal shortly before he died. But what a legacy he left – his chairmanship transported the Pittodrie experience from domestic struggle to unthinkable triumph on a world-wide stage. He and his vice-chairman, Chris Anderson, had the vision, courage and magical way with finance to put Aberdeen at the forefront of football, with the first all-seated, all-covered stadium in Britain, while keeping their bank balance in the black.

The story of the Donald family started humbly enough in the east end of Aberdeen from where Dick's father, James F. Donald, emerged to capitalise on a modern craze by opening Donald's Dancing Academy in North Silver Street. He lived above the premises and that was where he reared his four sons.

One by one, James, Herbert, Dick and Peter joined their father and learned to teach dancing. When father sensed the next entertainment craze was going to be moving pictures, he struck the forefront once more and built a chain of a dozen or so cinemas, with memorable names such as the Capitol, Majestic, Kingsway, Astoria, Belmont, Queens and Cinema House, and the largest of all, the 2,500 seater City Cinema in George Street. Add to that His Majesty's

Theatre and the ice-rink in Spring Garden and you begin to get the picture of the Donald empire. Dick's brother Peter went to London and became chairman of the Howard and Wyndham theatre chain and the family commanded respect as far away as Hollywood, where the legendary Sam Goldwyn would drop everything to entertain a visiting Donald from Aberdeen.

Developing as a footballer, Dick was signed by the Dons in 1928 for a career that stretched over ten years, with a break at Dunfermline. In the 1940s, the shrewdness of the young businessman was recognised by the Pittodrie board and he was called upon to join the directors. It was the beginning of a gradual course towards chairmanship and all the heady success that culminated in the European Cup Winners' Cup triumph over Real Madrid in 1983.

But peaks don't last for ever and towards the end of the eighties the Dons suffered not only the departure of Alex Ferguson but the tragic death of vice-chairman Chris Anderson. Dick Donald was soon past his best and an historic era was clearly at an end. The funeral service for Dick Donald, held in St Mark's Church, next door to His Majesty's Theatre, drew the full panoply of football figures, from old Dons George Hamilton and Archie Baird to directors and managers of all the leading clubs.

Touchingly, the Dons squad of the time paid their own quiet tribute, surveyed by such former managers as Jimmy Bonthrone, Ally MacLeod, Billy McNeill, Alex Smith and Jocky Scott. And who had more right to be a pall-bearer than the former hero of Pittodrie, Alex Ferguson, to whom Dick Donald became a substitute father and guiding hand for personal and professional conduct? It was a fitting end to a wonderful life.

With the death of Dick Donald, his son Ian took over as chairman, with Aberdeen stockbroker Denis Miller as vice-chairman and well-known Aberdeen lawyer Gordon Buchan on the board.

Growing up in the shadow of his father, never an easy role, Ian Donald had more of a footballing pedigree than people realised. Born into that well-known family, he had the rhythms not only of a dancing father but an even more distinguished dancing mother,

Betty Shaw, a popular professional who used to appear with visiting companies at His Majesty's.

Ian went to Gordon's College, captained the Scottish schoolboys and was pursued by Manchester United from the age of fifteen but completed his highers before joining up at Old Trafford in 1969, in the days of Bobby Charlton, George Best and fellow-Aberdonian Denis Law. He had his best spell in the United first team around 1972 but eventually returned to the family business. He was also involved in hotels with his sister Sheila and her husband, Stewart Spence. They owned the Atholl, the Queens and the Belvidere before consolidating with the Marcliffe-at-Pitfodels.

A more articulate man than his father, Ian became managing director of James F. Donald, which had moved from cinemas to pubs, clubs and bingo halls. He also followed his father to Pittodrie where he was a director before the age of thirty, in the early days of Alex Ferguson.

As chairman, he sought to further strengthen the board by co-opting Scotland's biggest private house-builder, Stewart Milne, a man who had been around the fringes of the club for some time and who was delighted to have a more official connection. In view of the crucial role he would soon be playing in the future of Aberdeen Football Club, he needs a chapter to himself.

5

STEWART MILNE

I F Stewart Milne was a newcomer to the Aberdeen boardroom, he was not exactly a stranger to the environs of Pittodrie. He had scarcely got to know Dick Donald in person but his company had won the contract to build the Richard Donald Stand.

There was no small irony in the fact that he had been the main beneficiary of that £3.5 million contract which put the Dons into real debt for the first time. Soon it would be his responsibility to rescue the club from that plight and to see they did not land in even deeper financial trouble. With the benefit of hindsight, he might have tempered his pleasure at becoming a director of the club and considered more carefully the step he was taking.

So who was this modest little man who would instigate dramatic events in the history of Aberdeen Football Club? And how did he appear on the scene? Stewart Milne was born at Tough, near the village of Alford, in 1950. His father, who was engaged in draining and ditching at farms around the district, didn't marry until the age of 53, thereafter producing five sons, to whom he was more of a grandfather than a father figure.

Young Stewart left Alford School for Aberdeen at fifteen to become an electrician with Andrew McRobb. After five years he and a friend went into partnership as plumbers and electricians but they went their separate ways and Stewart established his own business with three employees, involved in kitchen and bathroom conversions.

By 1975 he had formed Stewart Milne Construction, bringing his brother Hamish into the business. Hamish had gone to be a teacher in Cowdenbeath but now he was recruited for his mathematical brain to look after the company's finances. The third key figure was Hugh Mackay, who remains with the company to this day. They concentrated on house-building, timber-frame production and commercial development, and expanded to a payroll of 1,300 people.

Formerly based at Hartington Road, Stewart Milne bought a fifteen-acre croft at Westhill in 1975, adjacent to the plush head-quarters of today, and developed the business from there. The little byre that once housed the cattle became the construction factory. By the end of the century the firm had three major bases, one at Westhill in Aberdeen and one in Oxford, each producing 6,000 houses per year, and at Tannochside (Glasgow). The annual turnover exceeded £170 million, with profits of over £8.5 million. Stewart Milne personally owns 95 per cent of the business.

So how did he arrive at Pittodrie? A promising footballer himself, playing for Inverurie Locos in the 1960s, he nevertheless chose to devote himself exclusively to business. But once he had three sons of his own, growing up in their sumptuous home in Bieldside, he found himself running a boys' team. It was not until the lads were older that he finally managed to become a regular attender at Pittodrie. By then he was involved in sponsorship and corporate entertaining but was still an outsider when his company won the contract to build the Richard Donald Stand.

The invitation to become a director was accepted in a mood of adventure but he was soon to realise that he was entering a type of business operation very different from the one that had rocketed him to success. Unlike his accustomed strategy, he found that foot-ball operated on a day-to-day, week-to-week basis of short-term planning, which he found frustrating in the extreme. As he learned the ropes, however, he could see that football was about to enter an era close to revolution. It had already started in England but many Scottish clubs were slow to recognise what lay round the corner. Whereas football had always controlled its destiny from the inside, external forces were now at work, which would change all that.

Television was set to become the major factor, along with the Bosman ruling on players' contracts and the consequent appearance of that new breed of middleman, the football agent, who might range from legitimate negotiator to parasitic vulture.

Aberdeen Football Club had to move forward if there was to be any hope of re-establishing itself in European football. It must also play its part in changing the face of Scottish football. As a first step, the club became a principal instigator of revamping the Scottish Premier League into an entirely new organisation in which the top clubs gained control of their own affairs. Under the previous umbrella of the Scottish Football League, the tail could regularly wag the dog, with the lesser lights among the forty Scottish clubs simply exercising their majority vote.

So the big guns formed their own body, with Robert Wilson (later Lex Gold) as chairman, Roger Mitchell as chief executive and three board members, including Stewart Milne from Pittodrie. There was an early financial effect – those top teams had previously shared between £2 million and £3 million per annum of outside money (television, radio and sponsorship), but now they were sharing nearly £20 million.

This would be no more than a beginning. Some of the change would depend on the aspirations of Rangers and Celtic who, although failing to sit down and discuss it with the rest of the clubs, were making noises about joining other leagues, the English Premiership being the preferred option.

Public opinion was divided on the possible loss of the Old Firm but Stewart Milne shared the view of many other Aberdeen supporters that the absence of Rangers and Celtic might be no bad thing for Scottish football. In face of the power imbalance that had lasted throughout the entire twentieth century, the prospect of Rangers and Celtic taking flight to another football planet at least gave hope of an equitable future in Scotland. Any one of eight teams, competing on a level playing-field, could reasonably hope to win a prize. In reality, it was unlikely to happen but those who could recall that farcical domination by the Old Firm – and it was on course to happen again – were quick to suggest that a repetition of such monotony would threaten Scottish football with death from boredom.

Back in Aberdeen, the directors secluded themselves in the Marcliffe-at-Pitfodels one day to sort out the future of the club. That day ended with agreement about development plans and the fact that somebody had to take charge of it all. That person, they decided, would be Stewart Milne, who agreed to take on the role of executive vice-chairman, on the understanding that the club would begin to think in terms of a full-time chief executive.

Pushing ahead with an ambitious three-year expansion plan, he aimed to double the turnover. But the club was still buying players it could not afford and Ian Donald became deeply uncomfortable with the debt, concluding that the original plan was a disaster. He stepped aside to let Milne take over as chairman.

6
TOUGH TIMES
FOR WILLIE

Now in his second full season as manager, Willie Miller had to devote himself to the task of challenging the dominance of Rangers and seeing if he could better the recent achievement of landing the runner-up spot in the League. His ill-fated predecessor, Alex Smith, had taken on Rangers and Celtic in Glasgow in one season, beating them both and bringing home the Scottish Cup and the Skol Cup. Willie Miller had already tried to repeat those triumphs – and suffered defeat on both occasions.

Consequently, he entered season 1993–94 with much to prove. Once again he managed to snap at the heels of Rangers, but once again landed in that runner-up position and this time without a Cup final to contest. By now, Willie was sampling managerial stress. Paul Mason had gone back to England (Ipswich paid £400,000) while Joe Miller returned from Celtic for £250,000.

The outlook seemed promising when the Dons went top of the League but it did not last. The galling fact was that Rangers were by no means at their best that season and if the Dons, who were now the main challengers, could only have achieved the same points as the previous season, they would have been league champions this time round.

There was further gnashing of teeth in the Tennents Scottish Cup when the Dons, playing Dundee United in the semi-final, were just two minutes away from victory at Hampden when Welsh snatched an equaliser. United won the replay and went on to win the Cup. Morale in the Pittodrie crowd was dipping but the reserve of goodwill from an adoring public ensured that Willie Miller had maximum support from the fans in his bid to prove himself an able manager.

'Being put out of the Scottish Cup by Dundee United, when we were so close to the final, was a turning point for me,' Miller reflects. 'I decided to revolutionise the playing staff and see if I could take the team forward. It didn't work out.

'We were trying to replace players such as Alex McLeish and me and thinking we could find them in Scotland, but that was a struggle. Having brought in Lee Richardson, Billy Dodds, John Inglis and Peter Hetherstone among others, I was also bringing through youngsters including Stephen Glass.'

Changes were afoot for season 1994–95 when the Premier League went from twelve to ten teams and the relegation battle was to be spiced up with the introduction of play-offs. In future, the First Division champions would be promoted and the Premier League's bottom team would go down, while the second-bottom team would face a play-off against the First Division's runner-up.

It was, of course, unthinkable that any of this would be of concern to the Dons of Pittodrie. They were, after all, the only team apart from the Old Firm that had never been relegated. It was a distinction they would surely never surrender. Similarly, they stood proudly shoulder to shoulder with Rangers and Celtic as the only Scottish teams to have carried off European trophies.

Change was in the wind at Pittodrie, with the robustly effervescent Lee Richardson returning to England, Mixu Paatelainen heading for Bolton and Jim Bett for Iceland while Alex McLeish, Willie Miller's stalwart partner through the glory years, took his first manager's job at Motherwell. Among the arrivals, Billy Dodds cost £800,000 from Dundee, Peter Hetherstone £200,000 from Raith Rovers, Colin Woodthorpe £400,000 from Norwich and John Inglis the same sum from St Johnstone.

Having been second to Rangers in the League in an incredible five out of six seasons, rumblings of discontent began to be heard at Pittodrie. Elimination from the early round of the UEFA Cup at the hands of Skonto Riga of Latvia sparked a sense of crisis.

Adding insult to injury, erstwhile hero Alex McLeish brought Motherwell to Aberdeen in search of their first Premier League win in thirty visits – and they achieved it. Miller and McLeish were now rivals. McLeish would proceed to advance his managerial career, gaining further kudos in 1998 as boss of Hibernian. In contrast, his old playing partner presided over the Dons' descent to bottom place in the ten-team league. Relegation was not a word that had previously existed in the Aberdonian vocabulary, but now the club hovered perilously close to that reality.

Further defeats brought the whole sorry matter to a head. The doubts and fears of wise old owls had been justified and Aberdeen supporters had to face the unpalatable fact that their all-time hero, the incomparable Willie Miller, was the latest casualty in what was becoming an unacceptable decline. From the heights of Europe just a decade earlier, this was a sad impasse.

But the braying force of fan-power that had hounded Alex Smith to the exit door three years earlier and brought Miller to the manager's chair would have been hypocritical this time around. The board had answered public demand so the public must now take its share of responsibility. Willie Miller's departure in February 1995 was observed largely in respectful silence, ensuring that the simmering frustration would have to find a target elsewhere. In three years, Willie had won nothing but was twice runner-up to Rangers in the League and runner-up in the Scottish Cup and League Cup.

If the Dons were truly destined for relegation, at least the galling task of taking them down would not be borne by the club's greatest living legend.

7
AITKEN TAKES OVER

S o Willie Miller was gone from Pittodrie, saddened by his departure but taking a philosophical view of the experience: 'As a
manager, I didn't have the kind of players we had in the 1980s. We
had nobody like Alex McLeish, Jim Bett or myself. So it all came to
an end after three years and latterly there was disagreement.

'In that position you are under pressure and need one hundred
per cent backing from the board. I didn't feel I had that backing. I
suppose every manager thinks it is an injustice to be sacked though
I wouldn't say I was bitter about it. But it is certainly one of the
worst days of your life! I'm realistic enough to know that these things
happen in football.'

There were still twelve games to go, for which assistant
manager Roy Aitken was given full charge on a caretaker basis.
But still the crazy pattern continued. The players gave Roy a
splendid baptism with victory over Rangers at Pittodrie but were
then knocked out of the Scottish Cup by Stenhousemuir. Was
there no end to cruelty?

After a temporary revival, the Dons were back at the bottom of
the table by the end of April, four points adrift of Dundee United
with only three games to play. What a plight for the two teams that
had cracked the domination of the Old Firm in the 1980s and were
proud to call themselves the New Firm. Even Partick Thistle were
now five points better off than the Dons.

All seemed lost for Aberdeen as they entered those final days of
season 1994–95. A visit to Tynecastle was not a heartening prospect
yet two goals from Billy Dodds brought precious victory.

The last home game of the season brought Dundee United to Pittodrie for a nail-biting encounter. If the Dons could make ninth position, they would live to fight in the play-offs. The excitement over this dire situation, a wholly new experience for players and fans alike, was more suited to former triumphs at the top of the table than a rearguard action at the bottom. But at least it stirred enough interest to bring out an incredible crowd of over 20,000, who rallied round to give their team one last burst of vocal support. After all, there was a matter of Aberdonian pride at stake.

Pittodrie was alive with atmosphere on that May day in 1995, when the name of Houdini was much in mind. Could the Dons really escape the ultimate disgrace? Well, Billy Dodds, a great favourite with the crowd, scored first and created a second for Duncan Shearer. A future Pittodrie player, Robbie Winters, pulled one back for United but the Dons gained those valuable three points, which took them clear of the bottom position. There was still one more league game to play, against Falkirk, who were then in the top half of the table. The mathematicians told us that, if the Dons could win and Hearts lost to Motherwell, they would have climbed totally out of trouble, even beyond the play-offs. Dream on, Houdini! Stephen Glass and Scott Thomson certainly responded to the 7,000 fans who travelled south to roar the Dons to a 2–0 victory. But Motherwell beat Hearts and plunged Aberdeen right back into the play-off slot.

The deciding home-and-away encounter would be against a Dunfermline team that had narrowly missed automatic promotion and was playing with confidence. Once again the crowd topped the 20,000 mark for the vital home leg and once again Stephen Glass, emerging as one of the brightest talents seen at Pittodrie in years, put the Dons ahead. A Duncan Shearer double gave them a 3–1 victory. Surely they would now survive in the top flight, depriving Dunfermline of promotion.

For the second leg at East End Park, the fans were out in force once more and it took a Billy Dodds goal just after the interval to convince them that all was well. Joe Miller and Stephen Glass wrapped up a 6–2 aggregate. Aberdonian nerves had seldom been stretched this far, promoting prayers that it would not happen again. For the moment at least, there was the ecstasy of sheer relief, albeit a different kind of celebration from those that had become the accepted habit of the previous decade.

Having negotiated the route to escape, Roy Aitken was rewarded with the manager's job, bringing in an old Pittodrie favourite, Tommy Craig, as his assistant.

In the perpetual comings and goings of footballers, the Dons lost talented full-back Stephen Wright to Rangers, a move which deprived the North-east of a gifted player and did absolutely nothing for the lad's own career. Where have we heard that story before? Down the years it had been a habit of the Ibrox club to fashion success with a double-edged device. Apart from the Catholic boys, who were not welcome anyway, they could take first pick of Scotland's young talent, those lads being naturally attracted to the country's most powerful club. Any who happened to escape the Ibrox net, to be nurtured by another Scottish club, could always be gathered in at a later date by means of a transfer fee. That would not only strengthen Rangers but weaken their opponents.

It had happened most noticeably in the late sixties when Rangers bought almost every Scottish team's outstanding player, including Aberdeen's Dave Smith, in a desperate attempt to counter the spectacular success of Jock Stein at Celtic. The ploy failed so miserably that Stein marched on to his famous nine-in-a-row championships and Rangers sacked their distinguished manager, Scot Symon – on a day when they were actually sitting at the top of the League!

Of course, the biggest sufferer was Scottish football, those other clubs whose hopes were diminished by the loss of a star attraction. More recently, Rangers and Celtic have cast their nets to the far ends of the earth, bringing back assorted talents for wage packets in excess of £25,000 a week, sometimes when the player is not even on the substitutes' bench. But that has not dissuaded them from creaming off the best of other Scottish clubs' talent. Kenny Miller of Hibs, for instance, was scarcely given a place in the Rangers team before he was on his way to pastures new down south, lost to the domestic scene in Scotland. And they wonder why the rest of us shake our heads.

HAMPDEN JOY AT LAST

I N 1995, with the scare of the springtime play-offs still fresh in the memory, the Dons looked set for better times. League results improved substantially and in the League Cup they beat St Mirren, Falkirk and Motherwell on their way to a semi-final against Rangers on a wet night at Hampden.

Two goals from Billy Dodds gave them a 2–1 win and so, within months of potential disaster, they were heading for a Cup final, such are the vagaries of football. Dundee had beaten Airdrie in the other semi-final and the deciding clash took place at Hampden on a Sunday afternoon in late November. Eoin Jess and Stephen Glass had a field day, with Glass laying on the cross for Dodds to score and again for Duncan Shearer to blast home a header. After five years, there was at last a trophy heading north to Aberdeen.

While league performances fell away, the scene was enlivened by the purchase of Dean Windass from Hull City, a rumbustious character reminiscent of another age, who was to gain something of that cult rating enjoyed down the years by players such as Don Emery and Doug Rougvie. Windass could not only score goals but surprise you with the deftness of his skill. The coincidence of his name was also good for a joke or two, such as: 'Why did the Dons need to buy Windass when they already had Glass!'

Roy Aitken bought Paul Bernard from Oldham for a record-breaking £1 million, while the mercurial Eoin Jess, the lad from Portsoy who promised so much but only rarely delivered, was on his way to Coventry for £1.7 million – but not for too long. After a mediocre time in England, Jess came back to Pittodrie, as did Gary

Smith, who had gone continental with Rennes but returned to familiar territory. (Jess left again later for Bradford.)

Nicky Walker was added to the goalkeeping staff while other newcomers included Tony Kombouare, a stylish Frenchman, and a little Bulgarian called Ilian Kiriakov, who had caught the eye during Euro '96 and gave hope that the Dons might have found someone in the mould of Gordon Strachan. It did not exactly turn out that way although his ball skills were undeniable.

In the summer of 1997 there could have been no more welcome return than that of Jim Leighton, away for nine years but now back to the setting of his glory days. He took over as captain and was destined to become further established as Scotland's most-capped goalkeeper by far.

The League Cup win of 1995–96 took the Dons into the UEFA Cup but, after disposing of Vilnius of Lithuania and Barry Town of Wales, they went out to Brondby of Denmark, whose manager was a chap called Ebbe Skovdahl.

In 1997–98, the Dons were plunging as they had done three seasons earlier and the fate that befell Willie Miller in 1995 now seemed to await his successor. On 9 November 1997, Aberdeen suffered a 5–0 defeat by Dundee United, a disaster which was there for all to see on television. Time was up for Roy Aitken and Tommy Craig. Their departures were officially announced the following morning.

The chairman, Stewart Milne, remembers it well: 'Roy had won the League Cup but was struggling a bit and we began to have doubts about him. After that 5–0 defeat the directors met in my house and decided that that was the end of the road. I undertook the most difficult task of my life in going along to Roy's house to break the news. He was expecting it and took it very well. Roy was one of the nicest and most conscientious guys in football.

'He had been desperate to be manager but didn't want to seem disloyal to Willie Miller in taking over his job. But it was Willie who persuaded him to take it. We said we would give him the back-up of experience and brought in Keith Burkinshaw, former manager of

Tottenham Hotspur, who played a major part in revamping our youth development throughout Scotland and giving us the best youth operation in the country.

'We had known that Roy was a high-risk appointment, being young and lacking in experience, but his man-management skills were ahead of Willie Miller's and he was more receptive to ideas.'

Stewart Milne remains a firm supporter of Burkinshaw, claiming he was recommended by Alex Ferguson. Certainly he had done well with Spurs but not everyone around Pittodrie was so convinced that he was worth his wages and the fans never seemed to take to him.

So the unsatisfactory tale of the 1990s continued. Pittodrie's first three managers lasted for fifty-two years, but the latest three had been sacked in five years, even though their combined record of achievement was comparable to the first three! Much more than an interesting statistic, that fact tells us a broader story about the changing attitudes of society. Success needs to come soon, and there is little room for patience or understanding. That outlook will further change the face of football in the twenty-first century and almost certainly put some clubs out of business.

Keith Burkinshaw, who had become Director of Football at Pittodrie, bridged the management gap until the board appointed Alex Miller, the former Rangers player and manager of St Mirren and Hibs, who had recently been assistant to Gordon Strachan at Coventry as well as Scotland's assistant manager.

Miller found his own assistant in Paul Hegarty, who came straight from Hearts but was best remembered as a stalwart defender for Dundee United in the 1980s, when he and Dave Narey were two of the biggest names in Scottish football. For a modest fee, Miller also brought Derek Whyte from Middlesbrough. A former Celtic defender, he became captain of the Dons.

But in the matter of choosing managers, the Pittodrie board was stumbling from one disaster to another. In Alex Miller's case there were rumours of rows over lack of money for new players, and he never did gain the confidence of the fans. As he was shown the door after a year, Jim Dolan of the *Press and Journal* was writing: 'There is little that can be said in defence of Alex Miller's record, which is clearly the worst of all the five managers at Pittodrie since the heady days of Alex Ferguson. His tenure was ended by a succession of not only poor results but miserable performances, which suggested he was unlikely to turn things around.'

Paul Hegarty was given the chance to work alongside Keith Burkinshaw on a caretaker basis and in January 1999, just six games later, he had the pleasure of accepting a trophy in rather novel circumstances.

In honour of that great servant Teddy Scott, Alex Ferguson brought his full-strength Manchester United team for a testimonial match at Pittodrie. The ground was so overflowing with fans, it was reminiscent of Fergie's heyday at Aberdeen. With the rarity of a full-house, the crowd roared as he emerged from the tunnel with Teddy Scott, a man for whom Fergie had the greatest admiration and affection. Indeed, there were few people for whom he would have gone to such lengths of recognition.

The crowd roared again as the Gothenburg heroes appeared for a 'bounce' game with the youth team, raising lumps in many a throat. Gordon Strachan was among those who looked as if they could still find a place in the Aberdeen side.

For the match, United's goalkeeper Peter Schmeichel was in top form, and Beckham, Irwin, Giggs, Scholes, Yorke and Cole displayed their skills to an appreciative audience. Ronny Johnsen's goal was cancelled out by Mike Newell, who steered a header past Schmeichel, and it came to a penalty shoot-out. Derek Stillie made a diving save to bring the Teddy Scott Memorial Trophy to Pittodrie and Ted was richer by £250,000. No servant of the club was ever more deserving of his night.

As for Paul Hegarty, that turned out to be the only silver he brought to Pittodrie. He lasted out that caretaker season but did not realise his ambition of being confirmed as manager, going the way of so many others in the final decade of the twentieth century.

WELCOME, MR HANSEN!

9

As the revolving door kept turning, Paul Hegarty was replaced by Aberdeen's first-ever manager from overseas, a name well-known in Scandinavia but less so in Scotland. Ebbe Skovdahl arrived from his native Denmark at the tailend of the century, by which time foreign talent was the fashion.

Rangers and Celtic had imported so many players that the sight of a Scot in either team became a novelty. No one else could compete with that level of expensive import in a football scene growing more and more remote from the real world of the average supporter.

Skovdahl brought the credentials of a man who had raised the sights of modest-sized Brondby of Denmark in something of the same way as Fergie had done for the Dons.

The first intriguing fact about Ebbe is that Skovdahl is not his surname. Born in Copenhagen in 1945, he grew up as Ebbe Hansen, a promising footballer who had a team-mate called Ebbe Johansen. To avoid confusion, he agreed to use his middle name, and that was how he came to be known as Skovdahl, which means 'valley of the forest'. In real life, he and his charming wife are officially Ebbe and Lene Hansen.

Ebbe played football until the age of thirty-two and ended his playing career with Brondby, the team he eventually went on to manage. He led them to five Danish league championships and three Danish Cup wins, including three successive league titles, before moving to Aberdeen in the summer of 1999. On three occasions, he took Brondby to the quarter-final stages in Europe. When you add the fact that he also had a spell as manager of the great Benfica and took them to runner-up spot in the Portuguese league, you begin to get the picture of his track record.

Perhaps most important of all from a Pittodrie point of view, he gained a reputation for bringing through his own young players, an impressive list including the incomparable Brian Laudrup and Peter Schmeichel.

In Laudrup's case, he didn't have far to go to spot his brilliance. As a youth, Ebbe introduced a team-mate to his sister Lone. She proceeded to marry the young man and gave birth to the famous Laudrup brothers, Brian and Michael. Their father, Fenn Laudrup, had more than fifty caps for Denmark.

Uncle Ebbe used to watch the Laudrup children kicking a ball around the garden with his own two sons and was not slow to spot a blossoming talent. He introduced Brian Laudrup to the Brondby first team when he was just seventeen and the rest is history. In his time at Rangers, he was the most stylish and talented player in Scotland, a fact acknowledged by even the most fervent Aberdeen supporter.

With the demise of Alex Miller and Paul Hegarty, Aberdeen went in search of Skovdahl who, after seven years in his last spell at Brondby, was ready to add a second European country to his overseas experience.

While Brondby was regarded as the Rangers of Denmark, it was only slightly bigger than Aberdeen in terms of financial turnover. Skovdahl knew he was taking on a formidable task at Pittodrie although he didn't reckon it would be quite so formidable. But he soon settled to the job in hand, adjusted to the faster, one-pace Scottish football and expressed himself happy with his new situation.

'I knew all about Alex Ferguson's great record at Aberdeen,' he said, 'and I also knew that Graeme Souness had subsequently changed the Scottish game by bringing in so many top players from outside to play for Rangers. There was no way teams like Aberdeen could compete with Rangers and Celtic in buying that kind of player. But that did not mean there was no way you could compete. We could fill that gap with knowledge, tactics and good young players.'

With a lack of money to buy anyone, he experimented with newcomers and used his continental connections to seek out afford-able talent. He brought the Norwegians Thomas Solberg and Cato Guntveit, and Arild Stavrum from Sweden, as well as two young men from Morocco, Rachid Belabed and Hicham Zerouali. There was an initial burst of enthusiasm, particularly for Zerouali, a little bag of tricks who could suddenly raise spirits with a flash of genius and did just that with a memorable free kick in the Scottish Cup at Love Street in January 2000. He bent a magnificent shot into the net with a flair so seldom seen in Scotland.

But Skovdahl's first season got off to the worst possible start with a run of seven games without a goal and nine without a win. What had been regarded as bad was in danger of becoming even worse, and the club that had been voted Europe's number one in 1983 was offi-cially classed as the worst in Europe in 1999, ranked at number 273.

Yet the fans sensed a quiet promise in Ebbe Skovdahl, and that held their patience when it might otherwise have cracked altogether. Piece by piece he began to build confidence, always playing it low-key and conducting his interviews in a calm, gentle manner which commended him to people all over Scotland, even those who cared little about football. There was an inner strength here.

The league position was still dire. The Dons were firmly rooted at the bottom with no sign of catching anyone. But a few results began to appear and the League Cup of 1999–2000 offered a turn in fortunes when they dismissed Rangers at Pittodrie and went on to reach the final against Celtic at Hampden on Sunday, 19 March 2000.

By then, a most extraordinary match had captured the headlines. Rangers and Celtic were now ridiculously out of the reach of all others in the Premier League, and Celtic had a home draw against Inverness Caley-Thistle in the Scottish Cup. It would, of course, be just a formality – except that it wasn't. Caley-Thistle went to Parkhead and beat the mighty Celtic 3–1 no less. Nobody could believe it. Celtic were losing the league race with Rangers and were now out of the Scottish Cup.

But the giant-killers from Inverness were not finished yet. Drawn against the Dons in the next round, they came close to disposing of them too in their northern homeland. A Bobby Mann goal seemed likely to create another sensation until Cato Guntveit rescued the Dons with a late equaliser. Aberdeen won the replay at Pittodrie but not without a few missed heartbeats, when the acrobatics of Jim Leighton saved the day. Having knocked out Dundee United in the next round, they were drawn against Hibs in the semi-final.

But first, there was that unfinished business in the CIS League Cup final. Celtic now had nothing else to play for but this. Incredibly, towards the end of the club's worst-ever season, the Dons now had two Cup opportunities while Celtic had just one.

On that March day at Hampden, some amazing scenes took place. So astonished to have reached a Cup final in such a depressing year, the fans decided to travel south to Glasgow for a glorious day out, win, draw or lose. It was a beautiful spring day as the buses streamed south from Fraserburgh and Foggieloan, from Byth and Ballater. There were 20,000 joyous North-east folk on their way to the final, an occurrence now paced out to once in five years as opposed to those fairytale days when it happened at least once a year. If the sweet taste of success had sometimes palled a little in the halcyon days, there was no fear of that being repeated at the tailend of the century. Any crumb of comfort was a bonus and the fans were on their way to enjoy themselves.

As they filled the western half of the brand new Hampden Stadium that Sunday afternoon, they raised a party atmosphere that outshone and outshouted the larger Celtic support. The air was electric, reminiscent of the great days and in such contrast to the reputation developed over the years, that Aberdonians were too reserved to support their team.

For the first twenty minutes the Dons more than held their own and looked as if they might take advantage of a nervous Celtic team. The Celtic fans seemed edgy, too. Eventually, a bad defensive error gave the Parkhead side a goal before half-time but faith was not lost.

In the second half, Thomas Solberg was shown a second yellow card before Zerouali was stretchered off. Now it was an exercise in damage limitation, and a young Dons team held out remarkably well with Mark Perry filling in bravely for Solberg.

Celtic scored a second goal and victory was assured. But the real victors on that spectacular day at Hampden were surely the Aberdeen supporters. They stayed and cheered and celebrated almost as if the day had really been theirs. In a sense it was. I looked around that stadium and marvelled that an Aberdeen crowd could behave so well and so triumphantly in the circumstances. As they left the mighty slopes of the new Hampden, there was a feeling that this had been the best defeat they had ever known!

Few had expected the Dons to win, or even dreamed that they would be there. So, all things considered, this wasn't a bad day at all, and better times might well lie around the corner. There had been no trouble, no hard feelings, just support for an inexperienced team, which had gained in confidence and would surely take heart for the future. It was the mood in which football should generally be regarded although the reality seldom reaches that particular level of sanity.

But the season was not yet over. In this extraordinary year, there was still the exciting prospect of the Scottish Cup with the semi-final against Hibs – and the dire prospect of a play-off to escape relegation.

Mercifully, the latter possibility was avoided by the fact that Falkirk had to opt out of the promotion stakes because they did not yet have a stadium suitable for the Premier League. The Dons would surely have survived the play-off – then again, they might not!

Meanwhile, they tackled Hibernian in the semi-final of the Scottish Cup at Hampden on Sunday, 9 April, fought back from a Russell Latapy goal to equalise through Arild Stavrum and went on to reach the final when Andy Dow crashed home the winner from the edge of the penalty box. Having avoided relegation, Ebbe Skovdahl led his men to their second Cup final in a matter of weeks, this time against Rangers, who had coasted to a 7–0 semi-final win over Ayr United.

Once again the Red Army of Pittodrie marched south, now liberated from the ghosts of the 1980s and adopting a more positive attitude to supporting their team through thick and thin. The contrast of a relegation battle and two Cup finals at the end of the same season produced its own emotional abandon, a carefree sense of joy that would see them through no matter what the outcome.

What's more, this Scottish Cup final would mark the swan song of Jim Leighton, not only the most-capped Scottish goalkeeper of all time with ninety-one appearances, but the last of the Gothenburg heroes to pull on an Aberdeen jersey. Now in his forties, he was the last remnant of the golden age of Pittodrie and the supporters were determined to make it Jim's day, win or lose. But if they had visions of a farewell lap of honour, ideally with the great man carrying the Scottish Cup, the dream was shattered within three minutes of kick-off.

As Rod Wallace of Rangers came in to challenge on the ground, there was a collision with Leighton's head – and a stunned silence as he lay stock-still on the Hampden turf. It was not like Jim, who usually stirred even in the worst of moments. Older fans who knew what happened to Celtic's Johnny Thomson in 1931 when he collided with Rangers' Sam English said it was an exact replica of that fatal incident. Thankfully, Jim came back to life and was carried from the stadium on a stretcher, suffering from a horrendously broken jaw. There were grown men and women near to tears at the sight of the great Pittodrie servant ending his distinguished career in such an undignified and heart-breaking fashion.

With no goalkeeper on the bench, the brave-hearted Robbie Winters donned the jersey and performed with honour, pulling off good saves from Kanchelskis and Wallace. But the game had been stacked against Aberdeen before it started, and it was now little more than a farce. It was to the credit of the Dons players that they held out so defiantly until half-time, when they were down by a single goal.

The final score was 4–0 for Rangers and the Aberdeen team that day was: Leighton (Winters); Anderson (Belabed), McAllister,

Solberg, Whyte, Guntveit, Bernard, Rowson, Dow, Jess, Stavrum (Zerouali).

Once again the fans stood solidly behind the team and were thankful that Jim Leighton at least survived to take on the role of goalkeeping coach at Pittodrie. There he remains, a fine influence on a new generation of players to whom, he says, he wants to give the same kind of care and guidance as was shown to him when he arrived as a raw youngster in those distant days of the 1970s.

10

GOODBYE PITTODRIE?

B Y 1998 the new Scottish Premier League was in operation and Stewart Milne was spending long hours away from his building business to seek a better future for Aberdeen Football Club.

When he first came on the Pittodrie scene in the mid 1990s, he was struck by the fact that the club was suffering from complacency. The general view was that the post-Fergie syndrome was at the bottom of the malaise but he felt it went deeper than that. The players had certainly lost the influence of the greatest manager in Britain but there was an attitude that success could still be delivered without further effort.

'The reality in life is that there is only one way to success,' says Stewart Milne, 'and that is if you have a hunger for it. At Pittodrie, I found the hunger had disappeared and we went through a period without it. I like to think that Ebbe Skovdahl had the courage to clean out players who were with the club for all the wrong reasons and gather around him a group of youngsters in whom he restored that hunger which is essential.'

In season 2000–01, those youngsters carried off the Scottish Under-18s Cup in a Hampden final with the much-fancied Celtic, and Milne could revel in the joy and satisfaction that shone from their faces. They were young men with a fresh appetite for their football.

These were indeed the first fruits of the plan he was determined to put into practice. That plan had three main objectives, starting with a reconstruction of the football operation, which had lost its momentum. The emphasis would be on youth policy. Then came the business operation, with a target of doubling the club's revenue within five years, which was essential if Aberdeen FC was to regain its former glory.

Finally – and most dramatically as far as the Dons supporters were concerned – came the question of Pittodrie and its future existence. Should the club stay in its spiritual home at the foot of Merkland Road East or move out to Kingswells, on the other side of the city?

The question was addressed in 1999, when the directors looked at the options for providing a home for Aberdeen FC in the second century of its existence. Accepting that the siting of the Richard Donald Stand, with its unbalancing effect, had been a costly mistake, there was the further complication that the old main stand on Pittodrie Street had a limited life and would have to be replaced. Indeed, within a few years, all three of the lesser stands would have to be renewed.

On top of that, there were new rules about the distance between the pitch and the spectators, all stretching the boundaries of the stadium, which was already being hemmed in by housing development. The technical difficulties of re-shaping Pittodrie were presenting a major headache. For all its traditional shrewdness, the club had failed to buy up the neighbouring land essential to its future expansion. Perhaps the final nail in the coffin came when they were beaten to the purchase of the derelict gasworks next door.

The successful bidders, Morrison the builders, were said to have an established business arrangement with the Gas Board but there were those who felt that Aberdeen Football Club, in its determination to leave Pittodrie, did not try hard enough. Whatever the truth, they would still have to consider the supporters and their emotional attachment to the only home they had ever known for their beloved Dons. Leave Pittodrie? Unthinkable!

If the directors were truly set upon the unthinkable, they would have to achieve a major conversion of public opinion. Business people can generally pay lip service to their customers and proceed with their plans if they believe a change will succeed in the end.

Football directors have to be more circumspect. If they were to proceed on a shareholders' vote only, they could carry the day with ease. Of the 5.8 million shares, Stewart Milne and his company owned 1.6 million, Aberdeen Asset Management (directors Martin Gilbert and Hugh Little are on the board) had 2 million and the Donald family, through Ian Donald, controlled 500,000.

That overwhelming power speaks for itself. Yet little of it would count if the mass of Dons supporters decided they were not going to trek out to Kingswells for their football. In short, the directors had to convince the vast bulk of the fans that a move from Pittodrie was essential – and that it would not be such a bad thing to join a massive complex incorporating much more than the football stadium.

So what did they have in mind? And how did it all arise? Back in the 1980s, and long before he had any involvement with the Dons, Stewart Milne the developer took a buying option on Robbie Mann's 150 acre farm of Bellfield at Kingswells, out beyond the city's crematorium on the left-hand side. (Cynics might feel that moving from an adjacent cemetery at Pittodrie to a crematorium beyond Hazlehead was not the best omen for the stimulation of a vibrant football club!) The long-term vision was for the creation of a new village, a settlement of 1,500 houses and 3,500 people, for which plans were pending. Into that equation at a later date came Aberdeen Football Club, which had an option on 110 of those acres.

Elaborate plans were drawn up in which a modern football stadium would be surrounded by a soccer academy and training ground with playing pitches and 2,500 parking spaces, as well as a major facility for a community leisure and sports centre.

Aberdeen Football Club would take the lead but the local authorities of Aberdeen city and county, Grampian Tourist Board and Scottish Enterprise (Grampian) would be involved, with an Olympic-sized swimming-pool and a wide range of other sporting facilities. The complex would be completed with a hotel, restaurants and bowling alley. Everything was guaranteed, in fact, except that other matter of a successful football team!

In 2001, the development became more urgent when Scotland was putting together its bid to host the 2008 European Championship, for which it would need a set number of suitable stadia. With Hampden, Ibrox, Celtic Park and Murrayfield already earmarked, the two Dundee clubs agreed at long last to share a stadium and Hibernian and Aberdeen would surely come into the reckoning. Plans had to be submitted by the end of July 2001, and that was when the Dons directors finally put their cards on the table. Irrespective of the Euro bid, however, they had also decided that they must come to a conclusion about the future of Pittodrie within a fairly short time.

If it all went ahead as part of the European plan for 2008, the total cost of £35 million would hopefully attract substantial Scottish Executive funding, leaving the club to find perhaps £20 million. About £10 million of that would come from the sale of Pittodrie, most likely for housing development. Because of Stewart Milne's business interest, that would have to be handled by outside consultants, with the chairman bidding on an equal footing with others. Much of the balance would likely come from further share capital.

The Scottish bid was lodged in May 2002, UEFA's inspection of facilities began in September and the final decision was due in December. If that bid failed, the directors would have to decide if they still wanted to leave Pittodrie. So massive decisions lay ahead as the club reached the crossroads in its centenary year. As chairman, Stewart Milne declared himself firmly in favour of leaving Pittodrie, irrespective of the European decision, and he had strong support on the board. All that, of course, would be subject to planning permission.

'The club wants to do more in the community,' he said, 'to reach out to youngsters who will become attached to the club. We have already built up a community coaching department, in which one of the Gothenburg heroes, Neil Simpson, plays a leading part.'

Harnessing the loyalty and passion of local heroes in the backroom of football is always a sensible idea, successfully employed by Rangers and Celtic down the years. In that respect, Dons fans fully approved of the fact that well-remembered stars such as John

McMaster and Ian Fleming still played supporting roles for the club in Glasgow and Dundee. Approaching the second century, the Dons directors were planning to have ten full-time coaches working throughout the North-east. Part of the centenary focus, in fact, was to raise funds which would be ploughed into the soccer academy,

Stewart Milne was well aware that his board would have to weigh up the emotional attachment to Pittodrie. So he went out to canvass the views of the supporters and came to the conclusion, after a number of road shows, that up to 80 per cent of them were in favour of the move.

Of course, that did not include too many people around Kingswells, who held meetings to protest about this intrusion upon their way of life, particularly in relation to traffic congestion on matchdays.

Several other possible sites were considered but an alternative suggestion for a new stadium at Charleston, near Nigg, was a non-starter since the site was zoned for business use and would have cost £20 million.

Stewart Milne also acknowledged that, before the Richard Donald Stand was built at all, the directors should have drawn up a comprehensive plan for the future of Pittodrie. That would have been a better tribute to the greatest chairman in the history of the club. But the likely fate of the Richard Donald Stand is that it will have to be pulled down after ten years of existence, as some builder (perhaps even Stewart Milne) moves in to clear the site for houses.

The proposed stadium at Kingswells was planned to be ready in 2004, in time for the following season. In the event of Scotland's Euro bid being rejected, the directors were ready with a scaled-down version to be built at their own expense. So, one way or another, they were determined to say 'Goodbye Pittodrie!'

But that was thrown into further confusion in 2002 with the collapse of ITV Digital, which had financed so much of British football. With Sky Television's new offer being rejected – and the Scottish Premier League's own televison plan voted down by Rangers and Celtic – the Scottish clubs were now trapped in the biggest financial crisis of their existence, no longer able to depend on television money to bolster unrealistic wages.

In the longer term, such a heavy dose of realism would put football on a more workable basis. In the shorter term, there was a new question to consider: could Aberdeen FC now afford to bid Pittodrie farewell?

11
EBBE'S SECOND SEASON

I N Ebbe Skovdahl's second season, his team remained in the bottom six when it came to the new formula of splitting the League at the tailend of the season. But in 2001–02, the wisdom of the youth policy began to shine through. Kevin McNaughton, Philip McGuire, Darren Mackie and the Young brothers, Derek and Darren, became first-team regulars, clustering around captain Derek Whyte and new arrival Roberto Bisconti, a commanding midfield player from Belgium who was with Standard Liège and AC Milan before coming to Pittodrie. Leon Mike was recruited from Manchester City and Peter Kjaer, Denmark's number two goalkeeper, from Turkey. Add to that the growing maturity of Russell Anderson, back in the game after a year off through injury, and the future began to look more promising for Ebbe Skovdahl and his young team.

The manager, who was winning friends with his intelligence and charm, surveyed his array of talent and spoke of the balance required in a football team: 'You need the artist and the tradesman. Artists like Zerouali will lift a crowd and win you games. But it is the backbone players who will win you trophies.'

After three straight defeats by Rangers, Hearts and Hibernian at the beginning of 2001–02 – and a humiliating 6–1 dismissal from the CIS League Cup at the hands of up-and-coming Livingston at Pittodrie – the Dons suddenly found themselves on a run of home wins which took them well up the table. That run would stretch to seven if they could beat Alex McLeish's Hibs.

The match was petering towards a goalless draw that November day. The ninety minutes were already up and all the drama took place in the three minutes of injury time. First, Robbie Winters scored what seemed likely to be the winner. Stirred from their acceptance of a draw, Hibs went in desperate search of an equaliser and forced a corner, which would be their last throw of the dice.

In this all-or-nothing assault, Hibs goalkeeper Nick Colgan ran up to swell the numbers in the Aberdeen goalmouth, which was filled with everyone except Zerouali, who lingered near the halfway line. But the corner kick was cleared and the ball despatched to the little Moroccan. When he ran into the Hibernian half of the field, there was not a soul there but himself. Picture the scene as Zerouali, cheered on by a home crowd that had seldom enjoyed such long anticipation of a certainty, trundled towards an empty goal, with the hapless Colgan galloping back but running out of steam and being overtaken by team-mate and former Don Gary Smith, who made a brave attempt to save the situation.

Zerouali rolled the ball into an empty net, and performed a victory somersault, to give the Dons a 2–0 win and Alex McLeish a bad dose of apoplexy. (Even though his Hibs team was floundering in the League, ten points behind the Dons, Big Alex had the consolation a few weeks later of being appointed manager of Rangers, in succession to Dick Advocaat.)

Two weeks later, that winning run at Pittodrie was extended to eight games with victory over St Johnstone. Just one more win would equal Alex Ferguson's nine home wins in a row during season 1983–84.

Ah, but the next home opponents were the all-conquering Celtic, unbeaten in the first eighteen games to November, suffering only one draw and already running away with the title, leaving even the high-powered Rangers out of sight. Fergie's record seemed safe enough but nothing is certain in football. Out went the Dons, determined to keep the run going and leading by a Robbie Winters penalty when the ninety minutes were up. Into injury time, with Celtic throwing everything into attack, Valgaeren sent a pass back to his goalkeeper, Rab Douglas, who didn't bargain for the speed of young Darren Mackie. Failing to control the ball, Douglas lost possession as Mackie rounded him and ran it victoriously into the net.

Important beyond the 2–0 result was the confidence instilled in young players who could see that the will-to-win can overcome a top team even in one of its greatest seasons. Appropriate for such a celebration, it was also the Dons' one thousandth league match since the concept of Premier League football was introduced to Scotland in 1975.

Mind you, after Alex Ferguson's home record had been equalled, the attempt to beat it came unstuck when the bogeymen of Livingston came back to haunt Pittodrie. They had surprisingly entrenched themselves in third position, behind Celtic and Rangers, with the Dons pitching in at number four. Away victories were harder to come by, but the incentive of gaining entry to the UEFA Cup kept Aberdeen going to the end of the season, when they finally caught up with Livingston to claim a place in Europe for the centenary year.

After all the damage inflicted by the West Lothian club in recent years, there was the satisfaction of knocking them out of the Scottish Cup in 2002. That joy was short-lived, however, when Celtic came along in the quarter-final to put an end to further ambitions.

Ebbe Skovdahl was keeping his feet on the ground, making the point that the Dons were still fragile. It would always be difficult, he said, to retain the good young players who might be lured away by the bigger money and challenge of England. The aim should be to keep them at Pittodrie until their mid twenties and make sure that the conveyor-belt of youth was always ready with quality replacements. Alex Ferguson was among those who endorsed these views and confirmed that this was the only way a club such as Aberdeen could now compete.

In 1999, Skovdahl had arrived on a two-year contract at a salary of over £300,000 a year. When that expired in 2001, the club was on a wage-cutting exercise which had to include the manager. Players were no longer on substantial signing-on fees and had to accept a basic wage of less than £2,500 a week, with appearance money and win bonuses giving them a chance of doubling the basic over a season. In other words, money for nothing was no longer an option. Everything had to be related to performance, a policy that fitted in with the matter-of-fact days of Dick Donald.

By now deeply involved with building his young team, Ebbe was anxious to see how far they could progress and accepted a cut-back to £225,000 a year. The contract could be ended by either side with six months' notice but Ebbe expressed himself happy with life at Aberdeen. At the same time he was keen to advise on who should succeed him when he eventually returned to Denmark. (His former club Brondby had always said they would welcome him back any time.)

He had a high regard for his assistant, Gardner Spiers, who succeeded Tommy Mollers-Neilsen when he left after a bout of illness. Spiers had signed as a schoolboy for St Mirren when Alex Ferguson was manager and played alongside future Dons Peter Weir, Billy Stark and Frank McDougall.

Ebbe was insistent that whoever followed him as manager should be in place before his own departure, gradually taking over the reins so that continuity would be maintained. He wanted to avoid a situation like the one that arose at Manchester United when Sir Alex Ferguson's intention to leave his manager's job became widely known a year in advance. That would always create problems, especially when the successor was unknown. Fans so accustomed to success could react badly if the team struck a lean spell, as happened to United in the autumn of 2001, and Ebbe sympathised with Sir Alex over what he felt was unjust criticism. Fergie subsequently changed his mind and decided to stay on.

However long he stays at Pittodrie, Ebbe has formed such an affection for the club that he will always keep in contact. He is in no hurry to leave. His wife Lene enjoys living in Aberdeen. She has visited most of Scotland's castles, enjoying in particular her trips to Balmoral, and the two have explored the surrounding countryside. A favourite way to spend days off is to drive to Inverness, stay overnight and continue next day to Loch Ness and on to Fort

Augustus. With a fine appreciation of the national beverage, Ebbe has done nothing to discourage their visits to the distilleries of Banffshire and Speyside. Back in Denmark, their two sons are pursuing successful careers, Henrik as a psychologist and Rene as a teacher of English and sport, and they visit their parents as often as they can.

12
PRESSURE GROUP

I N 1998, Peterhead businessman John Stephen read in the *Press and Journal* a letter from Edinburgh-based journalist Sarah Nelson, a passionate Aberdeen fan, eloquently expressing her frustration at what was happening at Pittodrie and calling for action from her fellow supporters.

It was the catalyst for Stephen to gather together a number of friends, including Chris Gavin, an active watchdog of the Aberdeen board (of whom more later), and form AFC 2000 for the purpose of becoming a pressure group. This body of a dozen people took the rather extreme view that Aberdeen FC was heading for oblivion, and sought a meeting with Stewart Milne to press home their opinions.

By March 2000 they had set up a Shareholders' Association, inviting people with shares in the club to join in giving some power to the elbow of those who felt they had no influence in the affairs of Pittodrie. If enough supporters clubbed together, the argument went, they could try to raise their voting power to 10 per cent of the total shareholding, at which point they were entitled to call extraordinary general meetings of Aberdeen FC and put the directors under all sorts of pressure.

Any idea that fan-power had not already had its effect could be contradicted by the events of 1992, when it played a significant part in removing manager Alex Smith and propelling the popular choice of Willie Miller into the hot seat. Now, however, they were seeking a more formalised kind of power. They changed the name of the group to Aberdeen Football Club Supporters Trust, and gathered a membership of around 700 with a voting power in excess of 7 per cent.

Buying shares had become so much easier since the club went to the stock market in the mid 1990s. Until then, it had been a private limited company, with a face value of 100,000 shares at £1 each. £100,000? Farcical surely, when you could hardly have bought an Aberdeen bungalow at that price, never mind a whole football club.

Those shares belonged to a mere 166 people, held mostly for sentimental reasons by families with a long connection with the club, sometimes by dear old ladies who had never seen Pittodrie in their lives. When shares did become available, which was very seldom, the transaction was a private matter and the buyer had to be approved by the directors, who were not obliged to give a reason for their veto.

Although the shares had a face value of £1, they were changing hands for anything up to £20 each in the late 1980s. In those days, chairman Dick Donald, his son Ian and son-in-law Stewart Spence held between them a total of 24,000 shares. The next largest shareholder was local fish merchant Alex Whyte with 8,900, followed by the descendants of the late Charles B. Forbes, former headmaster of Middlefield School and chairman of the Dons. The family of the late Chris Anderson, Dick Donald's vice-chairman until his death in 1986, held 5,500 shares.

That structure was a matter of local discussion but the massive power of the Donald family caused only minor ripples among the supporters, who were glad to have the benefit of Dick Donald and his outstanding chairmanship, which had laid the foundations of such a well-run and successful club.

But all that had changed and now the fans were calling for a more democratic way of football life. The Westminster government had announced a scheme called Supporters Direct, which gave advice and funding to help fans towards a greater say in the running of the national game. However, devolution had excluded the Scots from such bounty and a campaign got under way to squeeze similar generosity from the politicians of Holyrood.

Back in Aberdeen, the AFC Supporters Trust strove for that 10 per cent shareholding, knowing full well it would hardly compare with the combined power of Martin Gilbert and his Aberdeen Asset holding of 36 per cent, Stewart Milne and his 28 per cent and Ian Donald with 9 per cent. That did not deter the Trust in its bid to snap at the heels of the directors and bring radical change to the Pittodrie scene. In particular, they wanted rid of chairman Stewart Milne, casting doubts on his leadership and calling for his resignation in October 2000.

They had already lined up the man they wanted to be chairman. He was an Edinburgh-based Aberdonian, Jim Cummings, who ran a successful business supplying software to the legal profession. He had no greater admirer than John Stephen, who had told him many times that he was surely destined to lead the Pittodrie board.

An initial step was taken at the annual general meeting in 1999 when Stephen proposed Cummings as a board member. With a big turn-out, he had overwhelming support in a show of hands but the chairman needed only to call for a count of the shareholder vote to show where the real power lay.

The point had been forcibly made, however, and if Cummings was not acceptable then, he was invited to join the board in the autumn of 2000. He hoped to effect change from the inside, while hardly disguising that he was no fan of Stewart Milne or vice-chairman Ian Donald. John Stephen and the Trust looked forward to better times, with their chosen man on the board along with the new chief executive, Dave Cormack, an Aberdonian who had returned from the United States to succeed Gordon Bennett. The first chief executive, Bennett's short tenure came to an end in a burst of unwelcome publicity about his personal life.

13
CUMMINGS – AND GOINGS?

J IM CUMMINGS was one of several people appearing on the Pittodrie horizon who were likely to affect the affairs of Aberdeen Football Club. He was born in 1948 and went to school at Causewayend, Powis and Aberdeen Academy before leaving at sixteen to work in the time office at Hall Russell's shipyard. From there he moved to the Donside Paper Mills, joining Olivetti in Aberdeen when he was twenty-one. It was early days in computer technology and for the next seven years he worked his way up the company ladder before returning from London to start on his own.

What began as a one-man business in a little shop in Wallfield Crescent grew to a substantial computer organisation, specialising in providing software for lawyers' offices, for which he chose the adventurous name of Pilgrim Systems. Considering its position as the legal centre of Scotland, he decided to move the headquarters to Edinburgh in 1985, before opening further offices in London and Singapore and heading for the American market as well.

Business commitment on a world-wide scale did not divert him from a lifelong devotion to Aberdeen Football Club – and an ambition to become involved in the running of it. Through supplying equipment to what is now Robert Gordon University, he came to know and admire the late Chris Anderson and joined the 50 Club at Pittodrie in the aftermath of Gothenburg.

His serious interest in joining the board surfaced when he became openly critical of chairman Stewart Milne, lamenting the premature death of Chris Anderson and declining health of Dick Donald as the root of a malaise at Pittodrie. Cummings criticised the way the club was being run, felt there was a lack of ideas and ambition and thought the Supporters Trust was a good way of bringing greater democracy to Pittodrie.

By then, he was well established as a champagne socialist, a capitalist member of the Labour Party with his top-range Jaguar, a string of racehorses and skiing holidays abroad, while regarding himself as one who could bridge the gap between boardroom and supporter.

If his name was little known on the slopes of Pittodrie, he came more into public focus when he sold a 20 per cent share of his business to the Clydesdale Bank and became richer by £2 million, now clearly a man of some means. In turn, that stake in his business was re-sold to Aberdeen Asset Management, the biggest shareholder in Aberdeen Football Club, with Martin Gilbert and Hugh Little on the board.

In his criticisms about lack of leadership, he was also against the proposed move to Kingswells, complaining about what he regarded as the chairman's conflict of interests. He regarded the Euro 2008 bid as a nonsense, a kind of Trojan horse that would deliver Aberdeen FC to the new site, and believed they should re-develop Pittodrie and stay where they were.

From Edinburgh, Cummings kept in close touch with his native city, where his son James owned Heavenly Pizzas and also ran Josephine's Restaurant with brother Keith.

With Cummings on board, Aberdeen FC seemed set for stirring times. However, he was not alone in sparking the next boardroom drama down Pittodrie way.

14

TALK OF A COUP

M ARTIN GILBERT was founder and chief executive of the biggest financial institution the North-east of Scotland had ever seen, originally called Abtrust but later renamed Aberdeen Asset Management, which handled more than £36 billion for institutions and individuals. It had twenty-six offices around the world and employed 1,200 people.

With him on the Pittodrie board was Hugh Little, one of his right-hand men at Aberdeen Asset, who was responsible for all private equity activities in the group. The two of them had met up as students at Aberdeen University in the 1970s.

Martin Gilbert was born in Malaysia in 1955, of Aberdonian parents who had gone out to the rubber plantations, as did many people from the North-east. He was sent back, aged eight, to be educated at Gordon's College, living as a boarder at Sillerton House in Albyn Terrace.

Eventually graduating MA. LL.B, he worked as a lawyer first with Meston's and then on the investment side of Brander and Cruickshank, and it was when that firm broke up in 1983 that he created Abtrust.

Hugh Little was also a Gordonian, more of a football enthusiast than Gilbert, with vivid memories of his first visit to Pittodrie in 1967, when the Dons beat Reykjavik 10–0 in a European Cup Winners' Cup tie. Any notion that such margins of success were normal was soon dispelled. He did, however, become a ball-boy at Pittodrie and there is television evidence of a Celtic match in which goalkeeper Evan Williams dived round the post and crashed into the helpless Hugh Little!

Under its original name of Abtrust, the company had been sponsors of the Dons in the early 1990s and was impressed by the profile it had provided. By the mid 1990s, football clubs were moving into the stock exchange and investors were paying attention to the money coming from Sky Television.

Suddenly, football seemed a good bet and when the Dons sought their first share issue in 1995, Aberdeen Asset decided to invest. Of course, there was an element of local sentiment but philanthropy was not the motive. This was clients' money being placed in what could turn out to be a sound investment. An initial stake of £1.5 million rose to £2.5 million and made Aberdeen Asset the biggest shareholder.

Martin Gilbert explained: 'I wanted to do what I could for Aberdeen Football Club because it is a vital part of the community and gives the city a focus and a confidence.'

It was to represent the company's interest of 36 per cent that Gilbert became a director in 1997, to be followed by Hugh Little in 2000. But football was changing out of all recognition, setting wage levels which bordered on the obscene. The television money was there all right, producing annual sums of £20 million for top teams in England and across Europe, and virtually bank-rolling those players who could command as much as £100,000 a week. But the anticipated bonanza did not materialise for the Scottish teams. Only Rangers and Celtic topped £2 million of television money and teams such as Aberdeen had to settle for a million.

From 1995 onwards, the Dons had raised new share money of £9 million but had exceeded that figure in total losses. The financial position was far from good and was not helped by the mediocrity of team performance on the field.

The sequence of trading losses coincided with the purchase of players the club could not afford and there would surely come a day of reckoning. Martin Gilbert made this observation: 'For a spell, the board embarked on a policy of expansion, trying to buy success. But history shows that that doesn't work.

'I can take the very dispassionate view that I don't care if we win next week as long as the longer-term prospects of the club are secure. In fact, I'm frightened of success coming too quickly if it is not going to be sustainable.'

The first hint of a possible coup came in March 2001, in the wake of a second humiliating departure from the Tennents Scottish Cup at the hands of the so-called lowly Livingston, the most recent precocious child of Scottish football. The West Lothian club, which had grown from the previous incarnations of Ferranti Thistle and Meadowbank, had not yet revealed itself as a potential power, but it would soon be taking its place confidently in the Scottish Premier League, tucked in behind Celtic and Rangers.

In the spring of 2001 there was still a sense of affront that the Dons of Pittodrie could be dismissed from the major Cup competition by a comparative tiddler. With recently reported losses of £3.3 million, the Dons could well have done with the £500,000, which was the immediate tally of what that defeat had meant in loss of revenue.

Soon the *Evening Express* was sniffing around for conspiracy theories and sportswriter Charlie Allan came up with the story that Stewart Milne was fighting for his survival as chairman, after learning that Martin Gilbert, Hugh Little and Jim Cummings were 'plotting' to have him replaced.

Cummings was, of course, the new boy on the block, openly ambitious to be chairman one day. No supporter of Stewart Milne, he now found himself in alliance with the two financial experts on the board. Cummings was already known to Gilbert and Little because of that 20 per cent stake in his Edinburgh software company.

What worried Gilbert and Little was that, having already been three times to the City trough to raise money with virtually nothing to show for it, the club would not be treated so kindly if it went back yet again, showing the same faces as before. With credibility at stake, the big investors in the City take a hard line on such attempts. Assuming that more new investment would have to be found, it followed that someone new might have to be at the helm when that time came. Were Stewart Milne's days therefore numbered? For Gilbert and Little at least, this was a wholly pragmatic conclusion.

As an astute businessman, the chairman was not unaware of the investment problem. When he got wind of an alleged plot to replace him, he conceded that the question of a new face could have been discussed. If there was someone ready to assume his role, giving full commitment to the club, he was ready to stand aside. After all, being chairman of a football club these days was hardly a bundle of laughs.

He was not, however, enamoured of the fact that talks had been going on behind his back when there was ample opportunity for any concerns to be raised. Whatever the situation, it was time to bring matters to a head. Now that the story was finding its way into the headlines, the financial men from Aberdeen Asset Management were deeply embarrassed to find themselves cast as alleged conspirators. They had reputations as men of integrity to maintain and had no wish to be dragged into the realms of intrigue. There were frank confrontations and hints that Gilbert, Little and Cummings might all leave the board. Whatever Stewart Milne thought of Cummings, he did not want the others to go.

When it came to the crunch meeting at Stewart Milne's house, he told his fellow directors he was ready to step down as chairman unless they gave him 100 per cent support. You could rock the boat only so far without damage and he was anxious to establish a united board which could operate on a basis of mutual trust.

It was time for decisions. Martin Gilbert and Hugh Little agreed to give the chairman their support, and despite his views, Jim Cummings apparently gave that undertaking too. But the chairman was not alone in believing that Cummings would fail to give him the required backing and the directors were ready to go public and vote him off the board. Instead, he was asked to resign and promptly did so.

'I decided to let the club off the hook,' he later mused. In all truth, he had no option.

He had arrived with the hope of effecting change from the inside but hardly hiding his disapproval of Stewart Milne and Ian Donald. He thought Martin Gilbert should be chairman but that was impracticable in his business circumstances.

Cummings was impatient on several matters. Considering what Ebbe Skovdahl had been earning at Brondby, he thought his Pittodrie salary was excessive. He also believed the club should be preparing for the next manager and he had no doubt about who that should be. He knew that his friend and near-neighbour in Edinburgh Alex McLeish still had Aberdeen at heart and might be lured back to Pittodrie from Hibs, even though his eventual aim might be the English Premiership. (That, of course, was overtaken by McLeish's move to Rangers.)

Refusing to be swept along by Stewart Milne's enthusiasm for Kingswells, Cummings also believed that, as chairman, he could not only give better leadership but knew the people who would be prepared to support him with substantial investment in the club. For the time being, however, Cummings had to withdraw to the wings to study developments, a fervent Dons fan who had by no means lost his ambition to lead the club one day. Time alone would tell.

While embarrassed by the situation, Martin Gilbert did not shirk an explanation of the part he and Hugh Little had played: 'What we were trying to do was for the good of the club, in that we felt a change at the top was necessary. It was nothing personal against Stewart Milne, who works hard for the club. But if you fail to deliver and have huge losses to report, someone has to be accountable and that has to be the chairman.

'Stewart Milne clung to the chairmanship by the skin of his teeth but got such a shock over that incident that he definitely changed. He was surprised that Hugh and I would do what we did but we had to look after our shareholders. Hugh and I were prepared to resign but the board felt it would be damaging if the three of us went. The

Supporters Trust also pleaded with us to stay. We have got over all that now and have reached an understanding about how we can work together.'

However, Gilbert had not lessened his admiration for the departed Cummings: 'Jim was like a breath of fresh air on the board. Having him as a director was an important step forward for the club and I believe it was tragic that it ended as it did.

'But he spoke out of turn and placed the three of us in the role of villains. I was going to suggest that, if we were raising more equity, we needed a fresh face as chairman and I don't think Stewart Milne was against that. If it was necessary for the sake of the club, he would have gone.'

Gilbert was also in favour of the Supporters Trust, which backed Cummings, and said, 'If you don't have people like Jim on the board, there is a public suspicion that you are hiding something.'

That idea developed in the spring of 2002, to the point where the directors invited the maverick figure of Chris Gavin, a founding member of the Trust and founding partner in the wildly satirical fanzine *The Northern Light*, to join the board.

There was a time when the searing attacks and colourful adjectives of Chris Gavin's articles, written under the name of Old Beach Ender and enough to frighten a maiden aunt, would have burned holes in the Pittodrie boardroom, debarring him from setting foot in the place. But democracy was on the rampage and there was no doubt that the fans were gaining a clear and intelligent voice in the inner sanctum of Pittodrie power.

Chris Gavin was born in 1951 and after an early childhood at Muchalls and Mackie Academy, Stonehaven, he moved with his parents to Broughty Ferry and Grove Academy, Dundee, later training as an insurance surveyor. When his parents were killed in a car crash, he moved back to Aberdeen and the main thrust of his career has been with BP at Dyce, where he works in a specialised branch of the oil industry as a hydrocarbon accountant.

His Pittodrie pedigree is lifelong, upholding the Aberdeen end in Dundee, where he founded the local branch of the Supporters Club in 1974. Since then he has been in on the ground floor of the fanzine movement and the Supporters Trust. In the early eighties, Chris opened a Comic Shop, selling American comic books and science fiction novels, and gained a diploma in management studies at Robert Gordon's. He is married with one son and lives in Aboyne.

Meanwhile, coinciding with the departure of Jim Cummings, the recently appointed chief executive of the club, Dave Cormack, was also resigning and heading back to America. The health of his young daughter was given as the explanation for his departure, but that was not the whole story.

A former pupil of schoolteacher-cum-Dons-hero Bobby Clark at Harlaw Academy, Cormack had gone to America and built up a network recruiting business in health care, eventually selling out in a deal which made him a millionaire. Attracted back to his native city by the job at the football club, he set about the new business plan, helping to cut wages and other costs by nearly £1 million and advocating a leaner, meaner organisation. His young daughter's arthritic condition was certainly going to create problems in moving from Atlanta to the cooler climes of Aberdeen, but Cormack had another reason for leaving Pittodrie after such a short time.

Back in Atlanta, where he began to re-establish himself in business, he made it clear he was unhappy with the situation in the Aberdeen boardroom: 'I could see there were two camps and it is very difficult for a chief executive to operate when a board is not united.'

Cormack's arrival, in the wake of so much disastrous publicity about the private life of his predecessor, Gordon Bennett, had been hailed as a new hope for the shrewd guidance of the club's affairs. In the event, he was not there long enough to play a significant role.

With a sound track record in England, Bennett had also brought high hopes that he was someone who could breathe new life into the running of the club. So, for the third time in eighteen months, the directors sought to establish the powerful new post of chief executive so strongly advocated by Stewart Milne, hoping that this time they might be lucky.

From an impressive list of candidates they finally chose Keith Wyness, a tall, imposing figure who, like his predecessor, was an exiled Aberdonian returning from adventures overseas to the club he had long supported.

Wyness was born in Aberdeen in 1956, son of a Scottish Amicable insurance man whose job took him around Britain. The boy's schooling followed his father's career, from Ashley Road School to Elgin, Solihull and Southampton, before his parents eventually returned to Aberdeen.

Keith Wyness graduated from Nottingham University with honours in industrial economics before embarking on an entrepreneurial career. His first stop was British Airways, where he worked on the Concorde marketing team and was given the job of starting the airline's Executive Club.

Moving to Miami to work for international businessman and chairman of the British Horse Racing Board Peter Savill, Wyness then branched out with a partner to form a cruise-line company, raising $125 million to build the luxury liner Radisson Diamond. Radisson bought them out and Wyness made an unsuccessful bid to buy Cunard.

In 1997 he moved to Australia to be managing director of The Olympic Club, an ambitious membership scheme for people who hoped to see the Sydney Olympics of 2000. But it ran into serious problems and Wyness parted company with the venture in 1999. Even after landing the Pittodrie job in 2001, he found himself obliged to parry media questions about the ill-fated scheme before tackling the job in hand.

Keith Wyness's immediate task was to sort out the options for the future of Pittodrie. Beyond that, his responsibilities stretched from helping to advance the youth and community programmes to providing the resources for the manager and seeing they were used wisely.

He gave early warning that the gravy-train of televised football would not last for ever and that any departure of Rangers and Celtic from Scottish football, much as it might please the fans, would further lessen the attraction of the Scottish Premier League to the TV companies. To retain a television appeal in an age of TV saturation, it would be necessary for Aberdeen FC to find its way back to European football without delay.

The run of nine home wins in a row, coinciding with Wyness's arrival in the autumn of 2001, was taken as a good omen for the man whose task it was to guide the Dons towards a new age of prosperity, on and off the field.

Wyness spelled out the harsh financial fact that Aberdeen could not offer wage packets it could not afford, and followed through with some drastic action. At the end of season 2001–02, for example, he was unable to offer contracts to captain Derek Whyte, top scorer Robbie Winters, talented midfield man Cato Guntveit or those entertainers from foreign climes, Eugene Dadi and Hicham Zerouali. If the supporters had been given a choice of keeping one player at the club, it would probably have been Winters for his goal-scoring abilities.

Wyness's desire for an early return to Europe was achieved in May 2002, even if the Dons were pipped for third place in the League on the very last day when they were beaten by Celtic at Pittodrie, and Livingston won 3–2 against Hearts. Even in fourth position, however, there was at least a place in the UEFA competition, ironically at the very moment when those departing players would have enhanced the prospects of getting beyond the preliminary stages.

At least Ebbe Skovdahl had taken the club back to a European scene that was once so familiar as to be taken for granted. Now, as Aberdeen FC reached its centenary celebrations, there was no fear that such a nonchalant attitude would ever again be allowed to prevail.

By the year 2000, football clubs had lost their fashionable appeal to investors, with few dividends on show, yet in the approach to the

Dons' centenary Martin Gilbert was becoming optimistic again, on the basis that Aberdeen FC had faced financial reality ahead of most others and was putting its house in order. Hearts, Hibs and even Rangers were beginning to follow the example. The Aberdeen directors had embarked on a plan to eliminate trading losses by 2003. Costs had to be cut, not least in the wage bill, and the revenues increased. Ian Riddoch of Wigan Rugby FC came north to take charge of sales and marketing.

So even when the Aberdeen shares dropped below 80 pence, just half the purchase price, there was no question of Aberdeen Asset deserting the ship. Hugh Little said: 'Though the economic argument for investing in football is not what it was, we don't intend to walk away. We'll stick around and make sure the club returns to a non-loss-making situation, hopefully getting the share price back to where it was.'

With the on-going discussion about the future shape of football, Hugh Little was also convinced that the Scottish Premier League would not remain in its original form beyond a few years. Change was inevitable, either with Rangers and Celtic playing in another league or with the introduction of a whole new set-up, with a number of Scottish clubs, including Aberdeen, competing with English clubs. Either way, there would be potential for Aberdeen FC, still the third force in Scottish football, to be significantly involved.

So everything was in the melting-pot as Aberdeen Football Club prepared to celebrate its centenary in 2003 – a new ground, a new manager to succeed Ebbe Skovdahl when he eventually goes home to Denmark, perhaps new names at the top, with the possible scenario of Aberdeen's very own Open golf champion, Paul Lawrie, a diehard Dons supporter, pursuing a dream to become the majority shareholder in the club.

What a different world from the one inhabited by our ancestors, those enthusiasts who gathered in the city centre one evening in 1903 and decided to form the club that has been commanding our love and loyalty ever since, breaking our hearts and raising our spirits to ecstasy.

We have crystallised our emotions in one familiar phrase that has been ringing around Pittodrie down the century and will no doubt find echo in some distant place: C'mon the Dons!

THE EARLY YEARS

15

THE BLACK AND GOLD

ABERDEEN Football Club as we know it today came into existence in 1903, a latecomer to the big-time scene of Scottish football which had been developing through the last quarter of the nineteenth century. It had become obvious that a city the size of Aberdeen should be involved at national level and the way to achieve it was surely a merger between a number of smaller local clubs. The precise origins of Aberdeen FC can be confusing because a club of the same name was already in existence, one of three that merged into the new club.

Let's briefly follow that limb of the story back to an October afternoon in 1881 when a dozen people gathered in the Albert Hall in Correction Wynd to form the very first Aberdeen Football Club. The meeting had been called by three teachers at Woodside Public School who were determined 'to start the dribbling game in Aberdeen'.

Eight of those present were teachers, two were bookbinders and the others were a medical student and a tailor. They elected Mr W. Stewart, one of the Woodside teachers, to be the secretary and despatched him forthwith to buy a dozen maroon jerseys, two balls and one inflator. That was how they brought the dribbling game to the North-east of Scotland and played it wherever the opportunity arose – at the Links, at Hayton, then Holburn cricket ground and, more permanently, in a beautiful setting at the Chanonry, by which time they had discarded the maroon jerseys and become known as the 'Whites'. A picture of the day shows the team in typical Victorian pose, complete with white jerseys and knickerbockers and in some cases sporting bowler hats.

By the late 1890s, however, the club was being forced to vacate its Chanonry home and the search for a new ground began. Close by the old North Turnpike Road, which we now know as King Street, the former Gallows Marsh had been converted into a dung-hill for police horses, which were stabled at Poynernook Road. The land on which the dung-hill stood had been leased to the city by Mr Knight Erskine of Pittodrie, in the Chapel of Garioch, but in February 1899 its tenancy was transferred to Aberdeen Football Club on condition that the Whites restored the ground to its former agricultural state, repaired the cart road and dealt with the rubbish heap.

With great spirit the club set about its task, levelling the ground, building a terrace at the east end and holding a bazaar to raise the minimum requirement of £550. By the end of the summer of 1899, everything was ready for the grand opening. Pittodrie Park was a new name on Aberdeen lips – Pittodrie is a Celtic word which can mean 'the place of manure'! – and the crowds who flocked to that first game against Dumbarton, some of them on tram-cars which ran a shuttle service from Market Street, were caught up in a festive atmosphere, with music provided by the band of the 1st Volunteer Battalion, the Gordon Highlanders.

Aberdeen won the match but the appearance of a brand new football ground in the city merely emphasised that they were by no means the best team in town. In the Northern League of the day they invariably had to play third fiddle to Orion, who were known as the 'Stripes' and played at Cattofield, and Victoria United, who were the 'Blues' and played at Central Park.

Wouldn't it make sense for these three clubs to band together and take the Granite City out of its Grampian isolation and into the mainstream of Scottish football? There was bickering among the three but the logic of pooling their resources and making an assault on the Scottish League finally triumphed at a meeting in Aberdeen Trades Hall on 26 March 1903, when the chairman was Mr John Clarke, lecturer in education at Aberdeen University.

They agreed to form a limited liability company with a capital of £1,500, taking over the removable assets of the three clubs. Of course, there was no guarantee that they would gain admission to the Scottish League or that they could afford the £50 a week required to survive, but the move had been made and the club came into being officially on 18 April 1903. The constitution set out 'to promote the practice and play of football, cricket, lacrosse, lawn tennis, hockey, bowling, cycle-riding, running, jumping and the physical training and development of the human frame', a breadth of vision that gave loudmouths the chance to say, on a bad day, that the footballers didn't know which game they were supposed to be playing.

The new version of Aberdeen Football Club first showed face at Pittodrie Park on 15 August, a dull afternoon when Stenhousemuir came north to share a 1–1 draw. For the first season, Aberdeen FC had to content themselves with a place in the old Northern League, a secondary affair which took in an area from Aberdeen to Fife and included teams such as Montrose, Dunfermline, St Johnstone, Forfar, Dundee A and Lochgelly United.

Solid Aberdonians were not exactly bowled over by the new arrangement, and the directors were soon under fire for poor results. A letter to the *Evening Express* came from a disgruntled gent who complained: 'Twice since the season opened I have seen members of the team dawdling about the town, apparently doing nothing. Now lads, a football life does not last very long and Satan finds some mischief, so try and get something to do during the day.'

Some excitement was generated by the signing of Bert Shinner from Middlesbrough, an early idol at Pittodrie, and Duncan McNicol from Arsenal, who became one of the best backs the club ever had.

McNicol was of magnificent build and was said to take the ball from opponents with ease and grace. At the scoring of one of his early goals, 'hats and sticks were thrown in the air'. The team won the Aberdeenshire Cup that season and, when they were drawn against Arbroath in the Qualifying Cup, the mob of Aberdonians who travelled south for the game caused such chaotic scenes at the local railway station that they promptly built a better one!

Towards the end of that first season the directors decided to make a bid for entry to the First Division. The Scottish League of the time consisted of two divisions of fourteen teams each but as yet there was no automatic promotion and relegation. Instead, the top twelve clubs in the First Division were asked to vote on who should make up the numbers, choosing between the two bottom clubs and the two who topped the Second Division.

To complicate matters, Aberdeen FC was asking to be considered and Jimmy Philip, who had been appointed the first manager, was despatched on a canvassing trip with the plausible argument that a city as important as Aberdeen should surely be represented in the principal showcase of Scottish football.

Meanwhile, the spring holiday of 1904 brought north the popular attraction of Newcastle United, giving the Pittodrie fans the chance to see those legendary figures of their day, Bobby Templeton and R.S. McColl, the former Queen's Parker who later became famous for his chain of sweet shops. Newcastle won 7–1, which was hardly surprising when Aberdeen had managed to finish only third in the mediocrity of the Northern League. So what chance the First Division?

It was the custom in those days for crowds to gather outside newspaper offices to gain first hint of major events. Many years ago, old Willie Benton gave me a vivid description of the scenes outside the *Aberdeen Journal* office in Broad Street when he, as the office-boy, came out to display the bills announcing the Relief of Mafeking in 1901. In much the same way, the crowds gathered in Broad Street on the day the Scottish League was voting on whether or not to admit Aberdeen FC to the First Division. Such was the fanaticism of the time.

Manager Jimmy Philip had returned from his expedition south with the promise of enough support to carry the day but, when the news came through to the crowds outside the offices of the *Evening Express* and *Evening Gazette*, there was an outburst of boos and groans. The promise of support had not materialised and Aberdeen FC was elected to the Second Division in the company of Hamilton Academicals, Clyde, Leith Athletic, St Bernard, Falkirk,

East Stirlingshire, Abercorn, Ayr United, Albion Rovers, Raith Rovers and Arthurlie.

It was better than nothing and the onus was now on the club to prove it was worthy of the top grade. That could be done only by producing a winning team and to that end Willie McAuley and Jimmy Robertson had already been signed from Middlesbrough. The Tees-side club also produced the former Celtic goalkeeper, Rab Macfarlane, for a total treble fee of £210. Rab turned out to be one of the characters of the game, indulging in a free exchange of banter with the crowd behind his goal.

On one occasion, when he failed to get in the way of a fierce shot which landed in the back of the net, a wag roared, 'Hey Rab, foo did ye come tae lose that goal?' Picking himself up, Rab looked round the post and shouted back, 'Better tae lose a goal than a goalkeeper!'

In trying to build a team that would take them to the top, Aberdeen also signed Ecky Halkett from Dundee, who was to become captain before being killed in the First World War.

At the first annual general meeting in July 1904, Councillor Alexander Milne (his son Vic became a popular centre-half as well as a doctor) announced an income of £1,927 which, together with the profits from the bar, left a surplus of £319 11s. 9d. The directors recommended a dividend of 10 per cent. That bar, incidentally, was in existence for twenty years before someone discovered it was not legally licensed!

At the start of season 1904–05, the big talking point was the abandonment of the old white jerseys, which had given the original club its nickname, and the introduction of a fancy new black-and-gold strip which drove the old faithful to distraction. Aberdeen became known as the 'Black-and-Gold Brigade', or more appropriately the 'Wasps', a name disliked by the players because it gave a ready weapon to the terracing wits when there was little sign of sting in their play.

The eleven who had shaped up into the first recognisable Aberdeen team were: Macfarlane; Willox, J. Mackie; Halkett, Strang, Low; Knowles, Mackay, G. McNicol, Ellis, Johnstone. By now the

Pittodrie reserves had taken the place of their seniors in the old Northern League.

As in the previous season at Arbroath, the Qualifying Cup became a cause for great enthusiasm in 1904–05. Aberdeen were drawn to play at Cowdenbeath and the Fife team were firm favourites to win. Once again the crowds gathered outside the newspaper offices and when the word came through that Aberdeen had won, 'staid and sober men hugged each other in their ecstasy. Reckless partisans threw their go-to-meeting hats in the air and everybody, with one voice, "let her rip" at the fullest pitch of their lungs.' Quite disgraceful behaviour in 1904 – and all because of a win over Cowdenbeath.

Crowds thronged the Joint Station for the team's return and, in the enthusiasm of the period, nearly all the share capital was snapped up and Aberdeen Football Club bought over Pittodrie for the sum of £5,668. They also signed Johnny Edgar from Arsenal, another great favourite with the supporters, and prepared for the semi-final of the Qualifying Cup, an event that could arouse much emotion in those days.

The opponents were Clyde, who came to Pittodrie for the tie and brought with them, in the customary way, their own linesman. The poor chap took dogs' abuse from the home crowd although one commentator did agree that the man 'would have tried the patience of a Job-and-a-half'. During that game the Clyde skipper interrupted proceedings to hand over a note to Aberdeen captain McNicol protesting that a certain player was ineligible for the match. Aberdeen won and the SFA did not uphold the protest.

The Qualifying Cup euphoria reached its climax at Dens Park, Dundee, on 26 November 1904 when Aberdeen won the trophy with a 2–0 victory over Renton, a club that had taken its place in football history by winning the Scottish Cup in 1888 and being hailed as 'champions of the world'. The team on duty that day was: Macfarlane; Murray, D. McNicol; Halkett, Strang, Low; Robertson, G. McNicol, A. Lowe, McAuley, Ritchie.

The 1,500 Aberdonians who travelled to Dundee on a Caledonian Railway special saw their team slithering about in the snow during the first half. Trainer Peter Simpson had a change of boots awaiting them at half-time and that paved the way for victory. The Cup was handed over in Wood's Hotel, Dundee, before the team returned to Aberdeen, where seemingly the entire population was out in full ecstatic force. The players were carried shoulder-high from the station through the streets and the din lasted long into the night. Players and officials celebrated in the old Palace Hotel at the corner of Union Street and Bridge Street (the site was later occupied by C&A), which was the social hub of Aberdeen's smart set until it was burned down in 1941.

In contrast to modern methods, isn't it rather appealing that the training preparation for a major game in those days consisted of a tram-car ride to Mannofield and a brisk walk to Culter and back to the terminus?

That Qualifying Cup win was modest enough but it did at least show that the emerging Aberdeen FC was capable of winning something, which was a better advertisement than its league position at the end of the 1904–05 season. To finish seventh out of twelve teams in the Scottish Second Division was bound to raise doubts about whether the club could reasonably aspire to the First Division. But that did not prevent the manager and directors renewing their efforts to drum up support and submitting their application once again. Seven other clubs were also forward with applications, including Motherwell and Morton, who had ended up at the bottom of the First Division, and Clyde and Falkirk, who were champions and runners-up in the Second.

Aberdeen pinned their faith on having friends at court and when the league meeting was held on 22 May 1905, Celtic sought to ease the dilemma by proposing the League be extended from fourteen teams to sixteen. That opened the way for four teams to gain a place in the top division. But who? When it came to the voting, Aberdeen were top of the poll. Motherwell and Morton were re-elected and Falkirk landed the fourth place, which was rough justice on Clyde, considering they had just won the Second Division championship.

Their ambition now realised, the Aberdeen directors set about improving both ground and team. The board at that time consisted of Councillor Milne as chairman, with James Rae, James Weir, John Mackay, Harry Wyllie, Willie Jaffrey and Tom Duncan, who was the last survivor.

The terracing was extended and due notice was taken of the burgh surveyor who had been scathing about the condition of the old Orion grandstand which had been transplanted from Cattofield. A new pavilion at the North-east corner was fitted with two large dressing rooms and an ornamental front. You might have expected a cricket team to emerge, such was the style of the place, with a balcony where gentlemen used to recline on a Saturday afternoon as if they were watching a Test Match at Lord's.

On the playing side, the staff of twenty-seven now included the great Willie Lennie, former Queen's Park, Dundee and Rangers player who had gone to Fulham but failed to settle. Willie was a brilliant left-winger who seldom played off form and later became the very first Aberdeen player to be capped for Scotland.

The people who would shape the new club's destiny were beginning to emerge. The first man of influence was Jimmy Philip, the original manager, whose first fourteen months of work earned him the princely sum of £116 3s. 4d.

16

PHILIP IN CHARGE

Jimmy Philip was in business as a wood-turner when he was given the job as part-time manager of Aberdeen Football Club in 1903. Among all the men who have guided the Pittodrie fortunes during the first century he was the only one who could call himself an Aberdonian until Jocky Scott became co-manager in 1988.

His son George, who lived in Counteswells Road until his death in 1977, remembered the early days of the family home at 13 Erskine Street and how as a child he would be hurled to Pittodrie on the back of his father's bike. There he would examine, with the wonder of a child's eyes, the jerseys and boots of the men who filled them, names that would take on a legendary ring – Donald Colman, Jock Hume, Rab Macfarlane, Bobby Hannah.

The choice of Jimmy Philip as manager was no random happening. From a broad base of sporting interest, he had a particularly far-seeing view about football. For example, he proposed the very first overseas tour by a Scottish international team, telling the SFA that he would foot the bill if there was a loss and that they could keep the profit if there was one. Also a talented referee, he was invited to officiate at the Olympic Games of 1912 in Stockholm. His son George kept the silver memento to prove it.

In our more sophisticated world of professionalism, such an invitation would be unthinkable. But attitudes were less rigid in those days; players were allowed to develop their own colour and personality – and there were some characters. Can you imagine an Alex Ferguson putting up with a little Irishman called Flanagan, who was signed by Jimmy Philip from Maidstone in Kent? Flanagan worked for Sharpe's cream toffees, which may have given him a thirst. He would collect his pay at Pittodrie on a Friday and head straight for the nearest pub, frequently landing in the privacy of a police cell. It was not unusual for Jimmy Philip to bail him out on a Saturday morning, bring him back to his senses and produce him in the dressing room in time for kick-off. To his credit, Flanagan could go out there and play down the left wing with all the assurance of a man who had spent the Friday evening at a temperance meeting. There was colour if not stability in some of those old-time worthies.

There was one popular Don of that period before the First World War whose colour was invariably black. Bobby Hannah worked as a coal-dunter at the harbour, finishing his shift at one o'clock and catching a tram-car to Pittodrie, still covered in coal-dust. He may have been the only professional in the history of British football who had to be put in the bath *before* the game! Bobby had a brand of two-footed tackle that was all his own. He also had a particular experience which hardly bears re-telling. In a game with Rangers, the full-blooded boot of the famous Tommy Cairns connected with his private parts and that, painfully and understandably, put a virtual end to the top-class career of Bobby Hannah although he did turn up later in America.

Meanwhile, manager Philip was guiding Aberdeen into the mainstream of Scottish football. The Black and Golds, who had not yet been called the Dons, made their entry to the First Division against Partick Thistle at Pittodrie on Saturday, 19 August 1905. The graceful Duncan McNicol was absent through injury, which explains why the team on that historic day was: Macfarlane; Murray, Brebner; Halkett, Strang, Low; Robertson, Henderson, Ward, McAuley, Lennie.

Aberdeen went under 1–0 but had to wait just another fortnight to register their first win in the top division, a 2–0 result against Kilmarnock at Pittodrie. That season, they finished in twelfth position of a sixteen-team league. During that first season Bailie Milne resigned through pressure of business, leaving us with the coincidence that the first century of Aberdeen FC began and ended with a chairman called Milne. He was succeeded by Harry Wyllie, while a local painter called William Philip, who had been associated with the old Victoria United in 1888, became a director.

The popular Duncan McNicol did not recover from that injury and by season 1906–07 had given up the game, later to become the professional at Murcar golf course. The movement of players, that eternal feature of football, had already begun. Willie McAulay was transferred to Falkirk and Rab Macfarlane had turned down terms so the manager went off and signed a big-name keeper of the time, Willie Stead from Southampton. He had also fixed up a prominent local goalie, Cody Mutch from Inverurie, who turned out to be the star of the pre-season trial match – and Willie Stead never played at Pittodrie again! Cody later distinguished himself with Huddersfield, a dominant English team in its day.

Jimmy Philip was never afraid to carry his spotting missions into the heart of English football and on one of those occasions came back with Charlie O'Hagan, the Irish internationalist who played for Middlesbrough. Charlie was a real broth of a boy who loved the acclaim that came from the Aberdeen crowd. At inside-left he teamed up with the great Willie Lennie and there is a strong case for saying it was the best left wing ever seen at Pittodrie. They became such an attraction in themselves that football followers in other parts of Scotland would turn out just to watch the beautiful rhythms of O'Hagan and Lennie.

Season 1906–07 ended with the Black and Golds in twelfth position, a repeat of the previous year. In the close season they lost Henry Low, who had been a fine servant from the start but was now on his way to Sunderland. That merely signalled the arrival of other new names, players who would write themselves indelibly into the Pittodrie story.

The first to arrive was a young man from the West Lothian club of Broxburn Athletic, distinctive from the start because he was inseparable from his clay pipe. His name was Jock Hume and few could have guessed that he would become one half of a full-back partnership which remained the backbone of the Aberdeen defence for fourteen years. He also became one of the characters of Pittodrie.

When he finally left Aberdeen in 1921 he became player-coach to Darwen, a small town near Blackburn, then played for Arbroath and Peterhead before emigrating to America, where he became trainer to Brooklyn Wanderers. Some say it was on his recommendation that Aberdeen later signed the incomparable Alec Jackson, whom he played against when the latter was with Bethlehem Steel.

Jock finally turned to refereeing and for twelve years handled the games at New York's West Point Military Academy. That was where they buried General George Custer of Last Stand fame, and there were no doubt a few who wanted to 'dig a hole' for the Scots referee as well. But the solid figure of Jock Hume was not for intimidating. He finally returned to Aberdeen, and died in 1962.

If Jock Hume was destined to be one half of a famous partnership, the other half appeared with even less of a hint that glory lay ahead. In the latter part of 1907, unheralded and unsung, a man of small build and modest manner slipped quietly into Pittodrie to become one of the most influential figures in the entire history of Aberdeen Football Club. His name was Donald Colman.

17
DONALD COLMAN

Donald Colman was one of the most remarkable men in the entire history of football. Those who remembered him would glow at the very mention of his name, such was the power of this quietly impressive man.

Colman was born in Renton, Dunbartonshire, in 1878 and the first surprising fact is that, just as in the case of Ebbe Skovdahl, his surname was not what it seemed. Donald Colman was really Donald Cunningham. Well brought up in a poor but proud home, young Donald spent a lot of time at his grandmother's, fired with a passion for football, which was not then regarded as a sensible choice of career. So when he first put pen to paper in local junior circles, he anticipated parental disapproval by using his granny's name. In later years, when he had made a career of football, his mother suggested he should resume his own name, but by then it was too well established and remained with him until he died of tuberculosis in Aberdeen in 1942, aged sixty-four. In the years between, he chalked up a career which is hard to believe.

As a boy, Colman had carried the hamper for his local Renton team, which had gained fame by winning the Scottish Cup. He played at full-back for Glasgow Perthshire, Tontine Athletic, Renton and Glasgow Maryhill (the team that produced Willie Lennie) and developed into a player of some class, gaining a record number of junior caps. But senior clubs fought shy of his small build. Sunderland tried him out against Hibs but the Roker Park boss, Tom Watson, handed him his expenses, patted his head and said, 'You're a first-class little back but be advised by me, my mannie, you stay with the juniors. You're too little for senior football.'

What part that played in hindering his career is hard to say but Donald Colman did remain a junior until he was twenty-seven. Finally, in 1905, he was given the chance to sign for Motherwell but lasted just two years before he was considered to have entered the twilight of a mediocre career. The Fir Park club gave him a free transfer and that seemed to be the end of the line for Donald Colman.

Incredibly, at the age of twenty-nine, it was just the start. Two of his former team-mates at Maryhill, Jimmy Muir and Dinger Drain, were by then at Pittodrie and Donald travelled north with them one day for want of anything better to do. It was Jimmy Muir who asked for a quiet word with manager Jimmy Philip and suggested he might give Donald a run.

To his everlasting credit, Philip took the gamble and before the 1907–08 season was ended the Motherwell discard was established in the Aberdeen team, succeeding at last as a senior footballer just before his thirtieth birthday – and about to embark on a partnership with Jock Hume that would last for nearly fourteen years.

By the age of thirty-three he was being hailed as the best right-back in Scotland and in that same year won the triple honour of being capped against England, Ireland and Wales. Where had Aberdeen found this man and, having been found, was there no stopping him? The football world was baffled.

Two years later he was still going strong for Aberdeen and Scotland and it took the First World War to prise him out of football and away to the battlefields of France. When that war ended Donald Colman returned to Pittodrie and was still playing in 1920 at the age of forty-two.

After that he 'voluntarily severed his connection' with the club, as befitted a gentleman; but this remarkable tale is far from over. Still a bachelor, Colman went home to Vale of Leven but only to become player-manager of Dumbarton, and the records show that he was still turning out as a player when he was forty-seven. At the

immy Philip, Aberdeen's first manager, was appointed in 1903 and retired in 1924.

Jock Hutton, heavyweight full-back of the twenties.

Aberdeen team of 1904 – winners of the Qualifying Cup. *Left to right, back row*: J. Philip (manager), A. Lowe, E. Halkett, T. Strang, R. Macfarlane, G. Ritchie, P. Simpson (trainer). *Front row*: J. Robertson, G. McNicol, R. Murray, D. McNicol, H. Low, W. McAulay.

Aberdeen team of 1928–29 with an array of local trophies. *Left to right, back row*: Merrie, Cooper, Donald (Dick), McHale, McLaren, McKenzie, Legge. *Middle row*: Ritchie (assistant trainer), Black, Smith, W.K. Jackson, Blackwell, Yuill, Love, McLeod, Livingstone, Russell (trainer). *Front row*: Robertson (secretary), Polland, Wilson, Falloon, McDermid (captain), Muir, Yorston, Cheyne, Hill, Travers (manager).

Alec Jackson – the Wembley Wizard.

Willie Mills and Matt Armstrong, deadly duo of the thirties.

Aberdeen FC's 1937 tour of South Africa, pictured in Durban. *Left to right, back row*: Willie Cooper, Billy Scott (father of Jocky Scott), Herbert Currer, Bob Temple, Billy Strauss. *Middle row*: Jackie Beynon (he died a few days later), Johnny McKenzie, Frank Dunlop, George Thomson, Eddie Falloon, Johnny Lang. *Front row*: skipper Bobby Fraser, S.V. Kimber (South African team manager), Frank Whitehead (chairman), Paddy Travers (manager), Donald Colman (trainer).

A poignant picture of fashion – cloth-capped Dons fans jam Merkland Road East for a Celtic match in 1937.

This was the Dons' first-ever trophy – the Scottish League Cup of 1946. Pictured (*left to right*) are George Taylor (he scored the winner against Rangers), Andy Cowie, George Johnstone, Archie Baird, Frank Dunlop, Pat McKenna, George Hamilton and Alec Kiddie.

Popular faces of the fifties – (*left to right*) classy forward Bobby Wishart, Davie Shaw, ever-smiling Harry Yorston, and in army uniform, Hughie Hay, clever ball player and protégé of Tommy Pearson.

Stan Williams scored the winning goal for the Dons in the 1947 Scottish Cup final – but the hero is out of the picture. Archie Baird and Billy McCall are there and so are Hibernian's Jimmy Kerr and Jock Govan.

Captain Frank Dunlop is carried shoulder high with the Dons' first Scottish Cup. Also pictured are (*left to right*) George Taylor, Billy McCall, Pat McKenna, George Hamilton, Joe McLaughlin, Stan Williams, Tony Harris, Willie Waddell and Chairman William Mitchell.

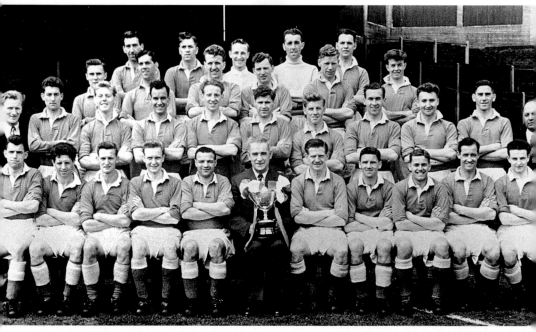

The Dons won their first League Championship in 1955. They also won the Reserve League and the Second XI Cup. *Left to right, front row*: Allan, Davidson, Jimmy Brown, Paterson, Buckley, D. Halliday (manager), Mitchell, Young, Yorston, Hamilton, Mulhall. *Second row*: D. Shaw (trainer), Ingram, Wilson, Glen, W. Smith, I. Smith, John Brown, Wishart, Allister, Wallace, B. Alexander (assistant trainer). *Third row*: Clelland, O'Neil, Clunie, Hay, Scott (Teddy), McNeill. *Back row*: Kelly, Dunbar, Morrison, Martin, Macfarlane. Missing: Leggat, Caldwell, Hather.

A champion of 1955 – Graham Leggat.

The man who won a fortune – Harry Yorston.

The Dons' stalwart half-back line in that 1955 championship-winning season – (*left to right*) Jack Allister, Alec Young and Archie Glen.

Davie Shaw, Aberdeen trainer and later manager, carries off left winger Jackie Hather.

Tommy Pearson had the ball skills of a magician.

Johnny Pattillo (*centre*) and Archie Baird (*left*), seen here with Ernie Ewen. Approaching the centenary, Pattillo is the oldest known surviving Don.

risk of breaking the chronology of the Dons story, let us follow through the rest of the Colman saga.

By 1931 another Dunbartonshire man and former Pittodrie player, Paddy Travers, was well established as Aberdeen's second manager and in need of a trainer-coach to succeed the late Billy Russell. What better candidate than you-know-who? By then fifty-three, and having spent the last ten years visiting Norway to teach them football, Donald Colman re-enters the Pittodrie story to begin a chapter that was perhaps more glorious than the first because it was one of innovation and influence.

Players who came under his guidance marvelled at his brilliant football mind, which was capped by a delightful personality. Colman had developed a philosophy about the game that was ahead of its time and shows that some so-called modern thinking is not so modern after all. He was giving lectures about use of the 'open space', running off the ball and experimenting with possession football.

He went to endless trouble to mould football boots to fit the feet and encouraged the use of both feet by having his players wear one boot and one sand-shoe in training, to coax the reluctant foot.

When Celtic goalkeeper John Thomson died after the collision with Rangers' Sam English at Ibrox in 1931, Colman set out to invent a head-gear for keepers. Unfortunately, it proved too cumbersome. But his inventive mind was always at work. It was Colman, for example, who invented the dug-out, a novelty which so intrigued Everton when they came to play Aberdeen in a friendly in the 1930s that they went back and built the first one in England.

An artistic full-back, he was also a boxing enthusiast and an accomplished all-round dancer, pointing to the common factors of balance and rhythm. There was one Aberdeen player above all whom he privately idolised because he personified his own dreams of football at its artistic best. Fair-mindedness would never allow him to show favouritism but I was later given the name by his daughter Edna (she became Mrs Brown of Summerhill Terrace) and his only son Donald (Cunningham, of course) who became a lecturer in English at Aberdeen College of Education.

It will not surprise fans of the 1930s to learn that his special player was Willie Mills, another product of the Vale of Leven and the perfect example of all that Colman had tried to teach. His admiration for Mills survived the criticism that he should have clinched the 1937 Scottish Cup final for Aberdeen.

Colman did not marry till 1924 when he was forty-six, keeping up his reputation as a late starter. For Edna and Donald, time with their father was therefore all too short, but they kept happy childhood memories of accompanying him to Pittodrie and helping to mark the pitch. They fondly remembered his talent as a singer and finally rationalised that he was simply a wonderful father. What better epitaph for Donald Colman, the man who showed that all things are possible? It is certain that no finer human being ever crossed the threshold of Pittodrie.

18

MADAM BOOTS
THE BOBBY

T HE arrival of Donald Colman did more than anything to bring
stability to the fledgling football club of Aberdeen and by March
1908 the team was heading for its first major experience in the
upper echelons of Scottish football, a Scottish Cup semi-final.

In those days there were no neutral venues before the final so
imagine the excitement when the game was announced for Pittodrie
and the opponents were to be Celtic. It was the year Aberdeen had
a player capped for Scotland for the very first time – outside-left
Willie Lennie – but the Parkhead club, already twenty-one years in
existence, was brimful of international players, on top of which they
were Scottish Cup holders.

The interest built to an unprecedented enthusiasm as Pittodrie
prepared for its first-ever 20,000 crowd on 21 March 1908. Amid
much publicity, Celtic came north to stay at the Murtle Hydro and
on the eve of the game both teams attended a performance at the
Palace Theatre, Aberdeen. On the big day, the band of the Royal
Engineers was there in all its glory to play before kick-off. The team
that took the field was: Macfarlane; Colman, Hume; Halkett,
McIntosh, Low; McDonald, Muir, Murray, O'Hagan, Lennie.

With all the ingredients of a great game, it turned out to be a sad
anti-climax of dirty play in which, according to the commentators,
Aberdeen got the heavy end. It was duly reported that Charlie
O'Hagan was fouled six times in five minutes and when the popular
Irishman protested, the referee threatened to send him off. This
roused the anger of the crowd and the referee went across to lecture

them too! When Celtic had scored the only goal of the game and it was all over, a hostile crowd pelted the visitors with stones for what they felt had been an exhibition of dirty tactics.

So crowd trouble is nothing new. In that same period there was a notorious riot at a Rangers–Celtic game at Hampden and the Pittodrie patrons were themselves now proving to be no angels. In that same year, Hearts came north for what Aberdeen thought was a North-east Cup tie. Arriving late, Hearts apparently told the referee they were there for a friendly and he took the liberty of cutting the second half to thirty minutes. The crowd checked their pocket-watches and, in their bewilderment, invaded the field, smashed the pavilion windows, tore down advertising hoardings, pulled the King Street gate off its hinges and – shades of Wembley 1977 – tried to uproot the goalposts.

Although their favourite goalkeeper, Rab Macfarlane, had now gone, the crowd had taken to local lad Cody Mutch, who had developed into a top-class keeper. What's more, the team was now sitting at the top of the Scottish League for the first time and, in the gathering interest, more and more women were showing up at Pittodrie. Until 1908 they had been admitted free of charge but with their numbers rising significantly there was little sense in turning chivalry into insanity. So the ladies were charged for admittance to the grandstand, such as it was.

Superstition was rife in those days and in their journeys south, Aberdeen players would never cross the Tay or Forth railway bridges without casting their coins. On his way to the Joint Station, Colman would never pass a certain blind beggar without giving him money. Aberdeen fans swore that a particular cup-tie in the south was lost because their train killed a black cat at Cove. A local versifier wrote to the *Evening Express*:

> Poor cat, we mourn your awful fate
> No more will you be seen
> But why, I ask, should your demise
> Bring woe to Aberdeen?

In 1910, Aberdeen FC paid its first benefit cheque to the man who brought its first Scottish international honour, Willie Lennie. He collected a sum of £150. Wilfie Low had gone off to Newcastle and Aberdeen received in part exchange a splendid right-winger called Jimmy Soye, but that was only the start of a series of comings and goings. They also acquired W.D. Nichol, an Englishman serving with the Seaforths who became known as the 'Thunderbolt' for the power of his shot. Charlie O'Hagan refused Aberdeen's top terms and ended up with Morton. The Pittodrie management replaced him with someone who would figure largely in the affairs of the club.

Patrick Travers came from Clyde and established a left-wing of Travers and Lennie, which became just as effective as the O'Hagan –Lennie partnership. Later, when he had played for Celtic, coached in Norway and trained Dumbarton, he returned as Aberdeen's second manager when Jimmy Philip gave up in 1924.

But in that close season of 1910 his thoughts were on playing football and among the new arrivals was one of his former team-mates at Shawfield, Jock Wyllie. It did not take the Pittodrie crowd long to realise that in Big Jock they had a new personality, robust but nimble and with a head of iron, which he used to fine effect when coming up for corner-kicks. He is reputed on one memorable occasion to have scored with a header from the halfway line! After two years Jock left for Bradford but didn't take any more to English football than the Pittodrie faithfuls did to losing him. So to everyone's satisfaction, he was welcomed back with open arms.

In more innocent days, football produced incidents which would be unthinkable today. Picture Pittodrie on 3 September 1910, and a game with Hamilton Accies. The ball was kicked into one of the garden plots adjoining the terracing, and a youth who went to retrieve it was warned off by a woman of substantial girth. Peter Simpson, the trainer, made an attempt but he too was driven into retreat. The joy of the spectators, now standing with their backs to the pitch, reached its peak when a policeman went to bring some order to the situation and the formidable madam grabbed hold and bodily threw him out. Finally, somebody tumbled on the wisdom of producing another ball.

Two weeks later Aberdeen, who had not saved a single point at Ibrox in five seasons of First Division football, went to Glasgow in determined mood and collected them both, an accomplishment that raised new pride in the Granite City. The team that broke the Ibrox duck was: King; Colman, Hume; Wilson, Wyllie, Millar; Soye, McIntosh, Murray, Travers, Lennie. That was Colman's hundredth game since joining the club in 1907, having missed only one.

Still with unusual incidents, spectators were baffled one Saturday to see Arthur King, who had taken over in goal from Cody Mutch, grabbing a shot from the Falkirk left-winger while standing well inside his goal-net area. It didn't seem possible from that angle. Falkirk claimed a goal but the referee discovered the ball had reached King's hands after bursting through the side netting.

Aberdeen were now top of the Scottish League and became the target for others to beat. Incentives were not uncommon in those days and when the team travelled to play Partick Thistle, a Firhill player mentioned they were on a £4 bonus if they could be the first team to beat Aberdeen that season. The Pittodrie players sought a similar bonus from chairman Tom Duncan, who said he could not commit his board to that kind of offer but promised reward if they put up a good show. That was all they did. The Partick players collected their £4 bonus and the men from the north were awarded an extra ten shillings for their first defeat.

The commercialism of 1910 had little to learn from today. In that same year a Greenock butcher offered a lamb to any Morton player who could score in a game against Rangers. With a liking for a tender chop, former Pittodrie player Charlie O'Hagan went out and scored five for Morton and collected his little flock of sheep on the Monday! It was a different world.

When Rangers came to Pittodrie, they had never been beaten in the Granite City. The question of whether Aberdeen could bring off the double was unresolved with three minutes left and still no scoring. Then Willie Lennie took a corner-kick on the left and Angus McIntosh came up to head home the winner.

Neutral linesmen came into force on New Year's Day 1911 and soon it was Celtic's turn to appear at Pittodrie. They too came a cropper, with a last-minute goal from Jimmy Soye, who said it was the best goal he had ever scored – and Jimmy scored some remarkable ones. So Aberdeen had notched up an Old Firm double, largely inspired by Donald Colman, now in his thirty-third year but just at the start of his international career. He was growing in stature by the week, a small body with a shrewd brain and a brave heart, sparking off a plague of verses including this one:

> We hae a back in Aiberdeen
> His like this toun has never seen
> For sterling pluck and judgement keen
> There's nane can match wi' Donald

There was promise in the air in the spring of 1911 when Aberdeen once again found themselves in the semi-final of the Scottish Cup, due to play Celtic at Parkhead this time and still joint league leaders with Rangers. But the Old Firm took the respective titles and the best that could be said of Aberdeen was that they were making their mark on Scottish football and being noticed on the continent.

The outcome was an invitation to tour the romantic lands of Bohemia, Moravia and Poland and off they set to play eight games in two weeks, with a total strength of just twelve players. They lost the first game but won the other seven and full-back Jock Hume distinguished himself when he was drafted to centre-forward and scored eighteen goals.

Back home there was disappointment that Paddy Travers, who had business interests in Glasgow, was being transferred to Celtic along with W.D. Nichol. But the most notable incident of 1911 – 12 was that, after stone-throwing at an Aberdeen–Rangers match in which visiting half-back Jimmy Gordon was set upon by spectators and saved only by the intervention of Aberdeen players, the SFA decided to close Pittodrie for two weeks. In fact, the punishment was ineffective since they were due to play away from home on both weekends.

It was in that close season that Jock Wyllie was transferred to Bradford City for £300, a move that caused ructions in the board-room despite the consolation that Paddy Travers was returning from Celtic.

On the national scene there was an imaginative move to cater for supporters who were unable to see football on a Saturday. The six top teams – Rangers, Celtic, Aberdeen, Dundee, Hearts and Hibernian – formed themselves into an Inter-City League for midweek games. But they fielded under-strength teams and treated the games as friendlies and the whole thing flopped.

More substantially, Aberdeen had now established a second team to play in the Highland League along with Buckie Thistle, Elgin City, Forres Mechanics, the 93rd Argyll and Sutherland Highlanders and the four Inverness clubs, Clachnacuddin, Caledonian, Thistle and Citadel.

In the First Division, however, Aberdeen had landed in the doldrums and there was general unrest and talk of transfers. Manchester City came north waving a cheque for £1,000 to secure the signature of the illustrious Colman but Donald drew himself to his full height and, with touching loyalty, made it plain he had no wish to leave Pittodrie and that was that.

19
ENTER THE DONS

So far in the story from 1903 there has been no mention of the Dons because the popular name of today had not yet found its way into the local vocabulary. People have argued about how it arose, some pointing to the many schoolmasters involved in the early days, including that don of education, John Clarke, who chaired the founding meeting in 1903. It is an unlikely theory. They may speak of dons at Oxford and Cambridge but it is not a word you heard in Torry or the sharny byres of Buchan. More likely it came from the simple contraction of 'Aberdonian', turning it first into 'Come on the Donians!' and then 'Come on the Dons!'

If there is doubt about how it arose, at least there was one man of my acquaintance who claimed he could pinpoint the very day when it was first used in print in the local press. The meticulous George Sleigh, a sportswriter with Aberdeen Journals in the first half of the last century, maintained it first appeared, for some unaccountable reason, after an Aberdeen–Celtic match at Pittodrie on 15 February 1913. Before then they were the Black and Golds or the Wasps. Now they were the Dons, celebrating the occasion with a 3–0 win over Celtic in a game which marked the first appearance of one of the worthies of his day, Dod Brewster from Mugiemoss, whose signature was obtained just an hour before a Sunderland man arrived on his doorstep.

Throughout this period that other popular Don, the incomparable Colman, was playing with splendid consistency despite his thirty-five years and there was local disappointment when he was chosen as a reserve against Ireland in Dublin. On the morning of the match, however, the selectors decided not only to include him in the team but to appoint him captain and Colman, the legend finding fame in the twilight of his career, strode out to play yet another magnificent match and to lead Scotland to a 2–1 victory, maintaining his record of never having played in a losing Scottish side.

In that season of 1912–13, the Dons utilised twenty-one players whose names, for the record, were: Arthur King, Andy Greig, Donald Colman, Jock Hume, Bobby Hannah, Stewart Davidson, George Wilson, Jock McConnell, Dod Brewster, Fred Watson, Wilfie Low, Jimmy Soye, Pat Travers, Davie Main, Johnny Wood, Willie Lennie, Johnny Scorgie, Joe Walker, Willie Milne, Bertie Murray and Angus McIntosh.

Financially, the Dons were going through a lean spell and were in no position to buy. If Colman and Hume had turned down offers to tempt them away, Stewart Davidson was off to Middlesbrough, Willie Milne to Third Lanark and goalkeeper Arthur King to Spurs, having taken a lot of barracking from a section of the crowd. Meanwhile, there was a cry to bring back Jock Wyllie, who was then captain of Bradford City but sorely missed at Pittodrie. The manager and chairman were despatched to see what they could do, and they succeeded.

After eight years, Aberdeen's first internationalist, Willie Lennie, had been transferred to Falkirk for what seemed the ridiculous fee of £30 and there was much public unrest about the poor form of the team. Showing more public-spiritedness than journalistic judgement, the editor of the *Evening Express* announced that he had been receiving a lot of critical mail but, in view of the club's lowly position and poor attendances, didn't think it was in the interests of the game to publish it.

In the spring of 1914, flagging interest was revived with a benefit match for Johnny Edgar in which the team of the day faced a selection of former Dons and won 4–2. The line-up that April day was: Greig; Colman, Hannah; Chatwin, J.J. Simpson, Low; Wyllie, Walker, Main, Travers, Scorgie. The former players lined up: Rab Macfarlane; George Macfarlane, Jimmy Gault; Ecky Halkett, Wilfie Low, Henry

Low; D. Taylor, Bertie Murray, Dr Jock Sangster, Charlie O'Hagan, Willie Lennie.

During that close season, Travers went back to his native Dumbarton and Aberdeen signed a new personality, a goalkeeper who had been with Newcastle and Sunderland. His name was George Anderson, a man who was soon taken to the hearts of the Pittodrie crowd and later became a leading citizen of Aberdeen – town councillor, businessman and wartime manager of the Dons before masterminding Dundee and projecting the talent of the famous Billy Steel.

Another signing of the time was Bert MacLachlan, whose wish to return from Aston Villa to Scotland was picked up by the intelligence service at Pittodrie. Bert, who was a cousin of future manager Davie Halliday, became captain in a period of the 1920s that produced some of the top names in the Pittodrie story. For the moment, Bobby Archibald arrived from Third Lanark and John Robertson, a city tinsmith and good judge of a player, joined the board and later became chairman.

But the assassination in Sarajevo had sparked off the First World War and if a lifestyle that had survived for centuries was about to be destroyed for ever, little wonder that football began to feel the ripples. Fearing the game might have to be suspended altogether, the Scottish Football Association consulted the War Office and it was agreed they should carry on for as long as possible. The players were members of the Territorial Army and some were off to the war. Bobby Hannah was mobilised for the 7th Gordons and Alec Wright for the 4th Battalion. There was fleeting excitement for the visit of a Queen's Park team including an outside-right called Alan Morton, before he transferred to the other wing and became the Wee Blue Devil of Ibrox, the most venerated Rangers player of all time.

In the movement and uncertainty of wartime, the Gordon Highlanders appearing in Aberdeen jerseys included Mungo Hutton, later to become a famous Scottish referee as well as Aberdeen scout in the west of Scotland. As the nation began to feel the effects of war, the crowds fell away and there was a need to cut spending. The

League and the Players' Union agreed that footballers receiving £2 10s, and over would take a reduction of 25 per cent. The Scottish Cup was abandoned and by 1916, with events leading up to the unspeakable horrors of the Somme, the war news was so bad that the public could raise little enthusiasm for football.

Mourning armbands became a regular feature, reflecting the fate of young men in the glaur of some foreign field, too far removed from the swaying cornfields of Aberdeenshire. The first of the black bands was for John Mackay, a Dons director and quartermaster in an Aberdeen company of the Royal Engineers, who was killed at Flanders. Then came CSM Charlie Neilson from Ellon, an outside-left who was killed with the 5th Gordons.

The war brought an unfamiliar look to the team as well as chaotic incidents, like missing a connection to Kilmarnock, having to change on the train and running on to the field twenty-five minutes late, only to be beaten 7–0. But there was the friendliness and help-fulness which became a feature of both world wars. Raith Rovers arrived at Pittodrie without a goalkeeper at a time when they were bottom of the League and the Dons were second bottom. The home team obligingly gave Raith the services of Andy Greig for the day – and he helped to inflict defeat on his own team!

The Dons struggled on through the turmoil of war but finally the burden became too much and it was agreed that Aberdeen, Dundee and Raith Rovers should drop out of competitive football until condi-tions improved. From 1917 until 1919 there was no senior football in Aberdeen and the club turned its attention to the local amateur league, giving it a great deal of help and encouragement. Much of the success of that competition was due to a man called Billy Russell, who did more than most to foster the game of football in Aberdeen. Eventually, he gave up his job as a tinsmith to become the Dons' trainer.

With the war drawn to an end in what was called victory, although the carnage left little room for celebration, Aberdeen Football Club began to pick up the threads of normality again. The very first player signed after the First World War was to become one of the most famous Dons of all, Jock Hutton, the most jovial chap who ever wore a football jersey. (Later generations will get the picture if I say he was much the build and style of Don Emery.) Just 5ft 8ins in height, Jock was reckoned to be well in excess of fifteen stone, not that his actual weight was ever published in those days. He didn't use that massive bulk and strength to unfair advantage although there were occasions when he exercised a perfectly fair shoulder charge and launched an opponent into orbit. But Jock was a happy, likeable man, romping through a game with the same jolly abandon he showed in life. Money, they said, burned a hole in his pocket yet Jock would come up smiling even when he couldn't lay his hands on a shilling.

For all his size, Jock was a soft and kindly soul and not a little gullible. On the Pittodrie payroll of the 1920s was a wee Glasgow joker called Johnny Paton, who sometimes went back south for the weekend. He would return on a Monday morning with a greeting for Jock: 'I've something here to interest you, Jock – a gold watch.' Jock would look at it and ask the price. 'Ach, just £3 to you.' Three days later the 'gold' would peel off, no more than you would expect from a so-called bargain at the Glasgow Barras on a Sunday. But all that happened later.

When Partick Thistle came to Pittodrie on 21 April 1919 for a friendly, which was intended to help Aberdeen restore contact with the game after the war, the Dons fielded the sturdy youngster from Bellshill Athletic. He played with a scarf round his neck but whatever amusement that aroused the Pittodrie crowd was soon engrossed in his performance. Jock Hutton may have been destined to be Scotland's right-back but he was fielded at inside-left that day, opening the scoring with a perfect header before rounding several Partick players to score again with a fierce shot that had everyone talking.

That cannonball kick would become the hallmark of Hutton's play. Manager Jimmy Philip realised after the game that he hadn't signed him and hastened to Motherwell on the Monday morning, thankful that the Partick party, with whom he travelled south, had failed to discover he was not already an Aberdeen player.

So the war was finally behind them and at the annual general meeting in August 1919 chairman Tom Duncan reported that thirty-three players and officials of Aberdeen Football Club had served in the forces and eight of them had died: Dr J. Ellis Milne, John Mackay, Herbert Murray, the brothers Charlie and J.H. Neilson, John Munro, Angus McLeod and Fred Watson. The Scottish League gave £1,130 towards the costs for the two blank seasons and the club decided to increase the share capital from £1,500 to £5,000, bringing in many new shareholders.

Big-time football in Aberdeen resumed on 16 August 1919 with a Scottish League game against Albion Rovers, for which the club dared to introduce the shilling gate (five pence today). That represented a doubling of the entrance money but did not deter 9,000 people from turning out to see an Aberdeen victory. The team on that historic return was: Anderson; Hannah, Hume; Wright, Brewster, MacLachlan; C.G. Watson, Caie, Hutton, Robertson, Archibald. Jacky Connon, one of the best local players ever seen at Pittodrie, was also edging his way into the team and Jock Hutton was soon to be moved to full-back.

The wider world had been turned inside out in history's greatest upset and football was suffering from a sense of lost continuity; but if anything could restore a touch of normality to the slopes of Pittodrie it would surely be the return of Donald Colman. Demobilised from the forces, he was back in Aberdeen by the end of 1919, past his best (not surprising when you consider he was then forty-one) but still a stabilising presence and a welcome link with an age gone for ever.

If Colman was back, another Pittodrie favourite was on his way to pastures new. The New Year's Day match (the rest of Scotland calls it Ne'erday, but not us!) against Dundee was Dod Brewster's last for the Dons before he was transferred to Everton for an Aberdeen record fee of £1,500, and that marked the start of another series of transfers which enabled the Dons to improve their ground and build a new stand. Dod became a big favourite in

English football and a year later was capped for Scotland against England at Hampden, playing alongside Stewart Davidson, another former Don who was by then captain of Middlesbrough.

Aberdeen's first Scottish Cup tie after the war was at Cowdenbeath on 27 January 1920, a day which produced yet another illustration of hooliganism on the soccer slopes of Scotland. Aberdeen's line-up at Cowdenbeath was: Anderson; Colman, Hume; Wright, Robertson, MacLachlan; Grant, W. Wyllie, Connon, Hutton, Archibald.

In the closing minutes of that match the Dons were a goal up when the home team claimed a penalty. The referee's refusal brought hundreds of Cowdenbeath supporters swarming on to the pitch and there was fighting and shouting everywhere. The Dons found their way to the pavilion barred by an angry crowd but the crisis produced its own hero in the shape of a gigantic sailor who jumped down from the stand and assumed the role of Popeye, the Pittodrie protector, cleaving a way to the dressing room with threatening fists.

Goalkeeper George Anderson had farthest to come and became isolated in an ugly scene, emerging so badly mauled that he had to be carried to the pavilion in a state of collapse. Meanwhile, burly Jock Hutton was employing the granite structure of his frame to rescue referee Stevenson, whose penalty decision had caused the riot. Mr Stevenson decided there was no time to resume the match anyway and the Dons were thankful to escape from the Fife town without further injury, through now to another round of the Scottish Cup in which they were drawn away to Gala Fairydean. For a financial consideration, the Border team agreed to switch the venue and that match on 7 February 1920, which drew a crowd of 15,000, was the first Scottish Cup tie seen at Pittodrie since 1914.

A month later, in a game against Raith Rovers, the Dons produced a lanky centre-half, an amateur called Victor E. Milne, a medical student at Aberdeen University, whose performance soon had the spectators in raptures. When he signed as a professional for the following season he was completing a half-back line of Wright, Milne and MacLachlan which subsequent players, including Willie Cooper, would claim to be the finest half-back line ever seen at Pittodrie. As it happened, Vic Milne was the son of that early chairman of the club, Bailie Milne, and football was by no means his only interest. Playing cricket for Aberdeenshire was just another of his sporting outlets, but football claimed him in the end and he became a big name in England after joining Aston Villa, retaining his connection in later life by becoming doctor to the Birmingham club.

In that year of 1920 Donald Colman was forty-two, long past the limit of a normal football lifespan. Any suggestion of a free transfer would have been an affront to a man of such stature, so it was left to the great little man himself to bow out gracefully, before embarking on his next big task of fostering the game in Norway. His partner of so many seasons, Jock Hume, left to be player-coach at Darwen, in Lancashire, and the veteran Jock Wyllie, for whom Colman had a great affection, went to Forfar.

The feeling that an era had ended spread from dressing room to boardroom where there were ructions among the directors, ending with the resignation of Tom Duncan, who had been chairman for fourteen years. The row centred around manager Jimmy Philip, who had reverted to a part-time role during the First World War. In restoring the job to full-time, some directors felt it should be advertised but the majority decided to offer it to Philip who had, after all, been there since 1903.

That was long enough in the eyes of some directors – not too surprising when nothing had been won in all that time – but Philip was offered his former status at a salary of £350 and he did not hesitate to accept. Tom Duncan was replaced as chairman by another Philip, this time William.

20

BLACKWELL'S UMBRELLA

D ONALD COLMAN played his last game for Aberdeen against Kilmarnock at Rugby Park on 21 April 1920 and, with the departure of his partner Jock Hume as well, the Dons were faced with the long-forgotten task of finding full-backs. Luck was on their side when they found a junior international from Glasgow Perthshire called Matt Forsyth. When it was also discovered that the young Hutton was really a full-back and not a forward, they came up with a new partnership of Hutton and Forsyth which turned out to be just as successful, if not as long-lived, as that of Colman and Hume. Forsyth had a fine football brain, much in the style of Colman, cool and calculating and the perfect contrast to the rumbustious Hutton, whose later international career owed much to the influence of Forsyth.

Matt had come back from the First World War, having been at the Somme, and was keenly pursued by English clubs but his mother was a widow and the deal with Aberdeen allowed him to stay in Glasgow and travel up for games on the Friday night. Working for a firm of railway company agents, he was able to get cheap tickets.

As a player he was stylish and adventurous, introducing the 'overlap' when neither the word nor the idea had gained currency. Indeed, full-backs who dared to cross the halfway line in those days were liable to be carpeted for their indiscretion. Matt trained with Third Lanark and travelled up with them for a game at Pittodrie. During the match he came forward on one of his adventures and unleashed a tremendous shot towards the rugged Jimmy Brownlie, a memorable character who kept goal for Thirds. The big keeper caught his hand between ball and crossbar and on the journey back to Glasgow, Matt was walking down the train corridor when a voice boomed out: 'Hey, young man, I want a word with you.' An apprehensive Forsyth stuck his head into Brownlie's compartment. 'What the hell d'ye think you are – a centre-forward? In future stay back where you belong, at left-back!' bawled the goalie, stabbing a fractured finger at the Dons player.

But not all the rumblings of big Brownlie could stifle the class of Matt Forsyth, who was the perfect thinking partner for Hutton. In later years he smiled when he recalled the likeable warmth of big Jock and said, 'As often as not his hefty clearances came straight back from where he had sent them.'

The pity of it was that Forsyth, a classier player, did not get the same international recognition as Hutton, who had seven caps during his Pittodrie years and several more after he left. By comparison, Matt had the doubtful consolation of being a Scottish reserve on no fewer than thirteen occasions.

He had been a schoolboy witness of the first big Ibrox disaster at the start of the twentieth century and was present again at Hampden in 1909 when the Rangers–Celtic Scottish Cup final ended in a riot, the crowd calling for extra time, invading the field, ripping up the goalposts and generally wrecking the place.

Matt later worked for the Admiralty at Scapa Flow and then in London but finally returned to Aberdeen, a lively octogenarian regaling a circle of friends with tales of long ago. Making friends had always been a talent of Matt Forsyth, whose own theatrical personality brought him into personal contact with music-hall legends Harry Lauder and Marie Lloyd and not least Dr Walford Bodie, the man from Macduff who became world famous for his extraordinary hypnotic and magical powers. Matt also befriended the great jockey Steve Donoghue during his visits to Scottish racecourses and went to see him win the Epsom Derby of 1922 on the back of Captain Cuttle (Steve won the Derby six times, three of them in succession).

Apart from Forsyth, there were other personalities gathering at

Pittodrie in the transition to the new era, including Sandy Grosert, later a dentist in the city, who came back from Hibs with a high reputation, having previously played for the Dons as an amateur. In his unpaid days at Pittodrie, Sandy had an unwritten stipulation in his agreement that the manager would provide him with a bottle of stout after his Saturday games. Jimmy Philip fulfilled the bargain.

There was also an attempt to gather up as many of the promising local youngsters as possible and these included George Sutherland, Alex Wright, Victor Milne, Arthur Robertson, Clarence Watt (Clarty), Walter Grant, Jacky Connon, Bobby Yule and Andy Rankin from Banks o' Dee, one of the best ever to come from Aberdeen's junior ranks.

With size and strength, the combination of Wright, Milne and MacLachlan was establishing itself as a brilliant half-back line. A young goalkeeper arrived from Scunthorpe to play a trial and was soon to become popularly entrenched. Harry Blackwell was a worthy successor to George Anderson and part of a back division which rolled off North-east tongues as 'Blackwell, Hutton and Forsyth'.

Out Bucksburn way, young Alec Moir was scoring forty goals for Mugiemoss in one season and a man from Leeds United arrived in Aberdeen one Friday night to sign him first thing next morning. Word reached manager Jimmy Philip, who headed out along the Great Northern Road at one o'clock in the morning and signed the lad on the spot. He played many fine games for Aberdeen but never did make the centre-forward position his own.

Jimmy Smith was brought from Rangers to be hailed by the Pittodrie crowd as the best left-winger since Willie Lennie, and behind the scenes Pat Travers was engaged as coach, having finished his playing career and returned to his native Dumbarton. Like his former team-mate, Donald Colman, Travers was far from finished with Aberdeen Football Club.

Meanwhile, in that season of 1921–22, the system of promotion and relegation had been introduced to Scottish football. Hearts came to Pittodrie desperately needing a win to escape the Second Division and they got it, but the match raised criticism that Aberdeen 'lay down' to make sure the valuable asset of the Edinburgh club would not be lost to the top division. The Tynecastle team continued to escape relegation for another fifty-five years until 1977, when the Scottish clubs that have yet to go down were reduced to an élite of three – Rangers, Celtic and Aberdeen.

But of all the talking points of the early 1920s, there was none so notorious as the Scottish Cup third-round tie of 1923, when the Dons were drawn against Peterhead in what turned out to be the craziest game of football ever seen at Pittodrie, or anywhere else for that matter.

With the tie due to be played in the Buchan town, the Dons nego-tiated a switch of venue. Peterhead drove a hard bargain – £250 guarantee, plus travelling expenses for players and directors and the promise of another match at Peterhead before the end of the season. In anticipation of defeat, the Highland League team was making sure of ample compensation. But matters were not as simple as that.

News of the deal brought a demand from the Peterhead players to be paid £10 a man. The club dug in its heels, refused to pay the money except for a win, and finally fielded a team without eight of its regulars. As small consolation, the management had been able to sign Jock Hume, the former Dons stalwart, just before the game but the rest were a motley gathering scraped together for the occa-sion. Among them were C.P. Murray and J.T. Wiseman, secretary and captain of the Aberdeen University side, who had to be listed under false names because they had already played in the qualifying stages of the Scottish Cup earlier that season – against Peterhead! However, small matters like an illegal team didn't deter them in those more colourful days.

The two players were widely recognised and if by some mischance Peterhead had won the game, Aberdeen captain Bert MacLachlan was primed to lodge a protest before it ended. But that was hardly necessary. Aberdeen's 5–0 lead at half-time became 13–0 before the end, by which time two Peterhead players, Buchan and McRobbie, had retired to the pavilion suffering from exposure! In wind and lashing rain, the Pittodrie fixture was farcical enough but Aberdeen goalkeeper Harry Blackwell set a new fashion between the sticks by wearing a waterproof coat – and raising a spectator's umbrella, which he removed on the one occasion when Peterhead ventured within shooting distance of his goal.

A gallant crowd of 3,241 huddled together for the miserable occasion, having paid a total of £181 8s. 11d. at the gate, a sum which left Aberdeen well out of pocket in view of the deal. The teams as published that morning (and note how the papers relieved themselves of responsibility for the false names) were: Aberdeen – Blackwell; Hutton, Forsyth; MacLachlan, Milne, Robertson; Middleton, Thomson, Grant, Rankin, Smith. Peterhead ('as supplied') – Drysdale; J.K. Allan, Hume; F. Thomson, J. Buchan, G. Slessor; W. Hutcheson, G. Allan, A. McRobbie, A. Hall, W. Milne.

The goals, for the interest of those with masochistic tendencies, were scored by Grant (3), Thomson (4), Milne (3), Rankin, Middleton and Smith. They should have saved some of the goals for the fourth round because they promptly went out of the Cup at the hands of Hibs.

21
HUTTON'S RUN
OF SUCCESS

J UST as Donald Colman had played in all three home internationals in season 1910–11, Jock Hutton was similarly capped in
1922–23, when Scotland took the championship with wins over
Ireland and Wales and a draw with England at Hampden.

The Wales game was played at Paisley and it was known that
Hutton was quietly worried about facing up to the famous Ted
Vizard, Bolton Wanderers' outside-left. On the forenoon of the
match, Aberdeen sportswriter George Sleigh met Jock walking in
Argyle Street, Glasgow, asked how he was feeling and was given the
confidential information that he was suffering from diarrhoea.

Suspecting the reason, George suggested a glass of good port wine
as a known cure for internal disruption and Jock was more than
receptive to the idea. But Scotland's right-back could hardly be seen
in a pub on the day of a big match so the two of them found a quiet
retreat where George administered the medicine. Jock said he felt
much better and proceeded to the game, only to find that Vizard had
pulled out at the last minute through injury. Jock played a splendid
game and went on to establish himself in a distinguished international career, diarrhoea or no diarrhoea!

Meanwhile the staffing position at Pittodrie was far from settled.
Centre-half Vic Milne, by then a doctor and a man commanding
great respect, was on the move to Aston Villa, leaving not only the
football scene but the cricketing fraternity of the Aberdeenshire club
for whom he had been a sound bat and effective change bowler.

But if they were losing a doctor, the Dons directors replaced him with a budding minister, Jimmy Jackson from Motherwell, who took up his divinity studies in Aberdeen and later played for Liverpool before taking over a Presbyterian church in the north of England. Stewart Davidson, who had gone to Middlesbrough in 1911, came back in 1923, clearly past his best but still a good influence on those around him. By now the Dons had shaped into a formation of: Blackwell; Hutton, Forsyth; Davidson, J. Jackson, MacLachlan; Moir, Grant, Miller, Rankin, Smith.

The movement of players had far from stopped (does it ever in football?). Jock Edward, a Glasgow junior, arrived in Aberdeen and had several fine seasons before moving to Portsmouth, later returning as player-coach to Huntly and settling in business in Torry, like his close friend Harry Blackwell. Among the other arrivals was little Johnny Paton (the one who sold the watch to Jock Hutton), an amusing chap who had played for Celtic and Third Lanark and could dribble through a defence with a bundle of tricks in his boots.

On a bitterly cold day he took the field in a match to be refereed by David Calder, brother of the famous Bobby, later Aberdeen's chief scout. Rubbing the cold out of his hands before the start, Johnny nodded to the referee with Glasgow perkiness and said, 'I'm cauld, ref – but you're Calder!' Mr Calder looked to see if anyone was within earshot and said, 'Watch it, you little bugger, or I'll send you off the park!'

Still eager to find local talent, manager Philip allowed his enthusiasm to land him in trouble. There had been a delay in signing Alec Ross from the local Richmond club and Dundee stepped in to sign him on a Sunday. Next morning the lad informed Mr Philip but confirmed that the signing had not been witnessed. Philip's eyes brightened. What's more, he reckoned a Sunday signature was illegal and persuaded the player to sign for Aberdeen instead, dashing off to register him in Glasgow and to announce he would play for Aberdeen reserves on the Saturday.

Ross returned his signing-on fee to Dundee, who were furious. They reported the matter to the SFA who held an inquiry and declared Ross to be a Dundee player. He was severely censured and

Aberdeen FC was fined £100, although the Association accepted Philip's explanation about his understanding of a Sunday contract.

With twenty years of history now behind them, the Dons were still searching for a national prize and hopes were rising in season 1923–24 when they reached the semi-final of the Scottish Cup for the fourth time. They had been there in 1908 and 1911, beaten both times by Celtic, and again in 1922 when Morton went through to win the Cup.

Now it was Hibernian who provided the opposition at Dens Park, Dundee, and a goalless draw was followed by a replay also at Dens, followed by extra time which still produced no goals. As the marathon continued, Hibs managed to score one goal amid protests that the talented Tim Dunn, later to become a Wembley Wizard, had steadied the ball with his hand. But the goal stood and Hibs went through to the Scottish Cup final, leaving Aberdeen fans to wonder when they were ever to savour the sweet smell of success.

On top of that, the club was running into trouble. Between those Scottish Cup games the Dons had to meet Queen's Park, who were deep in relegation trouble, and the team that took the field was without Hutton, Forsyth, Davidson, Miller, Rankin and Smith. It could have been argued they were saving their players for the gruelling Cup tie but the blunt accusation was that they were trying to help Queen's.

Charles Forbes, a future chairman, was playing for the Dons that day, in a team which showed no lack of effort to win the game. But Queen's Park were the victors and Clyde Football Club, who were also in relegation trouble, lodged a complaint about the weakened Aberdeen team. Jimmy Philip said his players had been left out on doctor's orders but it didn't wash and the club was fined another £100. At the end of the season, Queen's did escape and poor old Clyde went down.

In May 1924 Aberdeen toured Germany and on their return the big talking point was the resignation of manager Philip, the local wood-turner who had been given a part-time appointment in 1903 and had guided the club through those first twenty-one years. He had brought the city of Aberdeen into the mainstream of Scottish football, harnessed the talents of great players such as Colman and Hume and the club's first Scottish internationalist, Willie Lennie.

He had restored life after the barren period of the First World War and taken the Dons into the Roaring Twenties with the full-back partnership of Hutton and Forsyth. Admittedly, there was no silver to show for his efforts. They may have come of age and shown signs of maturing but it would take another twenty-one years and more before any kind of trophy was to grace the Pittodrie sideboard.

Yet, much as we rejoice in winning cups and flags, there is a romantic streak in football fans which lingers with great performances and personalities even when the period has passed into history. Colman-and-Hume, Hutton-and-Forsyth won nothing at all at club level and the same fate would befall other great Dons, such as Benny Yorston, Willie Mills and Matt Armstrong, as well as those famous half-back lines of Wright–Milne–MacLachlan and Black–McLaren –Hill. There wasn't a medal between them yet every one of those names stirred a glow in the hearts of Dons supporters according to their generation.

Jimmy Philip became a director after he retired. He also became involved with the MacGregor clan and its annual gathering and it was during a MacGregor day in Belfast in 1930 that he died in a road accident. His son George was diverted from a football career by his father's warning about committing everything to the sport. 'Look at the people who were once footballers and ended up as sandwich-board men on Union Street,' he used to point out. So George became a sea captain before returning to take over the Crown Bar in Woodside.

The choice of successor to Jimmy Philip as manager was almost predictably Patrick Travers, the Dumbarton man of stocky build and pawky humour who had played for Aberdeen and Celtic and finally returned to Pittodrie as coach. In that summer of 1924 he was about to embark on a fourteen-year reign as manager which would produce its own high drama and tragedy as well as an array of memorable footballers.

Before his departure, Jimmy Philip had begun negotiations for a transfer which would bring to Pittodrie one of Scottish football's greatest personalities. The fact that the deal was completed by Paddy Travers was appropriate, if only for the fact that the player had originated in his own Dunbartonshire. The first hint of it came at the annual general meeting when chairman William Philip announced that two forwards of whom much was expected would soon be joining the club. Pittodrie could hardly wait to hear the good news.

22

THE JACKSON FOUR

W HEN the mystery was unwrapped and the two newcomers to Pittodrie were revealed as the brothers Alec and Walter Jackson, the names produced little more than a shrug of anti-climax. Yet there can be no apology for devoting a whole chapter to the name of Jackson, if only because younger brother Alec turned out to be one of the legends of Scottish football, as sleek and delightful a figure as ever graced the game, immortalised with that élite who will forever be remembered as the Wembley Wizards.

Alec Jackson was the youngest of five brothers from the small community of Renton in Dunbartonshire. The eldest, John, had emigrated to America while Walter became a professional footballer with Kilmarnock and Alec with Dumbarton, where he played with such confidence that he suggested to his team-mates, when he was only seventeen, that they should hold a reunion celebration on the evening after his first game for Scotland.

But the promised land of the United States was calling and Walter and Alec Jackson decided to follow brother John, attracted by an early attempt to introduce soccer to the land of baseball. The Americans were offering well-paid jobs to people who could also play football and the Jacksons landed with Bethlehem Steel of Pennsylvania, whose senior executives included W. Luther Lewis, a fervent Welshman and the main inspiration of soccer in America.

Jock Hume was by then with Brooklyn Wanderers and is credited with sending back reports to Aberdeen about the tremendous talent of young Alec Jackson. Simultaneously, however, word was filtering through the connections of Donald Colman and Paddy Travers that the Jacksons were not so settled in the New World that they could not be lured back to the old country. Aberdeen wasted no time in making contact and the popular story has been that they wanted Walter, who refused to come without his young brother. It was an attractive story but found no support when I later talked to the Jacksons' nephews, John and William from Renton, who said Alec was the one who wanted to bring his brother.

In due course the two of them arrived in the city and were conveyed to the Caledonian Hotel in Union Terrace, which was the centre of much back-room activity connected with Aberdeen Football Club. Paddy Travers wasted no time in signing the Jacksons for £1,000, one of the best pieces of football business ever transacted.

It is always difficult to acquire the full flavour of a figure from the past and those who never saw Alec Jackson must depend on the judgement of those who did. Fortunately the evidence is everywhere. It does him poor justice to say he was tall, lithe, swift and beautifully proportioned but one of his contemporaries came close to the colour of his personality when he said he had laughter in his eyes as well as magic in his feet, a real dandy of a man who was blessed with a soft West Highland lilt.

Jackson's father had originally hailed from Fittie and now the son was back to delight the crowds with his artistry. Luther Lewis had given Alec a return ticket when he left America, with an open invitation to go back, but although he kept it in his wallet for a long time it was patently clear his future lay in the land where football was well understood.

Soon he was the automatic choice for Scotland at outside-right, chosen in 1925, at the age of nineteen, to play against England at Hampden in the first team since 1895 to be drawn entirely from home clubs. The Scots took the Sassenachs apart that day in a 2–0 victory which told little of their superiority. In the company of men such as Meiklejohn, McMullan, Gallacher and Morton, the man of the match was unanimously declared to be Alec Jackson, the teenaged cavalier from Pittodrie, a boy with dash and flair, and perhaps the first charismatic superstar of football.

In the black-and-gold of Aberdeen he went to Kilmarnock one Saturday and found his team-mates playing mostly to the left wing and suffering a 2–0 deficit at half-time. Jackson teased his colleagues at the break: 'If you would play more to the right-hand side of the park we might win this game you know.'

A cocky devil? But the Aberdeen players quietly took the hint, knowing it would need Jackson's genius to turn the game. So they played to his wing and he responded with three magnificent goals which gave them a 3–2 victory. As the players returned to the dressing room he just winked and said, 'I tell't ye!'

The Jackson brothers had made their debut against Rangers on 23 August 1924, when the crowd had the novelty of seeing the great Alan Morton falling back into defence to help his team-mates cope with the menace of the new winger. Johnny Paton and Walter Grant had to make way for the newcomers but Paton later returned to form an effective combination with the Jacksons, sandwiched between them at inside-right.

Aberdeen's signings were far from finished. Jock McHale arrived, a robust player who knew the game better than most and later was an inspiring influence on the rest of the team.

With Jimmy Jackson still playing in the half-back line, the Dons had three players with the same surname all appearing together. As if that were not enough of a headache for football writers of the day, Paddy Travers headed back to his home territory in the Vale of Leven and signed a fourth. This time it was Willie Jackson, more often known as W.K. or 'Stonewall', who came from the same little district as Alec and Walter but was no relation. As well as the four Jacksons there were also two Bruces in the Aberdeen team, which had taken new shape as: Blackwell; D. Bruce, Forsyth; J. Jackson, Hutton, MacLachlan; A. Jackson, W. Jackson, W.K. Jackson, R. Bruce, Smith.

But the idolatory was reserved for the thoroughbred on the right wing who was compared in later years with Stanley Matthews and would equate at this centenary point to Manchester United's David Beckham or Ryan Giggs. The high point of his career was to come in 1928 when he was chosen to play against England at Wembley.

The Scottish team was immersed in controversy from the start when it was discovered that the selectors had left out such names as Andy Cunningham, Bob McPhail, Jimmy McGrory, Willie McStay and the formidable Jock Hutton, who had by then moved from his great days at Pittodrie to Blackburn Rovers. Eight of those chosen were now playing in English football, including Alec Jackson, and a cartoonist of the time produced a drawing of the three home players, Jack Harkness of Queen's Park, Tim Dunn of Hibs and Alan Morton of Rangers, heading south by train, with one of them saying, 'If only we had another one we could have a game of solo!'

The Scots team which gathered at the Regent Palace Hotel in London's Piccadilly Circus included little Alec James of Preston North End, whose rougher mould was in sharp contrast to the smoothness of Jackson, often described as the Jack Buchanan of football. There was in fact a needle-sharp jealousy between James and Jackson. Both had the ambition to be stars of the London scene, which they achieved when James went to Arsenal and Jackson to Chelsea.

Both revelled in the limelight but it was the former Don who scored a point on the morning of the Scotland–England match when he and goalkeeper Harkness came down to the lounge of the Regent Palace. As they sat down for a cup of tea, Jackson employed an old trick much practised by Harry Lauder on his visits to the Waldorf Astoria Hotel in New York.

He summoned a page-boy and said, 'Here's half-a-crown, son. I want you to go through the hotel paging Mister Alec Jackson.' Half-a-crown ($12\frac{1}{2}$ p) was a sizeable sum and the page-boy performed his duty with loud diligence. Heads turned in search of a famous football name and the mischievous Alec grinned in delight and said to Harkness, 'I bet James will be wild about this.'

By the time the much-criticised Scottish team reached Wembley Stadium on that historic day, the two potential kings were prepared to back their self-confidence with a bet on who would score first, not that the team was given much chance of scoring at all. Out they went on to the hallowed turf of Wembley in a downpour to play a game of football which will be talked about for as long as Scotsmen have the breath of a boast in their lungs.

Careering on the right wing with guile and style, it was Alec Jackson who collected the winnings when he met an Alan Morton cross with a flashing header to put Scotland ahead in just three minutes. It was the first of a hat-trick, but the doughty James was not to be outdone and scored two more to make it 5–1 in the most famous Scottish victory of all.

Before that, however, Jackson had played with consistent brilliance throughout season 1924–25 which, ironically, turned out to be a thoroughly bad one for the Dons. They were lying equal bottom with five other clubs on the last day when they were hosts to a Motherwell team in the same plight. Would Aberdeen go down?

A crowd of 15,000 was there to cheer wildly when Walter Jackson shot home the opening goal. Then it was the turn of Jimmy Jackson to clinch victory and reports of the match said he was 'enthusiastically hugged by his delighted colleagues' – 1925, that was! – 'and around the arena bedlam was let loose'.

The Dons survived and so did Motherwell, as the crazy mathematics of goal average were worked out. With the skills of Alec Jackson clearly cut out for better company, it was hardly surprising when he headed south. Manager Travers was later to recall that Jackson had no sooner settled on 'Deeside', as he liked to call the North-east, than there was a series of English raids across the 'Tweed', as he liked to call the border, for the purpose of seeing 'this human greyhound', as he liked to call Jackson.

The privilege of signing him fell to the illustrious Herbert Chapman, later to mastermind Arsenal but at that time manager of Huddersfield Town, a club of little consequence in modern times but which dominated English football in the 1920s, when its most ardent supporters included a schoolboy called Harold Wilson, a future tenant of No. 10 Downing Street.

Huddersfield, which won the league championship three times in a row, lured away more Pittodrie players in due time and lowered its popularity with Aberdonians even further in the 1950s when it snapped up a bespectacled boy from his classroom at Powis School before local people had the chance to get to know that his name was Denis Law.

So Alec Jackson was off on the golden trail to England for a fee of around £4,500, a transfer which would have ranked among the astronomically obscene of today. The loss of those silken skills left a feeling of desolation in many a Pittodrie heart and that indelible impression is all the more remarkable when you consider he had been and gone from Aberdeen before his twentieth birthday. His Pittodrie career, which lasted less than twelve months, was mirrored nearly fifty years later in the fleeting presence of the great Zoltan Varga, regarded by a later generation as the best Dons player they had ever seen.

Jackson helped Huddersfield to another English championship but London was still his target and it was no surprise when he moved to Chelsea for £8,500 and became the highest-paid man in football, one of the very first to lend his name to advertising. London life suited his personality. For £5 a time he appeared on several days a week in the sports department of a big London store, while a fashionable hairdresser used to pay him to come in for his morning shave.

As one of the early superstars of sport he was soon spreading his interests outside football, taking over a popular public house in St Martin's Lane, London, and entering a partnership to run the Queen's Hotel in Leicester Square just before the war. In fact, his outside interests took him prematurely out of the game when there were still some years of football left in him.

But footballers had to make some provision for their later years although in the case of Alec Jackson those years were limited. The Second World War was breaking over us and he became a major and welfare officer with the Middle East forces. When the war ended Jackson, now a heftier version of the thoroughbred who had so graced Pittodrie, was driving along the dusty roads near Cairo when he was killed in a car crash.

Death is no respecter of genius and it came to Alec Jackson with all the swiftness which had characterised his life and movement, and for which he was remembered by older men with moisture in their eyes.

23
'STICK TO SINGING, SON!'

T HE Aberdeen directors relieved the confusion of names by selling not only Alec Jackson to Huddersfield but also Jimmy Jackson, the Pittodrie padre, to Liverpool. When challenged about these sales by angry shareholders at the annual general meeting, chairman William Philip said both players had complained about the criticism they had received from some spectators and pressmen, and this was the main cause of their departures.

If this was truly the case, it confirms the view that Pittodrie supporters are among the hardest to please. If the immortal Jackson was not to some people's liking, what did that leave for lesser mortals? Maybe we are a thrawn, ill-to-please lot.

Two of the four Jacksons were now gone and within months Alec's brother Walter was on his way to Preston North End, leaving only W.K. to carry the name. W.K. Jackson had arrived at Pittodrie in February 1925, having played for Everton before returning to Vale of Leven in the Scottish Second Division and working at the Singer sewing machine factory in Clydebank.

He was a kindly man in the father-figure mould, nurturing young players in much the same way as Bob McDermid. The latter came to Aberdeen after being in dispute with Rangers, and established himself as a tireless workhorse in the Dons' forward line. He was a natural choice as trainer when his playing days were over.

W.K. Jackson took over at right-back when Jock Hutton went to Blackburn in 1926 but later moved to left-back to accommodate an up-and-coming youngster called Willie Cooper. He also kept an eye on another local boy, Dick Donald, whose father was the cinema king of Aberdeen. On leaving school, Dick was given charge of the Cinema House at the corner of Union Terrace and Skene Terrace, a career which ran parallel to his football and produced a generosity of tickets for his team-mates.

Playing in front of W.K. Jackson, Dick Donald was having one of his lesser games when, after one particular move, W.K. sought to save the youngster from discouragement by calling out, 'Hard luck, Dick!' His voice carried to the terracing and brought immediate response from a wag who shouted, 'Hard luck, ma erse! Ye're just wantin a ticket for the picters!'

On another occasion, playing against Motherwell, W.K. said to a Fir Park player of his acquaintance, 'Don't be too hard on young Donald. He's a newcomer to the team.' By half-time the same lad had taken the visitors' defence apart with one of his finest performances and Jackson had to take an earful from his Motherwell friend.

Jackson was laid low with double pneumonia and pleurisy, which gave an opening to another Pittodrie favourite, Charlie ('Oor ba') McGill, a man inclined to claim every ball that crossed the touchline. Jackson had already made provision for the future with a shop in Rosemount, where his son carried on the family business while W.K. devoted himself to the bowling green. Like many a former footballer, he found the role of spectator unbearable, in his case landing in arguments until he finally would not go near a football match.

But he kept memories of warm fellowship and good discipline at Pittodrie, standards set by Paddy Travers and Donald Colman, who stood no nonsense. Internationalist Alec Cheyne turned up minutes late one day and found a reserve player already stripped to take his place. He still had time to change but the position was not to be reversed.

Travers had a way with him. Coming back from Hamilton one Saturday, the Dons players were having dinner on the Glasgow–Aberdeen train. A young Italian had played as a trialist that day and, when dinner was over, Travers said, 'I believe you are a bit of a singer. How about giving us a song?' The lad obliged with operatic arias and turned out to have a very fine voice. Travers was genuinely full of praise, then took him aside and said, 'You stick to singing, son. You'll do better at that than you will at football.' It was the tactful way of telling him his Pittodrie sojourn was over.

With three of the Jacksons gone, Travers signed Alec Reid of Third Lanark for a record fee of £2,000. The outside-right went a long way towards placating the supporters over the loss of Alec Jackson. Bob McDermid, too, added quality to the team.

The new offside law was introduced at the start of season 1925–26. This said that a player was offside unless there were at least two opponents between him and the goal. Previously the requirement had been three players.

Matt Forsyth's benefit match that year was an occasion for nostalgia, particularly when the players who took the field included not only manager Paddy Travers but the indestructible Donald Colman, still turning on the soccer style at the age of forty-seven. That was to be Forsyth's last season at Pittodrie before joining Forres Mechanics in the Highland League.

Still in the midst of his international career, Jock Hutton was transferred a few months later to Blackburn, where he became as much of a local favourite as he had been in Aberdeen. Pittodrie looked a good deal emptier without Jock but it was fitting that he should go when his partner had gone. With other famous pairings such as Colman-and-Hume and Cooper-and-McGill, or Armstrong-and-Mills to come, the names of Hutton and Forsyth went together as inseparably as Rolls and Royce and sometimes just as smoothly.

When Jock's playing days were over he landed a manager's job in Ireland but the first player he signed had already been signed by another club! His managerial career didn't last long. People argued about whether Jock was just a hefty kicker or a man of wider skills but the balance of my early inquiries showed that he really was a considerable footballer. Beyond all doubt, he was one of the most jovial and popular figures ever seen at Pittodrie.

Just as the Jacksons, the Forsyths and the Huttons had departed, new talents were creeping upon the Pittodrie scene, ready to burst forth as the idols of another generation. Alec Jackson was still an exquisite memory, despite the brevity of his time at Aberdeen, but soon there would be two others who would stay longer and carve themselves just as deeply in the affections of the faithful. One was Alec Cheyne. The other will take the vote of many an old-timer as the greatest Don of all. He was Benny Yorston.

24
BENNY – THE GREATEST?

DOWN the trendy length of the King's Road in Chelsea, in the days of psychedelic fashion, I went in pursuit of a legend. Some regarded him as the greatest Don of all but most believed he was long since dead. Suddenly there came word of a sighting in the World's End district of Chelsea and that was how I set out, with the air of a Sherlock Holmes of soccer, to see if I could find Benny Yorston.

Finally, I tracked down a likely block of flats and began a random quest for anyone called Yorston. A Cockney woman in curlers said, 'Try that door there.' I listened with fascination to the short step of the man coming to answer the door and there he stood in open-necked shirt and cardigan, a pale and rotund little chap with a tongue still as recognisably Aberdeen as his native Kittybrewster. Yes, it was Benny all right, recovering from a heart attack and apologising for the fact that a wartime knock on the head had affected his memory.

Benny Yorston, born in 1905, grew up at 68 Great Northern Road, one of six children attending Kittybrewster School. As a twelve year old he had played at Pittodrie in a schools championship and was scoring goals galore even then. He had completed a secretarial course at Webster's College when he met George Philip, son of the Aberdeen manager, who told him his father needed some help in the office at Pittodrie. Would he like the job? So Benny, who had been playing for Mugiemoss, took up work with manager Philip who gave him a run in the Dons' Highland League team and paid him a combined wage of £6 a week, from which he gave his mother £5.

Benny had a spell with Montrose whose chairman, desperate to win the Scottish Alliance Cup, said, 'I'll give you ten pounds for every goal you score.' 'Ten pounds?' said Benny. 'You must have more money than brains.' Out he went and scored four of those glorious goals that would become the hallmark of Benny Yorston. He collected the promised £40 from the Montrose chairman and elicited from his bewildered mother the question, 'What bank have you been robbing?'

Well-known referee Peter Craigmyle, who had no hesitation in nominating Benny as the Don who stood out in his memory above all others, saw him play at Montrose and told the Aberdeen directors they had better snap him up. They signed him for less than the cost of those four goals.

He proceeded to become the big name of the late 1920s and early 1930s, one of the smallest footballers of his day but capable of out-jumping the tallest centre-half and hitting his head on the crossbar if he was not careful. In four seasons he scored 102 goals, including a Dons record of thirty-eight league and eight Scottish Cup goals in season 1929–30. They came from left foot, right foot or head and often from the most incredible angles.

Little wonder he became the idol of his day, setting up a tradition of smallish centre-forwards which would be followed by Paddy Moore, Matt Armstrong, Stan Williams, Paddy Buckley and the man of the 1970s who echoed much of Yorston's idolatory of the 1920s, Joe Harper. Fans adored him, but colleagues on the park felt he turned on the brilliance only when he felt in the mood. None denied his supremacy on the day, as the leader of that dashing forward line: Love, Cheyne, Yorston, McDermid and Smith.

Mention of Alec Cheyne, who had arrived from Shettleston in 1926, stirs memories of a beautifully deceptive body-swerve and footwork artistry which made him a worthy choice for the Scottish team to play England at Hampden in 1929. He could hardly have guessed as he travelled south for his big event that he was about to write himself into the history books of football as the man who started the famous Hampden Roar.

In fact, he was a reserve that day and came into the team only because of a late withdrawal. Cheyne was to have the privilege of playing as inside partner to Alec Jackson, who had left Aberdeen just before he arrived. Sadly, the right-winger was carried off with a broken arm before half-time and removed to Glasgow's Victoria Infirmary. There was no substituting in those days so Scotland prepared to play the second half with ten men.

A hasty dressing-room plan sent Cheyne to the right wing, to carry the ball to the English corner flag and keep it there as long as possible in the hope of saving the match rather than winning it. With only a minute left to play, one of Alec's forays produced a corner-kick, which he took himself. Over came the ball from the right, curving in on the crossbar and dropping into the far corner of the net. A goal direct from a corner! The only score of the game – and less than a minute to play.

The eyes of 110,512 Scottish fans were turned on the big clock that graced Hampden in those days, aware that the English scarcely had time to equalise. So the Scots set up a mighty roar, designed to keep their team inspired until the end of the game. That roar did not flag by a single decibel before the referee drew breath for the final blast of his whistle – and not for a long time after it.

Just a year after thrashing England in the famous Wembley Wizards game of 1928, the Scots had won again, by a narrower margin this time but with ten men. Not only had Alec Cheyne brought a unique decider to an international match but he had given birth to the Hampden Roar, a sound which rang out thereafter as a thunderous symbol of Scottish support.

The story does not end there. Along Battlefield Road, less than a mile from Hampden Park, Alec Jackson was under chloroform at the Victoria Infirmary, having his broken arm repaired. I was indebted to the late Jack Harkness, Scotland's goalkeeper of the time, for the story which was later told by a nurse. She was standing by the player's side when the roar from Hampden resounded throughout the infirmary. Still under sedation, the mighty Jackson sat bolt upright in a sudden burst of consciousness and called out, 'Nurse, that's the winning goal for Scotland!' Then he lapsed back into unconsciousness.

As a last note to that memorable day, the English defenders complained that Hughie Gallacher had stood on their goalkeeper's foot and prevented him from rising to Cheyne's cross. But there's always somebody ready to spoil a good story!

Back in Aberdeen, manager Travers loved to recall that goal for years to follow and was indignant when anyone suggested it was a fluke. 'Cheyne was a master of the corner-kick,' he would remind them. 'I have seen him practise until he was satisfied he had the right angle. Like Jackson, he was the idol of Pittodrie for his artistic footwork.'

Travers' contention was borne out in the Scottish Cup of the following season when the Dons met Nithsdale Wanderers and Alec Cheyne scored two goals – both of them directly from corner-kicks! Such feats of accuracy, incidentally, had not been recognised as legal in football rules until 1928–29, when the law was changed in time for Alec Cheyne's moment of international fame.

The Aberdeen directors made a determined bid to keep their talented inside man but, with Chelsea in pursuit, he refused to be re-engaged and went off to Stamford Bridge for an Aberdeen record fee of £6,000. There he teamed up with Alec Jackson to continue the right-wing partnership that had lasted for less than forty-five minutes in the 'Cheyne International' of 1929.

25
McLAREN'S LUCK

I N the summer of 1927 Aberdeen Football Club blazed the trail
to South Africa with a tour which did much to popularise the
game in a country where rugby dominated. It was a memorable
experience for the players in an age when travel was little known to
the average citizen.

Their opponents were mostly of British stock and wherever they
went the Dons were fêted and fussed over, not to mention sunburned
by such a climate as they had never experienced. The main problem
was to master the lightness of the ball but once that was achieved,
the tour was a resounding success from the footballing point of view,
as well as the social.

It also revealed the full genius of young Benny Yorston, who was
leading scorer in South Africa and thereafter established himself in
the team. The players who undertook the adventurous journey,
along with chairman William Philip and manager Paddy Travers,
were: Harry Blackwell, Duff Bruce, Malcolm Muir, Willie Jackson,
George Ritchie, Mike Cosgrove, Jock Edward, Sam Spencer, Jock
McHale, Bob McDermid, Alec Cheyne, Bobby Bruce, Tommy McLeod,
Andy Love and Benny Yorston.

Paddy Travers could show great enthusiasm when unearthing a
player of high promise and, on discovering little Bobby Bruce, he
wrote to a friend that he had seen a player with the name of Robert
Bruce, who was likely to make his mark on Scottish football just as
his namesake had done on Scottish history. It was an ambitious
comparison but Robert the Bruce of Pittodrie did, in fact, develop
into a most accomplished and entertaining forward.

124

Unfortunately, he followed the well-worn path to England after four distinguished seasons, by which time he was still just twenty-one years of age. His departure for Middlesbrough was one of many lucrative deals to put a smile on the face of the Pittodrie bank manager from the mid to late 1920s. The great Dod Brewster had gone to Everton, Dr Vic Milne to Aston Villa, Alec Wright to Hearts, Alec Jackson to Huddersfield, brother Walter to Preston, Tom Pirie to Cardiff, Jimmy Jackson to Liverpool, Jock Hutton to Blackburn and Andy Rankin to Cowdenbeath.

The annual general meeting of 1928 was told that, whereas the club had once owed the bank £16,000, they were now completely in the clear and had a positive balance of £2,700. They now had a concrete wall around the pitch and an ornamental granite front at the Merkland Road end.

After the sale of Bobby Bruce, the club bought the ground behind the new grandstand, which became the car park. When Alec Jackson used to pay a visit to the city he would tease Paddy Travers about the grandstand, saying he had 'bought' it for the club with his transfer fee. Club captain Bert MacLachlan, who had been a mainstay of the team since coming from Aston Villa in 1914, bowed out in the late 1920s because of a persistent injury and his leadership was sorely missed.

In the eternal regeneration of talent, however, Paddy Travers was finding replacements. Scots exile Jimmy Black had come back from the gathering depression in America and developed into a top-class midfield man, interrupted only by an extraordinary suspension. Jimmy had played for an American club called Springfield. When it became defunct, another club took over the assets and declared that Black was one of them. Word that the American Football Association had suspended him indefinitely reached the SFA, which was asked to confirm the action. As both associations were members of the international body, the SFA had no option. The matter was eventually sorted out and the suspension lifted.

Travers signed Duggie Livingstone from Plymouth Argyle, Hugh McLaren from Nithsdale Wanderers and Frank Hill, who had been making a name for himself with Forfar. Although he was not aware of it at the time, the Dons boss now had on his books a half-back line that would mould itself into one of the best in Britain, with the familiar ring of Black, McLaren and Hill.

McLaren was unlikely to find an early opportunity at centre-half, where the powerful Jock McHale was still dominant, but his exclusion from the Aberdeen team led to an extraordinary piece of luck. Kilmarnock were doing well in the Scottish Cup of 1929 but they were short of a centre-half and asked if they could borrow McLaren for the duration of their Cup run.

Since he had not been committed to the Cup as an Aberdeen player, the laws allowed him to be loaned and the Dons management agreed. Whereas Aberdeen went out of the competition, Kilmarnock marched on to a triumphant final and Hugh McLaren, still an Aberdeen player, collected a Scottish Cup winner's medal and returned to Pittodrie to await his big-team chance!

The ever-active Travers beat off Rangers, Liverpool and Blackburn to sign Davie Warnock, a talented outside-right from the local Banks o' Dee who played some brilliant football for Aberdeen without getting full credit for his efforts (a fate that has befallen many local lads). In the same year Travers was in Glasgow signing the great Celtic and Scotland outside-left Adam McLean, who came to play out his veteran years in much the same way as that other memorable performer, Tommy Pearson, was to do nearly twenty years later.

In the autumn of 1930 Aberdeen mourned its first football manager, Jimmy Philip, killed in a car crash. His death was followed closely by that of Billy Russell, the esteemed trainer. Billy's death signalled the return of Donald Colman, by then fifty-three but ready to embark on a new career as a coach in the company of his old friend and colleague, Paddy Travers. Paddy described the return as 'a source of general satisfaction to Deeside'.

It was 1931 and the Travers–Colman combination scarcely had time to settle when they were struck by a sensational event so tightly veiled in mystery that it has not been officially explained to this day. It was all a matter of rumour until the original publication of this book in the 1970s.

THE GREAT MYSTERY

26

THE first hint of a big Pittodrie mystery reached North-east breakfast tables on the morning of 18 November 1931, with a baffling story on the sports pages of the *Press and Journal* under the headline 'Dons' Drastic Changes'. The report went as follows:

> Surprising changes have been made in the Aberdeen team to oppose Falkirk at Brockville on Saturday. Three of the recognised stalwarts, McLaren, Hill and Yorston, have been relegated to the reserve team. Last night Mr Travers, the club manager, declined to enter into the circumstances which have led to the players mentioned being dropped but admitted that it was on account of 'some domestic trouble'.

The media of today would soon have clarified 'the domestic trouble' but in 1931 puzzled Aberdonians could only turn it over in their minds and proceed to other pages where they found that large crowds had flocked to Marischal College to hear John Buchan, the novelist, talking about 'Truth and Accuracy'. Raggie Morrison's, that Aberdeen institution which graced St Nicholas Street where Marks and Spencer now stands, was advertising ladies' woollen combinations (soiled) for 1s. 9d. (less than 9p), frocks for 5s. (25p) and real mink marmot coats for £14 10s.

Sports fans cared less about John Buchan's 'Truth and Accuracy' than they did about the truth behind the mystifying events at Pittodrie. An under-strength team was beaten 3–1 in that Falkirk game and dismissed from the Scottish Cup by Arbroath. By now, more players had been drawn into the mystery with the dropping of David Galloway, a winger recently arrived from Raith Rovers, and Jimmy Black, the right-half back from America. The Dons were now without one of Britain's finest half-back lines as well as the centre-forward who had recently been Scotland's top scorer.

On Friday, 4 December 1931, the *Press and Journal* was still mystified. It reported:

> The continued omission of McLaren, Hill, Yorston and Galloway from the Aberdeen team has given rise to much conjecture in football circles as to whether they will be seen in their places again. Inquiries made have elicited that none of the players is on the open-to-transfer list but it is understood that the Aberdeen directors are willing to consider offers for them and for Black, who is meantime suffering from a knee injury. All are players of ripe experience and, until omitted a fortnight ago . . . were regarded as indispensable to the first eleven.

A shrewd man in most respects, Travers was trying to protect as many people as possible, but this was a classic case of how silence can damage the innocent. He should have known that a club such as Aberdeen could not hope to drop a collection of star players – they never did play for the first team again – and escape without explanation.

Rumours were rampant, including the inevitable stories of corruption, but no charges were ever brought. The directors were split and confused but Travers satisfied himself that certain players would never pull on that first-team jersey again. There is little evidence of protest about his decision.

In those depressing circumstances, great names began to disappear from Pittodrie. In January 1932 Benny Yorston was sold to Sunderland for £2,000. Frank Hill went on to a successful career with Arsenal and was later manager of Burnley. Jimmy Black died a young man, protesting his innocence. David Galloway died in the 1970s but I could find no trace of Hugh McLaren.

Frank Hill ended his days in California, where he became a

baseball referee and ran a chip shop. Many years ago I wrote to him seeking information about the Pittodrie mystery, hoping it might be time to clear the air, but had no response.

That left Benny Yorston, who had gone on to rescue Sunderland from relegation, sometimes on that same bonus of £10 a goal he had received at Montrose. Benny moved to Middlesbrough (how often that name crops up) and steered them clear of relegation as well. After the war he went into the business of rooming flats in London's South Kensington but fell on hard times.

When I tracked him down to that Chelsea flat, shortly before his death in 1977, Benny denied all knowledge of corruption – and even claimed to have no memory of the mystery which led to his departure from Aberdeen. He seemed still in full command of his faculties but his words had the hollow ring of untruthfulness. Perhaps it was that wartime knock on the head, with which he sought to preface our interview.

So what was it all about? From the Pittodrie dressing room of the time I gained the gist of what happened. A number of players decided to place fixed-odds bets with Aberdeen bookmaker Will Jamieson, on the basis that the Dons would be drawing at half-time and winning at full-time. Clearly, they could have some say in these matters and even if they hoped to win the match, the attempt to arrange the half-time draw was in itself a corruption.

A check on the scores in that period showed a coincidence of matches where the bet would have been successful. My own investigation revealed that, whatever the sinister implications, at least one of those half-time draws was pure coincidence. But it shows how easily an innocent player could fall under suspicion. In a Dundee United match, Aberdeen were leading 2–1 just before half-time when Willie Cooper, as honest a servant as the game ever knew, gave away a penalty which levelled the half-time score. It was only later that Willie discovered to his horror that he might have been seen as part of the plan. He was, of course, totally innocent.

Allegations of corruption in football are difficult to prove.

Nothing might ever have been known of the matter if someone had not invited former Celtic and Scotland outside-left Adam McLean to become part of the ploy. McLean conveyed his alarm to one other colleague and it all came to a head one day when the same player, by now convinced of manipulation, left the field making it known that he was not part of this plot. His words reached the ears of Travers and Colman, who began their own investigation and managed to keep it wholly within the privacy of Pittodrie. Even without police involvement, they became totally convinced that those five star players should never don an Aberdeen jersey again.

By coincidence, Percy Dickie left the Dons for St Johnstone in the aftermath of the incident and was appalled to find that the unfortunate timing of his move aroused suspicion. There was much scope for innocents to be hurt. Percy had been one of the most colourful characters ever seen at Pittodrie, his crinkly face bristling with humour as he entered into hilarious exchanges with the crowd. They loved him.

Percy joined the Dons from Mugiemoss in 1929 and played for Leicester, Chelsea and Manchester United during the war before returning to Pittodrie, by then in his late thirties but still the same old Percy. He bought a licensed shop in Bankhead and, when his Pittodrie days were over, continued playing for Peterhead in that post-war period when the Buchan club was dominant in the Highland League.

Percy belonged to the days when footballers still dressed to the nines. W.K. Jackson used to appear in a bowler hat and Hugh McLaren would convert it into a soft hat by putting a dent down the middle.

Donald Colman was still full of ideas about physical fitness and used to administer a body-building cocktail of sherry, honey and raw egg. Willie Cooper never forgot the taste of Gregory mixture, which Colman insisted upon for a weekly flushing of the bowels. Percy Dickie queued up for his Wednesday dose protesting there was nothing wrong with his inner workings. He was, after all, a plumber by trade! Inner rumblings were soon matched by the rumble of discontent among players who forced an agreement that the Gregory mixture would stop.

27
SMITH, COOPER AND McGILL

D EEP in the Bronx of New York I unearthed a solid man from Fittie whose name was remembered as the first leg of the defensive trio of Smith, Cooper and McGill. Steve Smith was retired from the New York Telephone Company, spending summers in the Big Apple and winters in Florida but still with a heart and tongue that belonged to Aberdeen.

Steve's connection with Pittodrie began in 1912 when he first raised voice inside the ground, with one eye on his business as a chocolate-seller and the other on the team, which he could still rattle off as: Greig; Colman, Hume; Wilson, Wyllie, Miller; Soye, Main, Walker, O'Hagan, Lennie. As he sold his chocolates, the lad from Fittie vowed he would play for Aberdeen one day. Progressing from chocolate-boy to programme-seller, he collected his supplies from Munro's of Crown Street and dashed back for lunch in Fittie before taking up stance at Pittodrie.

It was, of course, a vastly different Pittodrie. There was open terracing at both the King Street and Beach ends and the pavilion stood at the north-east corner, where the small East Stand was later situated. The grandstand, such as it was, stood next to the pavilion, where the main stand was later built, and along that same side there was a beer hut where men downed their draught and argued but generally kept themselves in good order.

On the opposite side, by the gasworks, there was another small stand close by the boundary wall at the halfway line, with open terracing all around. In the memory of former chairman Charles B.

Forbes, who played for the club in the 1920s, the dressing rooms were primitive, with six-foot-deep zinc baths in which players had to immerse themselves in ice-cold water.

Steve Smith remembered Pittodrie before the First World War as a neighbourly kind of place where everybody knew Dod Munro the groundsman and Peter Simpson the trainer. His own arrival at Pittodrie as a goalkeeper was a long way off, however. Playing for Hall Russell's in 1922–23, he emigrated to Canada where he played for the Toronto All-Scots. Then he moved on to Chicago where he teamed up with two of his old Pittodrie heroes from the chocolate-boy days, Bobby Hannah and Joe Walker, who were playing out their time in North America.

By then that other Aberdeen hero, Jock Hume, was established on the American scene and he asked Steve Smith to join the professional ranks of Brooklyn Wanderers. At that time there were Scots galore in American soccer, which had opened up a whole new field for immigrants. That enthusiastic Welshman, W. Luther Lewis, who signed the Jackson brothers, was building up his Bethlehem Steel team with men such as Bob McGregor, who had captained Morton to their Scottish Cup triumph of 1922.

Lewis moved on to be president of Chicago Pneumatic, the parent company of the Fraserburgh Toolworks, and you can imagine his delight some years later when, on a visit to his Scottish outpost, he met none other than Bob McGregor, by then back in Scotland as player-manager at Bellslea Park – and working for Lewis's tool company in the Broch.

Those early days of American soccer ran right across the prohibition period of the 1920s when thirsty Americans were driven to the shadows of the speakeasies to find their booze. As a poor relation of baseball, football had to make do with whatever dressing-room accommodation was nearest to a local park and, often enough, that turned out to be the basement of these illicit dens.

So the 1920s of the Charleston and prohibition went roaring towards the Wall Street crash of 1929 and in the chaos that followed, the American soccer scene fell apart. Among exiles looking for a boat home were Alec Massie, bound for Hearts, Charlie McGill, who would land with Aberdeen, Jimmy Black, who had reached Pittodrie a little earlier, and Steve Smith, who sailed into the Clyde with no fewer than 150 Scottish footballers on the ship.

Aberdeen had released goalkeeper Harry Blackwell the previous season so Paddy Travers signed two new keepers, Dave Cumming from Hall Russell's and that former Russell's man now back from America, Steve Smith. With the latter commanding the spot, Cumming was allowed to go off to Arbroath, from where he was transferred to Middlesbrough and became Scotland's goalkeeper.

The Pittodrie crowd had no complaint about Smith as the last line in a defence well remembered as: Smith; W.K. Jackson, Falloon, Black, McLaren, Hill. In the reshuffle after the troubles of 1931, Falloon became the centre-half and Cooper and McGill emerged as the full-backs in front of Smith – a full-back partnership, incidentally, which set up a Pittodrie record of 161 league games together without a single break.

With his American years behind him and approaching his thirtieth birthday, Steve was a latecomer to Scottish football but he played on until 1935. During the war he went back to work at Hall Russell's and looked after the Dons' reserve team, but he returned to the United States in 1947 to work for the telephone company.

Willie Cooper had signed for the Dons in 1927 for a fee of £20 and was paid £1 a week while he continued to play for Mugiemoss. A square-cut Aberdonian of leathery features and solid character, Willie must rank as second only to Willie Miller in terms of great Pittodrie servants, a key figure in that team of the 1930s, which many an honest witness regarded as the best they had seen: Smith; Cooper, McGill; Fraser, Falloon, Thomson; Beynon, McKenzie, Armstrong, Mills, Strauss.

To make good the deficiencies of the 1932 transfers, Paddy Travers was seeking a new blend and depended on W.K. Jackson and Bob McDermid to father the team through a difficult time. Eddie Falloon, a likeable little Irishman from Larne, had been successfully converted into a centre-half, at 5ft 4ins one of the smallest ever seen on a football pitch. But his height proved no disadvantage as he soared like a rubber ball to out-jump the tallest opponent.

Pittodrie has long been a meeting point for nationalities, whether English, Irish, Welsh, South African, Scandinavian, Dutch or Hungarian. Herbert Currer had set the pattern for a flow of South Africans and was followed by fellow countryman Billy Strauss, a splendid left-winger with such a shot that he was credited with literally bursting the net on at least two occasions while playing for Aberdeen.

A Strauss waltz down that left wing was one of the exquisite delights of Pittodrie during that decade although his movement was not so much a waltz as a quickstep, a very quick step indeed. While the South African took up the left wing, Welshman Jackie Beynon was signed from Doncaster Rovers to patrol the right, and he became a Pittodrie favourite for whom there was a tragic day ahead.

But of all the names of the 1930s, two symbolised the decade, just as Hutton, Jackson and Yorston had been synonymous with the 1920s. The names were as inseparable as bacon and eggs because they complemented each other so perfectly. They were, of course, Mills and Armstrong.

28
MILLS AND ARMSTRONG

WILLIE MILLS was widely regarded as the symbol of sporting glamour in the 1930s, smart and good-looking, the type to attract the idolatry of youth even before he had kicked a ball. When he did that, his appeal took on another dimension, just as had happened ten years earlier with Alec Jackson, whose personal style and appetite for living were reflected in his play.

Willie's skills were so pure and precious to manager Travers that he once said of him, 'Just give me five minutes of the real Mills and I'm satisfied.' As with many another thoroughbred, those five minutes could change the whole complexion of a match and when you teamed him up with the dash of Matt Armstrong at centre-forward, Aberdeen could boast one of the most deadly duos in British football.

So there was glamour at the heels of Mills and Armstrong, with Matt being likened to film star Ronald Colman and Mills being teased by Travers that he was too good-looking to be a boy. But it was the magic of their football that mattered most, and that was based on a twin-like understanding, developed during intensive afternoon sessions at Pittodrie, supervised by Donald Colman.

Travers' early impression of Armstrong had not been favourable and it took Colman to convince him that here was a future inter-nationalist. As for Mills, Colman never wavered from the view that he personified all he had ever dreamed about in the perfectly balanced footballer. That view was in no way coloured by the fact that the boy came from his own home corner and that he himself had played alongside Mills' father when they won the Scottish

Junior Cup with Ashfield at the end of the nineteenth century. Colman was too unbiased for that. He simply knew a great footballer when he saw one and Mills would rank among the best Pittodrie had ever seen.

The boy from Bonhill, Dunbartonshire, arrived in 1932 when he was seventeen, and played his first game in a reserve match against Celtic at Pittodrie. On that same day, the first team inside-left, Bob McDermid, was injured at Parkhead. So one week after his arrival, Willie Mills walked into the Aberdeen first team and stayed there for the next six years.

In that time he was credited with pioneering the long, sweeping pass, in an age when the tanner-ba' type of game was much in vogue. He in turn diverted much credit to Paddy Travers for thinking intelligently about the shape and form of the game. He also studied the methods of Bob McPhail of Rangers.

So the teenaged Mills was established in the Aberdeen team in 1932, earning a basic £5 a week (£4 in summer) with a bonus of £2 for a win and £1 for a draw, compared to the tradesman's wage of little over £2 a week. That gap has widened dramatically today but Mills merely judged it by the fact that he could go to the city's top tailor and buy himself the two most expensive suits for a total of £5. The boy had just come from the Vale of Leven where mass unemployment left men with nothing to do but gather in public parks and kick a ball around.

By the mid 1930s, the Pittodrie basic had gone up to £7 a week plus bonus and he was augmenting his income with a string of international appearances, including the Jubilee International against England and a place in the Scottish team that toured America in 1935. When he eventually left Aberdeen in 1938, his destination was none other than Huddersfield, that dominant team of pre-war England which had already lured away Alec Jackson. The fee was £6,500 but the wage that attracted him south was still only £8 a week.

With the Second World War only a year away, his career was cut short in the all too familiar fashion. Huddersfield told their players: 'Your contracts are finished. You are on the dole.' At the end of the war, Mills was playing for the British Army in Berlin, along with another name from Pittodrie, Charlie Gavin; then he returned to Aberdeen, by now into his thirties and with the best years of his career gone to waste.

He trained again at Pittodrie and played for Lossiemouth before teaming up with former Aberdeen team-mates Willie Cooper and Dave Warnock at Huntly. Latterly, living in Rubislaw Park Home, Mills used to ruminate about what separated people in the wide spectrum of talent. He was fascinated by the secrets of power and transmission as shared between brain and limb. He tried to convey to me the feeling of a well-coordinated body, and there was a pause as you remembered that those legs which once accepted the dictates of a brilliant football brain were now riddled with arthritis.

Willie would break into a smile and recall the occasion during his Highland League days when Huntly had an important game written up by Jimmy Forbes of the *Evening Express*. His report in the *Green Final* was a splendid one, except for a printer's error. That Saturday night thousands of people read that Willie Mills collected the ball outside the penalty area – and *shit* high over the bar! Willie's only complaint was that he didn't get his name in *The Guinness Book of Records* for such a feat of elevation.

Willie Mills used to look forward to the visits of his old buddy with the sleeked-back hair and neat moustache and the lively features creasing with good humour. Matt Armstrong, born in Newton Stewart and reared in Port Glasgow, was provisionally signed by Celtic when a telegram arrived at his home one day in 1931 asking him to keep an appointment with someone at the Central Hotel, Glasgow.

Matt turned up to find that the anonymous gentleman was none other than manager Paddy Travers of Aberdeen, anxious to know if Celtic had taken up their option. They hadn't. That option had actually expired the previous night but Matt thought he had better wait to see what manager Willie Maley had to say. The production of fifty crisp pound notes from the Travers pocket, however, convinced him that that was hardly necessary!

So he became an Aberdeen player, biding his time to succeed Paddy Moore at centre-forward and to strike up that telepathic partnership with Mills which stood for all that was skilful and exciting in the game of football. Matt could still savour the joy of it as he recalled the feats of his inside partner, saying, 'I have seen Willie do things with the old heavy ball of our time which nobody could attempt today.'

Armstrong went on to fulfil Donald Colman's forecast of playing for Scotland, including that Jubilee International when he scored in Scotland's 4–2 defeat of England at Hampden. Once again, a career was broken by the war and Matt's final departure from Pittodrie could bring a mischievous smile to his Hollywood features. It followed an incident when he and a friend had a night with Johnnie Walker – and a brick was thrown through a window down Pittodrie way. Perhaps it was time to leave anyway. He later played for Queen of the South, Elgin City and Peterhead.

Always the humorist, Matt recalled an incident at Elgin after former Pittodrie team-mate Joe Devine had succeeded, as few players ever do, in becoming a referee. Matt had committed a foul for which his old pal had no option but to book him. Mr Devine produced the notebook and said in the customary deadpan fashion, 'Your name please?' Matt looked in astonishment and then, realising Joe was only doing his job, sidled up to him and replied, 'My name? Tom f*****g Thumb!'

Matt became a car salesman before retiring to Kirk Brae, Cults, from where he ventured regularly to Pittodrie to be hailed by old-timers. He would also meet old friends, including Joe Devine, at the Carlton Bar or Jimmy Wilson's, and he would drop modesty and tell you the greatest of all Aberdeen teams was: Johnstone; Cooper, McGill; Dunlop, Falloon, Thomson; Beynon, McKenzie, Armstrong, Mills, Strauss.

Until the 1980s that view was widely shared. But one particular year of that era stands apart for high drama in the history of Aberdeen Football Club. It was 1937.

29
SADNESS IN THE SUN

T HE story of Scottish football has been such a two-horse race that you wonder how it has survived at all. Considering the power and resources of Rangers and Celtic, giving them dominance in an unequal struggle, it can be argued that the greatest achievements in Scotland are those outside the Old Firm, when some other team manages to snatch the candy from the big boys.

After thirty years and more in existence there was still no candy for Aberdeen FC and the supporters were beginning to wonder if they would ever know the sweet taste of actually winning something. It became a standing joke for North-east bachelors, being teased about not having a wife, to reply that they would get married when the Dons won the Cup. It was seen as a likely escape route for life. But their freedom came under sudden threat in 1937.

The Dons had started the Scottish Cup run with a tie against Inverness Thistle on such a cold and miserable day that most players wore gloves (very unusual in those days) and Donald Colman rubbed down the Aberdonian limbs with whisky, a sacrilegious misuse according to Matt Armstrong, who thought it would have been better inside them. Nevertheless, Matt rattled home a hat-trick in the Dons' 6–0 victory.

The next victims were Third Lanark, who came to Pittodrie that day led by Scottish captain Jimmy Carabine and that truly great inside-right Jimmy Mason. (Why did they have to destroy such a fine club as Third Lanark?) Billy Strauss scored twice in a 4–2 win.

Aberdeen had a third-round bye and beat Hamilton in the fourth, with only Morton standing between them and a historic moment for the club. Could this be the year? Were Aberdeen about to reach their very first Scottish Cup final? In the semi-final Billy Strauss, that streak of lightning with the lethal shot, scored one, Matt Armstrong the other – and the Dons were on their way to Hampden.

The excitement, which ran the length of Union Street and far beyond, was a foretaste of the scenes outside Hampden Park on Saturday, 24 April, when the crowds rolled up to see Aberdeen play Celtic in their first-ever final. They were two popular teams with a tradition of talented players but who could have foreseen that the crowd would set up an all-time record attendance for a club game in Britain?

Just a week earlier, the biggest crowd ever to see a football match in Britain (149,547) had turned up at the same ground for the Scotland–England clash and no one imagined there could be a repeat performance so soon. The turnstiles which clicked in this massive invasion closed their doors when the figure had reached 146,433. But that was only part of the story. At least one gate was broken down and thousands streamed in to join the official figure, while a further 20,000 were left stranded outside. Such was the enthusiasm for football in the 1930s.

So they stood with arms pinned to their sides, the green and white of Celtic, the black and gold of Aberdeen, awaiting the moment when they could greet the teams with the greatest burst of lung-power ever known.

Willie Cooper and Bob Temple, who were the Aberdeen full-backs that day, later recalled to Alastair Macdonald of the *Press and Journal* the feeling of awe when they trotted out of the Hampden dressing room. Said Bob: 'There seemed to be nothing but a sea of tammies and pink faces and the sound started in the middle of the stand and moved right round the enclosure. I'll never forget it.'

For two young men in particular that entry to the Hampden arena seemed like an impossible dream come true. Goalkeeper George Johnstone and right-half Frank Dunlop had been there just a year earlier as members of the Benburb team in the Scottish Junior Cup final. They went straight to Aberdeen and here they were, back at Hampden in the senior Cup final.

One man for whom it was a heartbreak before it started was South African Billy Strauss, who had done so much to make it happen. In the Morton game at Easter Road, Billy was badly injured and he had to watch the final from the sidelines, replaced by Johnny Lang. The teams were: Aberdeen – Johnstone; Cooper, Temple; Dunlop, Falloon, Thomson; Beynon, McKenzie, Armstrong, Mills, Lang. Celtic – Kennaway; Hogg, Morrison; Geatons, Lyon, Paterson; Delaney, Buchan, McGrory, Crum, Murphy.

Northern hearts sank when Johnny Crum put Celtic ahead in ten minutes but there was hardly time to draw breath before the Dons went on the attack. From the centre, the ball went out to Jackie Beynon on the right wing and the Welshman went off on his own. Matt Armstrong had a clear recollection: 'I remember seeing Jackie haring along the wing and I was saying to myself, "Matt boy, you had better get up there fast to meet that ball when it comes across. If you don't, you'll be in trouble." Fortunately, I made it in time to meet Jackie's low cross and I hit it first time into the Celtic net.'

But the glory was not to last. At the other end, Celtic went ahead through Buchan although Willie Cooper, not a man given to exaggeration, swore to his dying day that the great Jimmy McGrory flicked the ball on with his hand before Buchan scored. That settled it and Cooper shook his head and said it was a terrible way to lose a Cup. He explained: 'We were so built up for that final and were playing so well at the time that it was a dreadful disappointment. It took me a long time to get over it.'

Much as Willie shared the universal admiration of Donald Colman, he believed his enthusiasm for physical fitness did much to lose the match. All week he had emphasised that the more running they did in training the less they would have to do in the final. But it was a week of heat and Cooper recalled that the Aberdeen players were drained of energy before the big day.

So players and supporters alike suffered a crushing sense of anti-climax as they headed back home, arguing over chances missed but unanimous on the point that Billy Strauss would have made all the difference.

No one was more disappointed than Paddy Travers. Despite all he had done for the Dons since taking over in 1924, the great players he had discovered and nurtured, the imagination and colour he had brought to the Pittodrie scene, he had absolutely nothing to show for his efforts.

Two years later there was to be a reward for the pawky Travers when his team won the Scottish Cup. Sadly, it was not his Aberdeen team. With new directors on board, he felt his power was slipping and he moved off in the unlikely direction of Shawfield. Within a season, he collected the trophy that had eluded him in fourteen years at Pittodrie. The Clyde team that brought him the glory he richly deserved included a man who figured largely in his Aberdeen plans. That great little centre-half Eddie Falloon had followed his old boss south and he collected a Cup-winner's medal. It's a funny old game.

The gloom of Pittodrie that April weekend in 1937 was compounded on the day after the final when Dons director Bill Hay, a member of the lemonade family, collapsed and died. He was still in his forties. North-east folk tucked away their disappointment as summer approached and for the players there was the coming excitement of a tour to South Africa, a much-needed consolation after the Cup final, which didn't even provide runners-up medals. The match programme was their only souvenir.

The Aberdeen party headed for Southampton to board the *Stirling Castle* for the voyage to South Africa, where the heat was a new experience for men accustomed to the blast of a nor'easter breaking across the links. It was thoroughly familiar to Billy Strauss, now recovered from injury and pleased to be showing his Aberdeen team-mates the land he called home.

But the joy was short-lived when Billy went down with illness. The task of putting on a full side became even more difficult when the other winger, outside-right Jackie Beynon, was rushed to hospital in Johannesburg. The players knew that Jackie was sometimes bothered with stomach trouble but his pains were diagnosed as appendicitis, not a serious matter although it ruled him out of the tour.

Matt Armstrong went to see him in hospital and came back that evening with the opinion that Jackie looked far from well. Paddy Travers didn't want his players upset and cautioned Matt about speaking like that. But Matt was worried and his concern was well founded. Peritonitis had set in and Jackie Beynon died that night.

The Dons party was plunged into grief, with little thought for anything but their dead colleague. Jackie was part of their life together – how could he have been spirited away so swiftly? The tour would have to go on but first they would have to bury Jackie that Saturday morning.

The scenes in Johannesburg were almost without precedent. Traffic came to a standstill as people turned out in their thousands, including every exiled Welshman within travelling distance who had come to bring a touch of home to the farewell of as popular a Taffy as ever crossed the Scottish border.

Up at the cemetery on the hillside they gathered by the grave and raised their voices in such harmony as can come only from the soul of the Welsh. 'Land of My Fathers' rang out loud and clear in a ceremony that etched itself forever in the minds of those who were there. The players carried the coffin to a grave so far from the land of his fathers and from the grey streets of Aberdeen, his adopted city, where people shook their heads in disbelief. Wasn't it just a few weeks ago that they had watched him haring down the right wing at Hampden and sending over that low cross for Matt Armstrong to score the equaliser? The Dons lowered their colleague into the grave. He was later uplifted and brought back to his permanent resting place in the valleys, from where his heart had never departed.

'The players were broken-hearted, for Jackie was such a nice fellow,' Willie Mills recalled. 'I'll never forget the kindness of local people who felt deeply for us and couldn't do enough to help.' But broken hearts had to be patched over in the name of saving the tour and entertaining the people who had so looked forward to seeing the much-publicised visitors from Scotland.

So they played a match after the funeral and the tour continued, still beset with injuries. The Dons were due to play Lourenco Marques but matters were further complicated when goalkeeper George

Johnstone refused to play on a Sunday. The match went ahead on a sand pitch with the Dons wearing rubber boots. Within fifteen minutes a tropical thunderstorm broke over the ground and the pitch became a quagmire, just the conditions to give the local team a 3–0 lead at half-time.

The rubber boots were a disaster and at the interval out came the heavy boots and long studs. They were the secret weapon that produced the Aberdeen goals for a final score of 7–3.

On a free day in Cape Town, the Aberdeen party went along to watch a local football match and were greatly intrigued by a little fellow who was turning on the style for the railwaymen's team. He had already been following the Dons in South Africa, watching their style of play, studying their movements and wondering if he could emulate their skill. His name lies ahead in the story of Pittodrie but he accepted an invitation to come to Scotland in the following year, 1938. The wee man from Cape Town gave his name as Alfred Stanley Williams.

HITLER'S WAR

W HATEVER clouds may have been gathering over Europe, the 1930s and Aberdeenshire seemed as good a time and place as any to be a child – a mellow decade of foxtrots, saxophones and fine summer days. And into that fabric came the name of 'Pittodrie', a kind of magical sound to excite those who were still too young to share its glamour.

Any visit to Aberdeen was an adventure for the country child, when mothers would rummage in Raggie Morrison's before taking you to lunch at Isaac Benzie's in George Street, which had the sophistication of a little palm-court orchestra. Afternoons were spent at the Capitol or the brand new Astoria at Kittybrewster, with their glittering cinema organs, before fathers emerged from the Friday mart and you exchanged the glamour of the city for the gathering dusk and quiet of the countryside.

Pittodrie was still beyond my bounds but grown men brought home tales to stir delight, stories about Billy Strauss, Willie Mills and Matt Armstrong. One name above all caught my imagination, since his feats of the late 1930s and early 1940s seemed to match the rounded ring of 'Johnny Pattillo'. His name did not belong to any memorable formation but when I finally made it to Pittodrie it was the bow-legged run and natural flair of Pattillo that engaged my loyalty to Aberdeen Football Club.

Johnny Pattillo was born in 1914 and played for Hall Russell's before landing at Pittodrie, a wartime team-mate of the original Martin Buchan, to whom he bore a strong, middle-parting resemblance. He later played for Dundee and was manager of St Johnstone before he took over the running of the British Legion Club in Perth. At the turn of the century, Johnny Pattillo was the oldest known surviving player, in his late eighties but suffering from Parkinson's Disease and living in a nursing home in Perth.

After the ill-fated South African tour, there was little time to take stock of events before the looming presence of Adolf Hitler began pointing to the possibility of a Second World War. The First War of 1914–18 had turned the world upside down – surely it couldn't happen again? But the grim reality finally broke upon us that September Saturday of 1939 when Hitler invaded Poland. Like the rest of the country, the North-east buzzed with activity as young men who had joined the Territorial Army in the spirit of adventure found it was now for real.

Special trains collected them from the towns and villages of the North-east and rumbled in from places like Peterhead and Fraserburgh to mass at Bucksburn, from where the Gordon Highlanders marched off to war, many to be captured by Rommel at St Valery in 1940 and to spend the next five years in prison camps throughout Germany.

Some employers took the gloomiest view and sacked their workers, a fate that to all intents and purposes befell the Pittodrie players, whose contracts were terminated. In the break-up of the playing structure, Matt Armstrong, Billy Strauss and Andy Cowie went off to join the Royal Corps of Signals, reporting together to their depot at Canterbury. Others were called up for service.

The settled pattern of life fell apart and football went with it. The area beneath the Pittodrie grandstand became an Air Raid Precaution post (ARP) and the Dons were more or less shut out of their own home. But football, like life itself, had to go on in some shape or form and there was an attempt to provide public enter-tainment amid the chaos.

Aberdeen Football Club played a major part in creating an emer-gency competition called the Scottish North-Eastern League, covering a wider area than the name suggests. It included teams down the east coast from Aberdeen and Arbroath to Dundee United and Raith Rovers and even Rangers Reserves. Dons chairman William Mitchell donated the Mitchell Bowl to augment the competition and the Dons themselves had a lot of success in those limited times.

With Paddy Travers having moved to Clyde before the war, the Dons directors had been faced with choosing a new manager for only the third time in thirty-five years. The new boss at Pittodrie in 1938 was David Halliday, a Dumfries man well known as a Dundee forward in his day. That coach and club legend, Donald Colman, applied for the job and his daughter Edna remembered the suspense in their home at 342 King Street as her parents waited to hear. It would make a difference to their financial position. But Colman was approaching sixty and the directors felt he was too old, a fact he found hard to swallow. Edna recalled her father's disappointment that he had been passed over but he was not bitter and formed a good relationship with the new man.

In fact, David Halliday had scarcely warmed the seat when he was directed to the war effort and the job of caretaker manager fell jointly to Charles B. Forbes, the city schoolmaster who played for the Dons in the 1920s, and the ebullient George Anderson, complete with bowler hat and carnation, who owned the sweet factory in Rosemount and had been a notable Dons goalie in his day.

Deprived of most of their players, they were consoled by the large influx of soldiers and airmen who came to train in the North-east and who included many well-known footballers from the south. Those who passed our way and dallied to wear the Aberdeen colours for varying lengths of time included Dave Russell of Sheffield Wednesday, George Green of Huddersfield, Alex Dyer of Plymouth Argyle, Bobby Ancell and Jackie Dryden of Newcastle United and Joe Harvey of Bradford City. There were few better entertainers than that great little centre-forward from Crystal Palace, Ernie Waldron, who took no run at a penalty but seldom missed.

But of all the wartime visitors, who were officially known as 'guests', there was one whose impact was beyond all others. George Anderson went up to Lossiemouth to cast an eye over an airman who was being hailed as the great discovery of English football. His name was Stanley Mortensen, and he later became inside partner to that greatest of dribbling wizards, Stanley Matthews, with whom he played for Blackpool in three FA Cup finals after the war. In the last of those, in 1953, the veteran Matthews was making his final attempt to win an FA Cup medal. Blackpool were 3–1 down against Bolton Wanderers but the wizard himself inspired them to a memorable recovery against a team captained by Aberdonian Billy Moir, and in the final 4–3 victory Stan Mortensen scored a hat-trick.

More than ten years earlier, however, George Anderson had lured him to Pittodrie, where his electrifying runs and cannonball shooting put him regularly in the headlines. He arrived during season 1942–43 and played in the following season as well, averaging about a goal per game.

The Dons were playing a British Army team which was more or less an English international side in disguise, with Cliff Britton of Everton, Stan Cullis of Wolves, Don Welsh of Charlton, Tommy Lawton of Everton, Jimmy Hagan of Sheffield United and the Compton brothers, Leslie and Denis – yes, the same Denis Compton of cricketing fame who had the rare distinction of playing for England at both football and cricket.

By half-time the Army was leading by four goals to one but they reckoned without the great Mortensen, who was in the Aberdeen team that day, along with Tommy Walker of Hearts, Gordon Smith of Hibs and Jerry Dawson, Duggie Gray and Willie Waddell of Rangers. Having scored the first Dons goal, Mortensen went on to score three more, making it 5–4 for the Army. The fairytale seemed complete when he shot home a thirty-yard rocket to round off a perfect draw. But referee Peter Craigmyle blew for an infringement, for once lacking that sense of the dramatic which was usually his hallmark.

By 1947, when the Dons were approaching their second appearance in a Scottish Cup final, Mortensen was playing for England against Scotland at Wembley. Outside the stadium he ran into Charles B. Forbes, and Stanley, who enjoyed a bet, said, 'I've put my money on the Dons to win the Cup next week, Mr Forbes.' Then, more confidentially, the man who had always enjoyed his time at Pittodrie said, 'Any chance of Aberdeen coming to buy me?' Mr Forbes had to remind him that, much as that would delight everyone back home, the directors had no access to the Bank of England! And that would have been necessary to buy the Mortensen talents.

Charles Forbes recalled the pleasures and problems of wartime management: 'There were so many great performers around that George Anderson and I had to play trials to see who we wanted. In one of those games we had a goalkeeper who didn't seem good with high balls so we left him out after half-time and chose another contender instead.' Imagine their embarrassment when the man they rejected as Aberdeen's goalkeeper turned out to be the great Ted Ditchburn, Tottenham Hotspur and England keeper!

But they soldiered on, with Forbes and Anderson as emergency managers, William Mitchell as chairman and John D. Robbie as secretary. During a wartime Cup tie, George Anderson kept running to check with the treasurer how much they could afford as a bonus. From time to time he ran to the edge of the pitch and shouted, 'There's another pound in it for you, lads!' Such was the spirit of improvisation in wartime.

Thus the club marched on through the Second World War, with kaleidoscopic teams producing stars who could appear and swiftly disappear according to the secret movements of war. It certainly brought fresh faces to Pittodrie but for all the excitement, there was a longing for the return of football life as we remembered it.

The supporters talked wistfully of rising stars, such as George Hamilton, who had scarcely established themselves when they were off to war. Just as surely, Hamilton and many others were wondering how they were doing back on the beloved terracings of Pittodrie Park.

POST-WAR TO THE GOLDEN AGE

31

HAMILTON–WILLIAMS–
BAIRD

THE ten years between 1946 and 1956 were to be one of the best periods in the history of Aberdeen Football Club. After all the barren years, they would now carry off the Scottish league championship and the Scottish Cup once and the League Cup twice, with three other appearances in Hampden finals. Life was definitely set for improvement.

But nothing of that could have been foreseen when manager David Halliday came back from war service. A man of quiet disposition, Halliday never managed to convey his personality to the supporters but by deed rather than word he turned out to be by far the most successful manager in the club's first seventy-five years.

The North-Eastern League was still in existence as he re-occupied the seat he had taken up briefly seven years earlier, and prepared for peace-time football. He knew he could count on George Johnstone, Frank Dunlop, Andy Cowie, George Hamilton, Stanley Williams, Archie Baird and, of course, Willie Cooper, who had managed to play during the war because he had returned to his trade as a marine engineer in Aberdeen. These players were marking time before demobilisation and sometimes taking stock of how they came to be Aberdeen players in the first place. To every man there was a story.

George Hamilton, who belongs to that élite of great Dons, was playing for his local Ayrshire team of Irvine Meadow when Rangers invited him to play two trials before deciding he was on the light side. So instead of the marble hall of Ibrox, the lad with the skilful feet and head landed in the less fashionable surroundings of Palmerston Park, Dumfries, in season 1937–38.

He made a big impression on Queen of the South spectator Billy Halliday. Billy remembered that his brother David needed someone to replace Willie Mills, who was on his way to Huddersfield. The Aberdeen boss hastened to his home-town and Hamilton was summoned from his bed one morning and told to be at Palmerston Park by ten o'clock, when Halliday signed him for £3,000.

He arrived in season 1938–39, ready to play his part in beating Chelsea in the Empire Exhibition Trophy, a contest run in connection with Scotland's biggest-ever event, staged in Bellahouston Park, Glasgow, and drawing a total crowd of 13.5 million people. The Dons eventually went out in the semi-final to Everton.

Like many another, George Hamilton had the heart of his career cut out by the war, and he was twenty-seven before it really got under way. In the confusion of 1939, he had gone back to the local shipyard at Irvine before being called up to the Royal Engineers in 1940. He was a driver in the North African campaign but managed to play some Army football, forming a right wing with that Englishman of immortal fame, Tom Finney.

George had sailed abroad from Tail o' the Bank at Greenock and, in the German torpedoing of troop ships, his two closest friends had died. The young Hamilton took on a new appreciation of life, which affected his attitude to football. As he told me later: 'I used to wonder if I would ever see the lads at Pittodrie again. When the war was over you were just so glad to be alive and I was really looking forward to coming back.'

On the day of his return in 1945, we kept our eyes on the players' door to catch first glimpse of the pre-war wonder boy. Out of the ruck of dull civilian clothing around the doorway the bright red shirt emerged in that splendid moment that sets football hearts beating faster. They had appointed George captain for the day and out he came, waving to those fans he wondered if he would ever see again. We stood there swallowing hard in one of football's highly charged moments. Hammy was back and all was well. What the crowd didn't know was that his arrival had been hastened by the tragedy of his sister's death.

George Hamilton was back for the creation of one of the finest teams ever seen at Pittodrie. It would make history before that season was over. As much as anyone, he embodied the spirit of that period when a war-weary world gave thanks for survival and felt determined to enjoy itself.

As we breathed the fresh air of peace again, a normal crowd at Pittodrie ranged from 18,000 to 22,000, rising to 28,000 for Hearts or Hibs, 35,000 for Celtic and 40,000 for Rangers. Boom-time was here for Scottish football in general and for Aberdeen not least.

Hamilton's obvious love of the game and determination to play it skilfully and fairly earned him the name of 'Gentleman George', although in all truth he could look after himself if the occasion arose. Yet in eighteen years at the top, he collected just one booking – and that in a League Cup tie with Hibs when, with the score level at 5–5, the game went into extra time. George dared to say to referee Jackson, 'I don't think that was a foul, ref,' and down went his name. Referees today are hardly accustomed to such polite comment.

So George was back at inside-right after the war but what had become of Stan Williams and Archie Baird, to complete the inside-forward trio? Alfred Stanley Williams was the diminutive South African who was spotted in the aftermath of Jackie Beynon's death.

Stan didn't require a second invitation from Paddy Travers and arrived in Scotland in 1938, thrilled to be rubbing shoulders with Mills and Armstrong and fellow-countryman Billy Strauss. He was diverted to building Sunderland flying-boats at Dumbarton during the war and guested with Dumbarton and Clyde, by then managed by Travers. He was also chosen to play for Scotland against England at Wembley in a wartime international when rules about nationality were not so strict. Stan proudly remembered shaking hands with Winston Churchill when the Prime Minister stepped on to the sacred turf to meet the teams. He was still engaged on war service right up to the Scottish League Cup final of 1946, by which time he was established as a dashing centre-forward of 5ft 4ins.

There was no lack of height in his partner at inside-left, Archie Baird, who had also come to Aberdeen in 1938, in the same season that his team-mate at Strathclyde Juniors, Willie Waddell, went to Rangers. When Archie arrived at Pittodrie he found himself recruited on the same day as another Willie Waddell, who had come from Renfrew Juniors.

As the two boys settled into the same digs, both unknowns in the city of Aberdeen, they had no inkling of the part they would play in a historic moment for Aberdeen Football Club nine years later; nor could they have foreseen the interruption of the war. They were just fresh-faced boys with a lifetime ahead of them.

Archie had been an apprentice architect in Glasgow and continued his training with Jenkins and Marr in Aberdeen, which seemed like a sensible precaution, especially since his first season at Pittodrie left him with doubts about whether he was really going to make it as a professional footballer.

By 1940 he was *en route* to a wartime adventure that would turn him and many others like him into men overnight. Archie was earmarked for the field ambulance of the Eighth Army as it battled through the ferocity of the North African campaign, only to be ensnared as a prisoner-of-war by the Germans at Tobruk.

But that was not at all to the liking of the young man from Rutherglen (Archie was later to become the brother-in-law of television's Magnus Magnusson, who might well have found a Mastermind of escape in 1943 as the Aberdeen player sat down to work out a flight to freedom). With a characteristic body-swerve, Archie made a daring escape from the Germans and spent a year behind enemy lines on the Adriatic coast, with the assistance of an Italian peasant family for whom he ploughed, sowed grain and made wine.

When the Germans came, the family would hide him. He tried to break through to the British side of the battle-line but finally had to contain himself until the British troops pushed up the leg of Italy and he was free. (Archie wrote a splendid book about his war.)

It was a more mature and confident Archie Baird who returned to Pittodrie, having survived the terrors of war. He continued his experience of breaking through enemy lines and eluding tight situations on the football field to the point of being chosen to play for Scotland against Belgium.

He was also chosen for the famous Victory International at Hampden Park in 1946 but had to withdraw with cartilage trouble, his place going to George Hamilton who thus shared one of Scotland's finest hours. Baird's form, however, encouraged 'Rex' of the *Sunday Mail* to forecast that Gordon Smith and Archie Baird would turn out to be the best right-wing partnership Scotland had ever seen.

Unfortunately, his forecast was never properly tested. The troublesome cartilage was followed by a broken leg, broken jaw, broken nose and a variety of broken ribs in a career which Archie still maintains he thoroughly enjoyed. He is certainly remembered as a very fine footballer, tall, classy and distinctive in style, still an active citizen of Cove and joining Johnny Pattillo among the surviving octogenarians of Pittodrie.

As a postscript to the wartime connection, Archie took an honours degree in Italian at the age of fifty and, having been a PE teacher after the war, switched to languages and was latterly assistant head of Hilton Academy.

32
SILVER AND GOLD

S o David Halliday had his three inside men, Hamilton, Williams and Baird, and three survivors of the 1937 Cup final team, Johnstone, Cooper and Dunlop, as well as Andy Cowie and George Taylor from before the war and an outside-left who had come on the scene in 1944 whose name was Billy McCall.

There were not too many places left to fill. In a game against Dunfermline, he fielded a junior from Blantyre Celtic, who caught the eye by blotting out the Dunfermline winger who would become better known as Billy Liddell, for long the Liverpool and Scotland outside-left. That junior was Pat McKenna, and his signature was secured by David Halliday at half-time. With a stripling of a lad from the Dundee area, Alec Kiddie, he now had the personnel for one of Aberdeen's best teams although that had yet to be proved.

He signed up others. The all-powerful St Clement's junior team of the 1940s would surely have something to offer the Dons and Halliday signed three of them: goalkeeper Ian Black, left-half Johnny Cruickshank and inside-forward Martin Buchan. Ian Black went on to become Scotland's goalie but by then he had been called up for military service, guested with Southampton and decided to stay at the Dell. Martin Buchan was as good a ball player as Aberdeen junior football had seen in years, but he never did command the place his talents seemed to merit. If the beautifully balanced Buchan didn't reach his potential at Pittodrie (he later gave twelve distinguished years to Buckie Thistle), he was to make another contribution to the fortunes of Aberdeen Football Club. Within a few years he had a son, another Martin Buchan, who would grow up with his father's

160

instincts, follow his route to Pittodrie and become captain of a Scottish Cup-winning team, making him, at the age of twenty-one, the youngest-ever skipper to achieve that distinction. All that, however, lay twenty-five years ahead.

After forty years and more of Scottish league football, David Halliday was looking for a blend of players to bring some kind of prize to Pittodrie. The public was grasping at anything that enhanced the reality of peace and Scottish football made a brave attempt at restoring a pre-war face when it launched an A and B Division of a league programme on 11 August 1945, just five days after the atomic bomb had been dropped on Hiroshima, bringing about the Japanese capitulation.

The Dons team that ran out that Saturday afternoon to a special cheer of joy, relief and welcome home was: Johnstone; Cooper, Dyer; Bremner, Dunlop, Taylor; Miller, Driver, Pattillo, Baird, Williams. Against visiting Third Lanark, the Dons won 3–0, with two goals from Johnny Pattillo and one from Miller.

Before the season was out, a limited version of the Scottish League Cup had been instituted and Aberdeen beat Ayr with a team that had already altered to: Johnstone; Cooper, McKenna; Pattillo, Dunlop, Taylor; Wallbanks, Hamilton, Williams, McCall, Strauss.

The semi-final tie took Aberdeen to meet Airdrie at Ibrox Park, Glasgow, but the event was rather overshadowed by the fact that on that same day, 27 April 1946, Aberdonians were lining Union Street by the tens of thousands to give a hero's welcome to Winston Churchill, who had led the country to victory and was now on his way to the Music Hall to receive the Freedom of Aberdeen.

The Dons needed a replay and extra time to dispose of Airdrie but suddenly found themselves with a date at Hampden Park, Glasgow, on 11 May 1946 (a harbinger of Gothenburg?) for the final of the League Cup.

It was the first chance for a whole new generation of football supporters to visit the national stadium and when the Aberdeen party arrived in Glasgow, after three refreshing days at the Marine Hotel, Largs, they found the city seething with red and white. In heatwave conditions the Dons were given a tremendous welcome outside the stadium, while inside the terracings were already packed. The opponents, if I have forgotten to mention, were Glasgow Rangers. The Lords Provost of the two cities, Hector McNeil of Glasgow and Sir Thomas Mitchell of Aberdeen, shook hands with the teams before the start. Sir Thomas, or Tammy Mitchell as he was affectionately known, turned with characteristic pawkiness and gave the Dons players the Churchill V-for-Victory sign.

He had hardly reached his seat when the long-striding Andy Cowie sent one of his equally long throw-ins to Stan Williams, who headed it on to Archie Baird. The big inside-left completed the heading by scoring Aberdeen's first goal. This was the day when the slightly built lad from Dundee, generally referred to as A.A. Kiddie, played the game of his life, turning his own dream-like performance into a nightmare for Rangers' left-back Tiger Shaw, who was not accustomed to chasing shadows.

In yet another successful joust, Kiddie gained possession, raced ahead, crossed to George Hamilton, who guided the ball on to Stan Williams for the little centre to score a second. Rangers hit back with two second-half goals to draw level and might have been expected to snatch a typical Ibrox victory.

But that man Kiddie put a different complexion on things. In the very last minute the atmosphere was felt not only on the slopes of Hampden but in the common-room of Gordon's College boarding-house at Queen's Cross, where a group of us were clustered round the wireless, hanging on every word from BBC commentator Peter Thomson. He had just checked his watch for the number of dying seconds when suddenly Aberdeen were on the attack, the ball had been crossed by Kiddie . . . Cowie was going for it . . . Hamilton was going for it . . . George Taylor was going for it . . .

Peter Thomson had a good commentating voice but was privately known to be an ardent Rangers enthusiast. When his voice finally confirmed what the roar had already told us – 'Aberdeen have scored!' – it seemed suspiciously like a wail. Aberdeen had indeed scored and there was time only for the re-start before the final whistle. The sideboard of Pittodrie had its first national trophy, albeit a slightly limited honour because the makeshift contest did not include all the teams that would compete in subsequent years. The victory does not appear in the official list of League Cup wins but that did not inhibit the joyous celebrations, while the fact that it had been achieved against the might of Ibrox made it a worthy success by any standard.

Because of other fixtures in the south, the Dons went back to their Largs hotel and it was nine days before the Cup was finally brought north by train. A huge crowd waited at the Joint Station and Frank Dunlop just managed a hug from his wife before he was hoisted high and carried to the open-topped bus. Shop and office workers rushed to their doors and windows as the bus came up Market Street and Union Street on its way to the Caledonian Hotel. They were all there except Stan Williams, who had to return to his army base in the south, and George Hamilton, who still had military commitments at Maryhill Barracks, Glasgow.

On the following day the Scottish League Cup was displayed in the window of the *Evening Express* branch office at the top of Union Street, along with George Taylor's boot with which he scored the winning goal. The team sat down in that same office to sign autographs and the picture which appeared in the *Evening Express* showed a queue of autograph-hunters headed by a shiny-faced schoolboy who didn't dream that one day he would be writing a book about it all. Such is the fascination of life.

That heroic figure of the Dons' first trophy success, A.A. Kiddie, deserves explanation. A science student at St Andrews when he joined Aberdeen in 1945, Alec Kiddie was also a university athlete and wished to retain his amateur status until he graduated three years later. In those days, as best illustrated by the teamsheets of Queen's Park, all amateur footballers were referred to by their initials, thus A.A. Kiddie.

Sharing his football with a teaching career, Alec Kiddie found it hard to retain his outside-right berth in the Dons team, especially with the arrival of Tony Harris and Alan Boyd (both former initials men from Queen's Park), but he remained at Pittodrie until 1950. He never lived in Aberdeen and was transferred to Falkirk, later playing for Brechin City and Montrose.

A.A. Kiddie was a fleeting memory, dedicating himself to education and ending up as principal maths teacher at St John's High School in his native Dundee. He took early retirement, became an enthusiastic traveller and now, in his mid seventies, still talks happily of his Pittodrie days. As an amateur, he received no financial reward for his major part in bringing the very first Cup to Pittodrie in 1946. But chairman William Mitchell presented him with a gold wristwatch, which he proudly wears to this day.

33

SCOTTISH CUP
AT LAST!

T HE dust of the Second World War had settled on a jaded Britain
and people were searching for a return of some colour to their
lives. Everything good seemed to have happened 'before the war' and
now that it was over, there was a strange anti-climax of peace and
a fresh desire to express ourselves.

In football terms, that opportunity came to Aberdonians on an
April day in 1947, in the first full season after the war, when the
grey-granite hordes set out to cheer the Dons at Hampden Park.

For only the second time in history the club had reached the final
of the Scottish Cup and the northern army was on its way by every
form of transport, determined to fortify an attack on the Hibernian
of Edinburgh which would surely, at last, bring the first truly
national trophy to Pittodrie.

In the austerity of the time, most folk settled for a modest rosette
pinned to their utility coats but in the effervescence of youth there
were those of us determined to make more of the occasion. I can
still recall my mother in Maud converting an old red jersey into a
tammy, with the aid of knicker elastic and a tassel on top, and waving
me off in my blue trench-coat to the wilds of Glasgow.

The seething mob at the Joint Station was funnelled into train-
loads which rumbled southwards, excitement mounting by the mile
but sometimes muted in a scanning of the morning papers in the
hope of finding a sportswriter who would confirm our own high
hopes. Then we recalled that this Scottish Cup journey began, not
at the Joint Station that Saturday morning but three months earlier,

on Burns' Day. It was then that Partick Thistle came north for the first round of the Cup with a formidable reputation, having beaten Aberdeen in a league game at Firhill a few weeks earlier.

It was vital that Aberdeen should take advantage of the home draw to see them into the second round, but with the final minutes of that match running out, the score stood at 1–1. Partick were happily contemplating a replay on their own territory and Aberdeen were dreading that very prospect. To make matters worse, skipper Frank Dunlop was limping on the wing when the Dons were awarded a corner-kick on the left. The ball was cleared from the visitors' goal-mouth and seemed to be going to Willie Sharp of Partick. Aberdeen right-back Willie Cooper had moved up-field, however, realising he could get there ahead of Sharp – and hit a first-time, soaring shot from forty yards.

What happened next is part of Pittodrie folklore. There are still witnesses to tell you the ball seemed to be heading for the upper reaches of the Beach-end terracing, when there was no thought of an enclosure there. Jimmy Steadward in the Partick goal seemed to share that opinion. Whether it was a gust of wind or a downright act of God we shall never know, but the ball inexplicably drew to a halt and dropped nonchalantly behind the Partick keeper.

Willie Cooper denied it was a fluke but said it with a smile. He was too far away to see exactly what happened and it was a jubilant Tony Harris who turned to give him the news: 'You've scored, auld yin!' 2–1. The referee was checking his watch.

As he blew that final whistle, 34,000 people – think of that for a first-round tie with Partick Thistle – rose to acclaim the thirty-six year old who had given the Dons the right to prove they could make it all the way to Hampden this time. But if that winning shot owed anything to luck, that fickle lady would desert poor Willie before the contest was over.

In the worst winter in living memory, which left snow behind many a dyke in June, the Dons battled through a play-to-the-finish fourth-round tie against Dundee at Dens Park and returned to that same ground for the semi-final with Arbroath, which was played just one week before the final. In that game Willie Cooper pulled a muscle which had no time to recover before the big day.

So the journey south was more than tinged with regret that the old warrior, without whom there may have been no journey at all, had lost his very last chance of a Cup medal in twenty-one years of magnificent service to Aberdeen Football Club and to the game as a whole.

The team we contemplated that April morning looked strangely unfamiliar in defence. Pat McKenna had moved from left- to right-back; George Taylor had dropped back from left-half and the wing-half positions were taken by Joe McLaughlin and Willie Waddell. The teams were: Aberdeen – Johnstone; McKenna, Taylor; McLaughlin, Dunlop, Waddell; Harris, Hamilton, Williams, Baird, McCall. Hibernian – Kerr; Govan, Shaw; Howie, Aird, Kean; Smith, Finnegan, Cuthbertson, Turnbull, Ormond.

Outside Buchanan Street Station, Glasgow, toothless beer barrels with bow-legs and gravel voices stood ready for the business of selling red rosettes to the foreign invaders, offering free advice on how to get to Hampden Park. So we negotiated alien-sounding streets across the Clyde, through the Gorbals and up Cathcart Road to the spiritual home of Scottish football. In the gathering momentum, it would have taken an insensitive creature to resist the excitement.

Meanwhile, the Dons party was travelling up by bus from Largs, where they had gone to prepare. On the night before the match they had attended a whist drive (yes, a whist drive) at the invitation of Largs Thistle, and skipper Frank Dunlop won the miniature trophy. A good omen?

Willie Cooper never forgot the sense of emptiness at not being an active part of the day, sitting on the trainer's bench with Bob McDermid. But Willie was just emerging from the dressing room as the game got under way and had not reached his seat when disaster struck Aberdeen's bid to land the Cup.

Within thirty seconds, George Taylor was passing back to goalkeeper George Johnstone, who had stood between those same posts ten years earlier against Celtic. It seemed like a safe ball for the ever-dependable George, except that it slipped through his hands and legs and presented itself on a plate for any lurking opponent.

Without pausing to consider his luck, John Cuthbertson was round him like a man in a hurry to accept as generous a gift as Hampden ever provided. Within the opening minute, the great army of Aberdonians was shocked into silence. This was not what they had come all this way to see. At least the game was young and there would be time to make amends, as long as the Dons could prevent a second goal from a Hibernian team driven on by a man who would yet play a significant role as an Aberdeen manager: Eddie Turnbull.

They weathered the storm all right and in thirty-six minutes Tony Harris started a clever move. The ball went to Stan Williams, who side-flicked into the path of George Hamilton. Hammy, who was as good a header of the ball as the game had ever known, darted forward to head the equaliser. The Dons were back in business and what happened six minutes later was a feat that is still discussed by old-timers today.

If Stan Williams had done nothing else in his career he would have earned his Pittodrie pedestal for his achievement as he bore in on that goalmouth at the east end of Hampden. I asked the man himself to recall what happened: 'I liked the way we were fighting back after that early goal. We were clearly the better team and were confident, despite the setback, that we would get that Cup. After George Hamilton's equaliser, Tony Harris hit the ball down-field but it was too fast and seemed to be going for a goal-kick. However, I chased it in case there was a chance and managed to catch the ball before it went over the line to the right of the Hibs goal. As I cut along the line everyone expected me to cross to either Archie Baird or George Hamilton, who were better placed. One of them was shouting for it. Suddenly I spotted a small space between Jimmy Kerr in the Hibs goal and the near post. There was no time for careful aiming and no margin for error. I just remember saying to myself, "Here goes!"'

The rest of the story was lost in a red riot of jubilation. The consequences of fluffing that shot instead of passing to Baird would have been a howl of disapproval. Brilliance is tolerated only when it comes off! But brilliant it was, full of the cheeky confidence of Stan Williams, a goal in a million. The press pictures show disbelief on the faces of goalkeeper Kerr and full-back Jock Govan, and even Archie Baird, who had expected the cross.

But the match was not over yet. In the second half, the same Stan Williams was eluding the Hibs defence when he was brought down by Jimmy Kerr, who no doubt felt he had had enough of the little man's nonsense for one day. Referee Bobby Calder, who would later play a part in the fortunes of Aberdeen FC, had no hesitation in awarding a penalty.

This would surely settle it. But as George Hamilton placed the ball on the spot he was having mixed thoughts, as he later told me: 'When Stan was brought down he was injured and had to be taken behind the goal for attention. The delay gave me too much time to think and I remember looking round the crowd and saying to myself, "If I miss this and we lose, I'll be held responsible." At last I was able to take the kick and Jimmy Kerr saved it! After that, I was never so glad to hear a final whistle!'

Stan Williams, too, had agonising memories of being torn between his injury and an anxiety about the penalty. Behind the goal he kept asking trainer Bob McDermid if George had scored.

At 4.45 p.m. on Saturday, 19 April 1947 the Rt. Hon. Joseph Westwood, His Majesty's Secretary of State for Scotland, crossed the hallowed turf of Hampden and handed the trophy to Frank Dunlop, centre-half and captain of the first Aberdeen team to win the Scottish Cup. The presentation took place where presentations should always take place – out on the field, in full view of all who have come to see the match. Sadly, today's rowdier spirits cannot be trusted to stay behind the boundary walls and give everybody a proper view. So the ceremony goes up to the grandstand, where the high point of glory is reserved for those clustered around the directors' box.

Back in 1947, when the unruly would not have dared interfere with the rights of the majority, it was the privilege of all to share in the joyous moment. And so it was that April day, which is written in large red letters across the history of the Dons. Photographs show the crowd of 82,140, including 10,000 from Aberdeen, dressed in sober raincoats, soft hats or bonnets, well-dressed, well-behaved people intent on absorbing a memorable moment in their own personal history.

But the best was yet to come. Amid the scenes of jubilation, with Frank Dunlop holding the Cup for all to see, the crowd set up a chant of 'We want Cooper! We want Cooper!' From his place in the shadows of the south stand, the square-cut figure was coaxed out on to that same pitch where he had suffered the disappointment of Cup final defeat by Celtic ten years earlier.

Out he went to a thunderous reception which told him of the gratitude and affection of every living soul who supported Aberdeen. They handed the Cup to Willie, for to him it truly belonged, and there were grown men with red rosettes who blew their noses, for the solid folk of the North-east do not readily display their tears.

It was one of football's finest moments. Willie Cooper remembered it like this: 'It had been my day of greatest disappointment in a long career. Yet, when I heard the shouts from the crowd, it also became my greatest day. I tell you this, I was nearly greetin'!'

Willie played on for another year before retiring from big-time football in 1948. He went to work for Stewart's Cream of the Barley whisky, later part of Allied Breweries, and in his retirement became liquor storeman with the Cooperative at Berryden.

Looking back on his career, Willie told me he had never considered playing anywhere other than Pittodrie. He just played season after season for twenty-one of them, delighted when the manager asked him to sign for another year. It was another year's work, as Willie recalled, a guarantee that meant something in the 1930s when men were glad of any work they could find.

Willie's loyalty belonged exclusively to Aberdeen Football Club and the appropriate postscript to that 1947 Cup final was that, while there were no medals for a non-participant in those days, the SFA showed a commendable humanity in allowing the club to strike a special medal for a very special man.

Willie Cooper whom many nominated as a better footballer than his predecessor, Jock Hutton, stood out as the archetypal Aberdeen man. No player ever served a club more faithfully. That special medal was, in fact, all he had to show for his services to football. There had been no runners-up medals in the 1937 Scottish Cup final, nothing for the League Cup winners of 1946, because football had not resumed a peacetime footing, and now he had missed the 1947 final. But if football had offered him little silver, he at least had enriched the game.

Willie was there two days later when the players arrived back at the Joint Station. Not even torrential rain could dampen the spirits of the thousands who waited in the station forecourt. This time the open-topped bus made a longer detour by Guild Street, Regent Quay, Marischal Street and Union Street to the Caledonian Hotel, where the players were entertained to an early evening dinner.

Chairman William Mitchell thanked the players and Frank Dunlop replied that 'the boys could travel far and wide and still not find a club like Aberdeen. Personally I consider it a great honour to be a member of the club.' Afterwards, officials, players and friends were guests of Mr James Donald (Dick Donald's brother) at His Majesty's Theatre, where Dave Willis was doubling them up with laughter.

The fact that the Dons had been at Hampden just two weeks before the Scottish Cup victory, being beaten 4–0 by Rangers in the League Cup final, is something that few Aberdeen supporters can even recall today! The Light Blues may have avenged the defeat of the previous year but the game was played in a hurricane which had already blown away the memory.

The Dons had won the Scottish Cup after forty-four years in existence and that was enough to put a spring in the northern step and sustain the buoyancy of a patient Aberdeen support for many a day.

34

ALLISTER–YOUNG–GLEN

T HE team that brought the Scottish Cup to Aberdeen for the first time had been sadly robbed of a proper life span by the war, coming together only in the year before that triumph and beginning to disintegrate soon afterwards. After all, it was not a young team. Apart from the veteran Willie Cooper who had missed the final, George Johnstone and Frank Dunlop had been in the Cup final team of 1937, while Willie Waddell, George Taylor, George Hamilton, Stan Williams and Archie Baird were on the books before 1939.

Stan Williams was approaching his thirtieth birthday before the moment of Hampden glory. By the following year he had been transferred to Plymouth Argyle but he did not settle and returned to play for George Anderson's Dundee. He finally left Scotland in 1951 and spent two years in Malta before settling back in his native South Africa, this time in Johannesburg. It took twenty-five years for Stan to set foot in Scotland again, coming back to bring in the New Year of 1977 with his old friend and team-mate of 1947, Billy McCall, in Bishopbriggs, Glasgow.

Billy had been another great favourite at Pittodrie, a small, stocky left-winger, but he too left during the year after the Cup win. He claimed his departure arose from a row over a cigarette. On a matchday he was heading for the dressing room with an unlit cigarette in his hand when chairman Mitchell accused him of smoking before a game. McCall said he displayed the unlit fag but the chairman did not accept his word and reported him to manager Halliday. Some bad blood was generated out of a trivial incident until Billy McCall was transferred to Newcastle United in an exchange deal involving Tommy Pearson. Despite the unfortunate circumstances, however, McCall upheld Aberdeen as a place of great happiness to which people who left were eventually keen to return.

I had arranged to meet Williams and McCall in the Central Hotel, Glasgow, during that visit of 1977 and sat in the foyer, rekindling memories of the fair-haired Stan and the dark-haired Billy and wondering what the years had done to them. Through the revolving doors of the hotel came two small men with grey-white hair and the lines of age about their faces.

Stan had had one of those warning heart attacks and Billy had suffered a thrombosis but that did not inhibit a good old blether about happy days in Aberdeen. Football apart, Stan remembered dancing at the Palais in Diamond Street, for which Mr Bromberg used to issue complimentary tickets to Dons players. There was snooker with Tony Harris, Andy Cowie and Billy McCall and golf at Stonehaven, followed by swimming in the open-air pool.

For the Dons players, as for many people in Aberdeen, the Caledonian Hotel was the social centre of the city. Visiting teams stayed there, as did the stars appearing at His Majesty's, and the Caley became the place where Aberdonians went to see and be seen – a social crossroads with palm-court orchestra in the lounge and a staff of personalities, still remembered as Charlie Bultitude, head waiter, big Arthur at the door, Andy the cocktail king of the American Bar, the little Greek in the dining room, tall Mary in the lounge and the inimitable Jean in the back bar.

Stan Williams remembered it with affection: 'Back home they don't believe me when I tell them we were treated like film stars when I played for Aberdeen. People used to stop you in the street or on the tramcar to ask for your autograph.'

By the 1970s he was making parts for the rock drills that cut diamonds in the South African mines, working at Benoni, twenty miles outside Johannesburg. Every Sunday morning he would look in the papers for the Aberdeen result and give a thought to those other Sunday mornings when he would wake up in his digs at 9 Forest Avenue, the home of Mrs Ella Large.

Stan came to Aberdeen on a wage of £5 a week in the reserve team but by 1946 that had risen to £10 with a £2 bonus for a win. Inflation makes a mockery of such figures but Stan managed to save enough for a deposit account which rested in a South African bank awaiting his retirement.

He talked with respect of manager David Halliday, who had to cope with a high-spirited bunch of players, some of whom gave rise to rumours about drinking, dancing and outrageous hours. Half the stories were untrue, said Stan, but manager Halliday's tough line would have been justified if the other half of the stories *were* true!

Back at Pittodrie, George Hamilton became restless after the Cup final and put in a transfer request. He went to Hearts in exchange for Archie Kelly but had reached no further than the train to Edinburgh for the signing formality before he regretted his move. But he had given his word and that meant something in those days of greater integrity than now.

Still playing for Scotland, he was crossing on the boat for an international match in Dublin and leaning over the rail looking miserable when a voice behind him said, 'Are you happy, George?' John D. Robbie, an Aberdeen director travelling with the Scottish party, didn't have to wait for a reply. 'If I make the effort, will you come back?' George broke into a broad smile. 'You go ahead, Mr Robbie, and I'll be delighted to come back.' Thus a great Pittodrie servant returned to where he belonged and continued in a red shirt for another eight or nine years.

But the wheels of change were grinding out the old and in the new. Hamilton had already played a major part in paving the way for Aberdeen's future. After the 1947 Cup final he went to visit his parents in Irvine, where local people were glad to shake his hand and share pride in his success. Little did he think, as he wandered along to Kilwinning to watch a local junior cup final, that he was about to find a future captain of Aberdeen. In the Annbank United team that evening he spotted a player whose performance sent him scurrying to the phone to call David Halliday, just as Billy Halliday had made a similar call when he spotted young Hamilton at Dumfries.

Meanwhile, George's father made contact with the lad and confirmed that his name was Archie Glen from Mauchline. Halliday went hot-foot to Ayrshire and encountered young Archie's father who, true to his solid mining background, laid down the condition that his son could sign for Aberdeen only if he continued with his plans for a university degree in chemistry. Mr Halliday agreed and Archie Glen was heading north. He recalled: 'The club were even better than their word because they paid my fees for a BSc degree course at Aberdeen University and for that I was eternally grateful.

'I remember arriving in July 1947, looking at Willie Cooper and thinking he had been playing for the Dons three years before I was even born. I was soon to play with him in the reserve team and found him a tremendous competitor as well as a good teacher. He had basic rules which were very sound and which he felt you should learn.'

So the young Glen settled into digs with Mrs Petrie in Burnett Place, just round the corner from Willie Cooper in Leslie Road, and willingly paid his landlady £2 out of his wage-packet of £5. His first-team debut came in February 1949, against Falkirk at Brockville when he had the joy of playing on the same pitch as a childhood hero, former Rangers keeper Jerry Dawson.

By then he was also being inspired by the supreme artistry of Tommy Pearson, who crusaded for the belief that football had to be skilful and entertaining as a first priority and that, hopefully, the rewards would follow. Glen listened with rapt attention to the philosophies of Pearson, who was playing out his veteran days at Pittodrie, having given his best years to Newcastle United.

Archie remembered one afternoon session at Pittodrie during which he suffered the torment of many a defender as the master demonstrated his famous double-shuffle and showed how easy it was to put a ball through a player's legs. He said to Archie, 'I'll come up to you three times with the intention of putting it through your legs twice.' So with at least some forewarning, the exercise began, but when it was over the bewildered Archie found that he had been nutmegged on all three occasions. Such was the magic of Pearson, who was not only a juggler but an expert at taking up position.

It helped Archie to develop a special technique of tackling. As an opponent approached with the ball, he picked up the rhythm of his step, like the beat of a metronome, and tackled on the half-beat. Its effectiveness became part of his style.

Archie Glen attended university by day and trained at night, graduating in 1950. A year later he was off to do his national service and found himself playing in the British Army team alongside the great Welsh internationalist John Charles and that other superb footballer, Tommy Taylor, who was killed in the Manchester United air crash of 1958.

But a bad injury caused a bone to press on his Achilles tendon and the medical verdict was that he would have to find another occupation. His world collapsed around him in disbelief that his football career was over before it had properly begun. His army service over, Archie returned to Pittodrie without a word to anyone, found no ill effect in training and quietly asked a doctor friend to X-ray his ankle. The report confirmed the previous diagnosis but added that the bone had now slipped back into position – and to this day no one at Pittodrie has ever been told about it.

Glen returned to the fold at an interesting time of reconstruction when the Dons were coming close to having another good team. Jimmy Mitchell, the former Queen's Park and Morton defender, had come north to be captain.

Alec Young came late to senior football from Blantyre Victoria but turned out to be one of the finest centre-halves of them all, outjumping the tallest despite his lack of inches and gaining a reputation for his sliding tackles in which he not only did the splits but gave a heaven-sent opportunity for 'Chrys', the *Evening Express* cartoonist, to caricature him.

A stubby-haired Edinburgh lad called Jack Allister, who had gone to Chelsea after his army service, took over at right-half and Archie Glen completed a very competent half-line of Allister, Young and Glen. Before that, however, there were surprises in store for the Dons fans – and for Mr Halliday in particular.

35
PEARSON'S MAGIC

ONE morning in the late 1940s a telegram reached manager David Halliday which read: 'Request permission to play goalkeeper Martin, who is on your books. Sgd. Manager of Crystal Palace FC, London.' Halliday scratched his head, considered there had been some mistake and replied: 'Sorry, we have no goalkeeper called Martin.'

Thus arose one of those curious football stories. David Halliday was of course technically correct. He had only one Martin on his books and that was the big inside-forward he had signed from Carnoustie Panmure in 1946, a lad with height, strength and fine ball control who had played in the reserve team before going off to do his national service training.

Two months before his departure in June 1947, he had sat at Hampden with the entire Pittodrie staff watching that Scottish Cup win. But it was during national service that fate took a hand in the astonishing career of big Fred Martin. Playing for the British Army in the south of England, as a forward of course, he was drafted into goal one day when the keeper was injured. The regular man was out for several weeks and his deputy performed with distinction, so much so that he was spotted by Crystal Palace – and off went the telegram.

How could manager Halliday ever have imagined that the mysterious message was bringing him the first hint of a fairytale – the man he had signed for his outfield skills would, within a few years, be chosen as Scotland's first-ever World Cup goalkeeper! It was the stuff of schoolboy adventure stories but this time it had nothing to do with fiction.

All that, however, was still in the future when big Fred found himself as an Army goalkeeper, having committed himself to a professional career as a footballing forward. Recalling the dilemma, he said: 'Everyone has an idea of his own capabilities and when I went into goal that day I sensed that I had a certain aptitude for this part of the game. I was given permission to play for Crystal Palace, then came that day in 1949 when my national service was over and it was time to return to Pittodrie.'

Mr Halliday called him in and said, 'Well Fred, what are you going to do? Are you going to be a forward or a goalkeeper?' He left the choice entirely to Fred, who decided to take a chance on the latter.

George Johnstone was coming to the end of his career but there were others around, such as Pat Kelly, John Curran and Frank Watson. Out of that transitional period, however, it was Fred Martin who was to emerge as the goalkeeper of the 1950s, playing through three Scottish Cup finals, a League Cup final and a league championship season, as well as keeping goal for Scotland in the World Cup adventures of 1954. But more of that later.

Pittodrie was gathering up some remarkable personalities, some of whom would last through memorable times in the mid 1950s. Others would be best remembered by those who like to absorb the essence of a distinctive player and store it in the crevices of the mind for future bouts of nostalgia.

Two names spring readily to mind because they stirred public imagination in totally different ways: Tommy Pearson and Don Emery. If I were asked to nominate the players who had brought me the greatest amount of pleasure during sixty years of watching the Dons, I would turn to Johnny Pattillo, Ernie Waldron, Archie Baird, George Hamilton and come through the century to classical ball-players such as Charlie Cooke, Jimmy Smith, Zoltan Varga and Gordon Strachan. But if I were forced to name one player who satisfied the highest aspirations of football grace, intelligence and excitement, that man would have to be Tommy Pearson.

An Edinburgh man, he had been with Newcastle before and after the war but we caught the tailend of his genius at Pittodrie and

In jovial mood, Dons chief scout Bobby Calder, with manager Eddie Turnbull and chairman Charles Forbes.

Martin Buchan played a captain's part in the Scottish Cup final of 1970. The Dons beat Celtic 3–1.

Zoltan Varga, the great Hungarian who graced Pittodrie for just one season.

Billy McNeill with captain Willie Miller before the 1978 Cup final. McNeill took over from Ally MacLeod and did an excellent job for Aberdeen FC.

An anxious moment for Aberdeen's ebullient manager, Ally MacLeod. Overall, he proved to be a tonic for everyone at the club.

Willie Miller in a struggle with Frank McGarvey of Celtic. Miller became Alex Ferguson's 'mirror on the park'.

Bobby Clark, the Dons' long-serving goalkeeper and 'a great influence around the club', according to Alex Ferguson.

Jim Leighton took over from Bobby Clark in goal and became the Dons' most capped player. He made 91 full international appearances during his career with Aberdeen (twice), Manchester United and Hibs.

The Aberdeen directors are keen to show off their new young manager. *Left to right*: Charles Forbes, Alex Ferguson, Dick Donald and Chris Anderson.

Gordon Strachan – play-making genius.

In 1982, Aberdeen defeated Rangers 4–1 in the Scottish Cup final. A jubilant Alex Ferguson holds the Cup aloft.

In 1983, Aberdeen were again victorious in the Scottish Cup final, this time beating Rangers 1–0. Alex Ferguson lines up with the team before the game.

Pittodrie's greatest moment – March 1983 and John Hewitt scores the winning goal against Bayern Munich. The score is 3–2 and the Dons are through to the semi-finals of the European Cup Winners' Cup.

Mark McGhee in full flight in the semi-final against Waterschei of Belgium. Final aggregate score – 5–2 to the Dons.

were grateful for the privilege. For Pearson was one of the supreme artists of this maddening game, a barrel-chested dream of a player with the balance of perfection in his body and the sheer power of poetry in his movement.

With the deftness of a conjurer he practised a kind of sleight of foot that produced his famous double-shuffle. Others have tried it but never matched him. Knowing it would happen half a dozen times in a game, some of us would set out to observe precisely what happened. We kept our eyes riveted, waiting for the moment, but when it arrived and he weaved his magical deception, we were left none the wiser.

Then, like a conjurer who assures his audience that the trick is really quite simple and that he will let them into the secret, he was capable of taking on the same man again – or any other who cared to be demoralised – and beating him in precisely the same manner. Oh for the benefit of an action replay! (I wonder if Pearson exists anywhere on film.)

Some say Tommy Pearson would not be allowed to play like that today but great ball artists have always prospered in their respective generations, whether it was Bobby Walker, Stanley Matthews, Jimmy Johnstone, George Best or Ryan Giggs.

It is worth remembering that Pittodrie could draw crowds of 8,000 for a reserve game in the early 1950s, most of them there to savour the magic of Tommy Pearson and his protégé Hughie Hay. That kind of genius comes rarely in a lifetime and lingers like a perfume when so much else that seemed important is forgotten.

If Pittodrie remembers Pearson for his silken skills, the affection for Don Emery was rather different. Don was a colourful character with a cannonball kick whom one writer described as being built on the lines of a small rhinoceros. Others likened him to Jock Hutton, neither of them using their chunky frames to unfair advantage. However, anyone seeking to precipitate a collision would rebound like an arrow from a bow.

The late John Fairgrieve of the *Scottish Daily Mail* set the scene for a collision between Emery and Bobby Parker of Hearts, who believed that any winger with the temerity to go near the ball deserved all he got. It was uncommon in those days for left-backs to come in direct contact with right-backs but the Almighty had decreed that the question should be settled. As Parker and Emery went for a fifty-fifty ball, Fairgrieve described the scene:

> Tynecastle was hushed, the kind of silence often decreed in memory of some respected official. The ball bounced awkwardly but the ball was no longer of any importance. Parker and Emery were on their way and could not be called back. The impact itself was not particularly noisy; more a thud than a crunch. Emery had ground to a halt a fraction of a second before, the better to brace himself no doubt. That, of course, was not Bobby Parker's way and possibly his tactics were basically unsound. Parker stotted backwards and fell flat on his back. Emery stared down at him, expressionless, hands on hips. Parker rose, grinned, waved and loped away.

Don Emery's presence at Pittodrie was due to a local girl, Maude Cheyne, whose father was George Cheyne of the motor firm. Maude met Welshman Don when she joined the WAAF during the war and he was serving in the RAF and playing for the works team of Lovell's, the confectionery people, who paid him literally in sweets.

Don and Maude were married and when he resumed football at Swindon Town he ran into an exciting time in the FA Cup. As a Third Division team, Swindon were drawn against First Division leaders Burnley. Since the manager decided they didn't have a snowball's chance of beating Burnley, he took them off to Southport for a week's holiday and told them to enjoy themselves and forget about football.

On the following Saturday, Swindon knocked table-topping Burnley right out of the FA Cup by 2–0. Thousands welcomed them back to Swindon. In the next round Notts County were the opponents and this time the imaginative manager decided Weston-super-Mare was as good a place as any to forget about football. Once again Don Emery and his mates had a magnificent week of indulging – and came back to knock Notts County out of the Cup.

The recipe ran to the sixth round when Swindon were running short of seaside resorts and Southampton managed to stop the fun.

I cannot help feeling that such a civilised approach to a sport gone deadly serious deserved all the success it received.

Don might never have left the south but for the homesickness of his Aberdonian wife, which was a lucky break for David Halliday, who heard about it. Andy Cowie, that splendid wing-half who had come from Dundee in 1938 for £2,500 and played in the League Cup final of 1946, was out of favour at Pittodrie so Halliday arranged an exchange with Swindon's Emery, who took over the right-back position from Willie Cooper.

The Pittodrie crowd took him straight to their hearts, this solid chunk of a man who embodied those local emblems of granite rock and prime Aberdeen Angus. The power of an Emery free kick became absolutely legendary. Percy Dickie, who was coaching at Pittodrie, got in the way of an Emery ball at training one day and swore the manufacturer's name was imprinted on his backside for weeks thereafter. Fred Martin carried a badly bent finger into retirement, the result of an Emery practice shot – and the apologetic Don said he was only wearing plimsolls.

The statistics show that, in four seasons, he scored thirty-three goals, nineteen of them from penalties, while most of the others were free-kick balls, which keepers tended to see for the first time when retrieving them from the back of a shattered net. Tommy Gallacher of Dundee, later a sportswriter with the *Dundee Courier*, often reminded Don that his head had never been quite the same since he got in the way of one of his blockbusters.

Penalty kicks at Pittodrie were a matter of high anticipation, but there was no ceremony. The routine was that Harry Yorston placed the ball on the spot as the bulky figure came ambling down from his own penalty area. He didn't stop for any special aim but simply did what penalty-takers should never fail to do and blasted the ball with total ferocity to the back of the net. Goalkeepers who failed to touch an Emery shot were generally regarded as lucky. It was better than the infirmary.

Just after the famous 'Jimmy Cowan' international at Wembley in 1949, Morton came to Pittodrie and that heroic goalkeeper who had defied the English was given a standing ovation as he ran on to the field. But he was soon brought back to reality when the Dons were awarded a free kick thirty-five yards from the Morton goal.

Cowan signed to his defence to keep clear. But a Wembley reputation counted for nothing when Don Emery's kick went past him like a blur and had rebounded from the stanchion to the eighteen-yard line while Cowan was searching vainly in the net!

At 5ft 8ins, Emery admitted to a weight of only thirteen stone in his playing days although it looked a lot more. But he had a stout heart to match his bulk and, once again, John Fairgrieve used his wit to throw light on the Emery character when he alleged Don once played a game with a broken leg and might never have noticed if someone in the dressing room hadn't said, 'Excuse me, but isn't that a broken leg you've got there?'

Don went to East Fife, won a League Cup medal in the same team as future Aberdeen manager Jimmy Bonthrone then, broadening to a square-cut eighteen stone, became sales manager of the Webster Tyre Company, driving a Mercedes with the registration DON. What better insignia for one of the most colourful Dons of them all?

But Pearson and Emery were not alone among the fascinating figures of that era. Like Pearson, Jimmy Delaney, one of Celtic's greatest-ever names, came to spend part of his twilight at Aberdeen, a balding figure from Manchester United who could still turn on the style. He was followed to Pittodrie by another Old Trafford Scot, Tommy Lowrie, who idolised Delaney.

Aberdeen went on a tour of Norway in 1950 and Don Emery was sunbathing in a little boat with Delaney and Lowrie when the latter began larking about. One undergarment was thrown overboard and, in a tit-for-tat caper which went from bad to worse, Delaney and Lowrie ended up with nothing but their trunks and had to walk up the main street in a state of undress to buy new clothing, when clothes were still rationed.

Staying at the same hotel in Norway was the future President of the United States, General Dwight Eisenhower, who was at that time Supreme Commander of the Nato forces but had no command over the high-spirited Dons. The irrepressible Lowrie was investigating the layout of the hotel when he spotted smoke through the glass panel in a door. He immediately raised the alarm, extended the hoses and sparked off a full-scale emergency, only to discover the room with the glass panel was the hotel's steam laundry!

Pearson, Emery, Delaney and Lowrie were members of a transitional team and were not to figure in the exciting period ahead. But they were there when the Dons could field the oldest and one of the most talented forward lines in the land, in which only Harry Yorston was in his twenties. Just contemplate the market value of this quintet at the height of their fame: Delaney, Yorston, Hamilton, Baird and Pearson.

It was a period too when the distinctive styles of individuals gave tremendous scope to George Chrystal, one of the best cartoonists of his day working under the name of 'Chrys'. As an art student in Aberdeen he had submitted his early efforts to the *Evening Express* and later joined the staff, producing a regular Monday caricature of the Saturday action and creating that well-loved North-east character, Wee Alickie.

The popular belief was that he modelled Wee Alickie on Alick Murray, the fair-haired, pink-cheeked odd-job man at Pittodrie, who always danced about with excitement at the players' door and became a familiar face to every Dons supporter. Alick was an innocent soul who was first engaged by Paddy Travers. He stayed at 11 Linksfield Place with his mother, who turned flour bags into pants for the Dons players during the wartime scarcity.

Alick moved in with his brother Ernest when he retired to Carden Terrace from his antique shop in Ballater, and later lived in Fergus House residential home at Dyce. Chrys played down the idea that he had based his character on one man and claimed Alickie was an amalgam of young Dons fans. But Alick Murray was one of many in no doubt about the identity.

The up-and-coming players of the day included Frank Watson, the Peebles Rovers goalkeeper who not only joined up at Pittodrie but enrolled as a student at Aberdeen University. Frank played for the Young Dons against St Johnstone at Pittodrie on 6 September 1952 but was then taken to hospital suffering from poliomyelitis and was placed in an iron lung.

Public concern for a highly popular young lad eased with reports that he was improving and should recover. Frank was already married with one child and had completed the third year of his studies for an Honours MA in geography. It came as all the more of a shock when his death was announced on 5 November. The Pittodrie flag flew at half-mast as a token of sorrow for a young man and his family who had so much to look forward to.

George Chrystal also died in his early years but his twinkling humour and soft voice come alive every time I set eyes on Wee Alickie.

36

COURAGE OF HATHER

THE 1950s were bursting with a new vitality at Pittodrie as David Halliday came close to the blend he wanted. Sometimes a player would crop up on his own doorstep, as with the breezy boy who grew up just round the corner in Park Street and came bounding into Pittodrie to become one of Aberdeen's most controversial players. His name was Harry Yorston, not to be confused with Benny Yorston, who was a second cousin of his father.

Harry had stood on the terracing as a little boy before the war, idolising George Hamilton, whom he continued to regard as the greatest player he had seen at Pittodrie. Ten years later he could hardly believe his luck when he found himself playing alongside his idol and forming a partnership which was to assist him in becoming the Dons' leading goalscorer, a record which lasted through a generation until it was overtaken by Joe Harper in the 1970s.

Harry was the cheery-faced, good-looking golden boy of the 1950s who could raise ecstasy and exasperation in close succession, hitting glorious goals and missing glorious opportunities in a career of no half-measures. 'Maybe I didn't work at it as a career like some people,' said Harry reflectively, 'but I did enjoy my football.'

A section of the Pittodrie crowd fixed on Harry as a target of abuse, a fate not unknown to local lads. This caused anger among his fellow players who would tell you that Harry's work-rate took the burden off every other player in the team. Halliday signed him from St Clements A as early as 1946 and called him back from national service in Portsmouth to make his first-team debut during the Christmas games of 1948. Over that festive period he scored four

185

goals which were to prove vital in a season when the Dons were struggling to avoid relegation.

The manager didn't find all his players in convenient corners like Park Street. He showed great diligence in pursuing the players he wanted. The fact that a promising lad from the coalfields of Northeast England had turned down the chance to join Queen's Park Rangers didn't deter him from making the journey to watch him play for Annfield Plain at Horden. Annfield lost but Halliday had set his mind on signing their outside-left, a human flying-machine called Jackie Hather.

The player was in the bath when the secretary told him a man from Aberdeen wanted to see him. Hather sent back word he was not interested and later left for home. When he got there, who should be waiting but the same gentleman from Aberdeen who was not to be put off by a message from a bathtub.

Jackie, who had had a spell with Newcastle United before returning to semi-professional football, still refused to have anything to do with signing. Then his father stepped in and said he would like a private word with him. Whatever was said, Jackie Hather emerged with a change of heart and became an Aberdeen player in December 1948.

An injury to Tommy Pearson, whose talents he knew at Newcastle, gave him his first-team debut on New Year's Day 1949 and that was the start of a career which lasted for twelve years and is imprinted indelibly on the memories of all who saw him. Who could forget the flying winger, probably the fastest man Pittodrie has seen, as he took off down the wing or through the middle, lean and slightly hunched, his frail body suddenly accelerating into a sprint that would leave defenders floundering on a variety of wrong feet?

Jackie Hather, who eventually returned to live in Peterlee, County Durham, was so glad he took his father's advice. Until his dying day he spoke enthusiastically about the lasting impression made upon him by George Hamilton and raved about Aberdonians being the salt of the earth. After all, he married one and their son John returned to Aberdeen as a player before moving to Blackpool.

Jackie remembered well the day John was born. Aberdeen were

playing Queen of the South, whose goalkeeper was Roy Henderson, one of football's characters who had a memorable spell at Pittodrie at the end of the war. Hather was a left-footer who used his right leg for balancing only but on that particular day he was driven along the eighteen-yard line to an angle where he had no chance of using his left foot. So for once he tried the spare one and the ball flew past Roy Henderson for one of Hather's greatest goals.

It was a novel way to celebrate fatherhood. Roy found him afterwards to say 'Hey, who the **** taught you to use your right foot? I never expected that!' Hather played non-league football in the north of England until 1966 and there is one postscript to his career which illustrates the courage of the man.

All that speed and effort was achieved on just one kidney. The other had been removed when he was eleven and he was told he would not be able to take part in sport. Colleagues at Pittodrie were sometimes anxious about the risks and big Fred Martin can still wince at the memory of the screams which reached him at the other end when the boot of a well-known Scottish defender lunged dangerously at Hather's only kidney while he was lying on the ground.

But if the flying Englishman, who was known to his team-mates as the Hare, was the fastest Don over thirty yards or more, there was one player who could beat him on the ten-yard burst and that was Paddy Buckley, a dashing centre-forward who came from St Johnstone to become a firm favourite at Pittodrie. The fact that two of the fastest men the game had ever seen coincided in the same team cannot be overlooked when you consider what followed.

Six years had passed since Aberdeen had won anything but the team that Halliday had struggled to create as a successor to the one of 1947 was beginning to emerge. In the Scottish Cup of 1952–53 the Dons disposed of St Mirren, Motherwell and Hibs before making heavy weather of beating Third Lanark in a replay of the semi-final.

Now they were set to meet Rangers in what was still only their third appearance in a Scottish Cup final in fifty years of existence. In the Aberdeen team that day were three men who had played in the 1947 final: George Hamilton, still at inside-forward, Tony Harris, who had played his prime years at outside-right but had switched to right-half, and Davie Shaw, the Hibs left-back of 1947 but now occupying the same position for Aberdeen.

The line-ups were: Aberdeen – Martin; Mitchell, Shaw; Harris, Young, Allister; Rodger, Yorston, Buckley, Hamilton, Hather. Rangers – Niven; Young, Little; McColl, Stanners, Pryde; Waddell, Grierson, Paton, Prentice, Hubbard.

The full house of 135,000 people packing the slopes of Hampden saw John Prentice put Rangers ahead in eight minutes. It seemed as if that might be enough to see the Light Blues through, despite the fact that goalkeeper George Niven had been off injured for a spell and was replaced by big George Young. But with time running out, Harry Yorston swung a fine pass to Jackie Hather, who returned the compliment with an equally fine cross for Harry. He ran in to meet the ball with his head and that glorious equaliser gave the Dons a second chance.

In the customary imbalance of Scottish football, Rangers had an even greater crowd advantage for the Wednesday replay, which took place, as always, on their own doorstep. As many of us as possible made the second trip to Glasgow but the crowd of 113,700 showed clearly the drop in numbers from Aberdeen.

There was a popular belief that you were never given a second chance against the Old Firm and so it proved. Billy Simpson scored the only goal of the night and we carried our misery into the darkness of a long drive home.

But the Pittodrie players had developed a taste for the big occasion at Hampden and in the Scottish Cup of the following season they beat Hibs and Hearts with two first-rate performances to reach the semi-final. The mighty Rangers stood between them and a place in the Cup final but that at least gave the opportunity to avenge the defeat of 1953.

A lanky lad called Joe O'Neil was turning in some useful perform-ances but his chances of figuring in the Scottish Cup seemed to have vanished when he sustained a depressed fracture of the skull just three weeks before the semi-final. But Joe was built of hardy material and made a miraculous recovery, running on to the Hampden pitch with a close-shaven head to take his place against Rangers on Saturday, 10 April 1954.

Harry Yorston was suffering from one of his rare injuries that day and the Aberdeen team read: Martin; Mitchell, Caldwell; Allister, Young, Glen; Leggat, Hamilton, Buckley, O'Neil, Hather. A crowd of 110,939 could hardly have bargained for the spectacle that was to unfold before their disbelieving eyes that afternoon.

It all began with a typical cross from Jackie Hather, which was headed on by George Hamilton into the path of Joe O'Neil. Big Joe took it in his stride to put Aberdeen one goal ahead. But the fun had only started. Another cross from Hather sent goalkeeper Bobby Brown and centre-half Willie Woodburn rising together for the ball. But in stepped Joe O'Neil to head home a second goal with that skull which had so recently been fractured.

The example of big Joe was infectious and Rangers could make nothing of this Aberdeen team as Hamilton laid on the perfect pass for Graham Leggat to make it three. With eight minutes to go, O'Neil scored his own third and Aberdeen's fourth and was going through again when he was brought down in the penalty box.

Jack Allister had the privilege of making it five. Meanwhile, Aberdeen's hero had been taken off the field, causing some concern about that head injury, but he was soon returning to savour the final glory of his greatest day in football. That day reached its incredible climax when Paddy Buckley scored a last-minute goal to make the final result Aberdeen 6 Rangers 0. Six goals against Rangers and every one a beauty!

Before the final whistle, the blue brigade of Ibrox fans had drained from the Hampden bowl like water down a sink, leaving the red glow of success to the northern visitors who had wrought their sweet revenge. Aberdonians were unwilling to leave the scene of their triumph and many hung around Glasgow. John Cooper of Kidd Street, Aberdeen, had memories stretching back to 1919 when Jock Hutton made his first appearance for the Dons, wearing a blue scarf. On the night of the 6–0 win over Rangers, John and some friends landed at the Carntyne dog-track in Glasgow and crowned a wonderful day by backing five winning greyhounds. His success was the result of some excellent tips passed on to the red-scarved Aberdonians by appreciative Celtic supporters!

Before the teams left Hampden that day, frustration reached such a point with at least one member of the Rangers team that a boot went through the dressing-room window. By then Aberdonians were making the most of their big moment in the knowledge that the peak of pleasure might be short-lived. After all, it was not the final.

That ultimate encounter would bring them back to Hampden to meet Celtic, as it had done in 1937, when Britain's biggest-ever crowd looked on. On Friday, 23 April 1954 the Aberdeen party slipped quietly off to their Glasgow headquarters, with the hand-shakes of station workers and students out on their Charities' Week collection. On that same day Rangers announced they had given a free transfer to their famous centre-forward, Willie Thornton.

Demand was so high that a 2s. 6d. ticket was being sold on the black market for 15s. (75p) as 20,000 Aberdonians headed south in their red and white. Both Celtic and Aberdeen were quoted by the bookies at 2 to 1 but the news that depressed Dons fans was that Joe O'Neil, heroic figure in the rout of Rangers, had received an ankle injury in a league game with the Ibrox team the previous week and would miss the final.

Joe's hour of glory had come on his first-ever appearance at Hampden but now he was being denied the chance to follow through the success. Openly broken-hearted, Joe declared that he 'could hae a good greet'. What's more, Darkie, the Pittodrie cat, had to be destroyed that week after being involved in a fight and some shook their heads and said the omens were not good.

O'Neil's absence was the only change in the team, his place being taken by big Jim Clunie, a maintenance man from the Fifeshire coalmines whose real position was centre-half but who found himself at inside-left that day.

By now the outside-right berth was firmly in the grip of Graham Leggat, a product of Banks o' Dee who drew well-founded forecasts that he would be a truly great player one day. James Forbes of the *Evening Express* bracketed him with Willie Mills as the two best Dons he had seen. At nineteen, he was now playing in a Scottish Cup final alongside George Hamilton, the sole survivor of the 1947 team, who was nearly twice his age. Hammy and Fred Martin were in Scotland's World Cup party in Switzerland that same year and Leggat's turn for World Cup duty would come four years later.

But the business on hand on 24 April 1954 was the Scottish Cup final and the teams that took the field were: Aberdeen – Martin; Mitchell, Caldwell; Allister, Young, Glen; Leggat, Hamilton, Buckley, Clunie, Hather. Celtic – Bonnar; Haughney, Meechan; Evans, Stein, Peacock; Higgins, Fernie, Fallon, Tully, Mochan.

This, of course, was the Celtic team that had been revitalised under the captaincy of Jock Stein, the Lanarkshire miner whose years in the obscurity of Albion Rovers and Welsh non-league club Llanelli suddenly turned into a belated burst of glory at Parkhead.

Alas for Aberdeen, the match turned out to be a repeat of the 1937 encounter – Celtic scoring first, Aberdeen equalising from the re-start and the Celts making the final score 2–1. The only difference was that Celtic's first goal was scored by Alec Young of Aberdeen. Poor Alec! It was cruel luck for such a big-hearted player. He tried to clear a Mochan shot which was well covered by Fred Martin and sent it reeling past his keeper.

From the re-start, Paddy Buckley took a pass from Leggat, rounded Jock Stein, drew Bonnar and flicked home a magnificent equaliser. Sean Fallon, normally a full-back but playing at centre-forward that day, scored the winner. So the Cup went to Parkhead and the 20,000 followers from the North-east went quietly back to their trains and buses to reflect how easily the ecstasy of one week can become the dejection of another.

It was now fifty years since the present Aberdeen Football Club had entered Scottish league football and in all that time they had won the Scottish Cup once and the league championship not at all. But there would be another day . . .

37

WE ARE THE CHAMPIONS!

T HE Dons had now been defeated in two successive Scottish Cup finals but there was surely some substance in the team to get it that far. In season 1954–55 they were heading for yet another Hampden appearance when they were unexpectedly stopped by Clyde, whose penalty goal in the semi-final replay at Easter Road, Edinburgh, was enough to see them through.

By then, however, the Aberdeen players were caught up in the exciting prospect of the Scottish league championship being within their grasp. Was this, at last, to be their greatest year so far?

The Dons struck a new consistency in the early stages of the season, with everyone playing for each other and nobody resorting to backbiting if a goal was lost. The sixteen-team League of that period meant a programme of thirty games, and as they coasted towards Christmas the players began to sense that this could well be their year.

Winning the league championship was undoubtedly the greatest achievement in football and in half a century it had not been done by an Aberdeen team. The instant glamour may belong to the Cup but that could be won over five or six games in which good fortune could play an outrageous part. The League called for sheer consistency against the best and worst of opposition in all the upsetting variations, home and away, in sunshine, wind or driving snow.

This would be the real test of their mettle and these Dons were anxious to write their names into the Pittodrie history book as the first to do it. Harry Yorston recalled it like this: 'We played to a pattern as a workmanlike side, with confidence in each other, and we just knew we were going places.'

Throughout the season they lost five games with only one drawn result and it all boiled down to a day of decision in the undramatic setting of Shawfield Park, Glasgow, where football had a habit of looking like an intruder upon that other activity of Shawfield, greyhound racing. The Dons needed to beat Clyde to clinch their first-ever title and in what turned out to be a scrappy and otherwise forgettable match, the opportunity came with a penalty kick. Jack Allister and Archie Glen used to take the penalties time about and it happened to be Archie's turn. The photographs show that he shot high into the Shawfield net, past the left shoulder of South African goalkeeper Ken Hewkins.

Thus, without the noise and excitement of a big crowd and in a setting bereft of glamour, the Dons won the greatest honour of domestic football. On that historic day – 9 April 1955 – the *Green Final* was rolling off the printing presses of Broad Street and spilling into the streets by 5.30 p.m. with a deliriously happy Wee Alickie declaring: 'Cocks o' the North and Scottish Champs – Fa's like us?'

Back in the Shawfield dressing room the champagne corks were popping, David Halliday quietly surveying the joy of the lads who had achieved his most ambitious dream. More than twenty years later, Jackie Hather told me he still retained the vivid memory of Halliday's face when they came off the pitch. Pride was written all over it.

A carefree Aberdeen party boarded the train at Buchanan Street that evening, and big Fred Martin occupied the luggage rack all the way north, a fair indication of the mood of the occasion as well as a tribute to the endurance of the luggage racks. When the train drew into the Joint Station at 11.30 that night, there were ten supporters waiting to welcome them home. No crowds, no cheers, no sense of occasion – just home to a champagne sleep and up next morning to read the final confirmation that the Dons of 1955 had done what no other Aberdeen team had managed to achieve.

The champions of Scotland had won twenty-four of their thirty games, scored seventy-three goals and equalled the record by conceding only twenty-six. That record would have been broken if Fred Martin had not been injured one day. His deputy, Archie Glen, lost a goal that only an outfield man could have missed.

Those with longer memories would hesitate to say the championship team was the most entertaining they had seen at Pittodrie. It was more effective than attractive, perhaps lacking the panache of the 1947 team, but who can argue with its success? Archie Glen, who later became captain, gave me his assessment of the winning formula: 'Basically, the plan was to retreat as a team when under pressure, keeping the opposing wingers wide but always ready for the quick break, with long balls from Jack Allister and myself setting off those lightning darts of the front men, who could beat the best of defences for speed.

'It was the tendency to retreat which looked rather negative at times. When we did fall back to the penalty area I always knew if I forced a player to shoot from two or three yards in front of me that Fred Martin would get it. His reliability in goal had a tremendous influence on the rest of the defence, who could then get on with their own jobs. Fred was one of the best readers of a game I have ever known and I would put him in the top grade of goalkeepers I have seen.

'We had a fair pair of full-backs in Jimmy Mitchell and Davie Caldwell, Mitchell in particular being extremely fast. Caldwell replaced Billy Smith, who had broken his leg. The half-back line was good in the air and the wing-halves could give accuracy to passes of more than ten yards. Jack Allister was a tremendous player but the most under-rated man in the Aberdeen team was Alec Young at centre-half, who covered for everyone and did it so willingly.

'People still speak about his famous sliding tackle but he could do more than that. The fans were not in a position to know that Alec was an extremely thoughtful person, always concerned for the people around him. Up front we had those three fast men, Leggat,

Buckley and Hather, with Harry Yorston and Bobby Wishart slotting in between.'

The Dons had found a blend to allow for the exceptional talent of Graham Leggat, a thoroughbred from local junior football who was training to be a teacher of physical education at Jordanhill College, Glasgow. Leggat was a clean-cut figure with the college-boy look, fast, cunning, alert and instinctive, and capable of surprising even his fellow professionals with the skill of his movement.

His first touch of control was superb and the full extent of his talents was displayed in a game with Airdrie. By coincidence, this was also the first appearance of another Pittodrie favourite, the skilful Billy Little from Dumfries, who gathered many admirers from the 1950s to the mid 1960s and who later became a schoolmaster and then manager of Falkirk FC.

Aberdeen beat Airdrie 6–0 that day and Graham Leggat scored five, each with a distinctive character of its own. Billy Little had provided much of the ammunition and, in the rivalry of Glasgow evening papers for puns in their headlines, one of them declared 'Leggat goals come Little by Little'.

If there was a criticism of Leggat it was that he was better at taking the team from 1–0 to 3–0 than helping it out of a goalless rut but that was an aspect of his performance more evident to his fellow players than to the spectators. One goal in particular was recalled for years.

In training one day Leggat engaged Archie Glen and Fred Martin on the way goalkeepers, at a free kick near the penalty-box, tended to place the wall to cover the goal area nearest the ball, then concentrated their own attention elsewhere. So the most vulnerable spot lay behind the wall, if only you could chip the ball unexpectedly. Archie and Fred agreed.

Leggat practised all week and was ready to put his plan into action on the Saturday, when St Mirren were due at Pittodrie. The Dons were attacking the King Street end when the Saints gave away a free kick exactly where it was needed. Leggat looked at Glen to confirm his moment had come. Archie stood back and watched as Jim Lornie,

St Mirren's Aberdonian goalie, went through his routine.

By then Leggat was bending down to place the ball. He didn't move from that position until the whistle blew. Then, drawing back his leg from the knee, he released the perfect chip-shot which sailed over the wall and into the net before anyone had moved a muscle. It was a goal in a million but, like all feats of cunning, could not be attempted too often.

Graham Leggat's capabilities extended far outside football and many remembered him as a singer and impersonator, much in demand aboard the *Empress of France* when the Dons went on tour to Canada the following year. That tour must have sown ideas in his mind for after he had left Aberdeen and played for Fulham he eventually landed back in Canada, where he became general manager of the O'Keefe Sports Foundation. He lives in Canada to this day.

Apart from Leggat the entertainer, there is much about football stars that the average supporter seldom gets to know. Who would have thought that the solemn, unrelenting Jack Allister was also the life and soul of a social occasion? Harry Yorston seemed like a confident extrovert – some mistook his manner for big-headedness – yet Don Emery remembered him as a shy and diffident young man who would hardly venture into Lewis's store in Glasgow unless Don went with him. My own eventual meeting with Yorston brought the revelation of a modest, respectful and thoroughly likeable human being.

Paddy Buckley, on the other hand, was just the happy-go-lucky chap he always seemed to be, a proper joker in the Pittodrie pack – and if we are talking about packs of cards, he was also one of the best solo players in Aberdeen. With all their travelling, there has always been a card school among Dons players and in the 1950s it consisted of Davie Shaw, Alec Young, Archie Glen and Paddy Buckley.

Paddy didn't have to be an academic to have that special memory of the card player, which enabled him to chastise the scholarly Glen for not remembering the cards already played. Archie could only shrug and plead that he didn't have Paddy's brain-power! When I later met Buckley, those legs which made him the fastest man in football were scarcely able to take him for a short walk. He was by then a car-park attendant in Edinburgh, using a walking-stick and still in his forties.

In pinpointing the contrasting skills of that championship team, it is easy to overlook the contribution of Bobby Wishart, a clever manipulator of a ball whose ability to slide past an opponent with individual guile cleared the way for so many of those final runs by other forwards. The grace and prompting of Wishart stand out in many a mind as one of the richest recollections of that championship era.

38

CALL THIS A BONUS?

T HE Dons were champions of Scotland for the first time and the public front was one of joy and celebration for players, directors and supporters alike. Behind the scenes, however, it was a different story. The Pittodrie dressing room was seething with discontent after a head-on collision between players and the board over the question of financial reward for their historic achievement.

It had all boiled up during the final approach to the championship title when the players turned their thoughts to incentives. From other teams that had won the title they heard talk, and sometimes boasts, of what was offered for a winning spurt. The league programme was within weeks of completion when, with no move from the directors, the players decided to do something about it.

A deputation consisting of captain Jimmy Mitchell, Archie Glen and Fred Martin asked for a hearing at the regular directors' meeting in the Caledonian Hotel and that was granted. Archie Glen had reasoned that a team intent on winning the championship should win its home games anyway. The key factor was the away games and the proposition was that they should merit a special incentive bonus.

The case was put to the board and was followed by a pause. One director leaned across and repeated the proposition to make sure his ears were working before relaying it to the chairman, Mr Mitchell, who still wore an incredulous look. As far as the directors were concerned, the Scottish League would be paying the customary £1,000 to be divided among the winning players and enough was enough.

Well, if there was a day when footballers played for honour alone it didn't extend to the second half of the twentieth century. The Dons were looking for hard cash but all they got for their request at the Caley was a cool reception. There would be no incentive bonus for the final run-in, said the board. What is more, when the championship was finally clinched and the players had brought home the greatest honour in the history of Aberdeen Football Club, they did not receive a single extra penny from club funds.

All they got was the £1,000 from the Scottish League, divided into eleven parts – £91 for each position – which had to be further divided among players who had occupied those positions. For example, Fred Martin, as fine a goalkeeper as Pittodrie had seen, missed three games and was therefore subject to a deduction of three-thirtieths of £91. Big Fred contemplated a sum of just over £81 and was pretty disgusted.

Other Scottish players could hardly believe the story and for William Mitchell, who had done much to bring football glory to Aberdeen, it was an exercise in poor psychology, not to mention meanness, and it did the board no credit at all. It gave rise to resentment and left a sour taste for the start of the new season, and who can say what part that played in the subsequent decline of Pittodrie fortunes?

There were other factors which undermined the prospect of sustained success. The Dons' record under David Halliday had not gone unnoticed elsewhere. In that difficult period after the war, he had guided them to three major prizes and three more Cup finals inside nine years. That was good enough for Leicester City, who needed a manager, and before they had time to gather thoughts for a new season, Aberdeen were without the man who had transformed them from a club without a single national honour to one that had won everything available at the time.

In the tradition of giving a man the chance to prove himself, the board decided to give Halliday's job to club trainer Davie Shaw. Davie had been a clever left-back for Hibs, opposing Aberdeen in the 1947 Scottish Cup final and partnering his brother Jock, of Rangers, when

Scotland beat England in the Victory International of 1946. He had been transferred to Aberdeen and later became trainer, in which capacity he had done a splendid job.

His appointment as manager does not seem to have been unanimous, however, and James Forbes of the *Evening Express* told a story that hardly belonged to the school of diplomacy. Evidently, as Shaw entered the room to receive the good news, he was greeted by Mr Mitchell, the chairman, in the following terms: 'Well David, they have appointed you the new manager of Aberdeen Football Club – but you might as well know, it's against my wishes!'

Davie celebrated by taking his lads to Ballater for a day's golf. The players who had taken part in that championship year lined up for a photograph and their names are interesting to recall: F. Martin, J. Mitchell, D. Caldwell, J. Allister, A. Young, A. Glen, G. Leggat, G. Hamilton, H. Yorston, P. Buckley, R. Wishart, J. Hather, W. Smith, J. O'Neil, R. Morrison, J. Wallace, J. Brown, R. Paterson and J. Clunie.

It was virtually the end of the line for that great Pittodrie servant, George Hamilton. His colleagues from the post-war team had finally disappeared. Archie Baird was playing for St Johnstone, then managed by former team-mate Johnny Pattillo, before concentrating on a teaching career at Rosemount Secondary, Summerhill Academy and Hilton Academy. Tony Harris, another of the game's colourful characters, was well established as a dentist. Only Hamilton remained as a remnant of pre-war days. He was well through his thirties and feeling it was time to retreat to his newsagent's shop in Rosemount, a career which was followed by years as a traveller for Bell's whisky.

As he mulled over it all at his home in Hosefield Avenue, George told me Billy Strauss was the one who first sprung to mind among the great talents he had seen at Pittodrie. He remembered Strauss as fast and graceful and packing such a powerful shot. He followed Strauss with Archie Baird, Stan Williams, Frank Dunlop, George Taylor, Andy Cowie, Graham Leggat, Charlie Cooke, Zoltan Varga, Willie Miller and Gordon Strachan.

Not least, he mentioned Jackie Hather, who was not dissimilar in talent to Billy Strauss. He remembered the deep scar on Hather's back which told of the serious kidney operation. He classed Harry Yorston as a great-hearted player who was totally under-rated. ('People forget that, when we were bogged down, it took only a couple of flashes of Harry and we could win a game.')

George remembered the jokers in the pack – goalkeeper Reggie Morrison, who was not averse to spreading itching powder in players' clothes, and the formidable Don Emery, whose talent for planting stink-bombs once created a chaos of accusing looks among guests in Glasgow's North British Hotel. Morrison, incidentally, transferred his talents as a custodian from the Pittodrie goalmouth to Peterhead Prison, where he became an officer, keeping them in instead of keeping them out, as it were.

So George Hamilton bowed out at the end of a distinguished career that had earned him the deep affection of the Pittodrie faithful. In the troubled aftermath of that championship season, with dressing-room discontent and the manager gone, there was another factor that rankled at Pittodrie.

The Scottish FA had been considering allowing clubs to take part in the European Cup but it needed the pioneering initiative of Hibernian chairman Harry Swan to make continental football a reality at last. The European Cup (now the Champions Cup) determined the best club team in Europe and the fates had brought about a glorious coincidence as far as Aberdeen FC was concerned.

As Scotland prepared to make its entry into Europe in 1955, the honour of blazing the trail as Scottish champions would fall, of course, to the Dons of Pittodrie. Or would it? Nobody had bargained for the eccentricities of the Scottish FA who decided that, in gratitude to the man who advocated the move, Hibernian FC should be given the honour of representing Scotland in its very first venture.

It may have been intended as a noble gesture but it was an outrageous decision, when the Dons had won the right of entry in the place where it was supposed to matter – on the field of play. So Hibernian became the first Scottish club in Europe's premier

201

competition and Aberdeen, denied its proper place, had to wait another twenty-five years for the opportunity.

Davie Shaw didn't have his sorrows to seek as he embarked on his first season as manager but he did succeed in rescuing some of the championship euphoria for the Scottish League Cup, which came early in the season. The Dons beat Rangers in the semi-final and by 22 October 1955 they were heading for another League Cup final, feeling that Hampden Park was by no means as unfamiliar a place as it used to be.

The opponents were St Mirren and the fact that it was hardly a final to fire the imagination was reflected in the attendance of 44,104, which was more than 100,000 below the numbers who turned out for the Dons' first appearance at Hampden in 1937; nor was it a match to be remembered.

Mallan breasted the ball into his own net to give the Dons a lead before Holmes equalised for the Saints. Then Graham Leggat released a harmless-looking shot which Lornie seemed to misjudge and Aberdeen were winners of the Scottish League Cup by two goals to one. The Aberdeen team was: Martin; Mitchell, Caldwell; Wilson, Clunie, Glen; Leggat, Yorston, Buckley, Wishart, Hather.

Even if the game lacked distinction, a crowd of 15,000 turned out to welcome the team when they arrived at the Joint Station towards midnight, perhaps more of a belated salute to the Scottish champions of a few months earlier. As late-duty reporter on the *Press and Journal* that Saturday night, I went down to write about the welcome, watching as earlier train-loads of supporters arrived back to join the throng awaiting the team. I reported on the Monday morning:

> A miniature Hampden Roar nearly lifted the roof of the station as team captain Jimmy Mitchell stepped from the train and was lifted shoulder-high, carrying the Cup. A large cordon of police had to clear a way as the players were chaired, with great difficulty, through the seething mob to the bus waiting inside the station building.
>
> There were chants of 'We want Leggat!' but the popular outside-right was not with the party. Along with Jim Clunie, he had stayed

202

on in the south. At snail-pace the bus managed to leave the station but the crowd heaved forward and at one time there was a serious threat of people being crushed against the vehicle.

I was speaking from personal experience, having been pinned against a wheel of the bus as it started its manoeuvre out of the station.

It turned out to be the best moment of Davie Shaw's career as manager. He had little to cheer about during the rest of his time as boss at Pittodrie but on that night at least he could savour the success and say, 'I played for Hibs when they won trophies but never have I seen such enthusiasm as that displayed by the Dons' supporters.' Jimmy Mitchell, who had been swallowed up in the affection of the crowd, arrived home with his blazer torn but it was a small price to pay for his night of joy.

When the Dons returned to the bread-and-butter business of season 1955–56, the whole rhythm of success began to elude them. Alec Young, who had come so late to senior football, was one of the first to go out of the side and the effect of his departure showed how much the champions had depended on his shepherding influence.

The players themselves said they were unable to recover the comradeship of the previous few years and disintegration set in fairly quickly. Some semblance of the old feeling was still evident, however, when the Dons went on a tour of North America in the close season of 1956. Scrapbooks showed Jackie Hather playing piggy-back with Harry Yorston on the decks of the *Empress of France*; Archie Glen about to throw Paddy Buckley overboard; Fred Martin and Graham Leggat sporting straw hats with a background of Idlewild Airport. There were pictures of the Rockefeller Center and Times Square and the skyscrapers of New York, Niagara Falls and the racecourse at Winnipeg; and director Dick Donald carrying crates of Coke for the boys.

The *Empress of France* had to make a 200 mile detour on the outward journey because the normal route through Belle Isle Strait was blocked with ice and the Dons landed at Quebec instead of Montreal. Acting as part-time journalist for the occasion, Graham

Leggat reported that the Dons party was absolutely mesmerised by the size of everything. Television had only recently reached Aberdeen and Graham wrote, as a matter of surprise, that they actually had TV sets in their hotel bedrooms.

Paddy Buckley, also playing part-time journalist, sent a despatch about Alec Young and Jimmy Mitchell having taken New York by storm, turning out in their kilts and eliciting calls of, 'Gee, aren't they real cute?' from wide-eyed Americans.

The Dons played a series of draws with Everton, who were also on the tour, but chalked up victories of 8–0 over Montreal All Stars and 8–3 over Ontario All Stars. That included a brilliant hat-trick from that stylish ball-player Hugh Hay and an amazing overhead goal from Harry Yorston.

One columnist, observing an Aberdeen–Everton match in Vancouver, divided his attention between the actual game and the antics of another Vancouver journalist in the press box by the name of Jack Webster. My namesake was an exiled Glaswegian, a hell-raising broadcaster whose enthusiasm for the Dons' match sounded as if he was 'straining his voice through a bowl of porridge'.

39
GOLDEN HARRY

I N the superstitious way of footballers, Archie Glen liked to be last out of the dressing room and Harry Yorston was just in front of him. On the way to the exit, Harry would say to Archie, 'I bet that wee chap who shouts at me will start before I even reach the track.' Sure enough, as soon as Harry appeared this wizened little prune would begin his torrent of abuse.

Lamentably, he was just a symbol of that wider section of the support that picked on Yorston as an outlet for their frustrations, perhaps as much to do with their own nagging wives as any imperfections of the Dons' inside-right. Why did it happen? Local boys have often suffered in this way, on the basis that you can be harder on your own.

In Harry's case there was the added hazard of the 'golden boy' label, leaving him open to a Scottish propensity for pulling people down a peg. But there was no question of Yorston getting above himself. He was the golden boy of Pittodrie for the simple reason that he was the most prolific goalscorer Aberdeen had seen in more than fifty years.

But the much-maligned Harry Yorston gave them something else to talk about one day in 1957 when the *Evening Express* came out with a sensational story: Harry was giving up football at the age of twenty-eight. Basically, the story was that his father was a fish-market porter, a well-paid and much-prized job in Aberdeen, with a tradition of sons having priority in following their fathers. But the son could not leave it too late and the deadline had come for Harry's decision. It was a difficult one, as he recalled: 'I didn't know if I was doing the right thing. I had so enjoyed playing football that I was reluctant to give it up.'

He was at the peak of his career as a top-class professional foot-baller who might have expected to play to his mid-thirties. But privately, another element helped to swing the balance. Harry was such a thoroughly nice guy that he hesitated to criticise supporters but he did admit to me that barracking from the crowd played its part in driving him out of the game. There must be older men in the North-east today with Yorston on their conscience, perhaps now longing for those exciting dashes that were his hallmark.

So Harry made his big decision and exchanged his £16 a week as an Aberdeen player for the same £16 a week as a fish-market porter, with a security beyond the football life. Harry was finished with football but football was far from finished with Harry.

Over the spring holiday weekend of 1972 his attractive wife Joey, a former nurse at Foresterhill, added her 25p permutation to his Littlewoods coupon and thought no more about it. They had no high hopes when checking the results on the Saturday evening but sent off a claim and went away for the Monday holiday. On return, a phone call told them that Littlewoods' man was on his way from the station. Joey and Harry Yorston had won a resounding £175,000, a massive sum in 1972.

Harry gave up his job at the fish market but saw no good reason to leave their house in Burnieboozle Crescent in which they had lived for eleven years. They bought a nearby house for his parents. Idleness didn't suit Harry, however, and he was working for George Jolly, the printer, when he suddenly fell ill in 1992. A brain tumour was diagnosed and Harry was dead within the month, aged sixty-two.

Joe Harper was said to have overtaken Harry's tally of 171 goals in 1977 but, with no accurate records at Pittodrie, the position remains unclear. The fans are left with the memory of a player who, in some of his ten seasons at Pittodrie, had scored twenty goals before Christmas. They remember a great-hearted and eternally youthful player who deserved more gratitude than he received.

But Harry's good fortune did not make him the wealthiest of former Dons. That privilege fell to Dick Donald, followed by Willie Waddell, who played in the Cup final team of 1947 and was married to Betty Barlow, a nurse at Foresterhill. When Willie was released in 1950 he played out his days with Kettering Town, near Northampton. That team was run by people in the ball-bearing business, of which Willie gained a knowledge before starting his own enterprise. From modest beginnings, he built up a prosperous business and sold out to become an extremely wealthy man – all starting with a free transfer from Pittodrie!

With Yorston gone, the disintegration continued on a curve that can be gauged from the league positions in the five years following the title success. From champions in 1954–55, the Dons were runners-up to Rangers in 1956 but had dropped to fifth place in 1957, sandwiched between Raith Rovers and Celtic.

By 1958 that drop had continued to eleventh place, between Dundee and St Mirren, and in 1959 to thirteenth position, with Stirling Albion just above them and Raith Rovers just below. The fall from grace was complete in season 1959–60 when they ended up in fifteenth position, just three off the bottom in an eighteen-team League.

In three of those seasons, the Dons of Davie Shaw's management would not have survived in the Premier Division of a later date. For all his talents as player and trainer, the one thing he was not cut out to be was a manager. In the harsh world of football realities, he had to go.

There was a chance of reprieve in 1959 when the Dons managed to fight their way to the Scottish Cup final. Archie Glen had taken over as captain in those troubled times and faced the paradox of heading for the glamour of Hampden on the one hand and struggling to avoid relegation on the other.

Just before the Hampden date, Aberdeen had to face Rangers at Ibrox in a league game they desperately needed to win for survival, while Rangers needed the points to clinch the title. At the toss of the coin, captain Bobby Shearer joked with Archie Glen that they couldn't expect any favours from Rangers. But no favours were needed. The Dons won 2–1 and stayed in the top division – and Rangers still managed to win the title.

The prospects of winning the Scottish Cup must have seemed bright because St Mirren, the other finalists, were also at the wrong end of the table. The plight of the two clubs in the league programme lent a certain poignancy to the occasion, which was reflected in the respectable attendance of 108,591 at Hampden on 25 April. The Aberdeen team that ran out that day was: Martin; Caldwell, Hogg; Brownlee, Clunie, Glen; Ewen, Davidson, Baird, Wishart, Hather.

St Mirren had managed to score in the first twenty minutes of all their previous rounds so Aberdeen set out to prevent it this time. But you cannot bargain for everything. Early in the game David Caldwell, who had been converted from a forward with Duntocher Hibs to a left-back at Pittodrie, was badly hurt. There were no substitutes in those days so the Dons played the rest of the match with ten men.

In the emergency, Archie Glen called Jackie Hather from his raiding beat on the wing to fill the Caldwell vacancy and he reckoned it was a tactical error, for which he accepted responsibility. The game ran well for St Mirren, with Tommy Bryceland scoring before half-time, Miller and Baker increasing the total and Hugh Baird retrieving a consolation for the Dons in the last minute. By three goals to one, the Scottish Cup went to Paisley and the red-tammied brigade beat the northward trail with little to brighten their horizons.

Earlier that season the waning fortunes of Aberdeen Football Club had not prevented a takeover bid by that rumbustious architect and businessman, Mr T. Scott Sutherland. It was his second attempt. In March 1958 he abandoned a bid to gain control when he discovered that the reigning power lay with five directors whose families owned 60 per cent of the shares.

Sutherland, who had made a lot of money, was a tough character, short and stocky with a stubble of red hair, no candidate for a beauty contest but as dynamic a figure as Aberdeen had ever

produced. He ran an architect's practice among his various enter-
prises – he gave generously to the school of architecture that bears
his name – and found time to write a book called *Life on One Leg*,
which was all he had. Despite his handicap, he could play tennis
with such agility as to demoralise many an opponent with two legs.

Sutherland said he had offered £4 per ten-shilling share and that
he wanted to hold only 50 per cent. He would abolish the right of
the directors to ban the sale of shares by individual shareholders.
He said: 'My whole action has been altruistic, hence my willingness
to plonk down a small fortune for little or no return. I want to see
the Dons a happy and successful team always at or near the top. A
successful Pittodrie Park is a valuable asset to the city of Aberdeen.
Big gates and the influx of fans bring shekels to the city transport
department, country bus owners, taxi firms, shops, restaurants,
cinemas and pubs.

'I consider the directors' power to veto share transfer unsound,
bad for the club and minority shareholders. By exercising such a
veto, they can gobble up shares coming on the market at prices
around thirty to thirty-five shillings a share. They have complete
financial control, leaving outside shareholders with little or no say
in the club's affairs.'

But Sutherland's law came to nothing at Pittodrie and William
Mitchell and his colleagues continued to hold sway. The only change
to be made was that of manager, with Davie Shaw accepting a return
to his former job as trainer. His career as a manager came to an end
on 17 November 1959 and the pictures in the newspapers next
morning showed the new man shaking hands all round.

The sight of his familiar face and the news of his appointment
were enough to quicken the heartbeat of those who had long
admired his genius. The new boss was Tommy Pearson.

40

TIME RUNS OUT
FOR TOMMY

WITH the Dons struggling in the late 1950s, the devoted thousands who had brought record crowds in the post-war period were deserting in droves, many hinterland people heading instead for Highland League grounds on a Saturday afternoon. But fresh expectancy stirred at Pittodrie that November day of 1959 when the headlines told us that Thomas Usher Pearson, legendary footballer, was returning as manager to the scene of his twilight glory.

Since hanging up his boots, Pearson had not been far away. The intervening years had been spent as northern sportswriter for the *Scottish Daily Mail* and a large part of his week was devoted to writing about the affairs of Aberdeen Football Club. Now it was time to put his pen aside and see what he could do in reshaping a team in the doldrums.

His very presence raised hopes that the magical talent of his playing days might somehow reproduce itself in managerial terms, charming skill from mediocrity and moulding a team in his own distinctive image. It was, of course, an irrational expectation.

In the season of his arrival some key names were gone or going. Time was drawing to a close for that flying winger from the north of England, Jack Hather, and for centre-half Jim Clunie, who went on to coach Southampton to their FA Cup final victory at Wembley.

As the Dons embarked on season 1959–60, skipper Archie Glen was only fifteen seconds into a match at Kilmarnock when a collision with Willie Toner put him out of the game for nineteen weeks and virtually ended his career at the age of thirty-one. For three

The final of the 1983 European Cup Winners' Cup in Gothenburg. Dons captain Willie Miller exchanges flags with the captain of Real Madrid.

On that rainy night, Eric Black scores the first goal.

Above and below: John Hewitt scores the winning goal (again!), goes to ground . . .
Left: . . . and, later, gets his hands on the coveted Cup.

The team rejoice after their magnificent European victory.

Smiles all round for manager Alex Ferguson and his assistant Archie Knox.

The Dons' glorious homecoming from Gothenburg – 100,000 people took to the streets of Aberdeen to welcome their heroes.

Later that same year, the fabulous Dons went on to beat Hamburg in the contest for the Super Cup – the match played between the winners of the European Cup and the Cup Winners' Cup to determine which team was the Continent's best.

With the 2–1 Cup final defeat of Celtic in 1984, the Dons achieved their first League and Cup double.

The Dons celebrate another Cup final victory over Celtic, this time in 1990. *Left to right, back row:* Alex McLeish, Hans Gillhaus, Theo Snelders, Robert Connor, Graham Watson, Brian Irvine, Stewart McKimmie. *Front row:* Eoin Jess, Charlie Nicholas, Jim Bett, Paul Mason, David Robertson, Brian Grant.

Above: Hans Gillhaus causes problems for the Rangers defence in a 1991 Premier League game.

Right: Alex Smith managed the Dons, with Jocky Scott, from 1988 to 1992.

Below: The opening of the Richard Donald Stand. Vice-chairman Ian Donald introduces the Princess Royal to Roy Aitken, standing next to manager and club legend Willie Miller.

Willie Miller (*centre*) patrolling the dug-out in his first year as Aberdeen manager. He was assisted by another former Don, Drew Jarvie (*on his right*).

The Dons' Joe Miller surges past the Dundee defence during the 1995 Coca-Cola Cup final . . .

. . . which Aberdeen won. Stewart McKimmie lifts the Cup.

Chris Anderson, major influence with a tragic end.

seasons before that, Archie had been taking care of his future in a way not always open to footballers.

With a B.Sc behind him he had taken up a job as a quality-control chemist with the paint firm of Isaac Spencer and, while still a young man, rose to be managing director, with a very comfortable living to replace his football. Sadly, illness overtook him in the prime of life and he died much too soon.

Time was catching up a little prematurely with goalkeeper Fred Martin. In a match with Dundee, he rose to a ball with Andy Waddell and the collision broke his jaw. In hospital he was freely photographed with a face the size of a football. As with Archie Glen, that injury more or less put an end to the remarkable career of one of the finest goalkeepers ever seen in Scottish football.

Transforming himself from a professional forward to a World Cup goalkeeper had been a feat in itself. Fred Martin's international record did poor justice to a man who could be massively commanding in a style that was strongly reminiscent of England's Frank Swift. With his large frame he could clutch and palm and cut out crosses in a way that demoralised opponents and gave his own team the confidence to win the league championship. Like many another footballer, Fred went to work for the whisky blenders and rose to be a senior executive with Dewar's of Perth.

So those who had been fixtures since the 1940s were gone with the 1960s, but life never fails to turn up new talents and opportunities, high points and surprises as well as disappointments. Local lads Douglas Coutts and Dave Bennett were coming through. A bright young lad called Charlie Cooke had arrived from Greenock to come under the influence of Tommy Pearson, who could not have been long in detecting that Charlie, like himself, had the ball skills of an artist.

Dominant football figures such as manager Bill Struth of Rangers, Willie Maley of Celtic and Paddy Travers of Aberdeen, men who were never seen out of business dress, had all but disappeared and the age of the tracksuit manager was not quite established. But the 1960s produced a new breed of powerful manager, of whom Jock Stein was the most successful example. His sojourn with Dunfermline and Hibernian between 1960 and 1965 was merely the prelude to an incomparable career at Celtic. Willie Waddell guided Kilmarnock to a Scottish league championship and was later invited back to the Rangers camp of his playing days to balance the weight of Stein at Parkhead, and to help counter the Celtic domination of the domestic front and their spectacular achievements in Europe.

Pittodrie, too, was to benefit from the strength of one of the toughest and shrewdest men in team management, the aggressively dedicated Eddie Turnbull, who came from his coaching job with Queen's Park and was still remembered as the driving force behind the Famous Five of Easter Road in the middle of the century.

But first there should have been a golden era under Tommy Pearson, whose instincts would surely produce a Pittodrie team of football artists to warm our hearts on winter days. But such dreams did not materialise and, while it is true that he did improve the league position of the following five seasons, his performance as a manager was lacking in both lustre and silverware.

In fact, the novelty of floodlighting installed in 1959 was the brightest topic of conversation, while the balance sheet of 1960 showed a loss of £13,000 and a bank overdraft of £21,000.

Conversation would turn to matters such as the thorny problem of Norman Davidson and the fact that, whatever his deficiencies, he had scored twenty-seven goals in the 1957–58 season, which put him in the company of Graham Leggat, with twenty-nine in 1956–57, and Paddy Buckley, who scored twenty-eight goals in 1955–56.

Such talk in the hostelries of Aberdeen and the North-east was a suitable diversion from the fact that there was little to shout about at Pittodrie, not even a glimmer of relief from the Scottish Cup adventures, which can still work wonders on the football spirits when all else is despair.

In 1963, the Dons were dismissed from the Scottish Cup by Raith Rovers, despite a penalty save by John Ogston. In 1964, Ayr United may have been third from the bottom of the Second Division but they were still good enough to put the Dons out of the Cup at Pittodrie. As if such humiliation was not enough, the unthinkable became the intolerable in 1965 when East Fife held the Dons to a draw at Pittodrie and beat them in the replay at Bayview Park.

In the midst of all that, there had been a Summer Cup competition during 1964, in which the Dons managed to reach the final against Hibs. After two games the teams were still level so it went to a third and deciding tie. But before that could take place, Aberdeen had been thrust into the international headlines by an outbreak of typhoid. When the scare had finally cleared and the Summer Cup final went ahead, Hibs came to Pittodrie and won 3–1.

By 1965, Aberdeen supporters had been forced to thole an entire decade in which nothing at all had been won, all the more unpalatable since the previous ten years had brought every possible prize to the Pittodrie boardroom.

Time had run out for Tommy Pearson. His resignation was announced on 13 February 1965 and there were sixteen days of speculation before his successor was named. Eddie Turnbull needed no introduction to anyone who had been in touch with football in the previous twenty years.

Back from the war in which he had served as a sailor in the hell of the Murmansk convoys, he had played for Hibs in the Scottish Cup final of 1947. Soon after, that memorable forward line of Smith, Johnstone, Reilly, Turnbull and Ormond came into being, one of the best in the history of the game, in which he was the dynamic instigator. That type of player knows about responsibility and how to motivate others and frequently makes a good manager.

These were the basic qualities he brought to Pittodrie in 1965, complemented by a dour determination, a capacity for hard work and a penchant for bluntness – not an easy man but one respected for his knowledge and enthusiasm. His arrival heralded a whole new era for Aberdeen Football Club, in keeping with changes taking place elsewhere in the game.

The style of football at that time had been influenced by an extraordinary South American called Helenio Herrera, who took Inter Milan to three successive European Cup finals in the mid 1960s. The crinkly-haired Latin was already a legend in Italy, the full truth of which I discovered as a *Daily Express* writer flying to meet him at his home in Appiano Gentile.

Jock Stein, who was then manager of Dunfermline, and Willie Waddell of Kilmarnock had also come out to study the methods of the great Herrera and it was no coincidence that Waddell returned to lead Killie to the Scottish league championship of 1965 and that Stein then embarked on his fabulous career with Celtic – winning the European Cup in 1967 by beating the master's own Inter Milan in the Lisbon final!

Turnbull came to Aberdeen in the same month as Stein went to Celtic, a new breed of manager who would change Scottish football. He breezed into Pittodrie that March day of 1965 and by the end of April had handed out seventeen free transfers. Two years later, when the dust had settled, he was quoted as saying: 'I had had doubts about the wisdom of my move but it was such a shambles, and the lack of ability in many of the players was an eye-opener. I just had to weed them out. An immediate reorganisation of the scouting staff was imperative. I got men of my own and retained only Bobby Calder, the chief scout, for whom I had great admiration.'

By the time these quotes appeared, Turnbull had taken Aberdeen to fourth position in the Scottish League and into the final of the Scottish Cup. At any other stage in history his new-look Dons would have been good enough to win that Cup in 1967. Unfortunately for Aberdeen, it coincided with Celtic reaching their all-time peak. On 25 May 1967, Billy McNeill captained the very first British team to win the European Cup. The team lined up: Simpson; Craig, Gemmell; Murdoch, McNeill, Clark; Johnstone, Wallace, Chalmers, Auld, Lennox. Precisely that same formation had lined up twenty-six days earlier in the Cup final at Hampden Park to meet an Aberdeen team that read: Clark; Whyte, Shewan; Munro, McMillan, Petersen; Wilson, Smith, Storrie, Melrose, Johnston.

For skipper Harry Melrose it was a third encounter with Celtic in a Scottish Cup final. He had been in Jock Stein's Dunfermline team that won in 1961 and on the losing side with the Fifers four years later, when his former boss had just taken over at Celtic Park. Sadly, there was to be no luck in his third attempt for Harry or anyone else in the Aberdeen camp. Bobby Lennox scored three minutes before the interval and Willie Wallace added a second just after it, ensuring defeat for the team that the Celtic captain would be managing within ten years.

As if it were not enough to be meeting the best team in Europe, the Dons had other problems to cope with that day. Manager Turnbull had been ill all week and missed training. He started out from Aberdeen, intending to accompany his men to Hampden, and they all stayed overnight at Gleneagles Hotel. But he was too ill to start out on the Saturday morning and it was a pretty headless party that boarded the bus for Glasgow without him. The journey was further upset when the Dons' vehicle was involved in an accident. The party arrived late, with time only to change and take the field without a moment to gather their thoughts. It was a disastrous day altogether and the sole consolation for Aberdeen was that, by virtue of Celtic qualifying for the following year's European Cup, they were able to make their debut in European football as Scotland's representative in the Cup Winners' Cup.

Eddie Turnbull had at least restored contact with success and the kind of influence he had on the team deserves examination. That story really began back at Hampden Park, when he was still coaching Queen's Park and keeping an eye on a very young goalkeeper who, he knew, was going to the top.

41
TAKEOVER BATTLE

BEFORE Eddie Turnbull arrived at Queen's Park the training routine had consisted of running round the track, with one ball among them all. The new boss gave them a ball each and turned it into an exciting football experience. Among the youngsters whose imagination was fired by the new man was a Glasgow teenager who had been keeping goal for the first team since he was sixteen.

Bobby Clark, whose father was a director of Clyde FC and a well-to-do businessman, revelled in the fact that he was under the direction of a real coach for the first time. Turnbull taught him simple things, such as the intelligent throwing of the ball, and inspired him to think about football. But with his departure for Aberdeen, and Queen's losing their momentum, young Clark realised he had reached a point of decision.

I remember making my way to the Clark family villa to interview this boy who was being pursued by Britain's top clubs. A student of physical education at Jordanhill College, it remained for him to take his pick from Rangers, Chelsea, Tottenham Hotspur and several others and, as he talked idealistically about wanting to give his talents to Scotland, it seemed his choice was Rangers.

Suddenly I realised my Aberdeenshire accent was of special interest to him and I spared Bobby Clark the embarrassment of spelling out prematurely what I now knew – that he was going to follow his old boss to Pittodrie. Turnbull took both Clark and left-half David Millar to the Granite City, little knowing that he was moulding the young man who would become the most-capped player in the first seventy-five years of Aberdeen Football Club. Nor did I know, as I interviewed the boy, that I was talking to one who would so carve his name in the Pittodrie history – or that I would be here to write it.

Clark took over in goal from the larger frame of John Ogston, a local lad known as Tubby, whose career might have been more distinguished had he landed at a better time. Turnbull's team was beginning to take shape, running twelve games without defeat. Aberdeen had followed a fashion of the 1960s, begun by the colourful Hal Stewart of Morton, and imported Scandinavian players, notably Jens Petersen, Lief Mortensen and Jorgen Ravn.

Turnbull wanted players who would reflect his own distinctive personality. Tommy McMillan and Chalky Whyte were coming into their own, alongside Dave Smith, Ally Shewan, Harry Melrose, Jimmy Wilson and Billy Little, all poured into the Turnbull mould.

Pittodrie was buzzing and among the new excitements was eighteen-year-old Jimmy Smith, who had come from Glasgow Benburb, the junior team within shouting distance of Ibrox that had already given Aberdeen George Johnstone and Frank Dunlop. The fact that he earned the name of Jinky told of his special talent as a ball-player, a tall lad with deceptive movement who could work himself into trouble one moment as if to show how easily he could get out of it the next.

Turnbull was fielding a team which was emerging as: Clark; Whyte, Shewan; Petersen, McMillan, Millar; Little, Smith, Winchester, Melrose, Wilson.

Dave Smith, who had blossomed as a fine young player from local junior circles, was seeking a move and his opportunity came when Rangers went on a spree of buying up their opponents' best players, in an attempt to crack the Celtic supremacy. They denuded Dundee of Penman, Dundee United of Persson, Hibs of Stein, St Johnstone of MacDonald, Kilmarnock of McLean, Dunfermline of Smith and Ferguson (Fergie) and Aberdeen of Dave Smith – but were still unable to stop Jock Stein as he nonchalantly marched on to his nine-in-a-row league championships.

So Rangers gained nothing and the rest of Scotland lost its leading personalities, yet another example of the damaging imbalance of Scottish football. Dave Smith was off to Ibrox and Jens Petersen became 'sweeper' in the modern jargon, while Harry Melrose was classed a midfield man along with Francis Munro, who was signed from Dundee United.

It was a young formation with five contenders for Scotland's Under-23 team: Francis Munro, Jimmy Smith, Tommy McMillan, Jimmy Whyte and Bobby Clark. All except Munro found themselves chosen. By Christmas 1966 the Dons were challenging in second position in the League but the Scottish Cup began to dominate events and the league form shaded.

In the first round of the Cup Aberdeen went to Dens Park and beat Dundee 5–0, a game best remembered for a scintillating display by Jimmy Smith. St Johnstone were the next victims before the Dons met Hibs in the quarter-final at Easter Road. Hibs were in the lead when the silken Smith scored the equaliser with the last move of the match.

The replay at Pittodrie on the following Wednesday presented special problems for Bobby Clark, who was still a student at Jordanhill College and had an important exam due that day. After he put his case to the college, he was allowed to sit the exam an hour earlier, supervised by Roy Small, lecturer and occasional radio commentator. Bobby was put on his word of honour that he would not divulge the questions to anyone and he remembered that he had never been so popular with fellow students.

But the college knew he would not let them down. Mr Clark senior was outside with the car engine ticking over, ready to speed his son northwards for an evening replay that had aroused a fire of enthusiasm, particularly after that last-gasp equaliser. There might well have been a record crowd inside Pittodrie that night but they decided to close the gates when it reached beyond 40,000.

Jimmy Smith had been injured on the Saturday but Turnbull brought off a master stroke, which characterised his managership. He remembered that Ernie Winchester, the bustling centre-forward who first made his name as an Aberdeen schoolboy, had been highly successful against centre-half Madsden when the Dons played Morton. Madsden had since joined Hibs and Turnbull saw no reason why it shouldn't happen again. It did. Ernie had a tremendous game and the Dons won 3–1.

Fans queued all night at Pittodrie for tickets to see the semi-final against Dundee United at Dens Park and their wait was well worth it, for the match turned out to be an exciting cliff-hanger, with the Dons clinging on to a one-goal lead. Aberdonians thought the referee had lost his watch and in those dying minutes Chalky Whyte kicked the ball high into the stand on half a dozen occasions! On top of that, Jim Storrie missed a penalty.

Celtic provided the opposition in the final and, since the Dons had played them twice already that season and beaten them both times, there was no lack of confidence in the Aberdeen camp, despite the Parkhead team's triumphs in Europe. But the reality was different. Celtic won 2–0, as already described, and Dons supporters consoled themselves with the fact that Turnbull had at last brought them to the brink of success. His day would come.

At the end of that season the Dons went to America to take part in a novel experiment. The Americans, whose football is a very different game, decided to give soccer a chance and invited a number of sides including Aberdeen, Hibs, Stoke City and Wolves to become the adopted teams of American cities, playing out a contest in two sections with the winners meeting in a sudden-death finale.

The Dons became the Washington Whips and gathered up a new set of fans for their stay in the capital. Even President Lyndon B. Johnson was caught up in the event and gave the President's Cup as the winning trophy. Aberdeen did the US capital proud, winning the Eastern Section and qualifying to meet Wolves, winners of the Western Section, in the final in Los Angeles.

Jimmy Smith was sent off for a foul on Dave Wagstaffe and the ten-man Dons survived for a 4–4 draw at full-time. The game went to extra time, which ended at 5–5, and during a further period of extra time Ally Shewan, the lad from Cuminestown, put through his own goal to give Wolves the American President's Cup.

It had been a memorable experience. The Dons played in such places as the Los Angeles Coliseum and the Houston Astrodome, with its synthetic turf. Even more important, however, the tour had provided an opportunity to introduce the local lad who had followed his father to Pittodrie and bore the same name – Martin Buchan. Showing a special talent for marking an opponent out of the game, he would soon be here to stay.

Having taken over the European Cup Winners' Cup place from Celtic, the Dons launched themselves on their first venture into European competitive football, exactly twelve years later than they should have done when they were Scottish league champions.

In the preliminary round they beat KR Reykjavik 10–0 at Pittodrie and 4–1 in Iceland but faced stiffer opposition in the next round when they managed to beat Standard Liège 2–0 at home but went out on an aggregate of 3–2.

The following season, the Dons' league position gave them a place in the Inter Cities Fairs Cup, forerunner of the UEFA Cup, and it was there that Martin Buchan came into his own. Aberdeen were drawn against the highly rated Bulgarian team Slavia Sofia, which followed the familiar Communist pattern of those days in that the players were all soldiers.

As part of the new-fangled numbers game, Eddie Turnbull listed young Buchan at outside-left but as soon as the match began he took up the role of a double centre-half, alongside Tommy McMillan. His outstanding performances helped the Dons to a no-scoring draw in Bulgaria and a 2–0 win at Pittodrie. Thus Martin Buchan became the man who cleaned up at the back, a role he would play with distinction not only for Aberdeen but for Manchester United and Scotland. Unfortunately, that success was not maintained against Real Zaragoza of Spain and the Dons went out of the competition on a 4–2 aggregate.

Meanwhile, Eddie Turnbull was all but lured away to Rangers to take on a coaching role but the deal fell through and the North-east breathed again.

In season 1968–69 the Dons found themselves in an extraordinary position over goalkeepers. Bobby Clark had fulfilled all his early promise and had already collected his first few caps for Scotland. An injury gave a first-team opportunity to Ernie McGarr, however, and the reserve keeper was such a success that he not only kept Bobby Clark out of the Aberdeen team but went on to become Scotland's World Cup goalkeeper against Austria in 1969.

It was during his absence on World Cup duty that Bobby Clark was given a chance to show that he was still a top-class keeper, underlining Aberdeen's dilemma of having Scotland's two best men on their books at the same time. In the intervening period, Clark had not only contented himself with reserve-team football but developed an earlier talent as a centre-half. He actually had a spell in the first team as an outfield player in season 1969–70.

It was Fred Martin in reverse, a bizarre situation, except that Clark was clearly better suited to his former role. Turnbull told him so and allowed the situation to resolve itself. After a year in the wilderness, the former Queen's Parker was re-established as first choice and went on to build his record as the Don with the most international caps.

Ernie McGarr remained an exciting goalkeeper and it seemed rough justice that his career headed down the echelons of Scottish football instead of moving up to make him one of the bigger names of British football. He could surely have been a major personality.

For all his toughness, Eddie Turnbull was experiencing mixed health and the players felt he had lost his edge, reflected perhaps in the mediocre performance of 1968–69 when the Dons finished in fifteenth position in the League.

But whatever dramas were being enacted on the field, a greater drama was mounting behind the scenes where the board found themselves fighting off a takeover bid. The group that had designs on running Pittodrie consisted of well-known names in the Aberdeen business world. Gordon McIver was a Turriff man who had been the Dons' secretary in 1948 before developing business interests to become boss of Lawson Turnbull, the plumbing people. Sandy Mutch was prominent in local politics and was to become the first convener of Grampian Region. John Leiper was an insurance broker, Henry Robertson a fish merchant and Don Emery and Tony Harris were the two former players whose shadows had grown no less in retirement.

These were the men who signed a letter to shareholders indicating an offer of £8 for each ten-shilling share, but there were signs that someone else was behind them, a Mr Big who was keeping out of the way. Rumour said it was Peter Cameron, the wealthy builder and racehorse owner, but he flatly denied it. Several years later Gordon McIver assured me that he personally had the backing of £500,000 and that Peter Cameron was no part of it. 'I don't know if he was behind some of the others but he was not behind me,' he said.

One of the others in the group believed that Mr Cameron was involved, out of a genuine desire to see the Dons at the top, and that he not only planned a super-stadium at Pittodrie but intended to offer the manager's job to Jock Stein, with whom he was well acquainted. Gordon McIver weighed in with criticism of Pittodrie's public relations and a local scouting system that allowed players such as Denis Law to escape the net before their names were even noted.

Chairman Charles B. Forbes led the board's resistance to the take-over bid, helped by the fact that the current directors held 3,157 of the 10,000 shares. Richard Spain, boss of Henderson's, the King Street engineers, was soon to join the board with his 754 shares but, most important of all, there were three powerful ladies holding the balance somewhere in the shadows.

Mrs Mabel Callander, daughter of former Dons director John D. Robbie, had 268 shares. A regular attender at Pittodrie, she said she had been brought up with the club since she was knee-high to a kipper and was happy with the board. Miss Moyra Mitchell, daughter of former chairman William Mitchell, had 602 shares and she too saw no need for change. The third and most powerful of those ladies was Mrs Flora Duncan, widow of former director John Duncan, who held 838 shares and was also on the side of the ruling board. Petticoat power sealed the fate of the 1969 takeover bid and not even the great Don Emery, who seldom failed to score when he set his sights, could do a thing about it.

So the 1960s were left behind with a mixture of memories but nothing to show for them. Was it too much to hope that luck would change in 1970?

42

'CUP-TIE' McKAY

WHEN Bobby Clark regained his place in goal from Ernie McGarr after a year in the cold, he could not have returned at a more inopportune moment. In early 1970 the Dons were meeting the modest Clydebank in a second-round Scottish Cup tie and just managed to scrape through by two goals to one. Aberdeen supporters lost patience with their team that day and began booing and slow-hand-clapping.

As the third-round tie with Falkirk approached, a virulent flu bug put so many Aberdeen players in bed that manager Eddie Turnbull, himself a victim, had to seek a postponement. That minor epidemic played its own ironic part in the subsequent fortunes of the Dons that season. Directly because of it, a man from Gellymill Street, Macduff, has a strange tale to tell his grandchildren about how he gained a fleeting piece of glory in the history of Pittodrie.

After playing for Deveronvale, Derek McKay went on to Dundee but was given a free transfer before landing with Aberdeen. Sporting a George Best haircut, this North-east lad appeared from obscurity to have a splendid game at outside-right against Falkirk. Bobby Clark, wishing to encourage the boy, called out, 'Keep going, Derek, you can win the game for us.' The words were prophetic, as the rest of the story will show. For Derek McKay scored the only goal and put Aberdeen into the semi-final of the Scottish Cup.

He had more than earned his place at Muirton Park, Perth, where the Dons went to meet the Kilmarnock side which stood between them and another Cup final. Once again the boy from Macduff turned up trumps and scored the only goal of the match. No wonder they were calling him 'Cup-tie McKay', the lad who came from nowhere and carried Aberdeen to a memorable occasion at Hampden Park.

Once again the opposition was Celtic, the club that had thwarted Aberdeen's ambitions in 1937, 1954 and 1967 and was still the dominant force in the land. Just as Celtic had been on the point of becoming champions of Europe when they met in the Scottish Cup final three years earlier, the Parkhead men were due to play in that European Cup final again in 1970, this time against Feyenoord of Holland. But a crate of champagne gave Aberdeen a psychological boost – and not a drop of it was drunk.

The incident happened at Celtic Park, where Aberdeen were due to play a league game before the Cup final – it would clinch yet another league championship for Celtic if Aberdeen were suitably defeated. As the Dons party arrived they happened to see the champagne bottles being carried in for the celebration. The Celtic management would have been better to have kept their preparations private since the sight of the champagne was like a red rag to an Aberdeen Angus bull as far as Eddie Turnbull was concerned.

In no uncertain terms, he made it plain there would be no celebration at Aberdeen's immediate expense. Out went the Dons with their dander up – they fielded a seventeen-year-old from the Castlemilk housing scheme in Glasgow called Arthur Graham – and defeated Celtic by two goals to one.

The fact that the champagne had to be quietly stored away that night proved a tremendous boost to Aberdeen morale. They had learned that they were capable of absorbing everything Celtic could throw at them and coming out on top. Nevertheless, the public view was that Aberdeen had little chance of beating Celtic in Glasgow twice within ten days.

It was left to the superstitious to hope that the gods had Cup-tie McKay in mind to play some fateful part in the destiny of the club. He was not the greatest of footballers but was certain of keeping his place in the Cup final team. Two players who would not be there were the injured Alec Willoughby, whose partnership with his cousin Jim Forrest had been transferred from Rangers to Aberdeen, and former Dundee captain Steve Murray, who had recently signed for £50,000 but was ineligible for the Cup.

Whatever the outcome, it was certain to be a historic day for Martin Buchan, at twenty-one the youngest player ever to captain a team in the Scottish Cup final. Little of that excitement could have been foreseen by young Buchan when he left Cummings Park School for Gordon's College and found himself with the dilemma of playing rugby for Gordon's or football for the Boys' Brigade.

He was signed by the Dons while still at school but harboured a doubt about whether he was good enough to make the grade and vowed he would give himself until twenty-one to decide what to do with his life. At twenty-one he surely had his answer. Football was his talent even if his immediate prospects of Cup success were rated at about five-to-one against, compared with an odds-on Celtic quotation of two-to-five.

The bookmakers' reasoning was based on the solid evidence that Celtic had now clinched their fifth successive league title and were heading for the European Cup final, whereas Aberdeen's inconsistency had left them halfway down the table, with only twelve wins in thirty-two games. But every game is a new beginning, with the past melting away in the heat of fresh enthusiasm. Red scarves were washed and ironed, tickets bought and buses booked as the Northeast made ready to invade Mount Florida with optimism.

Spare a thought for this humble scribe whose Dons-daft days began in wartime boyhood and who vowed he would never miss a major event. This Buchan loon found himself on a journalistic assignment in Athens on the very day his team was liable to win the Scottish Cup for the first time in twenty-three years. Never have heart and body been in two such different places.

On the early afternoon of Saturday, 11 April 1970 I left the Hilton Hotel and went into the streets of Athens, walking off the nerves and checking my watch every few minutes, picturing the dressing-room scene at Hampden and the mounting excitement of the stands and terracings, where my ten-year-old son Geoffrey was playing proxy for his father to make sure the Dons wouldn't be a voice short.

I came upon the arena where the first of the modern Olympic Games was held in 1896, just seven years before Aberdeen FC was founded, and wandered inside to its stone terraces. Here at least was a stadium, in Greece perhaps but in Glasgow for all imaginary purposes, and from 3 p.m. until 4.40 p.m. I sat in the blazing heat, a lone figure in a historic but near-deserted stadium, kicking an imaginary ball, swaying, swerving, talking to myself, urging the Dons to victory and punching the air when it was achieved.

The outcome of my imaginary game was that Celtic scored once and Aberdeen three times. I rose with the final whistle, well satisfied with my performance and thought if the Dons had done half as well the Cup would be on its way to Pittodrie. When I learned the score next morning in the hotel foyer my leaps of joy and shouts of 'Up the Dons!' had startled Greeks scurrying for safety. There it was in a British Sunday paper – Celtic 1, Aberdeen 3 – just as I had played it.

The dream had indeed come true. Inside Hampden's bowl, 108,434 spectators had watched as Celtic stormed into the early attacks, only to see Aberdeen awarded a penalty in twenty-seven minutes because of a handling offence by Bobby Murdoch. The cross that preceded the penalty came from none other than Derek McKay. Before the penalty kick could be taken, left-back Tommy Gemmell landed in the black book by uplifting the ball and throwing it towards the referee.

That caused a delay but Joe Harper, the little man whose golden boots were already building him a reputation, replaced the ball on the spot and coolly scored. When Bobby Lennox had the ball in the Dons' net and the whistle blew for a foul on Bobby Clark, Jimmy Johnstone had his name taken for the vehemence of his protest.

The Dons were still ahead at the start of the second half but Celtic were once again storming the Aberdeen goal, bringing on Bertie Auld as substitute for big John Hughes. With only seven minutes to go, Joe Harper sent Jim Forrest away on the left wing and Celtic keeper Evan Williams could only partly stop his scoring attempt.

Who turned up to side-foot the ball into the net from a difficult angle but the Cup-tie expert himself, Derek McKay – 2–0.

But the drama was not yet over. Bobby Lennox scored for Celtic, a team that is never down till the final whistle. Could they still equalise? That doubt was settled almost immediately when Joe Harper laid on a ball for Derek McKay and the winger ran in to make the score 3–1.

The teams that day were: Aberdeen – Clark; Boel, G. Murray; Hermiston, McMillan, M. Buchan; McKay, Robb, Forrest, Harper, Graham. Substitute: G. Buchan (Martin's young brother). Celtic – Williams; Hay, Gemmell; Murdoch, McNeill, Brogan; Johnstone, Wallace, Connelly, Lennox, Hughes. Substitute: Auld.

Jock Stein and his players were quick to express admiration for the Aberdeen performance although the manager did not restrain himself from an outburst against referee Bobby Davidson of Airdrie.

Amid the jubilation of that Hampden scene there was no happier man than Aberdeen chairman Charles B. Forbes, former headmaster of Middlefield School, who was celebrating his three score years and ten in the finest possible manner. Academic discipline had taught him to control his emotions but he later explained: 'Put it like this, my tear ducts were not functioning properly. I have had my moments in sixty-odd years of being associated with the game, but this was the biggest thrill I have ever had. As I stood at the final whistle and realised exactly what had happened, I knew that this was the proudest moment of my life.'

The Dons players were still trying to accept the reality of a famous victory. Danish right-back Henning Boel had been magnificent in the way he had bottled up John Hughes. Jim Hermiston was a tower of strength in midfield and every other player emerged with distinction. But the greatest glory lay with the man from Macduff, Derek McKay, who came from nowhere, earned his brief moment of glory and disappeared again into the night, as if accepting that it couldn't last. His story came straight from the realms of Hans Christian Andersen.

Those who were there and shared the euphoria of that April day in 1970 were reluctant to let it go and those who stayed behind in Aberdeen wanted some part of the action. Good weather was the final encouragement for the massive crowd that turned out next day to welcome home its Hampden heroes. The players were completely taken by surprise at the size and warmth of the reception as half the population of Aberdeen, or so it seemed, filled Union Street all the way to the Castlegate.

This was the beginning of the modern-style reception and John Dunbar of the *Press and Journal* wrote that Aberdeen had probably never seen a day like it. From the balcony above the Town House door, Lord Provost Robert Lennox addressed the crowd: 'Today the sun is shining, the long winter is over, this is Eddie Turnbull's birthday – and we have won the Cup. What a perfect weekend!'

The crowd cheered as Turnbull held the Cup aloft, a broad smile lighting his normally rugged face. They shrieked as the Cup was passed to two-goal-scorer Derek McKay and then to captain Martin Buchan.

Eddie Turnbull, mastermind of the victory, had been brief in his instructions to the players: 'Play it on the carpet – and beat Celtic to the ball.' How well it had paid off.

As the bus had edged its way along Union Street, Bobby Clark pondered the route to the final and shouted to Eddie Turnbull, the man who brought him from Queen's Park, 'I wonder how many of these people were giving us the slow hand-clap in that game against Clydebank.' Turnbull shook his head philosophically and shouted back, 'Ay, son, that's football.'

What mattered was that Aberdeen, to whom so many had looked for a lead in countering the Old Firm, had won an award for the first time in nearly fifteen years. The Scottish Cup was here again. Inevitably, there were arguments in comparing the 1970 team with that of 1947. One man who put down his thoughts in lucid fashion was Archie Baird, popular inside-left of the first victory. In welcoming the players to the 'exclusive club' Archie pointed to the changes that had taken place in sport generally, with people running faster and jumping further. But the biggest change had come in the tactical field. He wrote:

> Now football has a new dimension, with the manager more and more pulling the strings. We had to do our own thinking, playing football that was almost entirely improvised and spontaneous. The present squad show many excellent qualities and much of the brashness of a computer age – a swinging, affluent society. Perhaps in trying to judge merit in two entirely different situations we are doing a disservice to both.
>
> In the end we are reduced to comparing personalities and individual ability, qualities which all the coaching in the world will never increase. Who, for example, in the present Aberdeen team comes anywhere near George Hamilton for sheer native football know-how? Gentleman George, the acme of correctness, pinpointing his passes and shots with deadly accuracy, was the best header of a ball Pittodrie has ever seen.
>
> Or Stan Williams, diminutive and tricky, with a needle-sharp football brain, ahead of his time and doing naturally the things which centre-forwards are coached into doing today. In defence there was Frank Dunlop, one of the best uncapped centre-halves of his time, an inspiring captain and dominant in the middle.
>
> But who can deny the sheer personality and power of the giant Dane, Henning Boel, the cool efficiency of skipper Martin Buchan and the sure hands and lightning reflexes of Bobby Clark in the present Dons? Nor did we have anything quite so jet-propelled as Jim Forrest and Dave Robb whose twin-striker role, curiously enough, was first being developed by Hamilton and Williams in the latter part of their careers.
>
> Let's say that a select from those two Cup-winning teams would have beaten the best. And we did have quite a lot in common – victory, champagne, rejoicing, then the triumphant journey back to Aberdeen with the football-mad city out to welcome us. There our glory ended. For us there were no fresh fields to conquer. For these bright young Dons of 1970, Europe and the world lies before them . . .

As a postscript to the Scottish Cup victory of 1970, let us return briefly to that deliriously happy Saturday night as the Aberdeen party made their way to Gleneagles Hotel, where they stayed the night in readiness for the triumphant return. Amid the heady celebrations, seventeen-year-old Arthur Graham, the Glasgow youth plucked from the anonymity of Europe's biggest housing scheme and thrust into football glory within a few weeks of joining the team, crossed the foyer of Scotland's most famous hotel to greet a lively little gentleman who had good reason to be sharing in the joy of the night.

'I want you to have my medal,' said Arthur, pushing the precious prize into his hand. It was the boy's way of expressing gratitude to a man who had played an exceptional role in the post-war success of the Dons. He refused the gift but it nevertheless remained the most touching moment in the lifetime of Bobby Calder.

43

CALDER & CO.

I T was the good fortune of Aberdeen Football Club that, for nearly thirty years, the heart and soul of Bobby Calder from Rutherglen were totally committed to the discovery of promising football talent for Pittodrie. Credit for that belonged to chairman William Mitchell, who invited Calder to become chief scout 'not just for a year or so but for the whole of your life'.

It was good foresight on Mitchell's part, designed to establish a loyalty that would not be broken by Rangers or Celtic when they discovered how good he really was. Calder would go on to prove himself the master spy of Scottish football, with an unsurpassed record of talent-spotting. Working as a railwayman in Glasgow during the week, he had rounded off a distinguished career as a top-class referee when he took charge of the Aberdeen–Hibernian Scottish Cup final in 1947.

Thereafter he had a spell as manager of Dunfermline and as a referee in America before returning to the Mitchell invitation. He liked the honesty of the approach and entered into a gentlemen's agreement. John Lawrence, millionaire chairman of Rangers for many years, would dine Bobby in the Central Hotel, Glasgow, hoping to persuade him to scout for Ibrox. But when it came to the crunch, the Pittodrie scout gave this response: 'What would you say, Mr Lawrence, if I had made the promise to you that I made to Mr Mitchell of Aberdeen and then you found that I had broken it?' John Lawrence knew when he was beaten and said, 'I can see where your allegiance lies, Bobby. I shall never ask you again.'

Calder's contacts were everywhere. A policeman stopped him in the street in Rutherglen one day and advised him to take a look at a lad in Lanark. Calder didn't expect much but followed up the hint – and that was how Ian Macfarlane, that fine full-back of the 1950s, arrived at Pittodrie before heading for England.

It was said that Calder was psychic and he did tell me of a bristling at the back of the neck when something was about to happen. Often he was about to track down another budding star for Pittodrie and, likely as not, would get there half an hour before another scout. The reputation he built up during the 1950s came to fruition during the 1960s when his collection of boys for Pittodrie ranged from Charlie Cooke and Tommy Craig to Jimmy Smith, Willie Young and Arthur Graham.

One thing led to another. On the day he turned up at Jimmy Smith's home to sign the young Benburb star, another boy in the background piped up.

'Maybe you'll come back and see me play, Mr Calder?'

'What's your name, son?' asked Calder.

'I'm Joe,' said the boy. 'I play for the school and I'm fifteen.'

'I'll be back next year to see you, son.'

And he was – and that was how Joe Smith went straight from school to follow his brother north. He became a key figure in the team of the mid 1970s that carried off the Scottish League Cup.

Across Glasgow, Bobby Calder spotted a red-headed boy who, like many another Glasgow red-head, had his sights set on Celtic Park. Tommy Craig was due, in fact, to meet Jock Stein so Calder wished him well but, as he turned to leave the Craig house, he asked for one promise. 'If by some chance you fail to sign for Celtic, will you come to Aberdeen?' he asked.

The promise was given. Calder's neck was bristling. A hunch was hovering to the extent that he decided to hang around in the vicinity of Celtic Park as Tommy Craig went for his interview with Jock Stein. When he emerged with his father, there had been no agreement on terms and Tommy was ready to sign for Aberdeen, one of the most talented boys ever seen at Pittodrie.

As in the case of the Smiths, Tommy's brother John followed him north – but not only John. Mr and Mrs Craig decided to uproot themselves from Glasgow and settle in the Granite City. As adopted Aberdonians they lived happily in Ashvale Place (daughter Ellen was married in the city) even when Tommy departed for the richer rewards of English football and John was transferred to Partick Thistle.

A phone-call from Edinburgh sent Bobby Calder scurrying to pass judgement on sixteen-year-old Willie Young. He took no time at all to decide the boy was a future internationalist. Another phone-call from a Rutherglen schoolmaster took him to one of the most exciting players of his generation, Arthur Graham.

Never arriving empty-handed, Calder armed himself with boxes of chocolates for the mother, cigars or cigarettes for the father and a pocketful of loose change for any brothers or sisters who might be dancing around the fringes. On the night he arrived at the Grahams' house in the Castlemilk housing scheme of Glasgow, he had hardly bargained for the size of the family. Calder's ready money was soon diminished as a swarm of children buzzed around him.

Gradually they buzzed off to bed and, as Mr and Mrs Graham watched young Arthur signing the papers, they heard Bobby Calder saying, 'You are signing for Aberdeen and signing for Scotland at the same time, son.' Stemming the boy's gratitude, he told him, 'I'll tell you what, Arthur, I'll have your first Scottish Cup medal!'

Within four months the boy who had gone to Pittodrie, played a few games in the reserve team and gone straight into the first eleven was taking that walk across the grand foyer at Gleneagles, holding out the medal he won in that afternoon's Scottish Cup final. The dream of a lifetime had come true. This was the promised medal but Calder said, 'Just you keep it, son. I'll get the next one.'

The next one came in November 1976, when Arthur held out his Scottish League Cup medal and the fatherly figure turned him away for the second time. His own reward had come in the transformation of a boy from the raw environs of Castlemilk to the status of a top-class professional footballer.

But of all the players Calder brought to Pittodrie, one name above all lit up his eyes. Charlie Cooke was indeed the master of finesse, about whom Calder would speak in the same breath as great inside-forwards such as Alec James. As a boy with Renfrew Juniors, Charlie was the hottest property of his day and the problem was not to spot him but to sign him. Calder won the race and phoned Aberdeen to say, 'I've signed the greatest ball-player you have ever seen.'

Unfortunately, the genius of Cooke did not produce any tangible rewards for the club during his stay from 1959 to 1964, nor did he establish himself with any permanence in the Scottish team. But that did not detract from the special place he held in the affections of Dons' supporters or of anyone who appreciated the artistry of a great ball-player.

Nor were Cooke's talents confined to football. He was a deep-thinking introvert, always ready to challenge you intellectually and bursting to express himself as a writer. But there were reports of friction between him and manager Pearson. Calder knew his greatest catch would soon be on his way but nobody anticipated that Dundee manager Bob Shankly (brother of the famous Bill) would be allowed to step in and pick up the bargain of the century at £40,000.

The transfer enraged Pittodrie fans who felt that, if Cooke had to go at all, he should not have been presented as a gift on the doorstep of the nearest rival. Dundee doubled their money within eighteen months when Charlie went to Chelsea, where he was welcomed as the darling of Stamford Bridge with the same warmth that Alec Jackson experienced in an earlier age.

But the Charlie Cookes of this world are rare gems and not every player despatched to Pittodrie by Bobby Calder made the grade. For those who fell short, however, the Dons scout told the consoling story of John Dick from Maryhill, who sparked off scouting activity in the 1950s. Calder headed the queue at the Dick household and sat late into the night. When the parents asked when he normally went home, the inexhaustible Bobby looked at his watch and said, 'Well, I start work at the railway at 6 a.m. and I would like to sign you before then, son.'

So John Dick signed for Aberdeen at 2.30 a.m. at the start of what would surely be a distinguished career. At Pittodrie, however, it was decided he had not come up to standard and within a year he was released to the free market. 'You must be daft!' was Calder's explosion. 'That boy will play for Scotland.' Turning to the lad himself, he said, 'Don't worry, son. They will be sorry they let you go.'

Calder made a phone-call to England and John Dick became a West Ham player. Imagine the joy of the Dons' chief scout as he boarded a train for London to see the England–Scotland international of 1959. There in the programme, as printed proof, was the name of John Dick, playing at inside-left for Scotland – the Aberdeen reject whose name could raise a blush at Pittodrie for a long time afterwards.

The early-morning signing of John Dick gave substance to the story that many an exhausted parent would advise a doubting son, 'Ach, you had better sign for Bobby or we'll never get to our beds!'

More accurately, Calder gained the confidence of parents who felt he would look after their sons' best interests. He extolled the wide open spaces and fresh air of Aberdeen, so they came to develop their talents, sometimes to stay, sometimes to follow the rainbow in search of gold; but almost invariably proving that a remarkable little man called Bobby Calder knew a footballer when he saw one.

While Bobby may still be spotting talent on the playing fields of heaven, his terrestrial role was taken by his trusted deputy, Jimmy Carswell, again based in Glasgow and a man who built his own reputation as a judge of youngsters. Carswell's eye was responsible for such discoveries as Willie Miller no less. Sadly, he suffered a stroke in the mid 1990s, when Roy Aitken was manager of the Dons, and the former Celtic captain looked no further for a successor than a man well known at Parkhead.

John Kelman had been Celtic's chief scout through the managerial careers of Billy McNeill, David Hay and Liam Brady. When Brady was under pressure, there were a number of departures from Celtic Park, including Bobby Lennox, Benny Rooney and John Kelman.

Kelman, who came from Carfin, near Motherwell, had been a Scottish schoolboy internationalist whose career did not flourish as expected. Nursing injuries, he began to develop an instinct for spotting talent, regarding Bobby Calder as the man who pioneered that art as a profession and stood supreme among football scouts. He and Jimmy Carswell were among the younger breed who kept an eye on each other as they scoured the land in search of football talent. John Kelman became chief scout for Bolton Wanderers in Scotland, coming across that great little ball-player and former Don Ian McNeill who was doing a similar scouting job for Bolton south of the border.

Today the scouting parish has broadened from Scotland to the continent of Europe, where John Kelman can be found any day of the week, reporting to Ebbe Skovdahl on affordable talent worth pursuing. Back home, he delegates the search for up-and-coming players to twenty other scouts, in a network that is regarded as one of the best in Britain.

Groups of youngsters from the West of Scotland are regularly matched against North-east boys in games designed to sift out the best in a never-ending process of producing the future stars of Aberdeen Football Club. As for the chief scouts, Calder, Carswell and Kelman have masterminded this vital function for well over fifty years between them.

44
FIREMEN SAVE THE CUP

THE Scottish Cup victory of 1970 was a tremendous boost to morale and the players could sense that they were on the verge of being a great team. The night of celebration at Gleneagles had ended with the directors gathering in a corner with manager Eddie Turnbull and chief scout Bobby Calder and talking through the night about where the Dons were going from there.

The aim would be to project the club over a five-year period; but how should they tackle it? With young Martin Buchan as captain, Turnbull had built a team of high promise so the first step towards consolidating the success of 1970 would be to keep the players together if at all possible.

After all, there was a rare blend of skills, starting with the stability of Bobby Clark in goal. Surveying it all with a shrewd eye from his goalline, Bobby reckoned Martin Buchan was the best defender he had played with. Steve Murray had arrived from Dundee to strengthen the pool and became Clark's choice as the best all-round performing colleague he had known, playing to an effectiveness of 95 per cent as opposed to other people's 50 per cent.

Murray was a thinking player, with a great awareness of the game. He moved on to Celtic but left football prematurely because of injury, later becoming a bank manager. Martin Buchan had a fine understanding with Tommy McMillan at centre-half; Jim Forrest, who had previously been Rangers' greatest goalscorer, and his cousin Alec Willoughby had developed a maturity which they had not attained in their twin-days at Ibrox.

With players such as Davie Robb and Ian Taylor adding their

contrasting styles, the Dons began season 1970–71 with great expectations. It looked as though these would be fulfilled as they went to the top of the League and threatened to halt Celtic's domination, which had been unbroken since Jock Stein's first full season in 1965–66. In a run of thirteen games, the Dons did not lose a single goal and the sense of invincibility was growing by the week.

In circumstances such as these, when things are going so well, in the curious workings of the world, that is so often when the unexpected happens. In the early morning darkness of Saturday, 6 February 1971, flames lit up the Aberdeen skyline. As the fire engines raced down King Street, it soon became clear that Pittodrie's main grandstand was in the process of being destroyed.

The fire, it seemed, had started after an explosion and soon the whole place was going up in smoke. Consternation! The Scottish Cup was in there! Firemen strove to rescue it as a priority. News of the outbreak reached the first team who had left the previous night for a league game at Dunfermline.

It is fair to say that the fire marked the turning-point in the route to the 1971 championship. The players were in disarray, without a home and forced into unfamiliar routines, training at Woodside and changing at Linksfield for matches at Pittodrie. The crowds, which had averaged 18,000 that season, restoring something of the post-war atmosphere, were still willing the team to victory but in the end the Dons were pipped for the title by Celtic.

There was no consolation in the European Cup Winners' Cup, which the Dons had entered with the confidence of having beaten the all-conquering Celtic to get there. In the first round they beat Honved of Hungary 3–1 at Pittodrie but lost by the same score in the away game. With a 4–4 tie, the second game went to penalties and out went the Dons on the cruelty of a 5–4 margin. So a season of much promise petered out without reward, other than providing the only real challenge to the superiority of Celtic.

Meanwhile, a new and refreshing force was emerging at boardroom level in Chris Anderson, still remembered from his playing days in the 1950s. Mr Anderson was part of a trinity of former Aberdeen players – with chairman Dick Donald and elder statesman Charles B. Forbes – who could claim to be the only football board in Scotland with the added authority of having played for their club.

Chris Anderson was born in 1925 and had grown up on King Street at the top of Pittodrie Street, where he would stare in childhood wonder at the big names of the 1930s as they went to and from the ground – Paddy Moore, Willie Mills, Matt Armstrong and the man with the distinguished air and the fine straw basher, Donald Colman.

Football was bred into the daily life of boys like Chris Anderson and fostered throughout the city by many a dedicated teacher, none more so than Mr Eddie Ross, headmaster of Linksfield School, to whom Aberdeen owed a deep debt. Young Anderson had been a lad of promise, chosen as a Scottish schoolboy international, but little knowing that his schoolmaster at Sunnybank, Charles B. Forbes, would one day welcome him as a co-director of Aberdeen Football Club.

His first step was to join the junior Mugiemoss and the second nearly took him to Ibrox Park. Manager Bill Struth despatched one of his players, former Moss man Duggie Gray, to try to persuade the boy south. But the ties down Pittodrie Street were strong and Chris joined the Dons in 1943 when he was eighteen. As ever in those days, war service intervened and it was not until the famous team of 1947 broke up more than a year later that Chris Anderson made his first-team debut along with Jack Hather.

Chris was soon good enough to be named for the league team and he had particular reason to remember a Scottish Cup tie against Celtic at Parkhead in 1951. In the days before that match, Don Emery received a letter threatening that, if Celtic did not win, the burly Welshman would have his features re-arranged by means of a razor.

If the poison-pen man had had the intelligence to check statistics he wouldn't have bothered with the threat because no one could trace an occasion when Aberdeen had beaten Celtic in a Cup tie at

Parkhead. But evil has a habit of recoiling on itself and the Dons went storming through that match with a glorious goal by Chris Anderson which put Celtic out of the Cup.

Looking back over his Pittodrie playing days, Chris picked out Frank Dunlop as the finest wing-half he had seen at Pittodrie although he had been converted to a centre-half by the time he captained the post-war team. He also credited Tommy Pearson with fostering a renaissance in Scottish football, encouraging a type of thinking that led to the successful Dons team of the mid 1950s.

Anderson's playing career suffered from that lean spell of the late 1940s and early 1950s but he played his most significant role as a young-at-heart director, up-dating the Dons' image of the 1970s and playing a major part in the creation of the Premier Division in 1975.

Having joined the board in the late 1960s, his first taste of success was the Scottish Cup final in 1970 and he was at Gleneagles that night, prominent in the discussion about the future and urging that the team be kept together.

Well, there was one departure no one had bargained for and it was the very first to happen. The players were back for their pre-season training in July 1971, still without a proper home after the fire, when Eddie Turnbull came among them and announced that he was leaving to be manager of Hibernian. A silence fell over the players and some, including Davie Robb, were visibly shattered by the news.

Behind his departure was the fact that a wealthy Edinburgh builder, Tom Hart, had achieved the dream of many a self-made man and gained control of the club of his lifelong affection. He was not going to settle until his friend Eddie Turnbull was back as manager in the place he had served so well. Chris Anderson took up the story: 'Eddie was going and nothing was going to stop him, so there was no point in being bitter. Though his health had been suspect, he and his coach, Jimmy Bonthrone, had been an excellent team. The calmer approach of Bonthrone balanced the rumbustious, dominant personality of Turnbull – and we decided to give

Jimmy a chance to prove himself. He got off to an encouraging start.'

That start was the Drybrough Cup, a new competition that opened the 1971–72 season. The Dons rocketed to the final against Celtic, which was to be played at one of the two home grounds instead of Hampden. Aberdeen won the advantage and it turned out to be a wonderful occasion. Pittodrie had been renovated after the fire and this return to normality drew a crowd of 25,000 on Saturday, 7 August.

Davie Robb scored the first goal, one of the greatest ever seen at Pittodrie, and Joe Harper's penalty kick gave the Dons the Drybrough Cup and a measure of consolation for the upheaval of the fire and all it had meant in terms of losing their grip on the league leader-ship earlier that year.

In the league programme, Celtic were once again dominant, *en route* to their famous nine-in-a-row championships, with Aberdeen snapping at their heels as the main challenger. Jimmy Bonthrone worked himself in as the new manager, changing the style to suit his own personality.

But although the Dons were repeating their performance of the previous year, it merely concealed the general unrest spreading in the dressing room. Chris Anderson remembered how Martin Buchan and Joe Harper were virtually saying to the club, 'We can collect a lump sum and double our wages by going to England, so you must let us go.'

The cracks were appearing in a potentially great team. Martin Buchan was allowed to pursue his southern ambitions and signed for Manchester United for a fee of £125,000, heading for the kind of fame and fortune his father could only have dreamed about. The son was a thoroughbred in the modern manner yet there are those who would tell you that the grace of the father remained a more distinctive memory.

So Buchan was gone (he was followed from Pittodrie to Old Trafford by younger brother George) and when little Joe Harper, who had come from Morton, was sold to Everton in December 1972 for an Aberdeen record of £180,000, the Dons had lost their star defender and the best striker in the land. When disintegration begins it can be hard to stop.

Bobby Clark was so conscious of the downward trend that he, too, asked for a transfer. Stoke City were seeking a replacement for Gordon Banks, their World Cup-winning keeper who had suffered a serious eye injury in a car crash, and Clark seemed to be their man. He travelled down to see manager Tony Waddington, who was keen to sign him on the spot. But the Dons were due to play Celtic on the Saturday and Stoke were told that he was not for sale until after that match.

Martin Buchan drove his former team-mate from Manchester to Stoke and told him that manager Frank O'Farrell was interested in taking him to Old Trafford, but his hands were tied at the moment. When the Dons played Celtic on the Saturday, a Stoke director came to cast an eye over the man for whom his club was evidently ready to pay £100,000. When the match ended, the visitor shocked everyone by announcing that the Clark offer was now £60,000.

Out of an unpleasant atmosphere, the good result was that Bobby Clark stayed at Pittodrie. Privately, he would have much preferred Manchester United to Stoke City but within a few weeks Frank O'Farrell had left Old Trafford in the familiar pattern of departing managers.

In 1972 the Dons went on a tour of North America, best remembered for some remarkable scenes when they met the Montreal Olympics. Trouble flared when the Dons were awarded a penalty and Joe Harper scored. You wouldn't have guessed it was a friendly. The crowd booing Harper's goal followed up by letting off fireworks and throwing stones, cans, shoes and a dustbin at the Dons players. Davie Robb, not known for cowardice, confessed he had never been so scared. Luckily, the field was fenced from spectators, who were trying to climb over. The referee took the players off the field and for thirty minutes officials tried to calm the crowd but without success; so the game was abandoned.

By 1972, Henning Boel and Tommy McMillan had left. Derek McKay, of Cup-tie fame, was in the Far East, Jim Forrest in South

Africa and George Murray had become coach. Drew Jarvie, who was to develop into one of the most stylish and talented of Pittodrie players, arrived from Airdrie for season 1972–73 and there were young players such as Joe Smith, Willie Young and Billy Williamson coming through from the reserve team. Several of the youngsters found a new maturity during a tour of Australia and New Zealand.

But the situation at Pittodrie had sunk into a trough, with further trouble building up in 1975. Big Willie Young, a red-headed boy from Port Seton Athletic who had established himself as the Dons', and Scotland's, central defender, was one of five Scots to land in hot water with the SFA.

It arose after an international match with Denmark in Copenhagen in September, when the players were alleged to have been drinking in a nightclub and to have been thrown out by the police after a rumpus over a disputed bill. The newspapers were full of it. There were reports of more trouble back at the hotel and someone was reputed to have felled Billy Bremner, the Scottish captain.

The upshot was that the five were banned from ever appearing in a national jersey again. Sadly, two of them were Dons, Willie Young and Arthur Graham. The others were Joe Harper, at that time with Hibs, having gone there from Everton, Billy Bremner of Leeds and Pat McCluskey of Celtic. The life ban was lifted in 1977 but at the time it had an upsetting effect on the players concerned.

For Willie Young, the trouble was not yet over. Back at Pittodrie and playing against Dundee United two weeks after the affair in Copenhagen, he was substituted for the first time in 234 games. The decision to take him off so angered him that he strode gigantically to the touchline, pulled off his shirt, threw it in the direction of manager Bonthrone and walked bare-chested along the track to the dressing room.

Before the final whistle had sounded he had left the Pittodrie precincts and that, believe it or not, was how Aberdeen's international centre-half literally left the club, never to wear its colours again. Before there was time to think of disciplinary measures the

244

matter was resolved the following week when Willie, a large and popular figure, was transferred to Tottenham Hotspur for £100,000. It was a sad end to his Aberdeen career but one that he brought upon himself.

The embarrassment of the touchline incident was one no manager could afford to tolerate. But if Young was going, the man who took him off was sensing that his own days in the job were also numbered. By October 1975, Jimmy Bonthrone was telling the board, 'I feel I can get no more from the players and, as Aberdeen deserves a prominent place in the game, I'm getting out.'

It was all very sad because, in the words of Chris Anderson, 'We were losing the most honest man I have ever met in football.' As one of his players told me, 'Jimmy Bonthrone gave everything he had but he tried to be so fair to everyone that he ended up being unfair to himself.'

So he bowed out with quiet dignity and withdrew to an occupation outside football altogether, back in Fife. His record had not been a bad one, but perhaps, like Davie Shaw fifteen years earlier, his strength had been as a coach and the sterner authority required by modern management was not in his nature.

If Bonthrone's era went sour on him, it should at least be remembered as the period when he introduced to the Aberdeen team a man whose individual skills were among the greatest that Scottish football had ever seen. Zoltan Varga was a slim-built Hungarian of such exquisite talent that canny Aberdonians wondered by what curious mischance he had suddenly materialised at Pittodrie. His last club had been Hertha Berlin.

Mystery was allowed to linger in the background, however, as Dons fans happily concentrated on the silken soccer of Varga, marvelling at the way he could guide the flight of a ball as if by remote control. The countries of eastern Europe had long provided the best juggling and balancing acts for the circus-ring so it was no surprise that an offshoot of that native talent should find its way into football.

Zoltan Varga predicted a bright future for young Arthur Graham.

'Bumper,' he would say in his fractured English, 'when I get the ball do not look at me. Just run thirty yards and ball will drop in front of you.' Sure enough, it would drop with perfection. Arthur's only problem with such unique service was that he couldn't always remember to keep running without looking back.

In assessing the skills that have graced the Pittodrie turf, from Alec Jackson to Tommy Pearson to Graham Leggat, some would argue that Zoltan Varga was the most truly gifted player who ever pulled on an Aberdeen jersey. If football were a wine, then here was the vintage champagne, a heady experience which was surely too good to last. And so it turned out to be.

The newspapers had been slow to get hold of the background story of why the Hungarian had left Berlin and landed in Aberdeen. There had been a bribery scandal and Varga was banned from playing in West Germany. His year in Scottish football had been an interlude in the wings before returning to the continental stage.

The newspaper stories came as no surprise to the Aberdeen directors, who were thoroughly acquainted with the bribery story. They were convinced that Varga was not the instigator of the corruption and that, having become involved in it, he had been suitably punished and could seek to restore his reputation in the service of the Dons. The directors deserved some credit for an enlightened view.

Having been tipped off about him by a German contact, Gunter Bachman, they promptly signed him for a fee which was no more than a token of his true worth. Towards the end of 1973, however, Hertha Berlin decided to buy back his contract for a similar sum and he became, technically, their player once again. But they did not buy him back as a practising footballer.

Ajax of Amsterdam had lost that immortal master Johan Cruyff to Barcelona for compensation of nearly a million pounds, and were looking for a replacement. It is the highest possible tribute to the former Don that Ajax turned towards Berlin and bought Zoltan Varga, the man who touched Pittodrie like a traveller in the night, playing his Hungarian rhapsody with masterly effect and sweeping on his way while an entranced audience gazed after him in wonder.

When his playing days were over we rather lost track of him, until that old familiar name turned up again in the 1990s, this time as manager of Hungarian team Ferencvaros, visiting these shores on European business.

45

ALLY'S MAGIC

I N the autumn of 1975, when Aberdeen were looking for a manager to replace Jimmy Bonthrone, director Chris Anderson was in Glasgow appearing on a television sports programme. At the studios he met a journalist who dropped a hint that, after ten years of solid achievement with Ayr United, Ally MacLeod was ripe for a move to a full-time club.

The Dons director raised his eyebrows. It was time for a bit of razzmatazz in the grey-granite citadel of the north, especially with an oil boom in progress and a latent support which was the biggest in Scotland outside Rangers and Celtic. MacLeod could be just the man to provide it. A super-enthusiast, he was the keen-talking motivating power for a new level of public relations among Scottish managers.

Growing up in the shadows of Hampden Park, he had played for the local Third Lanark as an entertaining winger and was later a member of the Blackburn Rovers side beaten in the FA Cup final of 1960. MacLeod had returned to Scotland as captain of Hibs before taking over as player-coach and then manager of Ayr United. His refreshing personality did so much to promote the team and the town that he was elected local 'Citizen of the Year'.

The Dons directors wasted no time in bringing him to Pittodrie but an initial burst of success was followed by a bad run, which was all the more noticeable since Scotland had just re-organised its football into a Premier Division of ten teams instead of eighteen. What had formerly been a mid-league position was now a relegation problem and that was where the Dons found themselves in the last days of season 1975–76, along with several others.

A death-or-glory game with Hibs at Pittodrie on the last day of the season would decide their fate. Aberdeen had never been relegated in the seventy-odd years of its existence. All seemed black when Mike McDonald saved a Davie Robb penalty kick but the Dons went on to win 3–0, and remained in the top division.

The new set-up had certainly sharpened competition, even if the terms involved revealed a curious interpretation of the English language. How could you explain to an outsider that Scotland had a 'Premier' (meaning first) division and a First Division? As an amusing piece of self-deception, it evidently made the second-grade feel better to be called the 'First', so who am I to disturb the illusion?

Starting his first full season as Aberdeen manager, Ally MacLeod was making his red-shirted players feel better, too. The early League Cup competition took the Dons into a preliminary section with Kilmarnock, Ayr United and St Mirren. They won it. In the home-and-away quarter-finals, Aberdeen were drawn against Stirling Albion in what turned out to be a nightmarish engagement. Having won 1–0 at Pittodrie, they went to Stirling on a night of gales and lashing rain and were beaten 1–0, just managing to survive a period of extra time. When it went to a third game at Dens Park, Dundee, the Dons won 2–0.

So to the semi-final against Rangers at Hampden and by then Ally MacLeod was beginning to establish the kind of confidence he had been looking for. The Dons had taken on the air of jet-setters, flying to their more distant fixtures in a charter plane and thus cutting the travel time, which had been such a built-in hazard of Aberdeen teams through the years that Chris Anderson assessed it as a practical disadvantage of eight goals per season.

There were no disadvantages on the night of 27 October 1976, however, as the Dons set about their League Cup semi-final at Hampden. This was the night they annihilated the Ibrox challenge in a devastating 5–1 victory. Jocky Scott set the pattern with a hat-trick, augmented by Joe Harper and Drew Jarvie, who volleyed home as spectacular a goal as the old stadium had seen in years. It was reminiscent of the drubbing the Dons had given Rangers in the Scottish Cup semi-final of 1954, when the score had been an even more emphatic 6–0.

On that occasion, Celtic had to be faced in the final and the Cup had gone to Parkhead. In 1976, Celtic were the opponents again but these Dons were not afraid of the prospect. The team had been gaining in depth and experience with the signing of Stuart Kennedy from Falkirk, surely an internationalist in the making, Dom Sullivan from Clyde and Joe Harper, fresh from his travels to Everton and Hibs and proclaiming himself happily back in the place where he felt truly at home.

King Joe was re-establishing himself as the goalscoring hero of the demonstrative Beach-end support, which was glad to call itself 'Ally's Army'. Three days after the midweek defeat of Rangers, the Dons were at home to league leaders Dundee United and Ally MacLeod felt there was little need to elaborate on that fabulous victory. His message in the Saturday programme was printed vertically down the page and simply said: MAGIC!

In preparation for the final, the Dons party stayed at the MacDonald Hotel on the south side of Glasgow, where long-serving colleagues Bobby Clark and Davie Robb shared a room. Robb, for whom Clark always had the highest admiration, was to be the substitute in the final. Suddenly, on the eve of the big game, Bobby said to his room-mate, 'Davie, you've been a workhorse for Aberdeen all these years and you haven't had much glory. But I have this strange feeling that you are going to come on tomorrow and score the winner. I can just see it.'

Well, the final raged on next day, with Celtic taking the lead through Kenny Dalglish, who took the penalty kick himself after he was said to have been fouled by Drew Jarvie. The highly talented Jarvie soon made amends when Arthur Graham's cross was headed on by Joe Harper to enable him to head the equaliser.

Davie Robb had indeed been brought on as substitute, to be greeted with a wave and shout from Clark: 'Remember!' At 1–1 the game went into extra time and only a hundred seconds had been played when Davie duly followed through the pattern of prediction and scored.

If that should turn out to be the winner, he would be left wondering if Bobby Clark had a future in the psychic business. But there were still twenty-eight minutes left for play and, as the fast-raiding Celts came storming into Aberdeen territory like the waves of a Chinese army, northern nails were bitten to the quick and nerves became frayed as a tinker's waistcoat.

In the burning excitement, something significant took place in the relationship between Aberdeen players and supporters. Sensing the plight of their heroes, the 17,000 Aberdonians at Hampden unleashed a vocal support such as I had never heard from the Pittodrie faithful. It rose to the rooftops of the national stadium and gave notice, for the first time, that mighty roars of football fervour would no longer be the exclusive preserve of the mob-rule hordes of Ibrox and Parkhead. It was the day when Aberdonians finally cast off their native reticence and, as they galvanised themselves to a deafening chant, while out-numbered three-to-one by the Celts, the referee drew breath for that final blast of the pea – and Davie Robb was hailed as the match-winner indeed.

Exactly a year after taking over as Dons manager, Ally MacLeod gazed across towards the Mount Florida street where he grew up and listened to the din of victory rebounding from tenement walls. The man who had given so much to football was gaining his first-ever prize and who would have grudged him his moment of glory? The city of Aberdeen, which had held its breath beside transistors and car radios, finally gave vent to the civic feeling as motorists drove the length of Union Street blaring out the Morse-code call of victory on car horns.

Some Celtic supporters were magnanimous in defeat but one of their number had yet to learn about the Aberdonian sense of poetic justice. A young Celt emerged from his little clique at the back of Hampden to throw a brick at a supporters' bus departing for Aberdeen. Without ceremony, four hefty Dons fans from Dyce bounded out to isolate the offender, warned off his mates, turned his brick-throwing arm up his back and marched him aboard the bus. 'Drive on,' they said. Somewhere in the region of Perth, so the story goes, the young Celt was given a lecture on the folly of throwing bricks at Aberdeen buses and released into the gloom of the night – with sixty miles or so between him and home!

The 'Scotsport' programme of Grampian-STV came live from Pittodrie next day when the players paraded the League Cup in front of 25,000 people. Ally MacLeod took a brief bow but for all the jaunty extrovert he had become, he refused the overtures of the chairman to address the crowd. They had merely wanted to hear the voice of the man who had brought them new hope. The team at Hampden had been: Clark; Kennedy, Williamson; Smith, Garner, Miller; Sullivan, Scott, Harper, Jarvie, Graham. Substitute: Robb.

Looking back on the MacLeod inspiration, Chris Anderson said, 'We had needed the buzz and froth and extravagant and sometimes outrageous comments – and that's what we got from Ally MacLeod. He cheered us all up, created a touch of the Barnum-and-Baileys and finally set the adrenalin flowing with the League Cup victory.'

Ally had proved a tonic to everyone. But something stronger than a tonic was needed for one piece of publicity MacLeod and his players could well have done without. On the evening of Wednesday, 2 March 1977 the Dons were surprisingly knocked out of the Scottish Cup by Dundee, in a replay at Pittodrie following a drawn game at Dens Park the previous Saturday. Later that night, an anonymous call to the *Press and Journal* made the serious allegation that three Aberdeen players – and the caller had names for them – had each placed a bet of £500 at odds of 8–1 that Dundee would win the match. The caller said he had it on good authority, but without evidence to back up the outrageous claim, the *Press and Journal* decided to ignore the matter.

Two weeks later, however, Grampian Television ran a Saturday night commercial about 'tomorrow's *Sunday Mail*' which would have a sensational story concerning Aberdeen players. The front-page headline that greeted readers next morning was: 'Players in "Soccer Bets" Shock – Cup-tie defeat sparks off police probe'. The story began: 'Detectives are investigating a sensational claim that three Aberdeen FC players bet a large sum of money *against* their own team in a Scottish Cup tie.' And on it went, on similar lines to the man on the telephone.

Grampian Chief Constable Alexander Morrison later explained that his men were furnished with a written statement, allegedly based on an overheard conversation, which they were obliged to investigate. The police were able to assess the betting on the match through Customs and Excise but came up with no evidence of any plot. So it was concluded that this was a figment of someone's imagination, a mischievous piece of work which nevertheless cast aspersions on the Aberdeen team

Chairman Dick Donald called a press conference and lashed out at the newspaper concerned. There was talk of legal action but the *Mail* had stayed within the limits of the law and the most Aberdeen could do was put the matter into the hands of the Press Council.

McNEILL TAKES OVER

46

THE betting story had scarcely settled in the spring of 1977 when the directors were at Pittodrie one lunchtime, having a chat with Ally MacLeod. Willie Ormond had just given up his successful run as Scotland's international manager to return to club football as boss of ailing Hearts. The question of the moment was who would get the job of guiding the Scots through the latter stages of qualifying for the World Cup in Argentina, the job already begun by Ormond?

The question was all but answered when Dick Donald was called to the telephone. He returned to the room and said, 'Well Ally, that was Ernie Walker on the phone. They are asking you to be manager of Scotland.'

Mr Donald made it plain that Aberdeen didn't want to lose him but, on the other hand, they would not stand in his way. Out of the doubt and confusion and the knowledge that his family had settled so well in Aberdeen, Ally MacLeod accepted the job and carried the Scots through to victories against Czechoslovakia and Wales and on to the World Cup finals.

The loyal battalions of 'Ally's Army' on the terracing of Pittodrie wished him well, sorry to lose him but grateful that he had brought new life to the club. The directors pencilled in the names of three men who would meet the requirements of a successor – Alex Stuart of Ayr United, Billy McNeill, who had recently taken over his first manager's job with Clyde, and Alex Ferguson of St Mirren.

Alex Stuart, an Aberdonian, was first to be considered but there were problems about his release from Ayr. At first, the choice of Billy

McNeill came as a surprise to those who forgot that, despite his shortage of managerial experience, he was a young man of character and stature who was surely a supreme authority on matters such as European football. As captain of the greatest-ever Celtic team he had spent a solid decade not only dominating Scottish football but playing in more top-class European matches than any other player in Britain.

In retirement he had become a successful businessman but the lure of football was too strong and he made a quiet return as manager of Clyde. Within weeks of that return, he was driving north in answer to a call from chairman Dick Donald, who felt confident he and his fellow directors had chosen the man for the moment.

The rendezvous point was Perth but the former Celt was soon driving all the way to Aberdeen, delighted to find himself in such an exalted position so soon in his managerial career. As the board had anticipated, McNeill grew into the stature of the job almost immediately, commanding respect and starting his first season by setting the pace at the top of the Premier Division.

As League Cup winners, the Dons were competing in the UEFA Cup in season 1977–78, drawn against the formidable Belgian team RWD Molenbeek and travelling to Brussels for the first leg. In a splendid display, the Dons held the Belgians to a goalless draw and brought this tribute from the official UEFA observer: 'It was one of the best performances, if not the best, by a British club playing in Europe that I have seen.'

High praise indeed to set Billy McNeill on his way. But the Belgians had a remarkable record in away games and finally won the tie by two goals to one at Pittodrie. So concentration returned to the domestic programme and the Dons found themselves with a clear lead, Rangers and Celtic having made poor starts to the season and Rangers landing in bottom position at one stage.

While Celtic continued to flounder, the Ibrox side made a steady recovery and by the first light of 1978, the League had resolved into a battle between the Light Blues and the red shirts of Aberdeen, with others trailing well behind. In one of the most exciting build-ups ever, Rangers pulled into a six-point lead, with the Dons keeping up the pursuit and embarking on an undefeated run of twenty-three games.

But the title was probably decided on 28 February by an incident that had nothing to do with the skills of football. On that day, Rangers went to play Motherwell, rejuvenated under new manager Roger Hynd. The Fir Park men went into a 2–0 lead and were playing with the confidence of winners when a chant went up from a section of the Rangers following: 'There's going to be a riot!'

It was the lunatic fringe at work again, the horde of hooligans whom Rangers' management condemned as a 'troublesome minority' but who turned out to be a very large and ugly 'minority'. These people had already brought disgrace to the Ibrox club at places as far apart as Newcastle and Barcelona and here they were again in their lager-laden aggression. 'There's going to be a riot' – and over the boundary wall they came, some perhaps escaping the beer-can ammunition of the main infantry but all on their way to the field. Whatever the depths of their gutter mentality, it did not escape them that a stoppage of play could disturb a winning rhythm.

The rhythm that day had belonged to Motherwell but, with blue scarves swarming around their ears, the referee had to take the players quickly off the field. When play eventually managed to resume, an unnerved Motherwell side had indeed lost its rhythm and Rangers went on to win the match.

The Scottish Football Association recommended to the Scottish League that the match should be played again but a gutless league committee took no such action and timidly fined the Ibrox club £2,000. It was not only Aberdeen supporters who passed the cynical verdict that the so-called punishment was cheap at the price. As it turned out, those points were exactly the number needed to win the title.

With the Fir Park win, Rangers kept their six-point lead and on the following Saturday the Dons were due at Ibrox for what was now conceded by manager Billy McNeill to be their last chance. If Rangers won and widened the gap to eight points (two points for a win in those days) they would be unstoppable. On a sunny March day, Aberdeen attacked from the start and scored a convincing 3–0 victory, with one goal by the irrepressible Joe Harper and two by young Steve Archibald, only recently signed from Clyde where he had been much admired by McNeill during his brief spell as manager.

That win cut Rangers' lead to four points and the Dons brought it back to level pegging, losing out on the last day of the season. Rangers had won the championship and the record-books credited them with one more achievement. By their weakness, the league committee had chalked up a decisive victory for hooliganism – and who knows how much they helped to sow seeds of bitterness for the future?

If Aberdeen had reason to feel aggrieved about the outcome of the League, they had none at all when it came to the Scottish Cup and League Cup. Once again, the power of Rangers put them out of both. In the League Cup the Ibrox men struck their best performance in years to avenge the semi-final defeat of the previous season, with a devastating 6–1 win in the first game of the quarter-final at Ibrox. The Dons won 3–1 in the return game but the Cup of 1978 was on its way to Glasgow.

In the Scottish Cup, the Dons went through the early rounds against Ayr United, St Johnstone and Morton and beat Partick Thistle 4–2 in the semi-final at Hampden. Having played those twenty-three games without defeat, and having just missed the title, there were high hopes that they would reap some reward for their efforts by lifting the Scottish Cup. In their weariness over monopolies, neutral Scotland wished it that way. But it was not to be.

In the Cup final of 6 May, the team that had played so well so often and had not been beaten since the previous December produced a miserable performance in which they failed to get to grips with the situation. Rangers were by far the better team, scoring through MacDonald and Johnstone. A late goal by Steve Ritchie, a full-back recently arrived from Hereford, merely put a better complexion on the final score.

So Rangers won the treble and the only token of consolation came the following week when the Young Dons beat Rangers in the final of the Second XI Cup, skippered by the popular Chic McLelland, who had recently lost his first-team place. The lack of silverware bit deep into the heart of manager McNeill, whose years of Celtic supremacy had conditioned him to nothing but success. The more objective judgement, however, was that he had done a magnificent job for Aberdeen Football Club in his first year as a manager. Until the last two weeks of the season, the Dons were still in a position to land the league and Cup double, which would have been a fitting act of celebration for the club's seventy-fifth anniversary.

The new manager had brought a feeling that, with such a man around, the moment of success would not be long delayed. He had strengthened the first-team pool by signing Gordon Strachan from Dundee and Ian Scanlon from Notts County, two fine ball-players, as well as Steve Archibald and Steve Ritchie. He had strengthened his own hand by bringing his former colleague, John Clark, from a coaching job at Celtic to be assistant manager at Aberdeen. Clark took over the role of George Murray, the coach who had twice cherished the hope of becoming manager.

McNeill encouraged local coaches to identify themselves with Pittodrie and he sought to improve his players' financial position through public appearances and so on. In fighting for his players, he demanded respect in return, a fact which was forcibly brought home to Willie Garner and Bobby Glennie when they stepped out of line at Hogmanay 1977 and found themselves fined and suspended by the manager.

Despite the trophy triumphs of Jock Wallace at Rangers, it was Billy McNeill who was voted Scottish Manager of the Year, no more than due recognition of his rapid progress from the starting-block.

Inevitably, the mediocre performance of Celtic in season 1977–78 gave rise to speculation that the up-and-coming McNeill might not be too long delayed in succeeding his old boss, Jock Stein, as manager at Parkhead. Public appreciation of his efforts to bring tangible success to Aberdeen was fully expressed on the day after the Scottish

Cup final when a dejected Dons party set out from Perth, having stayed overnight at the Station Hotel.

Win or lose, the plan had been to drive from the Bridge of Dee to Pittodrie in an open-topped bus but in view of the massive disappointment of the previous day the players were dreading that nobody would turn out. They need not have feared. The scenes in Aberdeen that Sunday afternoon of 7 May 1978 were remarkable for their enthusiasm. Around 10,000 people greeted them along the route and a further 10,000 had crowded into Pittodrie.

As captain Willie Miller and his players walked out to the arena in their red tracktops the place erupted. If this was the sound of defeat then what was victory? Chants of 'Aberdeen are magic!' overlooked the fact that they had been far from magic on the previous afternoon. But the thunderous vote of thanks was the supporters' appreciation of a team that had given Pittodrie one of its most entertaining seasons in seventy-five years of contest.

Player after player was singled out for chanted acclaim as they, along with Billy McNeill and his assistant John Clark, applauded the fans in return. Some players shed tears as they held out empty hands by way of apology for the absence of a trophy. The crowd responded to McNeill when he took over the microphone and said, 'Ladies and gentlemen, this reception is unbelievable. I am so disappointed for my players and for myself but most of all I am disappointed for you, the fans. All I can say is that we'll try very hard to bring you something next season.'

It was all the crowd wanted to hear, just as they had wanted Ally MacLeod to speak to them in the victory salute of 1976. McNeill had judged the mood more accurately and, in taking a rare opportunity for a manager to address the fans *en masse*, he enhanced his reputation still further.

The Aberdeen players vowed that these fans must be rewarded at the earliest possible moment. Three of them, Bobby Clark, Stuart Kennedy and Joe Harper, were bound for Argentina as part of their old boss's World Cup squad and the others were flying off to a well-earned rest in the Majorcan sunshine. At a boardroom reception, the directors expressed themselves well pleased with the impact of Billy McNeill and John Clark.

But alas, once more, that impact was never to know the test of time. The shock resignation of Jock Wallace as manager of Rangers on Tuesday, 23 May heralded a chain of events that diverted public attention from the fact that the Scottish international party was already flying into Argentina for the finals of the World Cup.

At home, John Greig's elevation from Rangers player to Rangers manager within twenty-four hours of Wallace's announcement hastened a shake-up at Celtic Park, where all was not well. When Dick Donald lifted the telephone in the early morning of Friday, 26 May, it was to be given due notice by the Parkhead board that they were about to offer their manager's chair to Billy McNeill in succession to the great Jock Stein, who was to be given another role.

McNeill had settled happily into life in the North-east but his regrets at leaving it so soon were outweighed by the temptation of a job that was, understandably, the peak of his personal ambition.

Within a few days it was all signed and sealed and the Aberdeen directors were back in the all-too-familiar position of finding a new man. Their enterprise deserved a better reward. However, they wasted no time in appointing Alex Ferguson of St Mirren, whose immediate task would be to instil in his players a belief that whatever had been achieved under Ally MacLeod and Billy McNeill could be improved upon under the new command.

47
ANNIVERSARY NIGHT

T HAT dramatic week in the early summer of 1978, which brought managerial changes at Ibrox and Parkhead and left Aberdeen looking for McNeill's replacement, also included the sacking of Alex Ferguson from the boss's job at Love Street, Paisley. The bickering there ended in the public forum of an industrial tribunal.

A freshly sacked manager of St Mirren being engaged for the more prestigious post at Pittodrie was scarcely going to stir wild enthusiasm among supporters in the approach to a new season. They found more to cheer about at the Capitol Cinema one rain-swept night when the original version of this book was launched on a wave of nostalgia for better times remembered.

The book was marking the seventy-fifth anniversary of Aberdeen Football Club, not that there was a great deal to celebrate in terms of silverware, with only five national trophies in all those years and nothing at all having been won in the first forty-three! (Imagine the Pittodrie crowds tolerating that kind of barren existence today.) Yet the Dons' achievements were not inconsiderable when set in the context of the twin giants, Rangers and Celtic, whose dominance down the century had virtually cast all others in the role of cannon-fodder.

Trophies were not everything in life, said the purists, and Aberdeen was celebrating a major milestone with a parade from the past, filing on to the stage of the Capitol to be greeted by a capacity audience of 2,000, waving red scarves in the air. From every decade they came – Matt Forsyth and Stonewall Jackson of the twenties,

Matt Armstrong and Willie Mills of the thirties, Archie Baird and Tony Harris of the forties and Fred Martin, Archie Glen, Harry Yorston and Jackie Hather of the fifties.

It was a glorious night of music, merriment and reminiscence, with players recognising themselves in old newsreel films of Hampden occasions and finishing off with a cocktail party in the restaurant area of the cinema.

At a more private gathering afterwards in the Atholl Hotel, Alex Ferguson crept quietly upon the scene, taking it all in, acknowledging a past that had been well and truly celebrated that night – a past in which he had played no part at all – and indicating that his task would be to build on those memories.

For all the rich history recalled that evening, who could have known that the real story of Pittodrie success was just about to begin? What a quirk of fate that the man sitting beside me with a drink in his hand, uttering modest platitudes, was destined to be the architect of that success, as well as the incomparable legend of the Pittodrie story.

Within a year that lonely figure, still reeling from the sacking notice of Love Street, would be inspiring a league championship that turned out to be no more than the forerunner of the Golden Age of Aberdeen Football Club. Looking back from this centenary point, it is already an exquisite memory, distilled in history. On the book-launching night of 1978 that history still lay in the future. Such is the fascination of mankind's continuing story.

— 48 —
ENTER THE
GOLDEN AGE

ALEX FERGUSON buckled down to his task. At thirty-five, he was one of the youngest managers in the game, with a margin between himself and the senior players that could prove perilously small. Indeed, there were said to be early signs of difficulty in establishing his authority. As a lad from the rough-and-tumble of Govan, however, he had learnt to look after himself.

His career had brought him prominence as a player with Dunfermline Athletic and then Rangers – he was part of that scooping-up of Scotland's best players in the 1960s, in a bid to counter the triumphs of Jock Stein at Celtic – and he had managed East Stirling and St Mirren. At Love Street he had fostered such talents as Tony Fitzpatrick and Frank McGarvey and, more significantly as it turned out, young players including Peter Weir, Dougie Bell and Billy Stark.

Now there was a sense of being in a bigger league of management as he surveyed the potential at Pittodrie and realised that the brief stewardships of Ally MacLeod and Billy McNeill had boosted morale and enriched the playing staff with such talents as Stuart Kennedy from Falkirk, Steve Archibald from Clyde and Gordon Strachan from Dundee.

The basic wage of £80 a week could be doubled with bonuses but was still not the kind of money to hold top players. So Alex Ferguson set about improving the wage structure. It was augmented for longer-serving players by the 'testimonial year', which had been established just before the manager's arrival.

Bobby Clark was the first recipient. That year of functions and a benefit match could raise as much as £20,000, a sizeable sum in those days.

Ferguson's first season at Pittodrie, 1978–79, was overshadowed by the last illness of his father and the bad odour of his tribunal, claiming unfair dismissal from St Mirren. It turned out to be a season without merit in Aberdeen performances, best remembered for the worst possible reason – a sending-off for big Doug Rougvie in the League Cup final against Rangers at Hampden, following an incident with Derek Johnstone.

Rougvie and his team-mates accused the Rangers man of playing to get a foul and making the most of it, a view endorsed in his own book by Alex Ferguson. Aberdeen had taken the lead through Duncan Davidson but Rangers equalised when Bobby Clark was awaiting attention for an injury. After Rougvie's dismissal, Colin Jackson (an Aberdonian to boot!) headed a last-minute winner.

Ferguson, whose name was already being popularly abbreviated to Fergie, appreciated a breather to gather his thoughts and prepare for his second season at Pittodrie. For all his genius, Gordon Strachan, who had arrived in 1977 at the age of twenty, had taken time to establish himself in the team. The new manager worked out his proper role and improved his confidence, and the player felt the better not only for Fergie's presence but also because assistant manager Pat Stanton was there. Stanton was Strachan's hero from boyhood days, when he followed Hibernian.

The Dons made an inauspicious start to the new season with defeat by Partick Thistle at Firhill. Morale was not improved in December when, having reached the final of the League Cup – for the second time in the same calendar year, as it turned out – they drew with Dundee United at Hampden but were beaten 3–0 in the midweek replay at Dundee, on a night of howling gales and lashing rain better suited to witches and warlocks than performing footballers.

The League Cup run, plus a severe winter, put the Dons well behind in their fixtures as the nights began to stretch into the early spring of 1980. Celtic were out in front and seemed destined to stay there, opening up a gap of ten points at one stage although Aberdeen had three games in hand.

The Dons made a late charge and, with six games to play, were still three points behind Celtic, who then took a dramatic 5–1 defeat at Dens Park. Aberdeen had beaten Celtic at Parkhead on 5 April and, in trying to catch up with postponed fixtures, were due there again on Wednesday, 23 April. Could it still be done?

A McCluskey penalty was cancelled by goals from Steve Archibald, Mark McGhee and Gordon Strachan and the football fat was now in the fire. The Dons still had four games to play. A home win over St Mirren was followed by three away fixtures. A draw with Dundee United on a Tuesday night teed up a situation where, if they could beat Hibs in Edinburgh on the Saturday, and if St Mirren could hold Celtic to a draw at Love Street on the same day, the Dons would almost certainly be league champions. What a setting for a grand-stand finish!

All routes that day led to Easter Road, which had proved an unhappy hunting ground for the Dons in recent years, in the knowledge that an away win was essential. As the action warmed up, Ian Scanlon, whom Billy McNeill had signed from Notts County, scored twice and Steve Archibald, Andy Watson and Mark McGhee brought the total to 5–0 in front of an audience that had its eye on Easter Road and its ear on the transistor for news of the Love Street match, which was running minutes behind.

St Mirren were indeed holding Celtic to the necessary draw but the Parkhead men were being awarded a penalty . . . no . . . wait . . . . the referee was consulting a linesman . . . it was a free kick outside the box. Hushed drama at Easter Road, where the final whistle had already gone. Nobody moved. The Aberdeen players waited on the pitch for signals from the crowd.

Yes, that was it! The final whistle had gone at Love Street. Unless Partick Thistle could beat the Dons next Tuesday by ten goals, the men from the North-east were champions of Scotland for the first time in twenty-five years. Bedlam reigned. As I wrote in the *Daily Express*:

Oh what a day to be an Aberdonian! I have lived through forty years of Pittodrie history but, make no mistake, this was their finest hour. Today's youngsters will tell their grandchildren about it. When the final whistle blew and the truth dawned through a mounting excitement, the whole frenzy of celebration exploded in a riot of red.

There was Alex Ferguson running about the field in a mad delirium, crying like a baby and hugging his players in disbelief. The coincidences began to dawn. It was fifteen years to the day that Bobby Clark, Aberdeen's most capped player [to that date], had signed for the Dons. It had seemed that this prize would elude him. But now, just recovering from the sudden death of his father, Bobby was able to shed a tear which told its own story.

Willie Miller's mother Jean was recalling the amazing fact that her son had been born exactly twenty-five years ago – his birthday was the previous day – just as Aberdeen had been celebrating their only previous league championship in 1955. Then came the champagne that flowed through the night and, yesterday, the most beautiful headache in the world!

Pardon the hyperbole but, as a *Daily Express* feature writer, I was unhampered by the restraints imposed on the even-handed sports-writer!

The Dons fulfilled their remaining fixture, drawing 1–1 with Partick Thistle in a miserable anti-climax at Firhill, officially declared champions at the very ground where they had been beaten on the opening day of the season. What an unpredictable game is football.

The team on that historic day at Easter Road read: Clark; Kennedy, Rougvie; Watson, McLeish, Miller; Strachan, Archibald, McGhee, McMaster, Scanlon. Naturally, there were arguments about the respective merits of the teams that won in 1955 and 1980. Certainly the earlier team had players who would rank with the all-time greats of Pittodrie, from goalkeeper Fred Martin and Archie Glen to Graham Leggat, Harry Yorston, Paddy Buckley and Jackie Hather.

The most significant comparison would have to be made on the quality of the opposition. In 1955, each of fifteen opponents had to be played twice, so that after you were clear of Rangers and Celtic you could look forward to Falkirk, East Fife, Queen of the South, Raith Rovers, Stirling Albion and Clyde, all of which were in the top division of those days and, in fairness, of better quality than they are today.

In the tighter set-up of 1980, the Dons had to play the best nine teams four times each. That would make the task of 1980 more formidable although cynics might say the regularity with which the Dons seemed to beat Rangers and Celtic made the 1980 task appear an easier one.

The point was that Alex Ferguson had made his breakthrough, winning the Premier Division championship, while his neighbour at Dundee United, Jim McLean, had won the League Cup. Sportswriters began to coin a phrase about the New Firm, meaning Aberdeen and United, as an east-coast threat to the dominance of the Old Firm. All neutral opinion wished that it could be so.

Meanwhile, the Dandy Dons arrived home to a tumultuous welcome, travelling down Union Street in their open-topped bus, setting the pattern for many similar scenes in the years ahead. The reception in the city centre was a prelude to the demonstration at Pittodrie, where 20,000 people sunbathed for hours until the team arrived.

One by one the players were announced to the crowd as they trotted out to acknowledge individual acclaim. First, captain Willie Miller, then Bobby Clark and so through the roll of special honour. Last player out was the man who had held a hero's place at Pittodrie for most of a decade. Sadly, Joe Harper had been out of the picture with a bad injury but he was not forgotten as he ran out to the scene of his earlier glories.

In that hour of triumph there was sadness not just for Joe Harper but for the fact that the supporters were seeing Steve Archibald almost certainly for the last time in the club colours. The dashing forward, who had blossomed towards international recognition since coming from Clyde, would soon be on his way to the greater rewards of Tottenham Hotspur. The transfer was already in motion and the chants of 'Stevie must stay!' came more in hope than expectation.

He looked embarrassed that he couldn't give the supporters the answer they wanted. On a gala day of informality, the Dons gave the crowd a sample of their training session, with Scotland's Player of the Year, Gordon Strachan, entertaining in goal.

With hindsight, we scribes should have kept a few superlatives in reserve, since what was happening that late spring day of 1980 was just the preliminary round of the Golden Age. We would need our excessive language in years to come; but who was to know? We lived for the moment, a truly glorious moment, and new forms of phraseology could test our talents at a later stage.

There was just one curious footnote to that memorable season, which was to surface much later. When Alex Ferguson came to write the first of his memoirs, *A Light in the North*, he speculated on whether or not Aberdeen would have won the league championship if Joe Harper had been fit. While acknowledging the talents of the little buzz-bomb who had become one of the all-time folk-heroes of Pittodrie, Ferguson made it clear that he had reservations.

By then, Fergie had established himself as the greatest folk-hero of them all and his assessment no doubt had the benefit of wisdom and insight. But considering the wee man's pedestal position in the hearts of a generation, I wonder how many would have agreed with Fergie's view?

To them, Joe Harper may have had a bit of a weight problem but he had that knack of creating a chance from very little and stirring the crowd with a sudden flash of individual flair. To fine effect, Harper managed to harness that low centre of gravity when turning in the penalty-box – and established a record with his 199 goals during two spells at Pittodrie.

49

LIVERPOOL LESSON

I F the dramatic events of 1980 gave promise of greater things to come, the surge towards the Golden Age of Pittodrie suffered an early hiccup. Season 1980–81 had started where the previous one left off – on an emotional high which landed a trophy before the season had even properly begun. A compressed Drybrough Cup competition reached its final on the first Saturday of August with a Hampden occasion scarcely worthy of the name.

A mere 7,000 people saw the Dons take on St Mirren, who were leading by a penalty goal with only seventeen minutes left. Then Gordon Strachan took command, made ground on the right and crossed for Drew Jarvie to head the equaliser. The winner brought a moment of glory for Steve Cowan, one of Fergie's boys from Love Street days, who scored against his old club with one of those long-range shots that delight the fans.

Next day the league championship flag was unfurled at Pittodrie by Alex Fletcher, the government minister, as a preliminary to a match with Arsenal who had come north to mark the official opening of the roofing for the south-side customers. The Gunners had recently been FA Cup finalists, suffering the double disappointment of being beaten at Wembley and also in the European Cup Winners' Cup final – on penalties. The Dons added to the misery and gave hint of their new-found aspirations by defeating them 2–1.

But that was about as much as you could say about season 1980–81, except that it became a learning process for the future. Handing out the lesson was none other than Liverpool, who were to be the Dons' round-two opponents in the European Cup – a contest to which Aberdeen had finally been admitted, having been done out of the pleasure exactly twenty-five years earlier when their right of entry as league champions was set aside in favour of Hibs, as discussed in the earlier chapter.

In 1980, Austria Vienna were despatched in the first round and the scene was set for the stiffest test of all, against the English supremos whose players included Ray Clemence, Alan Hansen, Kenny Dalglish and Graeme Souness. Cup-tie fever which had gripped the North-east in the build-up to the first-leg match at Pittodrie turned swiftly to stunned silence when, during John McMaster's absence for treatment, Liverpool's McDermott chipped the ball past Jim Leighton for the only goal of the game.

McMaster resumed and was starting on one of his mazy, diagonal runs towards the Beach End, beating one man after another, when he was felled by a high tackle from Ray Kennedy in what turned out to be one of the worst football injuries ever seen. Not only was McMaster put out of the game for a whole year but there were serious doubts if he would ever walk properly again. Incredibly, Kennedy was not even booked for his indiscretion and his name retained unpleasant connotations with Aberdeen people for many years.

Before the decade was out, however, the poor man was deserving of sympathy when he fell victim to Parkinson's disease and faced a bleak future of disablement. Miraculously, John McMaster did recover in time to share the plaudits of another day.

Liverpool emphasised their superiority in the return leg at Anfield with a 4–0 win which left the Dons in some despair. When you remember that that same season brought injury to long-serving goalkeeper Bobby Clark (making way for twenty-one-year-old Jim Leighton) and that Gordon Strachan, quickly becoming the creative inspiration of the team, suffered an injury in December which put him out of the game until the following season, you realise it was not Aberdeen's year, even if they did finish as runners-up to Celtic in the League.

50
ROBSON ON THE RUN

L IVERPOOL had been reigning supreme in English football, but
they were now being challenged by an Ipswich side fashioned
by Bobby Robson. The men from Portman Road had just won the
UEFA Cup and had taken over as leaders of the First Division when
they found themselves defending their European trophy in a first-
round tie with Aberdeen.

It was not a prospect to fill them with alarm but there was an
element of surprise about the Robson eyebrows when his team was
held to a 1–1 draw at Ipswich, the equalising goal for Aberdeen
coming from the emerging talent of John Hewitt. With touches of
that southern arrogance which irks the Scots, Bobby Robson
expressed doubts if Aberdeen could play any better. The presump-
tion was therefore that his own team would step up its performance
and win through to the second round.

Pittodrie was acquiring a taste for the big occasion. In a buzz of
excitement, the crowds streamed down Merkland Road East to see
if the UEFA Cup holders could be toppled. Penalties from Gordon
Strachan and John Wark maintained the deadlock at half-time but
it is the second period that will linger long in North-east minds.

Alex Ferguson had signed another of his Paisley discoveries, the
hugely talented but highly sensitive Peter Weir, who had been struggling to shake off the yoke of his £300,000 transfer fee. Suddenly,
in that second period Weir began to show his real power, running
at Mick Mills with such tantalising skill as to throw the international
defender into total confusion. Thus Peter Weir scored for Aberdeen,
a welcome event tempered only by the thought that an Ipswich

equaliser would put them through on the away-goal rule.

At a press conference afterwards Robson said he had been confident that that would still happen, even with only ten minutes to play. Peter Weir had different ideas. Running once more at Mills, he sealed the match for Aberdeen with a third goal, which not only dismissed the Cup holders in the very first round but rang early bells across Europe that a team from the North-east of Scotland was on its way. The Liverpool lesson had not been wasted on Ferguson and his men.

Next came the Rumanian team Arges Pitesti, which was despatched over the two legs but not before the Dons had to retrieve a 2–0 deficit in the away game. John Hewitt scored in both legs.

The greatest test of that season was to come in the third round, from the strong-running Hamburg, favourites for the trophy now that Ipswich were out. Could Aberdeen repeat the medicine for the German team? Making his European debut, Eric Black scored first for Aberdeen at Pittodrie before a harmless throw-out from Leighton to Kennedy produced an incredible mix-up which let Hamburg through to equalise. Andy Watson and John Hewitt restored the Aberdeen lead and it looked as if they might score more goals for a memorable victory, when Hamburg netted a second.

Although that goal put Aberdeen in a precarious position for the return match, Gordon Strachan was later to assess that Pittodrie night as the finest team performance in which he had ever participated. Hamburg clinched the second leg by 3–1, spurred on by that immortal of the soccer stage, Franz Beckenbauer, who had been with the German team in the 1966 World Cup final at Wembley and was still in command on the European field fifteen years later.

Even though the Dons were out in the third round, their tidal ebb of the previous season had turned to flow a little further into the European experience of 1981–82. A new sense of ambition was running through the corridors of Pittodrie.

In view of the chain of events that would catapult Aberdeen into football history, it is interesting to pinpoint a January day of 1982 when it all began unexpectedly at Fir Park, Motherwell. That was the day the Dons set out on the Scottish Cup trail. The match would have been eminently forgettable except that this young man Hewitt set some kind of record by scoring the only goal of the game in just 9.6 seconds from kick-off.

The second round brought Celtic to Pittodrie, where an incredible overhead kick by you-know-who sent the Dons on their way to further rounds with Kilmarnock and St Mirren before they prepared to face Rangers in the final. As excitement built up in the customary way, the players were training at Cruden Bay on the Thursday before the final when Alex McLeish gained possession on the edge of the penalty area and curved a beautiful shot into the far corner of the net. That was the stuff they needed on Saturday.

When the great day came – a day that would determine who would compete in the European Cup Winners' Cup of 1982–83 – John McDonald put Rangers ahead and sent the Ibrox legions into full song. As the Dons fought back, Alex McLeish appeared on the edge of the Rangers penalty area, with Gordon Strachan screaming for the pass. But no. Alex remembered Cruden Bay and, in an action-replay of his training feat, he curved the ball past Jim Stewart for the equaliser. That was how it stood at full-time.

So to extra time, an experience not relished by those who meet the Old Firm. The thought was there that while Rangers had won the Scottish Cup many times, Aberdeen had won it only twice. Three minutes after the re-start, however, Gordon Strachan lofted a ball into the path of Mark McGhee, who headed the Dons into the lead.

Ten minutes later, the strong-running McGhee returned the compliment by jinking along the by-line, beating Alex Miller and nutmegging John McClelland before passing across goal to Gordon Strachan, who guided the ball into the net. His somersault of delight remains a precious memory for Dons fans.

It was clearly Aberdeen's day and, as the Ibrox fans drained away to their watering-holes, the result was sewn up in the craziest of fashions. As Colin Jackson made a short pass-back to Jim Stewart, the Rangers keeper had to run out to kick clear. His kick rebounded off the advancing Neale Cooper and went spinning towards his own goal. The fair-haired Aberdonian ran past him and drove the fourth into an empty net with relish.

The Dons had now won the Scottish Cup for the third time. The first success had been in 1947, under the captaincy of Frank Dunlop, when the score was 2–1 against Hibs; the second in 1970, when they were led by twenty-one-year-old Martin Buchan to a 3–1 win over Celtic; and the third in 1982, when the trophy was collected by Willie Miller.

Ironically, the biggest victory of all, that 4–1 drubbing of Rangers, was the only one which needed extra time. More importantly, the Dons would be playing in next year's European Cup Winners' Cup competition.

51

PITTODRIE'S GREATEST NIGHT

APART from the natural optimism at the start of a new season, Aberdonians had very little sense of what might lie in store for them before the spring of 1983 was over. There is no crystal ball in football's locker, yet Alex Ferguson felt it in his bones that greatness beckoned.

For lesser mortals, the season kicked off on 17 August, more in hope than expectation, with a League Cup match against the bogey team of Morton. A predictable 2–2 draw at Cappielow was secured with an equalising goal from that inimitable character of Greenock, Andy Ritchie.

The following week, the little-known Sion of Switzerland came to Pittodrie for a preliminary round of the European Cup Winners' Cup and, in a 7–0 drubbing, the scoring honours for Aberdeen were spread among Black, Strachan, Simpson, McGhee, Kennedy and Hewitt.

At the start of what would be an historic season, it is worth looking at the composition of the Dons team: Leighton; Kennedy, McMaster; Simpson, McLeish, Miller; Strachan, Black, McGhee, Bell, Hewitt. Weir and Rougvie were substitutes.

The return leg in Switzerland was remembered less for Aberdeen's 4–1 win than for the fact that the team had never played in such a picturesque setting. Even the hard-nosed Fergie found time to reflect with poetic eloquence that his heart had been stirred by the Alpine splendour, with the twinkling lights of mountain villages providing a memorable backdrop to the progress of Aberdeen Football Club.

Fergie's poetic prose gave way to Anglo-Saxon bluntness on the Saturday, however, when the Dons kicked off their league programme with a defeat at Tannadice. Before the season was finished, that same Dundee United would dismiss Aberdeen from the League Cup and pip them by a single point for the championship. But there were other glories on offer.

All attention that season was focused on the European scene. The Dons were drawn in the first round proper against Tirana, the capital-city team from the hard-line communist country of Albania. John Hewitt, who was to become known as Super Sub for his uncanny ability to come off the bench and score vital goals, made it 1–0 at Pittodrie before a goalless draw in Albania took the Dons through to a second-round meeting with Lech Poznan of Poland.

Goals by Peter Weir and Mark McGhee at home and Dougie Bell in Poland put Aberdeen into the quarter-finals of a European competition for the first time. Only now was there a sense of coming up against the élite of Europe although there was to be a four-month gap between that November game in Poland and the next one in March.

The December draw left plenty of time for planning ahead, not least for the supporters who might wish to be present on some foreign field in case a moment of history was about to be made. That wish was not to be diminished by the news that Aberdeen's opponents were the powerful Bayern Munich, whose teamsheet included such famous players as Augenthaler, Breitner, Hoeness and Rumminegge.

The first leg was played in Munich and, if a 0–0 scoreline suggests something negative, the truth of that early March evening was very different. These are extracts from the report I despatched to the *Sunday Standard*:

> The lingering roar of celebration which rang around the great Olympic Stadium of Munich was more than a joyous expression of 1500 Aberdonians. It also marked the entry of Aberdeen FC into that upper echelon of continental football, with the announcement

that this city which is already the oil capital of Europe is now set to take its place with the best of them.

All the years of promise and disappointment were finally put aside as the Dons took on the legendary Bayern Munich on their own ground and taught them a lesson in the arts of the game.

Of course it was a night with an historical omen. The pitch on which this memorable game was played out marks the exact spot where Neville Chamberlain's plane touched down for his crucial meeting with Hitler in 1938. There may have been no 'peace in our time' for the Aberdeen defence as the Germans came at them in raids of growing desperation but, to quote Mr Chamberlain's successor, this was indeed their finest hour.

Curiously, against all the odds, you could sense the possibility of success from the time we all set out from Aberdeen on the Tuesday morning. It was the first time the Dons had taken more than a plane-load of supporters to a foreign fixture and as they boarded four jets (suitably painted in the original black-and-gold of Aberdeen) a feeling of unusual optimism was buzzing all over the airport.

By Tuesday evening the supporters had announced their arrival, not only in the beer-halls but, believe it or not, in the Bavarian State Opera House. Along with music buffs Robert Thomson and Bill Brown (Pittodrie season-ticket holders who lived in Glasgow) I found myself watching a spectacular production of Wagner's 'Lohengrin' in the sheer opulence of an opera house where elegant ladies dripped with diamonds.

We crossed the street, from the Opera House to the Hofbrauhaus, Munich's most famous beer-hall where Hitler used to gather with his cronies when they were cooking up the Nazi Party in the 1920s. That bustling beer-hall already belonged to the red-and-white scarves as Aberdonians raised their massive steins and sang 'The Northern Lights' as an alternative to the jolly rhythms of the oompah-oompah brass band. At least one puzzled German was hailed with the tradi-tional North-east greeting of 'Fit like, Fritz?'

As to the match itself, Aberdeen fans may not have seen their team move forward in the accustomed style. They may not have recognised the role of their current hero, Peter Weir. But who could argue with a team which not only stopped the great Bayern from scoring on their own ground but might well have scored themselves on at least three occasions?

After the match the focal point was the Sheraton Hotel, where the players mixed with supporters in the lounge bar, enjoying a quiet glass of beer. Two American oilmen who had worked in Aberdeen and had flown in from Cairo and Tunisia for the night, paid their own tribute. It was the least they could do for 'mighty fine people' they said. There might still be a long way to go in the second leg but, in Munich at least, Aberdeen had won 0–0.

The scene was therefore set for what was potentially the greatest night Pittodrie had ever seen. Having reached the quarter-finals in Europe, one more game could take the Dons to the penultimate stage of the competition. Was it too much to expect? They had prevented Bayern from scoring at home so why should they permit them greater licence elsewhere?

The excitement built up to unprecedented levels as the crowd converged on Pittodrie that March night of 1983. Within ten minutes, however, Bayern had shown what a dangerous team they could be when Breitner slipped a free kick to Augenthaler, whose thirty-yard shot merely touched Jim Leighton's fingers on the way to the net. Hopes were restored before half-time, however, when McGhee timed a perfect cross to Eric Black, whose header was blocked by Augenthaler. As Bayern's scorer made a second attempt at clearing, Neil Simpson ran in to equalise.

That half-time score would be enough to take the Germans through to the semi-finals, a possibility increased in the second half when Pflugler scored with one of those long-range, swerving shots in which continentals seemed to specialise. Pittodrie went quiet. Heads went down. Not even an equalising goal would save Aberdeen now. It would take two to reach the semi-final and what kind of crazy optimist would bet on that happening with only fifteen minutes left to play?

Alex Ferguson had already reacted by sending on his two substitutes, John Hewitt and John McMaster, replacing Stuart Kennedy and Neil Simpson. Without being wise after the event, Gordon Strachan maintained he had a strong sense of something about to happen. When you combined his own genius with that of John

McMaster, something was always liable to happen anyway. This is how Strachan remembered the subsequent events:

> With fifteen minutes left I was fouled to the right of the German penalty area at the King Street end. As we placed the ball for the free kick, John McMaster and I remembered that, though our double act was well known in Scotland, the Germans had probably never heard of it. Big Alex McLeish got the message and ran up to his spot in the penalty area.
>
> John and I started our run, bumped together, pretended to blame each other and turned away as if in disarray. That's the moment when I turned back quickly, apparently without looking where I was putting the ball, and chipped it to the spot where Alex McLeish was stationed. We had practised it dozens of times. With Bayern's defence still wondering what was happening, Alex rose like a bird and angled his header out of Muller's reach.

Pittodrie went wild. Back in business at 2–2, it would take just one more goal to see the Dons through. Were the gods on their side? The answer came within a minute. From the re-start, John McMaster gained possession and prepared for one of his long, left-foot lobs towards the Bayern goal area.

Eric Black was already in position to head towards Muller's right-hand side. The keeper did well to reach the ball at all, but managed only to palm it towards . . . who else but the enigmatic John Hewitt, who could wander mysteriously out of a game but just as quickly appear from nowhere at the vital moment. With consummate skill, John brought the ball down and sent it through the legs of the keeper as he sought to recover balance.

Pittodrie erupted but there were still thirteen minutes to play, and at least one moment of anxiety when Rumminegge threatened to spoil the party. The game in Munich may have been the cool, technical display, but in Aberdeen, when the referee drew breath for that final whistle, the grand old stadium witnessed an explosion of enthusiasm, confirming that 16 March 1983 was beyond all measure of doubt Pittodrie's greatest-ever occasion. I tried to capture the essence of it at the time, going over the top with verbal extravagance

for which I offer no apology. It was how we felt in the hour of glory.
This was the report:

> It went without saying that Wednesday's European epic produced the
> greatest, most emotional occasion in eighty years of Pittodrie history.
> Having danced in the streets until the early hours, wrung-out rags
> were trying to rehabilitate themselves as people and restore some
> rationale to a topsy-turvy world.
>
> Thursday was for throat lozenges as even the most nostalgic
> diehard conceded that, whatever periods of greatness had punctu-
> ated the Pittodrie story, no team from times remembered could stand
> comparison with the present squad. By the same token, their creator,
> Alex Ferguson, stands out as the most successful manager by far.
> Memorable talents like Charlie Cooke, Jimmy Smith and Zoltan Varga
> have peppered the Pittodrie story with artistry but no team has
> combined attractive football with the kind of drive, commitment and
> final achievement of these men of the eighties.
>
> Behind that team and its manager lies a boardroom structure
> which could be taken as a model of how to run a football club. Indeed,
> after their 3–2 defeat on Wednesday, officials of Bayern Munich
> expressed envy at the tightly run, three-man board arrangement,
> with its own compact ground providing more noise and atmosphere
> from a 25,000 crowd than they can muster from 50,000 in the vast
> Olympic Stadium, where they are only sharing tenants.
>
> With native shrewdness, millionaire Dick Donald runs the show
> quietly and efficiently, with vice-chairman Chris Anderson and Dick's
> own son Ian, all former professional footballers, providing able
> support. As the men of vision who have given Aberdeen the first all-
> seated and covered stadium in Britain and many other innovations
> as well, they took the congratulations of Wednesday evening with
> the modesty of men who know their business.
>
> But even they were showing beads of sweat in the aftermath of
> that European classic. And little wonder. For this was the kind of
> night to be talked about in fifty years from now, the night when people
> all over Europe were trying to find Aberdeen on the map, curious
> about a side which could rise from the dead, with fifteen minutes to
> play, and deliver a killer punch to the legendary Bayern of Munich.
>
> For those of us seeking to distil the memory of a great Scottish

occasion, assorted pictures keep flitting across the video-screen of the mind, like half-remembered dreams and nightmares. Shall we ever forget the cool, Teutonic precision of the Munich machine with its chilling art of suddenly converting half a chance into a lethal shot? What about the inspiration of Alex Ferguson in bringing on that foot-balling genius John McMaster as the substitute who changed the course of the game?

Or the hunch which made him produce young John Hewitt as another replacement to forge delirium from despair with the winning goal? When it was all over, we stayed to demand a lap of honour and to cling to one of football's finer moments. As the joy eventually flooded through the streets of the Granite City in rivulets of red, one of the focal points of celebration was the pub of former Dons player Jimmy Wilson, who was holding a fund-raising night for the blind. It was a fair measure of the exclusive preoccupation of an incredible night that the gyrations of a sexy lady disrobing to the raucous rasp of 'The Stripper' was hard put to divert doughty men from their Pittodrie post-mortem.

But in the end the analyses were exhausted, the emotions truly spent. Grown men who had believed that Roy of the Rovers belonged to fiction might have disputed the fact, if only they could have raised the energy. It would be time enough in the morning, after a restless sleep of action replays, to accept that their team had really joined the European élite.

We tend to suffer for euphoria in this life and the Dons came bumping back to earth on the Saturday with a home defeat by Dundee United, followed by a last-gasp win against Morton and a further home defeat by St Mirren. It was hardly the best prepara-tion for the semi-finals of the Cup Winners' Cup, in which the Dons had been drawn against one of the lesser names in Europe, Waterschei of Belgium.

From the town of Genk, Waterschei had quietly built a work-manlike side which was making up in effectiveness for what it lacked in glamour. They had come a long way from their origins in the 1920s, when they were founded by local coalminers, but were only just breaking into the European scene. Good reports preceded them and Aberdeen were faced not only with a slump in their own performance but the secret fear of going out to an unfashionable team when they had already disposed of a giant.

For the first leg at Pittodrie, Alex Ferguson decided to bring back Dougie Bell, prompted by a slight twinge of conscience at having left him out of the second Bayern match when the gangling, mercurial wizard of dribble had performed so well in the first. Fergie's instincts triumphed again.

No sooner had the game started than Bell, with that sergeant-major gait of his, gained possession and proceeded to take on the Waterschei defence on his own. There are still doubts about whether his parting ball was meant to be a pass or a shot. Either way, it streaked diagonally for the right-hand post at the King Street end and Eric Black arrived in time to slide home the first goal.

Before Waterschei had time to draw breath, the Dons scored again through the sheer determination of Neil Simpson, who survived three tackles to send a low shot into the net. The match had been running for only four minutes. The Belgians stabilised the situation until the interval and showed how dangerous a side they could be.

In the second half, however, Doug Bell launched himself on another of his extraordinary forays, leaving Mark McGhee to complete the third goal. Waterschei scored before Peter Weir restored the three-goal lead and the final score was settled at 5–1 during an incredible goalmouth scramble, when the ball seemed net-bound on four occasions before McGhee, now lying on the ground, managed to scoop it in.

No one doubted then that Aberdeen were set for the greatest event in their eighty years of history. The return tie in Belgium would surely be a formality but before then the Dons had to face Celtic in the semi-final of the Scottish Cup. The Celts were battling for both League and Cup, eventually losing out in both, so there was a lot of Parkhead pride to play for that day at Hampden.

It turned into a rough-house of an occasion with Aberdeen, just three days away from the Waterschei match, sustaining injuries to Gordon Strachan, Eric Black, Dougie Bell and Neale Cooper. Cooper had to be taken to Glasgow Victoria Infirmary while Bell's injury was to have a disastrous effect on his European hopes. All four missed out on the Belgian game, which Aberdeen lost 1–0, a minor matter which niggled as the only defeat on that European adventure but did nothing to alter the most exciting football prospect Aberdonians had ever known. The Dons were in a European final for the first time!

52

THE GLORY OF GOTHENBURG

W ELL before the semi-final was over, Aberdonians were making their arrangements for the European final. 'Are ye gyan tae Gothenburg?' became the most common question around the North-east and far beyond, as the Dons had gathered a remarkable number of new-found supporters.

Yes, they were going to Gothenburg all right, with much perusal of Scandinavian maps to see exactly where the damned place was. The majority would go by air – fifty plane-loads as it turned out – while the P & O ferry *St Clair* was drafted in to cruise across the North Sea with 500 supporters. Many went by car and coach, using the English ferry crossings to the continent before heading north to Sweden.

Personal stories abounded. An Aberdonian policeman in Edinburgh, Bryan Farquharson, a fanatical Dons supporter, had a typical story to tell. With a car-load of friends he set out from Edinburgh at 5 p.m. on the Monday, heading for Ramsgate and the Tuesday morning ferry to Dunkirk. A strike diverted them to the Dover–Calais crossing and Bryan was navigating his driver through Belgium, Holland and Germany towards Denmark when he realised they were running short of time to catch the ferry to Sweden.

As the car accelerated, under the direction of the policeman, they ran into a speed trap and were fine £70 on the spot by the local constabulary! Worse still, they missed the ferry but they managed to catch the last possible crossing to be in time for the match.

In the euphoric exodus, there was time to spare a thought for two men who had played a significant part in the Aberdeen advance of recent years. Dougie Bell, exciting ball-player with a temperament for the big occasion, was virtually out of contention for the final. The injury news was even worse for right-back Stuart Kennedy, a forceful character in the Pittodrie dressing room, who had seriously damaged his knee against Waterschei in Belgium. In one single stroke of misfortune, Stuart's career with Aberdeen came abruptly to an end. Such is the cruelty of fate.

Alex Ferguson put him on the bench at Gothenburg to give him a chance of a European medal. The substitutes' bench could not hold a second invalid, however, and the manager thought Bell might at least have another chance. Medals would therefore be going to some who had as yet played no part in the campaign at all and that seemed a poor sort of justice.

The sense of an army on the move gathered momentum that May weekend as the North-east prepared for the trip to Gothenburg. Before flying out on the very first plane from Dyce on the Monday morning, I was asked to set the scene for the *Evening Express*. This is an excerpt:

> As we stand on the eve of Gothenburg, by far the greatest event in the eighty years of Aberdeen Football Club, I doubt if too many of us have grasped the full significance of where we are going or what we are doing. For this is no mere walk to Pittodrie or bus journey to darkest Glasgow.
>
> This is the day when we set out in our thousands by aeroplane, ferry-boat or warship, as well as car, bus and bicycle, to meet the greatest club name in the history of world football – at a level of the game where few Scottish players have been privileged to compete.
>
> To say we are poised for the greatest occasion many of us will ever know may be tempting providence and running against the grain of North-east caution, which generally counsels us to 'flee laich, flee lang'. But to hell with caution! What time is this to 'flee laich' when we have already flown into the heights of the European élite and may be standing just ninety minutes away from the applause of a television audience estimated at around 800 million?

Of course, the Dons may lose but if we don't savour the moment now, when can we ever? It is wonderful just to be there. If someone had told us in September that the glamorous Cup winners of Europe, all the way from Scotland to the Soviet Union, from the Baltic to the Mediterranean, would knock each other out in furious competition and that the great Real Madrid would be left to face the Dons in the final, we would have directed him to a good psychiatrist. But it happened . . . and now I'm on my way to Dyce. Gothenburg, here we come!

Aberdeen Airport that Monday morning was a seething mass of red and white, a concourse of throbbing anticipation as one plane-load after another was called to the departure lounge and duty-free allowances were bought up for the great spree ahead. The Gothenburg airlift was on its way, a modest journey which soon had us flying over Scandinavian forests and losing height on the approaches to the airport.

In that *Express* article, I had paused to remember absent friends, those who had followed the Dons all their days but had not lived to see this. What would the late Jimmy Forbes of the *Evening Express* have been writing on this historic occasion? What would that other memorable colleague George 'Chrys' Chrystal have been preparing for his loveable cartoon creation, Wee Alickie?

Among those who later responded with their own experiences, none expressed the feeling better than Mrs Mary Gardner from Gray Street, Aberdeen. In this condensed version of her graphic letter to me she gives a striking picture of a woman's point of view:

In deciding we were going to the final, there was no thought in our minds as to who would look after the children, how we could afford it and so on. We were going, come what may! From the moment we touched down in that lovely city the welcome the Swedes gave us was quite overwhelming. There was no doubt who they would be supporting at the Ullevi Stadium. Our first stop on arrival had been at the stadium to savour the place. Workmen were putting finishing touches here and there and, as we watched, it was hard to imagine how this eerie, empty stadium would generate an electrifying excitement.

Wednesday came and the centre of Gothenburg was hotting up with the arrival of more fans. Familiar songs were being sung in the shopping precincts, new friends were being made, old acquaintances renewed. There was a continuous cluster of interest around the window of the bank where the coveted European trophy was on display. By afternoon the brief shopping spree was behind us (I had bought a tear-proof mascara which could come in handy that night!). I tried to grab a few hours' rest in preparation for the big match but sleep was impossible through sheer excitement.

I had been too young to understand and only now, in thinking of my late father, was I becoming aware of what a huge part this Aberdeen Football Club had played in his life. What would he have had to say today about a daughter of his going all the way to Sweden to follow the game which had deprived her of so much of his attention all those years ago? I smiled a quiet smile and felt I was here for him too.

That was how Gothenburg affected people. On the day before the match I wandered on to the pitch of Ullevi, an oddly designed stadium which was built for the World Cup finals held in Sweden in 1958. The eighteen-year-old Pelé gained his first World Cup winners' medal, scoring twice in Brazil's defeat of the host country but not in this stadium.

As the Dons went through a training session on a pleasant afternoon, onlookers took snapshots of casual little groups. My album contains one of Dons vice-chairman Chris Anderson, journalist Hugh McIlvanney and Scotland manager Jock Stein, who was lending a quiet word of advice here and there to Alex Ferguson, giving the benefit of his vast experience.

Everyone, it seemed, had come to Gothenburg on this great family outing. North-east journalist Jim Naughtie had managed to flee the confines of Westminster and appeared at the bar of the Europa Hotel, which was the centre of all Aberdeen activity. My youngest son, Martin, had finished his highers in Glasgow on the Tuesday, jumped on a bus north and caught the last plane from Aberdeen Airport to Gothenburg.

The carnival atmosphere built up until there was no doubt that the Swedish city belonged to Aberdeen. Locals stood back, mesmerised by the good-humoured invasion, then joined in with the tidal wave of red and white which seemed to generate a conviction that there could be only one result on the night.

That matter, however, would be resolved in the football arena and nowhere else. On second thoughts, privately entertained, were Aberdeen really capable of keeping this kind of company? That thought was allowed to drown in the deluge that descended from dark and thunderous skies as the hour of the match drew near.

The Aberdeen party was already on its way to the stadium by coach, tense and tight as bowstrings, some cutting themselves off from reality with Sony Walkman headsets, listening to the music and glancing nervously at the lightning that flashed across an ugly sky. As the fans made their way to Ullevi, the 12,000 or more Aberdonians out-numbering the Spaniards four to one, groundsmen began to haul away the massive tarpaulins which had surely saved the match from being postponed that night. As articulate in words as in his football artistry, Gordon Strachan neatly observed the dressing-room situation:

> In strange surroundings we changed into our familiar strip and realised that the great moment was ever so near now. An unusual hush descended on the dressing room as everyone went into his own thoughts, maybe his own prayers, and we just sat looking at each other.
>
> It was not until five minutes before we were due to take the field that reality returned. That was the moment when we all started screaming and shouting, like a bunch of schoolboys. Alex McLeish is always shouting. The lads began to shake hands and wish each other all the best. My style is to tell the boys to enjoy themselves above all else. I looked at the lads – Neale Cooper, Neil Simpson, Eric Black and John Hewitt – and wondered what was going through their young minds.
>
> The boss gave us his final words. All the planning was over now, he said. It was up to us out there in the Ullevi Stadium of Gothenburg.

Suddenly a bell rang and that was our signal to leave the dressing room. Out we trooped to line up in the tunnel and that was a curious experience. For we were standing just an arm's length from the Real Madrid players, across the passage, side by side, casting an odd glance at each other but never exchanging as much as a smile. This was time for serious battle. No time to be fraternising with the enemy.

Out they came, the all-red of Aberdeen, all-white of Real Madrid, in that parallel procession which brings a lump to the throat on great occasions. The eleven young men who lined up for Aberdeen were: Jim Leighton, Doug Rougvie, John McMaster, Neale Cooper, Alex McLeish, Willie Miller, Gordon Strachan, Neil Simpson, Mark McGhee, Eric Black, Peter Weir.

The formalities over, the game was soon in progress and in seven minutes the Dons were a goal ahead. Strachan took a corner on the right, and McLeish came up to power the ball goalwards with his head; it was blocked near the line but Eric Black swung round to drive it into the net.

The joy was short-lived. In attempting a pass-back to Jim Leighton, Alex McLeish misjudged the heavy ground and the ball drew up in the water. The dashing Santillana appeared from nowhere to accept the gift and was brought down in the box by the desperate efforts of Leighton. Juanito scored from the penalty spot and the rest of normal time was fought out on that basis.

Real were managed by their former playing star, Alfredo di Stefano, whose rather cynical approach to the game was revealed in his subsequent criticism of his own players. During extra time, he said, Real had attacked too much: 'They did not do what I told them to do. What I was hoping for was a result through penalties.'

Although Aberdeen had played well enough to win, the experienced Spaniards were clear favourites if it came to a penalty shoot-out. Matters seemed to be going their way when the teams started the second period of extra time. Just fifteen minutes left to avoid the sudden-death decision. Eric Black had gone limping off and on came the man who symbolised memorable moments in Cup dramas, young John Hewitt. Could he do it again?

In some ways, this had been Peter Weir's night. Once again the cultured left-winger managed to draw the attention of three Real players as he hovered near the dug-out. Then off he set, beating two of them before chipping a perfect ball to Mark McGhee down the left touchline. To the great credit of his skill, strength and determination, McGhee rounded his marker and crossed into the penalty box.

The Real goalkeeper, Augustin, came out to intercept the square-cut cross, missed it by inches – and who was running in on his own to head into an empty net but the man of destiny himself, twenty-year-old John Hewitt. As he wheeled to the right, performing a Middlefield version of the Highland Fling, he was acclaimed by the crowd as a hero yet again. He had started it all on a January day in 1982, with that nine-second goal at Motherwell, and he had finished the job sixteen months later in the faraway venue of Gothenburg.

There were still eight minutes to go and Real were soon awarded a free kick just outside the penalty area. The ball was blocked but the referee gave them a second chance because they hadn't waited for the whistle. This would surely be their last chance to secure their penalty shoot-out and the Aberdeen players lined up, desperate to foil them.

Gordon Strachan was suddenly aware of a prayer being intoned behind him: 'Please God, don't let them score. They don't deserve it!' In his infinite mercy, the good Lord cast down favours upon the red sea of support and answered the prayer of a man called Peter, who sought no more than justice. The Real player shot that free kick past the post and there was time for only a goal kick before the referee blew his whistle.

The Dandy Dons of Pittodrie had done it! Whereas they had once reached only for the heights of Scottish football – and arrived there very rarely – they had now adjusted their sights to the pinnacles of Europe and beaten the best that that continent could provide.

More immediately, they sparked off such a celebration as no Aberdonian had ever seen. In those gaunt stands of Ullevi we danced and sang and shouted and hugged and sought new ways of expressing ecstasy. Out there on the field, the players enjoyed their own frenzied performance as Willie Miller received the European Cup Winners' Cup and came with his team-mates to salute those faithful thousands who had come to share their finest hour.

Bedlam broke loose in that Swedish city as carefree Aberdonians splashed in the fountains. They were already drenched by the rain so what did it matter? It was reminiscent of VE night in 1945. Indeed, this *was* their VE night – a Victory in Europe which had come the way of Aberdeen Football Club for the first time ever and might not be repeated in a lifetime. That tear-proof mascara had come in handy for Mary Gardner.

When we had wrung out the last ounce of joyous expression from wilting bodies and drifted briefly into a sleep where dreams could not improve upon reality, there was the stirring of a grey dawn and a fleet of aeroplanes awaiting the red army to return us to the home shores like foot soldiers back from a victorious war.

My report for the *Sunday Standard* that weekend read:

As the city of Gothenburg sank out of sight and I sipped champagne from that Cup on the team plane home, it was time to close an eye and seek to clarify the dream of a thousand memories.

Finally convinced that there would be no waking up to some cruel joke, I could still see those 12,000 magnificent fans singing in the rain, dancing in the streets, putting the final touches to the greatest night of their lives.

I remember the agonies of those final minutes when injustice was still a possibility, and then the final explosion of relief, a moment when Aberdeen's biggest bookmaker, Bobby Morrison, stood beside me with tears in his eyes, not because of the money he had lost but through genuine emotion – no more than a symbol of all those granite men around him now, unashamedly admitting the softness of their hearts.

But when they dimmed the lights of Ullevi Stadium around 11 o'clock on Wednesday night and the Pittodrie party returned to their village headquarters of Farshatt Hotel, outside Gothenburg, it was there that some gems came dancing out as a gift to the collector of memories. For here was a scene of controlled celebration, totally in keeping with the reservation of the Aberdeen character.

When the players arrived back with the trophy, hotel guests suspended everything to form a guard of honour and applauded as Alex Ferguson and his men proceeded to the banqueting room. Here was a Government Minister, Alex Fletcher, proposing the toast and a leading European official talking from knowledge of the great clubs of the world and saying he had never known one with such a wonderful family atmosphere as Aberdeen.

Here was vice-chairman Chris Anderson, one of the great architects of football administration, moving from table to table in the role of discreet host. Here, too, was Dick Donald, who first arrived at Pittodrie as a player in 1928 and, fifty-five years later, was savouring his finest moment. He had not had a chance to speak to his captain, Willie Miller, and as they came together at the self-serving buffet table, I strained to hear their first exchange, wondering if there might be some historic words on this, the greatest night of their respective lives.

Without breaking stride or diverting from the business of shovelling on a slice of ham, some salad and tatties, the doughty Dick said, 'Well well, Willie, it's been quite a night.' To which the inscrutable Willie replied, 'Ay, so it has.' Two unflappable men of sterling character had surely said it all.

Others were less restrained and, when we touched down at Dyce, emotions which were already spent had to be quickly revived to meet a welcome which defied description. I remember as a boy running up Union Street, reaching out to touch Winston Churchill as he sat in an open car after the victory of World War II. But Winnie had nothing on this day, when Aberdeen laid down its tools and formed a crowd of at least 100,000 welcomes.

Like Pied Pipers of Pittodrie, the Dons team drew thousands in their triumphal wake to the ground they call home. Among those waiting to greet them was an old man with a wistful look in his eye. The great W.K. (Stonewall) Jackson, now 83, was playing for the Dons sixty years ago and has lived through almost all there is to tell about the club. Doctors no longer allow him to attend a match but there he was, holding out his hand to young Eric Black, who clasped it with a respect and courtesy and admiration which spoke volumes for the character of the boy.

What a moment that was. Two men representing the opposite ends of the Aberdeen story but united in a simple scene which told you everything about what is good and civilised at Pittodrie. That was the final lump in the throat for those who dreamed a dream and woke up to find it was all true.

53

DONS – NUMBER ONE IN EUROPE

T HAT night of Gothenburg glory left some haunting images. There was the picture in the *Press and Journal*, taken during the match and showing a totally deserted Union Street. Every soul in Aberdeen was at a television set. That picture was brilliantly contrasted with another from two hours later, which told a very different story of crowds spilling on to the same Union Street in high celebration, with cars reportedly blasting their horns in the codes of victory.

In the grey dawn of the following morning, an old lady in a back-street hovel in London turned on her radio and heard the celebrations in Gothenburg of the previous night.

'They're singing my song,' she said to herself. And so they were. Mary Webb, the forgotten lady who composed 'The Northern Lights of Old Aberdeen', shed a tear of joy for all things Aberdonian.

By then the great airlift was under way. After a sleepless night, it was time for the heroes to return. As the 'Welcome Home' banners went up, the city prepared for such a day as it had never seen before.

Aberdonians had been to the zenith of their footballing experience, rounding off with those truly amazing scenes when the city went on unofficial holiday and filled every inch of the route, from the airport right through Bucksburn and Woodside, up Anderson Drive and down Queen's Road and Albyn Place to Union Street. The scenes continued down King Street to Pittodrie itself, a homecoming where, perhaps for the first time, a certain truth began to dawn.

For those unaccustomed to it, ecstasy needs a soft landing. When you have just been to the top, you look around and wonder where the next step might be. Even a repeat of that ecstasy might never again have quite the same flavour. The immediate prospect at Pittodrie was a game against Hibs two days later, the last league fixture of the season, when it would still be possible to take the championship if Dundee United lost on the same day.

The carnival revived on the Saturday, with the Hibs team forming a guard of honour for the new Cup champions of Europe as they ran on to the field. The Dons proceeded to win 5–0 but, in the event, Dundee United went through that afternoon to win their first ever championship by a single point over Aberdeen and Celtic, confirming the impression that the balance of power in Scottish football had at last moved eastward to the so-called New Firm.

On the following Saturday there was still the Scottish Cup final to look forward to, the finale to the Dons' most remarkable season of all. The Gothenburg eleven lined up against a Rangers team which still had an all-Scottish look about it, before the advent of manager Graeme Souness, and contained one name which would yet figure in Pittodrie's scheme of things: McCloy; Dawson, McClelland; McPherson, Paterson, Bett; Cooper, McKinnon, Clark, Russell, McDonald.

It proved to be one of the most disappointing of Cup finals, with Aberdeen coasting to a 1–0 victory through an Eric Black goal in extra time. All things are relative, no doubt, but it seemed so tame in the week after Gothenburg, with the indifferent quality of the play leaving a strange feeling of deflation.

Yet the team had won the Scottish Cup, something they had done only three times in the previous eighty years – and they had beaten Rangers into the bargain. What more could people ask for? Clearly, Aberdeen had reached new planes of expectation, tasted the exquisite flavour of life at the top, and things might never seem quite the same again.

The mediocrity of the play that day brought a public outburst from Alex Ferguson, who felt that only Willie Miller and Alex McLeish had played as he wanted, and the party repaired to the Old

Course Hotel at St Andrews for a reception that seemed more like a wake than a celebration.

Upset by the manager's tirade, Gordon Strachan made his own protest that night by getting up and leaving the function, an act that was carefully noted by the manager who later fined him £250 for the discourtesy. Strachan apologised but made the very fair point that the players had given of their best against Rangers although, quite frankly, after a season like that there wasn't very much left to give.

Some of them were due to leave immediately to join the Scottish party for the home internationals, to be followed by a Scottish tour of Canada and an Aberdeen tour of Germany. It was all too much. Alex Ferguson had the grace to apologise to his players after breakfast next morning, not having fully appreciated how the emotion of Gothenburg had affected them.

The summer passed by and before that extraordinary year of 1983 was out, the Dons had been voted Best Team in Europe in the annual award made by the sports manufacturer Adidas and the magazine *France Football*. What's more, they had the chance to prove it in the established fixture between the holders of the European Cup and the Cup Winners' Cup, by which the argument could finally be settled.

The opponents in this Super Cup contest were Hamburg, who had beaten Juventus of Italy in the final of the European Cup and had shown their greater experience when knocking Aberdeen out of the UEFA Cup in 1981.

The Dons' development as a team was to be tested as they set out for Germany in November 1983. Forcing a no-scoring draw in Hamburg, they prepared for another of those great Pittodrie occasions when a full house was assured, offering the chance of a belated night of glory for those fans who harboured regrets that they had not gone to Gothenburg.

On a wet night, Peter Weir took control and one of his surging, left-wing runs towards the King Street end produced the cross which was cut back by John Hewitt for Neil Simpson to score. A corner kick from Weir and Willie Miller side-footed the ball to Mark McGhee, who made it two. With the bandwagon rolling, it could have been five or six but the 2–0 scoreline remained and Pittodrie had produced another of its phenomenal European nights – one of the rare occasions when the winning silverware could actually be presented at the home ground.

By then the Dons had recovered from the emotional strains of Gothenburg and its anti-climax and were now sitting at the top of the Premier Division. Having mastered the giants of European football by winning the Cup Winners' Cup and the Super Cup, there was still the target of the European Cup, which had been won by a British club for the first time in 1967, when Celtic triumphed over Inter Milan in Lisbon.

The passport to that trophy would be the Premier Division championship, which must now be the main ambition. The Dons strode through that season 1983–84 majestically, winning the League by seven clear points over Celtic and conceding only eighteen goals up to the last game.

Jim Leighton was set for a league defensive record if he conceded no more than two goals but Alex Ferguson put out half a reserve team for the final fixture at Love Street and St Mirren won 3–2, still leaving the Dons with a shared defensive record but rather taking the gloss off Leighton's magnificent performance. Next season they would be poised for that European Cup contest but success was now such a familiar element at Pittodrie that there was still much to achieve in 1983–84.

Back to defend their Cup Winners' Cup of the previous season, the Dons progressed with wins over Akranes of Iceland, Beveren of Belgium and Ujpest Dosza of Hungary to find themselves, by April of 1984, once more in the semi-final. Blasé though the supporters had tended to become, there was a rekindling of enthusiasm with the realisation that only one more team stood between them and another European final.

Where was it being held this year, we all began to ask. When do they start booking the flights? The Portuguese team Porto brought a 1–0 lead from the first leg to the deciding night at Pittodrie. That seemed no great obstacle for an Aberdeen squad that had learnt to rescue deficits and turn them into triumphs. Alas, the Portuguese managed another 1–0 victory at Pittodrie and those hopes of a repeat performance disappeared in the sea mist of that night.

But one exciting goal still lay ahead. Aberdeen had never won the league and Cup double and, with the League safely tucked away, they were due to meet Celtic in the Scottish Cup final at Hampden on 19 May. Eric Black put Aberdeen in the mood with an opening goal before the game was marred by an ugly incident. Roy Aitken made such a lunge at Mark McGhee that he was sent off and the Dons faced ten determined Celts, always a difficult challenge.

In the way these patterns work, Paul McStay scored a deserved equaliser with four minutes to go and the match went into extra time. Appropriately, it was Mark McGhee, victim of the earlier incident, who scored the Dons' winner, which would also prove to be his last goal for the club.

That season's end brought the expiry of several contracts. Gordon Strachan was considered the likeliest player to test his skills at a more lucrative level. Indeed, Alex Ferguson had already anticipated his star play-maker's departure by signing Billy Stark from St Mirren, another of the players he had nurtured in his Love Street days. After much sniffing around by those agents who make a living from shaking the football kaleidoscope, Strachan was diverted from a muddle about moving to Cologne and landed instead with Manchester United, in time to be part of its FA Cup-winning team of 1985.

Mark McGhee was also rumoured to be on his way and ended up with Hamburg although the matter was mishandled by Alex Ferguson. Clearly, the Dons players had reached their moment of maximum European exposure, with a shop-window value that was likely to be at its height.

Strachan and McGhee were free agents, with special talents that were much in demand. Big Doug Rougvie hardly came into that category but he was the third member of the Gothenburg team to depart in that close season of 1984, a matter to be examined later.

So the Dons had won the much-coveted double for the first time in their history and faced season 1984–85 with such new players as Frank McDougall from St Mirren and Tommy McQueen from Clyde, joining up with Billy Stark, who had already taken his place in the team, and another significant player for the future, Stewart McKimmie from Dundee FC. An Aberdeen lad, McKimmie had been signed during the previous season, in time to win a European Super Cup medal in his very first week as a Dons player, and would take over the raiding right-back role formerly held by Stuart Kennedy (by now forced into premature retirement) and latterly by Doug Rougvie.

The Aberdeen team in that Scottish Cup final against Celtic had still retained the highly recognisable look of: Leighton; McKimmie, Rougvie; Cooper, McLeish, Miller; Strachan, Simpson, McGhee, Black, Weir. But the departure of three Gothenburg heroes alone would have altered the shape of the team and soon we were having to accustom ourselves to the sound of new permutations.

In the autumn of 1984 the team was liable to read: Leighton; McKimmie, McQueen; Stark, McLeish, Miller; Black, Simpson, McDougall, Bell, Falconer. Other variations made room for Brian Mitchell, Ian Angus, Ian Porteous, Steve Cowan and, of course, Neale Cooper, Peter Weir and John Hewitt.

No matter the permutations, the Dons struck front from the first day of the season and by the beginning of December had won fifteen of their seventeen league games, with another one drawn. The form was quite devastating. Victories by a four-goal margin were not uncommon, including a 5–1 destruction of Rangers at Pittodrie. So it went on until the last day of the season when they established a new Premier Division record of 59 points, having gone two better than the 57 points record which they had achieved in the previous season.

Somehow, that stunning performance in the League was at the expense of all else. On a bleak August night at Broomfield, the Dons were sent spinning out of the League Cup in a first-round defeat by humble Airdrie, by now under the managership of the effervescent

Ally MacLeod. The occasion is best remembered by Dons fans for the fact that they were given their first sight of a promising new signing from Stirling Albion, Brian Grant.

They did manage to reach the semi-final of the Scottish Cup, only to be despatched by Dundee United. The high hopes of reaching for the European Cup took a disastrous turn in the very first round, after they had taken a 2–1 lead against Dynamo Berlin at Pittodrie. The Germans reversed the score on their home ground and after extra time the matter went to penalties.

Glued to their radios, Aberdeen fans went through the agonies of hearing the Germans missing one of their kicks and knowing that the next Aberdeen goal would take them through to the second round. Courageous as ever, Willie Miller took the responsibility of the vital kick. It was saved and Dynamo went on to win the extended shoot-out.

Despite the European disappointment, there was a sense of astonishment that Alex Ferguson had somehow managed to ride out the inevitable destruction of his Gothenburg team and, within a year, to come up with a fresh combination capable of winning the championship. Did the man have access to some kind of magic? If so, it had not produced the potion for winning the League Cup, the only trophy to have eluded the manager in his remarkable career at Pittodrie.

That missing piece of the Ferguson jigsaw was supplied in the early weeks of season 1985–86, when Aberdeen carved their way through the League Cup contest, beating Ayr United, St Johnstone and Hearts before gaining sweet revenge on Dundee United, who had thwarted their efforts far too often in this competition. It all led up to a final at Hampden Park on Sunday, 27 October, when they met Hibs.

Within twelve minutes the inimitable John Hewitt had laid on two goals for Eric Black and Billy Stark, and a second one for Black rounded off the victory. The Dons had scored thirteen times in that Cup run without conceding a single goal.

That Hampden day was particularly poignant for the club's

vice-chairman and former player, Chris Anderson, whose description of it comes in a later chapter. For Chris, a superbly fit man still in his fifties, had been shattered by the news that he was suffering from the incurable motor neurone disease.

In the previous month, Alex Ferguson had been assisting Jock Stein in Scotland's bid to qualify for the 1986 World Cup finals when, in the moment of victory at Ninian Park, Cardiff, the Scots manager collapsed and died. Stein had been undoubtedly the greatest figure in the entire history of Scottish football, mainly as the Celtic manager who had won the European Cup with a collection of local lads of his own grooming.

Now, in the hour of tragedy, the Aberdeen board agreed that their manager, who was already developing in the Stein mould, should take on the dual role of running the Dons and taking Scotland to the World Cup finals in Mexico. It was a generous gesture in the national interest but it worked to the disadvantage of the club, as Alex Ferguson later acknowledged.

Although still top of the league table in December, the Dons began to slip and ended in fourth position. Fortunes were revived for the Scottish Cup, however, when they reached the final without travelling further than the River Tay, having beaten Montrose, Arbroath and Dundee on the way to the semi-final against Hibs, which was also played at Dens Park. This had looked like being the year of Hearts, who seemed to be coasting to a league championship and a Scottish Cup final in their finest season for a long time. They had taken their cue from Aberdeen's success and all neutrals wished them well.

But a last-game defeat at Dundee, plus a high-scoring win for Celtic at St Mirren, pipped them for the championship on goal difference. On a day of tearful deflation, you sensed that their misery was not yet over.

Fate plays many a cruel hand and Aberdonians went south for the Hampden final wishing they were playing some other team. It took John Hewitt just five minutes to score and the Gothenburg hero added another before the stylish Billy Stark emphasised Aberdeen's superiority with a third goal. Poor Hearts went home with no more than a cup of woe and much sympathy from football people every-where, not least Aberdeen. Their noble attempt to join the Dons and Dundee United in trying to spread the honours more evenly had suffered a double blow, and you wondered how long it would take to get over the disappointment.

Meanwhile, Aberdonians pondered the extraordinary fact that, in the seven seasons between 1979 and 1986, the Dons had carried off no fewer than ten major trophies, had been declared the Best Team in Europe and were dominating events in Scotland. They had brought a much-needed breath of fresh air into a game that had been crying out for someone to crack the mould of Rangers and Celtic. In the continuing imbalance of wealth and power, it was always going to take a super-human effort to achieve it; so most fair-minded people rejoiced in what Aberdeen had done.

Honours had been coming so thick and fast that it was a temp-tation for the supporters to become blasé about success. They were in the European Cup again and the Dons set out to erase the night-marish memory of the Berlin shoot-out. Akranes of Iceland, oppo-nents of two years earlier, were duly despatched in the first round and Servette of Switzerland in the second.

When the quarter-finals came along in the early spring of 1986 you wondered if there was some kind of omen in the fact that Aberdeen had been drawn against Gothenburg of Sweden. Ah, those magical memories! Three years had elapsed since the great night and this time they would be playing the team that actually belonged to that curvaceous stadium of Ullevi.

The Swedes came to Pittodrie for the first leg and the crowd stood in a tribute of silence to their Prime Minister, Olaf Palme, who had just been assassinated. The Dons were leading 2–1 when the great Johnny Ekstrom equalised in the very last minute. That score would take the Swedes through if there were no more goals in the return leg and it was perhaps with a certain fear of tarnishing the memory of 1983 that the supporters, a much smaller band this time, flew out to Gothenburg.

It was March instead of May and the bulldozers were clearing snow into murky mountains by the roadside. From a different seating angle, the Ullevi looked a different place and I found my attention wandering from the match as I tried to regain my bearings and superimpose upon the stadium the memory of an exquisite night.

It would take only one goal to see the Dons through to the semi-final – and who knows what beyond that? Jim Bett very nearly achieved it but the match ended without a score and the Dons were out of Europe. We drank quietly in our hotel that night, knowing it had been an unreasonable expectation that Gothenburg could reproduce its magic. Jim Bett, a Hamilton lad, had been signed from the Belgian club Lokeren that season, having previously played for Rangers. It would take him a few more years to emerge as a major figure in the plans of both Aberdeen and Scotland. Later, the big-game favourite of Pittodrie crowds, Doug Bell, was transferred to Rangers and bit by bit the elements of the Fergie era were being whittled away.

54
REQUIEM FOR CHRIS

ALTHOUGH trophies were still being won, an air of malaise was descending on Pittodrie, symbolised by the death of Chris Anderson, whose fight against the dreaded motor neurone disease had finally ended. It was a sad day for football in general and Aberdeen in particular. As a journalist and a friend, I paid this tribute at the time:

> Scotland could ill afford to lose Chris Anderson, vice-chairman of Aberdeen Football Club and one of the game's ablest administrators, who has died at the age of sixty from the same motor neurone disease which claimed film star David Niven.
>
> Chris Anderson was the fair face of sport, an intelligent, articulate spokesman and the brain behind so much of the change, not only at Pittodrie but throughout football. Destined to be the next chairman of the Dons, he told me, in a deeply moving conversation not long before he died, about his sadness at being robbed of the chance to lead the club towards the twenty-first century.
>
> He was well aware of his fate and, with a courage which characterised him as player and man, he told of his last visit to Hampden Park and how he looked around and knew he was seeing the great stadium for the last time.
>
> The public knew less perhaps of his work as chief executive at one of Britain's leading polytechnics, Robert Gordon's Institute of Technology [now University], where he took immense pride in the provision of higher education for talented youngsters in the North-east. Indeed his OBE was awarded for his service to both sport and education.
>
> But it was football which brought wider recognition, first as an

Aberdeen player in the post-war era and then as the director who masterminded much of his club's off-the-field success, like building an all-seated, all-covered stadium with executive boxes and so on. He played just as big a part in laying the foundations of Aberdeen's rise to dominance of Scottish football in the eighties, leading to the success as Cup Champions of Europe in 1983.

He led the way to the creation of the Premier Division in 1975 and was advocating a British Cup and a Scottish National Soccer League when few could envisage the idea. But a cruel twist of fate struck at Chris Anderson soon after he took early retirement from his college post at fifty-eight.

While still able to communicate, he talked very frankly about how it all happened. I leave the man himself to make his last public utterances:

Now that I was taking early retirement, I looked forward to fulfilling my two remaining ambitions. I wanted to spend more time with my wife Christine, who is a great tennis buff, and to take Aberdeen Football Club into the twenty-first century as its chairman. I have always had strength, I had some money but I never had the time. Now I was making some for myself.

Always superbly fit, I could be found in the gymnasium at Gordon's College twice a week, even after retirement. I was always a fast mover, I suppose the fittest man for my age in the whole of Aberdeen, a teetotaller and non-smoker.

In September 1984 I had to go into hospital for a hernia operation but recovered from that. By the end of the year, however, I began to feel a stiffness in my right leg and hand. I was also beginning to lose too many games of head tennis! The trouble was diagnosed as motor neurone disease – and there was no known cure.

Damage or disease of the central nervous system apparently affects the nerve fibres, which then fail to energise the muscles of the body. So the muscles waste. Naturally we were shattered but decided not to tell anyone at that stage. We didn't want to upset people. So I soldiered on through last spring, getting stiffer and more restricted in my movement but still able to get about.

In July I went to Switzerland for the European Cup draw but my condition was becoming apparent. So in August I told my family and

Teddy Scott's big night, January 1999. He is surrounded by former Pittodrie managers and assistants, (*clockwise from left*): Jocky Scott, Drew Jarvie, Archie Knox, Willie Miller, Alex Ferguson, Jimmy Bonthrone, Roy Aitken and Alex Miller.

Captain Derek Whyte holds aloft the Teddy Scott Testimonial Trophy, which the Dons won by beating Manchester United. Alex Ferguson paid Teddy the highest tribute by bringing his Old Trafford stars to Pittodrie.

Ebbe Skovdahl and his wife Lene arrive in Aberdeen.

Goalkeeper Jim Leighton is carried off after a collision with Rangers' Rod Wallace during the Tennents Scottish Cup final, 2000. It was a sad end to a wonderful career.

Robbie Winters gamely took over in goal after Jim Leighton was injured. Here he takes his first goal kick.

Kevin McNaughton, seen here in a game against Hearts, won his first full cap in 2002.

Darren Young shows his pace against Celtic.

An open goal is an open invitation to Derek Young. Hearts are on the receiving end.

Peter Kjaer, Aberdeen's goalkeeper, was in the Denmark squad for the World Cup in 2002.

Hicham Zerouali, Morocco's magical box of tricks who performed too seldom.

Ebbe Skovdahl with his young hopefuls – (*left to right*) Phil McGuire, Darren Mackie and Kevin McNaughton.

Director Chris Gavin.

Former Director Jim Cummings.

In the driving seat – director and major shareholder Martin Gilbert with Open Golf champion Paul Lawrie, who has personal designs on Aberdeen FC.

irector Hugh Little.

Chief Executive Keith Wyness.

irector Gordon Buchan.

Vice-chairman Ian Donald.

Chairman Stewart Milne.

friends that I had this disease and was heading towards being unable to move physically. There was total disbelief. They were so devastated that I found myself having to cheer them up.

I had also been trying to avoid creating any alarm at Pittodrie but of course I had to tell the chairman, Dick Donald, and our manager, Alex Ferguson, who were both shattered. When I discovered there was nothing that could be done for me in Aberdeen I began to find out what else might be done and that was how I came to visit Newcastle, which is a major centre for this kind of disease.

I learned about research going on in Boston – and that there are between 4,000 and 5,000 sufferers in the United Kingdom. I found a pattern beginning to emerge, showing that the victims are generally fit and athletic people and that the trouble often arises after an operation. All along I felt some reaction to my hernia operation was triggered off in the body. The medical people say they might crack this disease in two or three years but time is not on my side.

Anyhow, I have faced up to my situation and, when people ask if I feel any bitterness, I can only reply that I don't. If it hadn't been me it would have been someone else. My mind is clear but I am now faced with the frustration of not being able to move and feeling I'm a burden on other people. I was always such an independent kind of North-east person.

We talked about the golden age of Aberdeen Football Club, the managership of Ally MacLeod in 1975, continuing briefly with Billy McNeill and brought to fruition by Alex Ferguson.

'What we have done is succeeded in shifting the football base from Glasgow to the east coast,' said Chris. 'In my illness I have been deeply touched by the reaction of the younger players at Pittodrie, who have sent me cards of encouragement.

'When I went to Hampden for the League Cup final in October and Willie Miller stepped up to receive the trophy, I found myself looking round the great stadium and knowing it was the last time I would see it. Afterwards I went to congratulate the players and found I could face them all with one exception. Somehow I choked up when I came face to face with Eric Black. And so did he. It wasn't just that he scored twice that day or that he set us on our way to victory at Gothenburg. I'm sure it was because he epitomised for me all that was good in football. He seemed to stand for all that Aberdeen had done in recent years.'

Too ill to go to see Aberdeen in the Scottish Cup final against Hearts, Chris watched on television and tapped out his prediction of the result. It was Aberdeen 3, Hearts 0, the correct score.

In facing up to his greatest battle so courageously, Chris Anderson remained conscious till his very last day. But he was trapped inside an immobile body without means of communication, except for the flap of an eyelid.

The man who loved fitness and freedom was finally a prisoner. And, in the fading minutes of Tuesday night, he was mercifully given his release.

55
THE END FOR FERGIE

WHEN Aberdeen agreed that Alex Ferguson could divide his time between club and country after the sudden death of Scottish manager Jock Stein, his commitment to the club was almost bound to suffer. In all truth, the era of Alex Ferguson had run its course. The supporters felt less conscious of his presence and sensed it was only a matter of time before he moved on to a club such as Manchester United, which still craved a return to the success of its illustrious past.

As in all things in life, there is a time to come and a time to go and, while it is hard to say so about your greatest-ever legend, Fergie's hour had arrived. His loyal and energetic assistant, Archie Knox, had meantime left to be manager of Dundee but was brought back as assistant, with thoughts that he would be the ready-made replacement.

In the event, Knox chose to accompany Ferguson as assistant at Old Trafford, a move which incurred the displeasure of the supporters who felt, understandably, that if he did not intend to stay as manager, he should perhaps not have bothered coming back from Dundee.

So Alex Ferguson went on his way to Manchester United, that fine old club which had lost its famous Busby Babes in the Munich air disaster of 1958. Their distinguished manager, Matt Busby, came back from the threshold of death and ten years later had created another magnificent team which won the European Cup, with legendary players such as George Best and Bobby Charlton (Aberdeen's own Denis Law missed out through injury).

By the time Ferguson took over, however, United had gone for nearly twenty years without winning the English League. Liverpool's dominance in that period went down very badly in Manchester and one manager after another had been sacrificed in the frustration of seeking a new Messiah. Ron Atkinson had just led them to an FA Cup victory with the team which included Gordon Strachan but that did not prevent him being displaced soon afterwards.

So in November 1986, as Fergie took on the biggest job in British football, Aberdeen was left without a manager and eventually settled on the surprise choice of Ian Porterfield, the former Raith Rovers player best known for scoring Sunderland's winning goal in the FA Cup final against Leeds United at Wembley in 1973.

On his departure, Alex Ferguson had suggested to the board that they should find an older man as manager, bringing in Willie Miller as his assistant, with a view to the future. Tommy McLean was offered the job but turned it down. 'Instead, they came up with Ian Porterfield – and that amazed me,' said Ferguson.

Almost immediately, the new man ran into some tabloid publicity about his private life and, for all his drive and dedication to the game, he was never fully accepted by the fans. He will be best remembered in Aberdeen for his Nicholas signings – Charlie from Arsenal for £425,000 and Peter from Luton for £320,000.

Porterfield's biggest moment was the Skol Cup final of 1987 when Aberdeen were beaten by Rangers in a penalty shoot-out, the culprit being the ever-popular and highly skilled Peter Nicholas, who missed his scoring chance. Peter went back south for family reasons, joined Chelsea and became their captain in the 1989–90 season, when the Stamford Bridge club made an early challenge for the English title.

Porterfield's time ran out in the spring of 1988, and he too went to Chelsea, as assistant manager, before moving to Reading as manager. After his divorce, he married a daughter of the memorable Jack Allister, a hero of the Dons' championship team of the 1950s.

Uncannily, St Mirren produced another of its eccentricities. Just as they had sacked Alex Ferguson in the week Aberdeen needed a replacement for Billy McNeill, so did they sack Alex Smith when the Dons needed a successor to Ian Porterfield. The timing was psychic!

Smith landed the job but, in the first few months, he ran into a repetition of Porterfield's misfortune with the Skol Cup. Once again it was Rangers who were the opponents and this time they managed a 3–2 victory without the agonies of a penalty-kick decider. As Smith worked quietly in the background, the supporters reserved judgement on the new management team.

Having lost Jim Leighton to Manchester United, Smith took a tip from his predecessor that there was a surplus of good keepers in Holland. Fergie also suggested to Smith that, while there looking for a keeper, he might give him a report on a Merseyside lad playing for Groningen. His name was Paul Mason.

When Smith arrived to cast an eye over the FC Twente goalkeeper, Theo Snelders, the big man had called off with an injury. In the opposing team, Mason impressed Smith, but not as the full-back Ferguson had been looking for. He passed on his report and, when the former Dons manager took no further action, Smith stepped in and signed him for a different role.

He did, of course, catch up with Mr Snelders and brought off a double Dutch coup which proved what a shrewd judge of a player he could be. Within a short time it was hard to find an Aberdeen supporter who would have exchanged Snelders for Jim Leighton, fine servant though he had been. The Dutchman became an instant attraction at Pittodrie, a stylish giant of a man with a superior bearing, who could make goalkeeping look so easy that he was voted Scotland's Player of the Year by fellow professionals in his very first season.

Smith was not finished with the Dutch connection. He paid £300,000 for the gigantic Willem van der Ark, a 6ft 5ins striker from the Willem II club, and followed that up with what looked like the most spectacular signing of them all. A tip from a contact in Holland brought news that Hans Gillhaus of PSV Eindhoven might be available. Back went Smith to buy him for £650,000, a record fee for an Aberdeen signing.

Gillhaus (the G was pronounced as an H) first appeared against Dunfermline at East End Park in November 1989, a dream debut in which he scored twice in the first sixteen minutes, the first being that spectacular overhead hitch-kick which sent the travelling support home in raptures.

On the following Wednesday, he made his home debut when Rangers came to Pittodrie and fought an even battle. They were beaten by another spectacular goal from the Dutchman, by now being acclaimed as the best of the foreign imports in a period when clubs such as Celtic, Dundee United, Hearts and Dunfermline were finding players in Poland, Hungary and Yugoslavia as well as Scandinavia.

The stimulating presence of Gillhaus electrified Pittodrie, players as well as spectators, with Charlie Nicholas rekindling his enthusiasm in the company of a kindred spirit. Hopes of a new inspiration, reminiscent of Zoltan Varga, were dampened when the Dutch player became an early victim of heavy tackling although no one doubted that here was a special talent.

By then, however, the Dons had signalled their intentions for the new season by winning the Skol League Cup in another exciting final against Rangers, the third successive meeting between the clubs in the same competition. Having lost out in 1987 and 1988, Aberdeen were determined to succeed. They had gone to Hampden for the semi-final and beaten Celtic with a spectacular long-range goal from Ian Cameron, another Aberdeen signing from Smith's former club, St Mirren.

Cameron, an honours graduate of Glasgow University whose culture extended to his feet, was injured before the final; but the cudgels were taken up by Paul Mason, now quickly establishing himself as a valuable member of the squad, who scored the first goal. Before half-time, however, Ally McCoist had backed into Willie Miller and been awarded the kind of penalty that would not have been claimed by the most diehard Rangers supporter.

All agreed that referee George Smith had suffered an aberration and given the initiative back to the Ibrox club. Was this to be yet another Skol Cup victory for Rangers? Happily, justice was finally done when Paul Mason shot home the winner – and Aberdeen had scored their first trophy success for three years.

The barren period was over and the delight of the support was reflected best on the face of Willie Miller, not a man to display emotion but confirming that it was one of his most satisfying moments. The Dons were back in business, shaking off the Ferguson era which had threatened to become an albatross round the necks of Aberdeen players. They were playing good football and success would surely follow.

Season 1989–90 ended in dramatic fashion when the Dons, having accounted for Partick Thistle, Morton, Hearts and Dundee United, reached the Scottish Cup final. With no scoring after extra time, it was down to the penalty shoot-out, the first time it had been used in this competition. Still level after the five regulation kicks, the teams went to a sudden-death decision. With Anton Rogan's kick brilliantly saved by Theo Snelders, it all rested on Brian Irvine. Hampden had seldom known a moment like it.

Big Brian, taking over from a semi-fit Willie Miller, strode majestically to the spot and sent the Cup to Pittodrie on a nail-biting margin of 9–8. As a born-again Christian, he said afterwards that God was with him as he took the kick. Not a single atheist in Aberdeen raised an argument against the timely intervention of the Deity.

There was no such heavenly support, however, to save the career of manager Alex Smith. Not even his considerable record of success prevented the swelling tide of criticism which began to engulf him within the following two years. His career came to an end in the early part of the decade. That was where our modern story began, in the opening chapters of this book. So we round off one hundred years of history at Pittodrie – and leave the rest to reflections.

ON REFLECTION

FERGIE REMEMBERS

C ASTING an eye down the century of Aberdeen Football Club, through all the ups and downs, the high dramas, distinguished players and glowing memories, the story is dominated by four names in particular: Dick Donald, Chris Anderson, Alex Ferguson and Willie Miller.

But, from this coincidence of human chemistry, it is Ferguson above all who takes centre stage as the most significant figure in the history of the Dons, the folk-hero who guided the club to the zenith of experience.

Growing up in the shadow of the shipyards in Govan, young Alex Ferguson began his senior career with Queen's Park but came to prominence in the 1960s with Dunfermline before he was snapped up by Rangers in their bid to counter Jock Stein's all-conquering Celtic.

His managerial teeth were cut briefly with East Stirling and then St Mirren, where he built the best team Love Street had ever seen. So to Pittodrie in the summer of 1978 – and the rest is history indeed. At different times between his departure for Old Trafford in 1986 and the centenary year he has given me his thoughts on the Pittodrie experience, most recently at the magnificent new training ground at Carrington, on the outskirts of Manchester, where we sat in his plush suite and reviewed the past.

Alex Ferguson arrives there at 7.15 a.m. and has ninety minutes of comparative peace before the bedlam of the day breaks out. The ringing of phones, the knocking on the door, reports from coaches on players' fitness, questions about diet and a thousand and one

317

other things which leave you wondering how a modern football manager copes with it all.

By the time he reached his sixtieth birthday on Hogmanay Day of 2001 he was planning to give up the daily grind at the end of that season, in exchange for a more ambassadorial role with Manchester United. But the attractions were still too strong for one who felt fit enough and ambitious enough to carry on. However, he was not unmindful of what happened to his friend Jock Stein, and the new contract which would keep him for three more years at Old Trafford would still take him out of daily management just before he reached sixty-four, the age at which Stein collapsed and died in Fergie's presence as Scotland qualified for the World Cup finals in 1985.

As we settled once again to the Pittodrie question, here is a selection of Fergie's own words:

> After the part-time of Love Street, the most important thing in coming to Pittodrie was the feeling of security. Dick Donald just said to me, 'You make your own decisions about the team and you will never get interference from us.' And that was how it remained. I wasn't long there when the *Press and Journal* carried one of those 'What's wrong at Pittodrie?' stories, seeking the views of the public. I was said to have had a fight with Willie Miller.
>
> The truth is the team was not playing the way I wanted and I did have arguments with individuals. I had a disagreement with Willie Miller. I felt his defence was staying far too much in the penalty area. It wasn't easy at the beginning, not helped by one or two personal problems like my father's last illness and the fact that I went ahead with my case against St Mirren for unfair dismissal. The Aberdeen directors advised me against going to the tribunal but I was impulsive in those days and only later realised it was a stupid thing to do. I have learned to curb that side of myself.
>
> In that first October, we played Fortuna Dusseldorf in the Cup Winners' Cup and lost 3–0 in Germany. I was still trying to bridge the gap between the players and myself and, inadvisedly, listened to their request for a night out after the match. I softened and let them go.

Well, they must have had a night out! On the Saturday they played Hearts at Pittodrie and were awful. After a 2–1 defeat, I went into the dressing room and rounded on Alex McLeish. Willie Miller spoke up and said, 'Why don't you get on to the older ones?' That started an argument but Willie did later apologise. We ended fourth in the League that season and at the end of it I told the players that if anyone wanted to leave the club they could go. Only one player responded. Willie Garner knew his place was in jeopardy anyway.

Having established his authority, Fergie proceeded to look around for the team he wanted to build. His first purchase, in the spring of 1979, was Mark McGhee from Newcastle. Gradually he got to grips with people and situations, as he revealed in this rare insight into the private world of a football manager:

As a young manager I worked by intuition and instinct. I have always tried to judge, decide and act quickly. If you have an injury on a Friday, for example, and the players are waiting to hear the team, you must go and tell them right away.

It was wonderful having the backing of a man like Dick Donald, who was capable of making a decision and sticking by it. He had a wonderful way. Before a Cup final he would say, 'It won't be the end of the world if we lose this one. The players are getting a bit carried away.' It was his way of saying to me, 'Don't worry if you lose. Your job is safe.' Dick would sit around the team hotel and just watch. He was a great observer.

Chris Anderson was the balancing factor, a complete contrast to Dick Donald. Looking forward all the time, he could see the way ahead for the televising of football. I may not always have agreed with his views but he was the kind of man we needed. Chris had big ideas for the club and wanted to promote it. He was also a great supporter of the players.

Willie Miller was my mirror on the park, the best player to emerge in Scotland in the fifteen years from the early 1970s to the late 1980s. He and Bryan Robson at Manchester United were identical types, the two best players I have dealt with. [In a later discussion, in season 2001–02, he gave top honour to Roy Keane.] The fact that Rangers and Celtic players were afraid of Willie's presence was a measure of the figure he had become in Scottish football. As a captain, he came into the class of John Greig and Billy McNeill, the three most successful team captains we have seen.

Willie Miller was the single factor at Aberdeen but he was surrounded by players of character, people such as Stuart Kennedy, Drew Jarvie, Mark McGhee and Gordon Strachan. Big Doug Rougvie was a character of a different type, well loved and part of the balancing act. So the team was full of characters, who combined to overcome the Rangers–Celtic dominance.

What about that great day at Easter Road in 1980?

Bobby Clark was a great influence around the club at that time, instilling discipline in the other goalkeepers – Jim Leighton and Bryan Gunn. Bobby was like a sergeant-major, with a fiery temper. He was a very good organiser but, in the end, the man he helped so much, Jim Leighton, became a better goalkeeper.

So we won the League that year and gained entry to the European Cup but the Liverpool experience which followed was an embarrassment – and a big lesson. The players didn't have the experience of Europe.

At what point did Alex Ferguson realise that his Aberdeen team might be going places?

I realised it when we beat Rangers in the Scottish Cup final of 1982. To go to Hampden and dominate an Old Firm team gives you reason to believe you have a decent team. The players sprouted wings then. Jock Stein was recognising their capabilities and by 1984 had five of them in the Scottish team – Leighton, Miller, McLeish, Strachan and McGhee. Jock played as big a part as anyone by doing that. Willie Miller had started getting his place over Alan Hansen and Gordon McQueen.

Of the twelve players who took the field at Gothenburg in 1983, six were at Pittodrie before Ferguson arrived: Leighton, Rougvie, McMaster, McLeish, Miller and Strachan. All but Strachan were home-grown talents. The other six were Fergie's own choices.

McGhee, who had gone from Morton to Newcastle, came to Aberdeen for £70,000, while the other purchase was Peter Weir, who came from St Mirren for £300,000. The remaining four were part of a crop of youngsters he himself had developed: Neale Cooper, Neil Simpson, Eric Black and John Hewitt. Others in that group playing their various parts included goalkeeper Bryan Gunn, Steve Cowan, Dougie Bell and Ian Angus. In reminiscent mood, Fergie recalled some names at random:

> Stuart Kennedy was a brilliant player and what a tragedy that he went out of the game as he did. He had that great belief in himself as the best back in the world! He was also the barrack-room lawyer at Pittodrie and a bit of a Pied Piper. People seemed to follow him around.
>
> John McMaster had a genius which was electrifying. Before that disastrous Liverpool game, Jock Stein had told me he was going to pick him for Scotland. Well, we all know what happened with his injury that Liverpool night. But he fought back and made it to Gothenburg. John had magnificent vision and stroked his left foot with all the smoothness of an artist's brush. You could have set it to music.
>
> Peter Weir could be mercurial but when he played, the whole team played, as witness Gothenburg, where he made so much of it happen. I thought Neale Cooper had a lot of promise but he should have turned out to be a better player than he did. He was a good tackler and aggressive and he and Neil Simpson protected the back four. In the end, however, I would have to say Simpson was a better player. Neither had great vision but they did have dynamism and natural enthusiasm.
>
> Mark McGhee had tremendous resilience and when he was leaving I remember standing on the park with Willie Miller one day and remarking on how much we were going to miss him. In fact, Mark was a bigger loss to the team than either Gordon Strachan or Doug Rougvie. John Hewitt was the scorer of big-game goals and Eric Black was at his best in the air as well as being a good finisher. But both Black and Hewitt were influenced by McGhee's game.

That team grew up together and if they had stayed together beyond the Gothenburg time, it is difficult to assess what damage they could have done to the Old Firm, perhaps for three more years. In the next season, when we won the league and Cup double, we knew that Gordon Strachan was going to leave us. He needed a new motivation.

In the summer after Gothenburg there were lots of inquiries about Gordon. Dick Donald suggested we phone Manchester United to see if they were interested in him at £500,000. Yes, they were interested but Ron Atkinson came back to tell us there was a problem – he discovered Gordon had already signed for Cologne! Evidently, he had signed some kind of contract and we didn't know. The matter was resolved, however, and he went to Old Trafford.

In offering re-signing terms, we were not prepared to go daft with money. We tried to have a strict financial set-up at Pittodrie but perhaps we took it all a bit for granted. After Gothenburg, Mark McGhee had given me his demands for staying. I said he must be joking. The season went on and I left it too late. It was really my fault that we lost Mark. It wasn't worth quibbling over the extra £5,000 or £10,000 to keep him. By March, Mark had decided to go and I knew I had made a mess of it.

In the case of Doug Rougvie, I made what I thought was a good offer. But he wanted the same as Willie Miller and I said I would take it to the directors. By the time I went back, Doug had left for London to sign for Chelsea but I think he made a terrible mistake in leaving Aberdeen. He may have done all right financially but he could have been there into the 1990s, the folk-hero he had already become.

As for my own career, there is no doubt that Aberdeen made me as a manager and I keep a very special place in my heart for Pittodrie. They were eight great years. When I left, I was surprised by the choice of Ian Porterfield as replacement. Do you know, he never once phoned me about anything.

As for the future, I have to say that the chemistry which brought together that particular talent and character might turn out to be a once-in-a-lifetime happening. Luck entered into it. It is possible that the Dons will never again reach that place in Europe. Manchester

United waited well over twenty years to find another Charlton or a Best. Celtic are still waiting for another Lisbon Lions of 1967. Rangers are waiting to repeat their European triumph of 1972. Aberdeen will still have success in Scotland but that is not the criterion any more. Having won in Europe whets your appetite.

57
ARISE, SIR ALEX!

I N 1985, towards the end of his time at Aberdeen, Alex Ferguson wrote a book about his Pittodrie years. It was frank and revealing and very much the man's own work. But it was not until 1999 that he produced the full autobiography, by which time he had grown from spectacular success as a manager in Scotland to become, arguably, the greatest football manager British football has ever seen.

By the end of the century, the man we all knew as Fergie had spent fourteen years as boss of Manchester United, overcoming early difficulties to forge teams that would eventually win the FA Premier League championship seven times, the FA Cup four times, the European Cup Winners' Cup and Super Cup, crowning it all with the European Champions Cup and World Club Championship in 1999.

Despite the feats of Jock Stein with Celtic, Bill Shankly with Liverpool and Matt Busby with Manchester United (all Scots from the same working-class mould), Alex Ferguson outstripped the lot as the only man who had swept the board in both Scotland and England.

At Old Trafford he did at least have huge financial support and the benefit of one of the greatest club names in the world. With the limited resources at Aberdeen, there was no option but to build his own team and his phenomenal success, having cracked the Rangers–Celtic monopoly and dominated the scene for eight years, extending that to become the top team in Europe in 1983, must rank as perhaps the greatest feat in the history of Scottish football.

It would have been no major surprise to attain all that as manager of Rangers or Celtic but to do it within the limits of a so-called provincial club was an unthinkable triumph. To this day, Rangers' ultimate success in Europe is exactly the same as Aberdeen's – one European Cup Winners' Cup, in 1972. Only Celtic have gone one better, with the European Cup, but even they have not been able to repeat their distinction of 1967.

That rise to fame in football was suitably crowned when Fergie, the working-class boy from Govan, became Sir Alex Ferguson, a millionaire with his string of racehorses and a name and reputation that were known around the world.

What a story there was to tell, and he told it in a rather remarkable book called *Managing My Life*, in which he had the collaboration of fellow-Scot Hugh McIlvanney, the distinguished sportswriter from *The Sunday Times*.

McIlvanney's brilliance as a writer could so easily have intruded upon the authenticity of the book. Instead, he cleverly melted into the background and simply shaped up the true spirit of Alex Ferguson, who had taken such an interest in the project that he provided his ghost-writer with no fewer than 250,000 words of hand-written notes!

Yes, this was the real Fergie all right, and he had by no means forgotten his years at Aberdeen. Interestingly, he pinpointed the first moment of unease which gave him thoughts of leaving Pittodrie. Having won the Scottish league championship in 1985, the Dons had coasted to the quarter-finals of the European Cup the following season, when they were drawn against none other than Gothenburg. Before a nostalgic return to the Ullevi Stadium there would be the home tie at Pittodrie, a night when the crowd stood in silent tribute to the Swedish Prime Minister, Olaf Palme, who had just been assassinated.

The Dons were leading 2–1 with just a minute to go when Johnny Ekstrom equalised to make the return game a difficult one. What diverted Fergie's mind that night, however, was what he regarded as 'the meagre attendance of 17,000'.

'It crossed my mind that perhaps the Aberdeen supporters were spoiled and took success for granted,' he says, 'and the suspicion planted seeds of restlessness in me.'

In the return game in Gothenburg, one goal would have sent the Dons into the semi-final of the European Cup and Jim Bett came within inches of achieving it. In the event, they went out on a goal-less night but Fergie was already on the road to discontent. His assessment of the fans' mood was, of course, an accurate one. Prolonged success can certainly induce a sense of monotony, although what would we give for some more of that monotony today!

By 1986 the vast majority of Dons' fans had already faced the inevitability of losing their manager and it would be surprising if it took that disappointing crowd of 17,000 to convince the man himself that it was time to leave. Within eight months, Alex Ferguson was gone from Pittodrie, lured to Manchester United who were lying second-bottom of the English League under manager Ron Atkinson. The opportunity to manage at Old Trafford had come at the right time although, surprisingly, the money on offer did not match what Fergie had earned at Pittodrie that year, such was his favourable bonus arrangement with Dick Donald.

In his new role, Fergie caught up with Gordon Strachan, who had arrived there two years earlier, and he added to the Pittodrie memory by signing Jim Leighton as his goalkeeper in 1988.

Sadly, both of those relationships went sour. The perky Strachan had long bordered on conflict with his boss and comes in for some strong criticism in Fergie's book. The Jim Leighton story is even more depressing, concerning the much-publicised drama surrounding the FA Cup final of 1990.

By then Fergie had begun to have doubts about Jim's confidence and only the support of assistant manager Archie Knox seemed to keep him in the team. In that FA Cup final against Crystal Palace, United just managed a draw and Fergie adjudged Jim to have had a poor game. When it came to the replay, Knox's support for Jim was over-ruled and Fergie decided to play Les Sealey, no better than Leighton but with enough of that East London cockiness to believe that he was.

Not unnaturally, Jim Leighton was shattered when his manager broke the news just before dinner on the eve of the replay. United went on to win the Cup and that was virtually the end of Jim's career at Old Trafford. He went on loan in England before going to Dundee and Hibs and finally returning to his natural home of Pittodrie.

Ironically, his international career continued unabated and he was to end up as the most capped Scottish goalkeeper of all time. He could have claimed Kenny Dalglish's place as the most-capped Scot if he had not decided to withdraw from the international scene.

As for Alex Ferguson, his pre-eminence in British football was rewarded with his knighthood in 1999, the year in which he led Manchester United to both European and World Club Championships. Accolades were coming thick and fast, including an honorary doctorate from Robert Gordon University.

In the year of his knighthood, Aberdonians had their best chance to welcome back the all-time legend of Pittodrie when he came north to receive the Freedom of the City, an honour that put him in the company of Winston Churchill, Mikhail Gorbachev, Nelson Mandela and Queen Elizabeth, the Queen Mother.

And what a night it was. From the moment Alex Ferguson left the Town House in a horse-drawn carriage, Aberdeen was ready to re-live its greatest sporting era, in which the lad from Govan won ten major trophies, including that Cup Winners' Cup and the subsequent European Super Cup, wresting domination of Scottish football for the only period in a century of monopoly by Rangers and Celtic.

It had been like a breath of fresh air and now, on this freedom night, they had closed off the main thoroughfare of Union Street, set up giant video screens and released a multitude of balloons, as thousands turned out to welcome home their hero.

Through a sea of red and white, Alex Ferguson was borne to the city's Music Hall for a ceremony dating back to the twelfth century. A fanfare of trumpets heralded the procession as Lord Provost Margaret Farquhar led the way to the platform. With a hymn and a prayer, two appropriate speeches and three cheers for the youngest-ever burgess, Alex Ferguson graciously accepted the Freedom of Aberdeen.

It was all deeply impressive, the boyish frame of Fergie now matured into a figure of substance, wearing his enhanced status with touching dignity and humility. From there, the party moved to the Beach Ballroom for a civic dinner in the grand manner, a glittering occasion which lured that memorable team Scotland the What? from their retirement in a hilarious tribute to the guest-of-honour. With George Donald at the piano, Buff Hardie and Steve Robertson stirred memories with a parody of 'This is Your Life'.

Those memories were further heightened by a dramatic video presentation of the golden years, watched by Fergie and several of his immortal squad – Willie Miller, Alex McLeish, Neil Simpson, Doug Rougvie, Stuart Kennedy, Dougie Bell and John Hewitt, who scored the winning goal at Gothenburg.

It was a night of pure nostalgia, emphasising how soon great moments can melt into history. Yet it all seemed no longer ago than yesterday. Alex Ferguson had become the living symbol of those inspiring times, an adopted son of Aberdeen to whom North-east folk would cling unashamedly for ever, for once casting off that reserve which veils their emotions.

58

MILLER LOOKS BACK

I F Alex Ferguson was the architect and inspiration of Pittodrie's greatest years, the man who translated the plans into action was of course club captain Willie Miller, without a shadow of doubt the most important player in the entire history of Aberdeen Football Club.

Described by his old boss as 'my mirror on the park', and the best penalty-box player in the world, Willie Miller was a stalwart of steel who became a legend in his own playing time. He was born in Glasgow's Duke Street Hospital on 2 May 1955, just as the Dons were winning their first-ever league championship, and grew up near Bridgeton Cross, not far from Celtic Park yet a Rangers stronghold in the east end of the city.

There was no background of football, scarcely even an interest in the early years, but his primary school needed a goalkeeper and the young Miller obliged, ending up as the keeper chosen for the Glasgow Schools Select to visit the United States. Back home, he became bored in goal and tried his luck at centre-forward.

That was where he was spotted by Dons scout Jimmy Carswell and signed on an S-form at the age of fourteen. Two years later, in 1971, he arrived at Pittodrie but was farmed out to Peterhead, where he proceeded to score twenty-three goals in the Highland League.

Recalled to the Dons' reserve team, he remembered being greatly helped by George Murray, Bobby Clark and the inevitable Teddy Scott. It was Teddy who spotted that he should be a defender, not a goalscorer, and Miller knew immediately that he had found his true position.

On his first-team debut against Morton at Cappielow Park on 28 April 1973, he came on as a substitute for Arthur Graham. The Dons won 2–1, with a team which read: Clark; Williamson, Hermiston; Thomson, Young, Boel; Joe Smith, Taylor, Jarvie, Varga, Graham. How strange that the future legend should play his first competitive game on the day that that other memorable figure, Zoltan Varga, was playing his last.

Miller's first honour in an Aberdeen jersey was a League Cup medal with Ally MacLeod's team of 1976, when the Dons beat Celtic 2–1 at Hampden. That followed the 5–1 demolition of Rangers in the semi-final, with the hat-trick from Jocky Scott and goals by Drew Jarvie and Joe Harper. It was in that final that Jarvie equalised a Kenny Dalglish penalty and Davie Robb scored the winner in extra time.

But Miller's greatest years lay ahead, with the arrival of Alex Ferguson. As two positive personalities, it has already been established that they did not hit it off at first although the reports of conflict were somewhat exaggerated. Willie Miller explained:

'When Fergie arrived, he used to keep on referring to his St Mirren players and that annoyed me. He had his ideas on how the game should be played and I had mine but we saw each other's point of view and there was compromise. Through the arguments we had a couple of head-ons and I felt the better for it.

'His aggressive style of man-management didn't bother me; in fact it helped. Perhaps he should have changed the style for other players who couldn't take it. His great strengths were his tactical ability and his motivation. He knew how to play the European teams and had the knack of choosing the players for the occasion, Dougie Bell being the classic example.'

When Willie Miller's contract was at an end in 1981, he went down to discuss terms with Sunderland, well remembered by a previous generation as an extremely wealthy and ambitious club. This was his reaction:

'I would have been substantially better off but I didn't like the place. It was a big club but it was like a mausoleum. They were living in the past and mainly on the memory of winning the FA Cup in 1973, with a goal scored by a player called Ian Porterfield!

'So I stayed with Aberdeen and did not regret my decision. The success we had has been more important than money. That success culminated in Gothenburg and it is only later that you realise how important it is to win a European trophy. You build up a reputation, become accepted in Europe and it doesn't go away overnight.'

As well as being the great footballer that he undoubtedly was, Willie Miller was also a role-model for young players, keeping a level head, conducting himself with impeccable good judgement, and never courting publicity or any other form of self-promotion. But what about his capacity for sleep?

'There was certainly a public perception that all I did was sleep – and give referees a hard time,' says Willie wryly. 'Yes, I did sleep a lot – usually ten hours at night, another couple of hours during the day and maybe half-an-hour before a match. As far as referees were concerned, I was only giving them the benefit of some good advice!'

By the time his playing days were brought to an abrupt end with injury in 1990, Willie Miller was already established as a businessman in Aberdeen, having had his own popular hostelry near the Green and running the Parkway pub at the Bridge of Don, as well as a number of nursing homes. He was married to Claire, a member of the well-known amusement family of Codora, and had become the North-east's most famous adopted son.

His return to Pittodrie as the successor to Alex Smith in 1992 raised a fear that the pitfalls of management, which claim so many talented footballers along the way, might one day tarnish the polished image of Willie Miller. There was an argument that the untouchable idol is better left on his pedestal. Willie Miller took that risk and, sadly, went the way of so many others.

Looking back on that situation, Alex Ferguson said: 'To expect a great player to be a manager is a nonsense. Yet anyone who worked with Willie would have seen his qualities and said he was among those who would make a manager. However, you must give people time to formulate a vision of the club. The issues of management are not clear-cut. In Willie's case, his shyness may well have been a problem.'

Miller himself reflected on his fate: 'At board meetings, Dick Donald never failed to support me and I could well understand why Alex Ferguson thought so highly of him. But by my time his health was failing and other people were taking over. I have always been in favour of giving people some time but, at Pittodrie, the first manager to be given that time since Fergie's day has been Ebbe Skovdahl. The board should have learned that lesson earlier.

'Roy Aitken and I had no managerial experience but we were followed by Alex Miller, who had plenty of experience, yet he was no more successful and he too was sacked. He was followed by Paul Hegarty, who was given a certain amount of time to prove himself but it was not long enough. I was sorry for Paul.

'Looking back on those sacked managers, it was not all down to them. You have to ask questions about the board that appointed them.'

Despite the disappointment, Willie Miller makes it clear that his heart is still with the Dons. There are those, including Teddy Scott, who believe that he now has the knowledge and maturity to be a successful manager, ten years after his first attempt. If he was not at his best in his relations with the media, he has since become a radio pundit of good standing and has a much fuller appreciation of how the system works. As to the opportunity of a second chance in management, he breaks into a wry smile of doubt but, interestingly, concedes that you never say never.

Whatever the future, Willie has his views on Scottish football and, as the man who bravely led the challenge in the 1980s, totally rejects the idea that nobody can break the renewed domination of Rangers and Celtic: 'Back in the mid 1970s they were saying that nobody could beat them but we did; and it is defeatist to say that it cannot be done again.

'As for Rangers and Celtic leaving the Scottish league and making it easier for other teams to compete, I don't believe it would be good for Scottish football. It is easy to convince yourself that life would be better without the Old Firm. But it would leave you with a second-class product, a poor substitute for what we have.'

On the future of Pittodrie, Willie had a novel idea for turning the pitch to run along the front of the Richard Donald Stand, giving a better balance to the ambience of the stadium. But surrounding space would still be a problem and the idea was unlikely to appeal to a board of directors who had their minds set on going elsewhere.

At this centenary point, Willie Miller's business interests are concentrated on the Café Continental at the Beach, along with the franchise which made him the Harry Ramsden of Aberdeen. That is all housed in what was once the Beach Pavilion, former variety theatre and home base of Aberdeen's internationally famous comedian, Harry Gordon. From Harry Gordon to Harry Ramsden tells you something of the changes that have taken place in the social life of the city.

As for Willie Miller, the quiet lad from Glasgow's east end who grew into the stature of a soccer giant, his name will march into the folklore and history of the North-east, engraved for ever in the hearts of Aberdonians who followed his leadership to the heights of a most unforgettable experience.

— 59 —
WHERE ARE
THEY NOW?

I N the Scottish Cup final of 2000, it was a heartbreaking sight to witness Jim Leighton being carried from the Hampden turf he had graced so magnificently down the years. The injury brought a tragic end to the career of Scotland's most-capped goalkeeper of all time.

But in the heat of the moment, our concern for the man's welfare deflected us from the significance of what was happening that spring afternoon in Glasgow. As the stretcher-bearers hastened their patient from his goalmouth, we were witnessing the very last of the Golden Age of Pittodrie.

Returning to his natural habitat, Leighton had sustained a playing career into his forty-second year, the last of the Gothenburg heroes to wear an Aberdeen jersey and now taking his farewell in the most disastrous of circumstances. In that moment, Alex Ferguson's team had finally gone.

JIM LEIGHTON was a braveheart indeed, born in 1958 and growing up appropriately in Elderslie, birthplace of another Scottish hero, William Wallace. After school he joined the Civil Service, working in the benefits office, but was spotted playing for Dalry Thistle and wooed by St Mirren in the management days of Alex Ferguson.

Instead, he took up the offer of the Dons' chief scout, Bobby Calder, and came to appreciate the way Aberdeen looked after their young lads, not least in their reassurance of parents. Ally MacLeod was the manager when he was signed in 1976 and promptly farmed out to Deveronvale. He made his first-team debut in 1978–79 when Bobby Clark was injured. After fifteen years, however, Bobby was still first choice in the championship year of 1980 but Leighton became his successor almost immediately.

He had been twelve years at Pittodrie before Alex Ferguson came into his life again, signing him for Manchester United in 1988 in that period when Fergie was struggling to establish himself in the rarefied environs of Old Trafford.

Jim was now with one of the greatest club names in the world, the second of the Gothenburg heroes to team up again at Old Trafford with their former boss, Gordon Strachan having gone there in 1984.

As already documented, the story ended unhappily for both players, Strachan falling foul of Ferguson before being transferred in 1989 to Leeds United, where he found a new lease of life and captained the Elland Road side from the Second Division right through to the English league championship of 1992. In doing so, Leeds just pipped Manchester United for the title, no doubt leaving Gordon Strachan and Alex Ferguson with their own distinctive thoughts!

Fergie had yet to prove himself in English football and concedes that, after three years at Old Trafford, he was reading obituaries of his sojourn down south. The pundits did not hold out any great hope for his survival as United entered the FA Cup of 1989–90.

Jim Leighton was still the first-team goalkeeper in January 1990, as United faced Nottingham Forest in the third-round tie. That morning, Fergie took the unusual step of placing a bet that United would win the Cup, at odds of 16–1. It was a major turning-point in his English career.

His team went right through to the final, meeting Crystal Palace at Wembley but managing only to scrape a replay in the dying seconds. Fergie reckoned Leighton had had a poor game and later revealed that he had already been worried about the keeper's recent form. Dropping him for the replay, Fergie replaced him with Les

Sealey, brought on loan from Luton Town as a cover for so many injuries. It was a shattering blow for the former Dons keeper, who could be said to bear the scars to this day.

Despite that horrendous injury at Hampden, Jim Leighton has not been lost to Aberdeen FC. At the centenary, he was well established as the goalkeeping coach, a fine influence on a new generation of young players to whom, he says, he wants to give the same kind of care and guidance as was shown to himself as a raw youngster in the 1970s. Jim had finally put down roots in Aberdeen, the city so beloved by his wife Linda and their two children, Claire and Greg, who were both born here.

There are two postscripts to Jim Leighton's career worthy of a thought. With ninety-one caps for Scotland, he was still first choice for manager Craig Brown's international team when he resumed playing for Aberdeen. That put him within easy reach of Kenny Dalglish's all-time record of 101 caps.

Forever a man of principle and strong opinions, however, he could not get on with the international goalkeeping coach, Alan Hodgkinson, and forfeited a chance of the number one place in the hall of fame by requesting that he should not be chosen to play for Scotland again.

The rift with Alex Ferguson has not been repaired to this day but that FA Cup final heartbreak of 1990 did nothing to damage his friendship with the man who replaced him in goal, the irrepressible Londoner, Les Sealey.

Just as Jim came coaching at Pittodrie, Les had gone on to a similar role with West Ham where, in the summer of 2001, he suddenly collapsed and died of a heart attack. He was forty-three, the same age as Jim Leighton, who not only went down for Les's funeral but was asked to help in carrying the coffin. Such are the emotional ironies which remind us from time to time that football is really no more than a game.

But if Jim was the last of the Gothenburg team to play for the Dons, seventeen years after that pinnacle event, he does at least have one former team-mate to keep him company at Pittodrie.

NEIL SIMPSON, who is back at his home ground as senior community coach, was one of the three strictly North-east boys in that famous team, Neale Cooper and John Hewitt coming from the city while Simpson was the only country boy, brought up at Sauchen and Newmachar.

Playing for the Aberdeen Schoolboy Select, he attended courses run by Bobby Clark and Lenny Taylor but was lured south to Sheffield United. By the age of sixteen, however, he had a call from manager Billy McNeill and that settled his future. He signed in 1977 and made his debut a year later, in Alex Ferguson's first season.

With other youngsters including Andy Watson and Neale Cooper, Simpson fought for his place and reckons his best-ever performance was reserved for Gothenburg, a view shared by Fergie himself.

If that was the high point, his worst memory concerned the clash with Ian Durrant of Rangers in 1988, when the Ibrox player sustained a long-term injury. Simpson was a good, robust but never dirty player, yet for the rest of his playing days he had to endure the vilification of Rangers supporters. His own career was affected just as badly as Durrant's and the irony was that the Rangers player survived in football, latterly with Kilmarnock, long after Simpson had gone. Since that depressing episode, the two players have never again exchanged a word.

Neil Simpson's first-team career ran the neat decade from 1980 to 1990, during which he played five times for Scotland. He failed to find a place in the 1990 Cup final team and was on his way to Newcastle, with two more seasons at Motherwell before returning to Cove Rangers in the Highland League.

With the phenomenal success in Europe, Aberdeen Football Club was hardly prepared for the fresh aspirations of the men who got them there, the heightened profiles which had given them a new earning value. Sometimes it was the least expected who were casting their thoughts elsewhere.

So what became of the other Gothenburg heroes?

Doug Rougvie was a rousing Pittodrie character, a player Alex Ferguson still believes should have stayed with Aberdeen. Arriving from Dunfermline United in 1972, the gigantic Rougvie may not have been the picture of sophistication but he would readily respond to the crowd's chant of 'Roog-vee, Roog-vee' and set off on a blood-tingling charge which delighted everyone, except perhaps the manager, who would wonder where he was off to now!

Flushed with European success, the big man went to discuss a new contract in 1984, after twelve years at the club, and asked for a signing-on fee of £15,000, with an increase in basic wage from £275 to £375 a week. He had missed out on the testimonial match he was due because of recent poor attendances for such events.

By the time the club responded, however, the big full-back had gone to London to discuss an offer from Chelsea, who were not only prepared to meet his £15,000 signing-on fee but were offering £600 a week, plus £6,000 for each year of service. That was tantamount to a weekly wage of £720. When he came back to report that, despite the Chelsea terms, he would rather stay with Aberdeen at £375 a week, he claimed the manager accused him of playing one against the other and told him bluntly where to go. So Doug went.

'He kicked me out of his office and, on the following week, wouldn't let me inside the Pittodrie door,' said Rougvie later. 'He slaughtered me in the press but I didn't respond, though I was hurt. My heart was at Pittodrie and I didn't want to leave. I have every respect for Mr Ferguson as a football manager but not for the way he managed people.'

If that was a sad ending to his glory days, one Rougvie incident helps to restore a smile. Fergie opened his *Evening Express* one day to read a headline: 'Doug signs up for the TT races'. Flabbergasted by this revelation that the big man had ambitions on a motor-bike, he watched him arrive next day in full leathers, to much ribbing from his team-mates.

But Fergie was not amused and gave him an ultimatum to get rid of that machine or go on the transfer list. Big Doug couldn't understand the fuss. When the manager put him right on the dangers, however, he soon replaced the motor-bike with a harmless pedal bicycle. But that was not the end of it. On the Thursday before the 1984 Cup final with Celtic, the same Douglas was knocked off his bicycle by a lorry – and had to be carted to hospital!

Professionally, he proceeded to Chelsea for the next three years and moved on to Brighton, Shrewsbury and Fulham before returning to his native Fife and Dunfermline Athletic to which his original boys' team had been affiliated. Doug and his wife Brenda had a house built at Kingswells in preparation for their return to the North-east which, with a little consideration, they might never have left. After a spell with Montrose, he was player-manager at Huntly and Cove and joined the Wood Group, where he worked in instrument designing. More recently he moved to Kelloggs, Brown and Root in a similar capacity.

On matchdays, however, Big Doug is still to be found in an official role at Pittodrie, entertaining corporate guests in the Richard Donald Stand.

JOHN MCMASTER, the boy from Greenock, was the exquisite ball player whose skills still linger in your memory when so much else has faded away. As Alex Ferguson said, he had magnificent vision and stroked his left foot with the smoothness of an artist's brush. You could have set it to music indeed.

That merely intensified the agony of that European match with Liverpool at Pittodrie when he was so severely crocked by Ray Kennedy. Gordon Strachan recalled the sickening spectacle of a lower leg which seemed to be hanging off, causing them all to reflect on how easily your career could be ended by a single tackle. Mercifully, in the case of John McMaster, there was a miraculous restoration which enabled him to resume the European adventure at a much later date and to collect his winner's medal at Gothenburg.

John was originally spotted in his home area of Greenock by a local scout, John McNab, and came to Pittodrie in 1972 at the age of seventeen.

In the crumbling Porterfield days he went back to be player-coach and then assistant manager to Allan McGraw at Morton. He failed to land the Queen's Park manager's job but turned his skills to coaching boys for Pittodrie at the Strathclyde Park centre, near Hamilton. Now employed by CIS Insurance, John devotes his spare time reporting to the Pittodrie manager on forthcoming opponents – and scouting for talent.

NEALE COOPER, born in India of Aberdonian parents – his father was a tea-planter in Darjeeling – was back in time for schooling at Airyhall Primary, Aberdeen, where he was spotted by Ernie Youngson, the janitor, who was a friend of Teddy Scott. Neale helped Teddy with odd jobs during school holidays, became a ball-boy and was signed by Billy McNeill, playing his first game for the reserves when he was still fourteen. As one of the young bloods groomed in perfect time for the success ahead, he made his first-team debut at sixteen, against Kilmarnock at Pittodrie, and had his first away match at Celtic Park, when the Dons won.

When it was all over, he had an ill-fated spell with Aston Villa before returning to Scotland and struggling to find a place in the Rangers team. Then he was signed for Reading by a manager he knew well, Mark McGhee, and had four years with Dunfermline before heading north to manage Ross County, taking them through the Scottish League system to the First Division.

ALEX McLEISH from Barrhead, near Glasgow, was another in the coincidence of bright young talent which became an essential part of the Ferguson chemistry, perfectly timed for the great years. His partnership with Willie Miller was one of the greatest, not only for Aberdeen but for Scotland as well. McLeish played in seventy-seven full internationals, third only to Kenny Dalglish and Jim Leighton, and was Scottish captain on eight occasions.

When his playing days were over he became manager of

Motherwell and moved on to Hibs in 1998 as they were slipping into relegation, but brought them back to the Premier League for a challenge on Rangers and Celtic. In season 2001–02, although his success at Easter Road had dipped considerably, he had built enough of a reputation to be offered the Rangers job, in succession to Dick Advocaat.

Throughout his managerial moves he took with him, as his assistant, another of the Gothenburg pool, Andy Watson, who was widely acknowledged as an essential cog in the McLeish success.

WILLIE MILLER has already warranted a chapter to himself as the playing legend above all. Because he was a few years older than McLeish, the golden era did not provide him with as many caps. But who can argue with his tally of sixty-five internationals, in which he was Scottish captain on twelve occasions? Good fortune may not have followed him into the manager's chair at Pittodrie but he has become a successful businessman in his adopted city of Aberdeen, and established as a regular voice of wisdom on BBC sports programmes.

GORDON STRACHAN may well qualify as the most exciting play-maker Pittodrie has ever seen. From a tough district of Edinburgh, he wisely resisted early attempts to take him to Manchester United so that he could mature nearer home. He joined Dundee and was captain by the age of nineteen.

A year later, in 1977, he was signed by Billy McNeill and it was Aberdeen's good fortune that he stayed for the next seven years. Apart from enjoying the best period of the club's history, he also shot to international fame in the 1982 World Cup in Spain when he not only emerged as Scotland's star player but was voted by the world press as the personality of the event.

In 1984, he preceded Alex Ferguson to Old Trafford, won an FA Cup medal the following year and later moved to English championship glory with Leeds. He amassed a total of fifty caps, twenty-eight

341

of them with Aberdeen. Gordon's venture into management ran into trouble with Coventry but in season 2001–02 he took charge of Southampton and hauled them clear of relegation with a run of spectacular results against England's top teams.

MARK MCGHEE, like Gordon Strachan, was born in 1957, a Cumbernauld lad who was with Bristol City at sixteen and played for Morton and Newcastle United before Alex Ferguson signed him for £70,000 in 1978. A strong-running attacker who provided the winning cross for John Hewitt at Gothenburg, Mark followed Strachan on the exit route from Pittodrie, going off to Hamburg, who were recent European champions, for a fee of £300,000.

Mark later returned to play for Celtic, then went full circle back to Newcastle United. His playing days over, he showed promise as a manager with Reading before moving on to Leicester, Wolves and Millwall. In his playing career he was capped four times for Scotland and remains proud of the fact that he scored against England.

ERIC BLACK's family moved from East Kilbride when his father went north to Alness to work in the oil industry. He was playing for the North of Scotland Schoolboys against Aberdeen when he was spotted by Bobby Clark, who always had a keen eye for a player.

Signed on a schoolboy form at thirteen, Eric was later farmed out to Nairn County in the Highland League before joining up at Pittodrie in 1979, when he was sixteen. Another player whose timing for the peak years was fortuitous, his high moments included scoring the first goal at Gothenburg. The late Chris Anderson claimed him to be the embodiment of all that was good in football.

Eric left Pittodrie in 1986, had a five-year run with the French club Metz but was out of the game by twenty-eight with a back problem. He joined the technical department of the Scottish Football Association in Glasgow in 1993 and was youth director at Celtic Park before teaming up with former Rangers captain Terry Butcher in a football recruiting agency. In season 2001–02, Eric became manager of Motherwell, with Terry as his assistant, but resigned in the financial collapse of April 2002 and became number two at Coventry under new manager Gary McAllister.

JOHN HEWITT goes down in Pittodrie history as the Super Sub who came on at all vital moments, like a hare out of a trap, to snatch victory for the Dons, all the way to the memorable goal that finally took the European Cup Winners' Cup to Aberdeen.

A local boy, John played for Middlefield Boys' Club, where he was wooed by managers Dave Sexton of Manchester United and Alex Ferguson of St Mirren. When the latter arrived at Pittodrie he made sixteen-year-old John Hewitt his first signing. The rest is history.

When John tired of the super-sub label in 1989, he sought a move, going to Celtic Park and later St Mirren. There was a brief spell in Ireland with Dundalk before he came home to be player and assistant manager to Doug Rougvie at Cove Rangers.

Back living in the Rosehill district of his childhood, he now works for the Aberdeen recruitment agencies of Team and Tulloch, who have a hospitality box at Pittodrie, where John Hewitt plays host to the company's guests on a Saturday afternoon.

PETER WEIR, like Alex McLeish, grew up in the small town of Barrhead, near Glasgow, but became a confirmed Dons supporter as a schoolboy, when his father happened to take him to the 1970 Scottish Cup final. Little did he know that his favourite team would later fork out £300,000 to bring him from St Mirren in 1981.

Peter's powerful running and delightful ball skills made him a rare talent, able to demoralise Real Madrid at Gothenburg. As Alex Ferguson said, when Weir played, the whole team played. But it was Peter's turn to be demoralised when Ian Porterfield succeeded Fergie as manager and he was transferred to Leicester City. Alex Smith tried to buy him back but Peter had given his word to Tony Fitzpatrick at Love Street and still regrets that he did not return to Aberdeen, a city he adores.

He finished his career with Ayr United and coached at Celtic and again with his close friend Billy Stark at Morton. He still hankers after a role in football. Meanwhile, from his home near the Erskine Bridge, he works as a driver.

That leaves two more players who should have shared the glory of Gothenburg but to whom the fates dealt a wicked blow.

STUART KENNEDY's career came to an end tragically in the European semi-final tie with Waterschei, when his studs caught on the wooden rim of the pitch and caused a twist in the knee. Ironically, the injury was exacerbated at the moment of victory in Gothenburg when he leaped from the dug-out in celebration – and caught his studs again! He had another eighteen months at Pittodrie, with surgical attention, but never played another game of football.

Stuart came from Grangemouth and played for the local YMCA before signing for Falkirk at eighteen. His special rapport with Alex Ferguson grew from his unique position of having played alongside him at Falkirk for two seasons. Stuart served his time as a marine engineer at Grangemouth, playing part-time football, and Fergie felt an affinity with people who worked in the shipyards, as his beloved father had done.

As a former team-mate, Stuart reckoned he was the only one entitled to call his boss Fergie! He would also point you to a notable event that took place two days after Hillary and Tensing reached the summit of Everest (29 May) and two days before the Queen's Coronation on 2 June 1953. That was the birth of Stuart Kennedy, who is therefore half as old as Aberdeen Football Club!

Stuart, who gained nine caps for Scotland, took over the Woodside Inn at Falkirk, which has been his livelihood since leaving Aberdeen.

DOUGIE BELL was similarly to miss out on the greatest moment but, whereas Fergie gave Stuart Kennedy a seat on the bench for the sake of his medal, he felt he could not afford a second invalid among the substitutes. He rationalised that Bell, unlike Kennedy, might have a second chance, however improbable.

But who can ever forget the mesmerising ball skills of the Glasgow lad, born in 1959, who was signed by St Mirren in Alex Ferguson's day and followed the boss north to play his way into contention at Pittodrie? The Waterschei semi-final at Pittodrie was just one of the memorable performances that will stir our appreciation of football when so much else has disappeared.

Bell's injury against Celtic in the Scottish Cup was followed by another against Hearts, creating some doubt about his condition. Still only twenty-six, he was sold by Alex Ferguson to Rangers. But that was just the start of a new phase in his career which would stretch for ten years. By the time Dougie was thirty-six, he had played for Hibs, Shrewsbury, Birmingham City, Hull City, Partick Thistle, Portadown, Clyde, Alloa, Elgin City and Albion Rovers, bringing his senior club total to thirteen. A compulsive football player, he returned to the junior ranks and was until recently manager of Baillieston Juniors.

Meanwhile Dougie Bell trained as a social worker and applies his discipline in what is now known as a 'residential school' in Glasgow, still playing football to keep the lads out of mischief.

In later years, it was a strange experience to see Mark McGhee and John Hewitt returning to Pittodrie in Celtic jerseys, Neale Cooper in a Rangers one, Doug Rougvie playing for Dunfermline and Peter Weir for St Mirren. There was something ill-fitting about the garb, stirring memories of their previous incarnations to which, you felt, they more properly belonged. Their glory days had slipped quietly into these pages of history and, as we bit our lips and swallowed hard, it was time to acknowledge Grassic Gibbon's reminder that nothing in this world abides. Nothing is true but change.

REMAINS 60 OF THE DAY

I f Jim Leighton and Neil Simpson are the last of the Gothenburg
men to be found at Pittodrie in the centenary year, there are
others from the more distant past who remain on the pay-roll of
Aberdeen FC and maintain the continuity that helps to fortify the
traditional strength of a football club.

Jim Whyte, better known as 'Chalky', is in charge of promotions and
lotteries. His Pittodrie connection stretches back to season 1962–63,
when he arrived from Kilsyth Rangers in the managerial days of
Tommy Pearson. He was there to take his place in the more
successful team of manager Eddie Turnbull, forming a sound full-
back partnership with Ally Shewan from Cuminestown (Ally now
works offshore in the oil industry) and playing for Scotland twice at
the Under-23 level.

In 1971, Chalky moved to Kilmarnock. When his playing days
were over he entered the licensed trade and found himself invited
by Bell's Whisky to move back to Aberdeen to take over the plum
representative's job as successor to another Pittodrie favourite, the
great George Hamilton, who was retiring. From there, it was a short
step back to the employment of Aberdeen FC.

Chalky had a football background. His father, another Jim Whyte,
was captain of Morton in the Greenock club's heyday of meeting
Rangers in the 1948 Scottish Cup final. The team included the
legendary goalkeeper, Jimmy Cowan.

346

CHIC MCLELLAND, who is now in charge of youth development at Pittodrie, attended the much-publicised Scotland Street School in Glasgow (designed by Charles Rennie Mackintosh) and arrived in Aberdeen in 1969 as a sixteen year old, playing at full-back alongside Jim Hermiston and Ian Hair.

He survived into the Fergie era but moved on to Motherwell, Dundee and Montrose, becoming an SFA community coach. Back at Pittodrie, Chic became involved in the highly structured and successful youth scheme, bringing on promising boys from the ages of eight to fifteen, with coaching centres all the way from Thurso to Hamilton. Former Don Ian Fleming coaches the boys at the centre in Dundee.

On Saturday mornings, there are friendly matches with corresponding age-groups from visiting Premier League clubs, after which the boys all go together to watch the seniors at Pittodrie. It is Chic's job to pass on promising talent to Drew Jarvie when the boys reach sixteen.

DREW JARVIE, highly gifted player and a hero of Ally MacLeod's 1976 League Cup-winning side, has responsibility for the Under-18 and Under-21 teams at Pittodrie. Like Chalky Whyte, Drew was a product of Kilsyth Rangers, signing for Airdrie in 1966 and coming on as a substitute for Scotland against England at Wembley in 1971, a team which included future colleagues Bobby Clark and Davie Robb.

Drew arrived at Pittodrie in 1972, just as Jimmy Bonthrone took over from manager Eddie Turnbull, and was still there in the early days of Alex Ferguson before returning to Airdrie. He was a player-coach at St Mirren, then assistant to former Dons colleague Jocky Scott, who was manager at Dundee. In 1988 the two of them came back to Pittodrie as part of the management team of Alex Smith.

The youth system, which began to bear fruit as the centenary approached, produced up-and-coming players Kevin McNaughton, Phil McGuire, Fergus Tiernan, Darren and Derek Young, Darren Mackie, Scott Michie, Ross O'Donoghue and Bob Duncan.

TEDDY SCOTT, who nowadays looks after the kit, along with Jim Warrender, is the man with the longest connection at Pittodrie, a unique figure who merits a chapter to himself.

Apart from these former Pittodrie players who are still full-time employees of the club, there are others with a part-time role, such as Sandy Finnie, who helps out in the community programme, and that irrepressible little character, Jimmy Wilson, a tricky winger from the Turnbull era, who assists Chalky Whyte on matchdays. Jimmy, who deservedly gained a Scottish League cap in 1967, runs a boarding house in King Street where he has the added influence of looking after some of the young lads who come to try their luck at Pittodrie.

61

TEDDY SCOTT

W ITH so many former Dons around Pittodrie at the centenary, the threads of the past still weave their way into the future of the club, in what is clearly going to be a vital time in the second century. With Rangers and Celtic out of sight financially, the rearing of their own young players becomes paramount as never before at clubs such as Aberdeen.

In the fostering and encouragement of young talent, no man has done more for the Dons than Teddy Scott, for whom the centenary brings the fiftieth year of loyal service to Aberdeen Football Club. No wonder the supporters filled Pittodrie in 1999 when Alex Ferguson brought his Old Trafford stars for a testimonial match which gave Teddy a handsome cheque for £250,000.

His main reward, however, has been the talent that has blossomed under his guidance in all phases of his career – player, trainer, valet, as well as guide, philosopher and friend to every youngster at Pittodrie since the 1950s. On top of all that, he represents the archetypal North-east man of his generation, a solid, hard-working, genuine, decent, likeable human being who does nothing but good for all around him. Such people are as indispensable as they are unfashionable.

His value was best summed up by the quick wit of Gordon Strachan when the Dons went to play Sion of Switzerland and arrived with the wrong pants. Alex Ferguson said in mock seriousness that he would have to sack Teddy Scott. Up piped Strachan: 'And where are you going to get the ten people to replace him?'

Teddy was born in Ellon in 1929, one of eight children whose father died before the last one was born. He left school at thirteen to work in the Ellon boot factory, later played for Bournemouth during his national service and returned to join Sunnybank and become part of history. For in 1954 Sunnybank became the first-ever Aberdeen team to win the Scottish Junior Cup and Teddy was the centre-half.

By then twenty-five, he was signed immediately by Aberdeen in the season of their first Scottish league championship. He was competing for a place with stalwarts such as Alec Young and Jim Clunie, and made it to the first team just once. He played one season with Elgin City, worked as an uncertificated PE teacher in Buchan but soon rejoined the Dons as trainer.

Incredibly, in the hundred years of the club's history, Teddy has served fifteen of the seventeen men who have managed the Dons. When he joined the reserves, his team-mates included Ian Macfarlane, George Kelly, Joe O'Neil, Hughie Hay, Norman Davidson, Reggie Morrison, Jimmy Hogg and that marvellous little ball-player, Ian McNeill. Teddy's recollections are an insight into Pittodrie's past:

> I started with Davie Halliday as the boss, followed by Davie Shaw and Tommy Pearson, another former Dons player, who talked a good game but didn't take part in training. He used to hold a team meeting on Friday to discuss last week's match and tomorrow's one. I always remember, there were ashtrays on the table and the players sat there smoking!
>
> Eddie Turnbull was our first tracksuit manager, and a very good one at that. His number two, Jimmy Bonthrone, who succeeded him, was a good tactician but hardness was not in his nature.
>
> Then came Ally MacLeod, a great personality and enthusiast who got the supporters going. He also brought Stuart Kennedy from Falkirk. But I always regarded his tactics as dodgy and never rated him as a manager. Billy McNeill was a gentleman, as well as a good manager and tactician. If he had stayed at Pittodrie I believe he would have achieved much the same as Alex Ferguson.
>
> Alex, of course, was the best of all the managers and he and Archie Knox were a good combination. Ian Porterfield was a nice man but

out of touch with Scottish football, after his years in England, and he was never right for Aberdeen.

I rated his successor, Alex Smith, very highly. I remember watching as he coached the boys at King's College one day and was so impressed by the way he could get them going that I went back to see it all again.

Willie Miller had been looking after the reserve team but he became the manager too soon. I think he could well have done the job at a later stage. He was followed by Roy Aitken but Roy didn't have enough for the job. He would have been better in the youth role, in which he later succeeded with Leeds United. Tommy Craig, a fine player in his Pittodrie days, came back as Roy's assistant but he didn't have the personality to be a manager. Both left together, having at least won the League Cup in 1995.

I was surprised when they let Alex Miller go. He went to Liverpool in a coaching role and had a hand in Gary McAllister moving to Anfield from Gordon Strachan's Coventry. When Paul Hegarty then became caretaker boss, his assistant was former Don Neil Cooper. Neil had been training the boys and when Paul was sacked, he hoped he would get his old job back. But he was removed along with Paul and I thought that was a mistake. He had brought along many of the good young lads.

Down the years, I have had the advantage of being with the reserves and seeing the youngsters coming through. Names which come back to me include Tommy Craig, Jimmy Smith, John Hewitt, Neale Cooper, Neil Simpson, Eric Black, Martin Buchan and, of course, Willie Miller, who turned out to be the greatest of them all. Eric Black would have been a lazy player in any other team but Stuart Kennedy made him work. My mind roams over other players – Peter Weir, who could hold the ball so well; Doug Rougvie, who was such a character; and who could forget John McMaster? I remember him coming from Greenock and being anxious to work on the ground staff through the close season, just to make a bob or two. Boys come from all kinds of homes and I can recall some well-known names arriving here with holes in the soles of their shoes.

You try to teach the youngsters good habits as well as skills and hope they will still be around when the club can reap the benefit. I had high hopes of Paul Wright, for example, but he was off to Queen's Park Rangers on freedom of contract.

We may never again see the kind of loyalty shown by Willie Miller and Alex McLeish. Looking back over the years, other names that spring to mind as exceptional players include George Hamilton, Archie Glen, Alec Young and Gordon Strachan. Mark McGhee did a lot of work here.

In the build-up towards Gothenburg, the secret was that Alex Ferguson and Archie Knox planned everything correctly. Archie would go to watch foreign teams and was brilliant at remembering players and what they could do.

Teddy acknowledges Gothenburg as the greatest moment in the life of every Dons fan. For him, however, that event must share the honours with another – that day in 1954 when he won a Scottish Junior Cup medal with Sunnybank at Hampden Park, Glasgow.

62

WE'LL SUPPORT YOU EVERMORE!

W HILE players, managers and directors come and go, the most
constant factor in any football club is its support, in
Aberdeen's case that loyal and sometimes long-suffering band of
people who trek to Pittodrie in all weathers to attach themselves
emotionally to their beloved team. It is a marriage of sorts, with all
that that entails in freedom to love, argue, criticise, fall out and then
make up again in moments of high pleasure.

They raise their own heroes and villains and speak of them with
a familiarity that belies the fact that they may never have been as
close as to exchange a word. For a hundred years now, succeeding
generations have followed that route to Pittodrie in all their various
styles and fashions.

The middle partings and baggy pants will fix us in the 1920s and
1930s, just as the clean-cut image of a George Hamilton or an
Archie Baird will tell us about wartime's young men. When the
heavy beat of rock 'n' roll produced Elvis Presley in America and
Tommy Steele in Britain, it sparked off a new vitality which was
reflected elsewhere. In 1956, when the tousle-haired Steele was
introducing the new craze at the Capitol Cinema, Aberdeen, that
other fair-haired lad, Denis Law from Powis School, symbolised the
same vitality on the football field, sadly at the distance of Bill
Shankly's Huddersfield, having escaped the local net.

Similarly, the Beatles of the mid 1960s were reflected in football
terms by their so-called fifth member, George Best, while the Bay
City Rollers of the 1970s brought change to the terracing, spawning

an army of youngsters in big boots and half-mast tartan trews.

Like life itself, football was undergoing a revolution and, with the endless choice of pastimes in the modern world, it is perhaps surprising that the beautiful game has retained such a hold on its followers, albeit on a smaller scale than in times gone by.

From its catchment area of small towns and villages and rural communities across the North-east of Scotland, Aberdeen Football Club has drawn a loyal support throughout its first century. Random groups began forming themselves into clubs but a more formal arrangement was reached in 1981 when they created the Association of AFC Supporters Clubs, a move started by the Dyce branch, with Gordon Robertson of Aberdeen taking on the role of first chairman.

He was followed by Euan Chisholm, a lawyer from Buckie, who served for three terms and confirmed his enthusiasm for the Dons by calling his house Fars Hatt, after the team's hotel on the outskirts of Gothenburg! Other chairmen have been Alex Hosie (Aberdeen Red Rosettes), Neil McDougall (Marischal Bar Reds), Roddy Arnott (Capital 1903, Edinburgh) and, most recently, Jack Douglas from Stonehaven.

In all that time there have been only two secretaries, the hard-working Isobel Fyfe from Dyce, and Susan Scott, a Yorkshire lass who came to live in Scotland. Susan was drawn to the Dons by her young son, and her daughter is married to former Don Gary Smith, now with Hibernian.

The number of clubs has hovered around the fifty mark, with a total membership of 3,500. Orkney can claim to be the largest branch and others are spread impressively around the world. You have to admire Mark Robertson, for instance, who runs the Dons Down Under club in Melbourne, Australia, and pulls in members from hundreds of miles away. Across in New Zealand, it is Dr Alistair Hayworth who rounds up his Kiwi Reds in Hamilton, while the North American Dons are organised by Ian Bremner in Toronto. The 1st Northern Ireland branch is run by Jonathan Lemon from Lisburn, outside Belfast, and London can produce two supporters' clubs, the

Rob Roy Reds (Iain Macdonald of Thomas More Street) and the London Club (Andrew Dewar of Potters Bar).

Back home, there are clubs all the way from Orkney, Wick and Thurso to Newton Stewart, Rothesay, Edinburgh and Glasgow and every corner of the North-east, while some, including Keith, Forres and Nairn, have dropped out of the picture. Some of the supporters' clubs are no more than ticket agencies but others hold regular meetings and are extremely active, Inverurie being a prime example.

The association, which holds an annual dinner-dance with players in attendance, took time to gain acceptance in the boardroom but now has regular meetings with chairman Stewart Milne.

The part played by the Supporters Trust has already been documented, ranging from shareholder power to watchdog activity. A key member of the Trust, Chris Gavin from Aboyne, now on the board at Pittodrie, was behind the fanzine satire.

The Red Final and *Paper Tiger* are the titles of modern times but the original fanzine was *The Northern Light*, cooked up in 1987 by Dave Watt and Chris Gavin. The former would write under the name of 'Major Marcus A. Reno' while Gavin's pen-name was 'Old Beach Ender'.

He explained: 'The fans needed an outlet to release the bile and frustration that gathers up while participating in the world's most irritating league and we were the men to provide it. Our fate was set in granite kippers.'

Gordon Reid's cartoons became an integral part of *The Northern Light* and sales reached an impressive 4,500 at one stage, selling mainly around the streets of Pittodrie on matchdays as well as in local shops. With the strong language of total irreverence and the printing of the unprintable, the fanzine prided itself on having a say in the departure of manager Ian Porterfield. They were hardly less critical of his successor, Alex Smith, while quite supportive of his assistant, Jocky Scott.

For a variety of reasons, *The Northern Light* was killed off in 1992, interpreted by some as a reluctance to vent their spleen on the incoming manager, Willie Miller, the all-time playing legend whose name was being hailed from the slopes of Pittodrie, along with the calls for Alex Smith's departure.

If a satirical fanzine had a legitimate place in modern society, there was no acceptable place at all for that band of so-called supporters who took pride in calling themselves the Casuals, a name taken from their expensive Pringle or Lyle and Scott sweaters. For these were not the under-privileged, kicking against society. Instead, they were the swaggering well-heeled, avoiding club colours in order to infiltrate the ranks of the 'enemy' at away games and engage in the gang warfare that was attaching itself to football in the 1980s.

While you might have expected it least from Aberdeen, they were some of the worst elements in Britain, causing embarrassment to the club they claimed to support and giving it a bad name throughout the country. By the approach of the centenary, some of their leaders claimed to have reached maturity, with wives and families, but on the Dons' recent visit to Dublin at least one well-known leader was kicking in a shop window once more.

The unwelcome presence of the Casuals had lessened with police surveillance but raised its ugly head again in season 2001–02 when Rangers fans came to Pittodrie and rained coins on Robbie Winters when he was taking a corner-kick. Instead of leaving the culprits to the police, the mindless ones invaded the track, spoiling for a fight and turning the focus of blame on Aberdeen. It is a depressing sickness of the age.

If the Casuals are a blight on Aberdeen Football Club, the desirable face of football support at Pittodrie is personified by Paul Lawrie, who became the best-known Aberdonian in the world in 1999 when he sensationally won the Open golf championship at Carnoustie. When the Frenchman Jean Van de Velde embarked on that bout of Gallic insanity in the river, setting up a three-way play-off, the worldwide television audience was holding its breath to see what would happen next.

I had never met Paul Lawrie but knew the face so well. It was typical of the farms and villages of Aberdeenshire, where nothing ruffles them. I said to my watching friends, 'The loon fae Aiberdeen will not be found wanting here.' And he wasn't. Calmly, he grasped the greatest opportunity of his golfing life and strode on to fame and fortune. It was an incredible moment, bringing a burgeoning pride to every Aberdonian.

Needless to say, the whole lifestyle of Paul Lawrie and his family was to change from that moment onwards although the man himself was made of the stuff that doesn't change so readily. He was still the solid lad who grew up in Kenmay and became a mechanic in his father's taxi business. At seventeen he became assistant professional at Banchory, earning £30 a week, but was with Newmachar Golf Club when he won the Open.

From boyhood, however, he has been an avid Dons fan. He shared the greatest moment at the age of fourteen when his father took him to Gothenburg. Today, while playing in tournaments for twenty-seven weeks of the year, he sees as many Aberdeen games as possible, home and away, and checks his watch wherever he is in the world on a Saturday, before calling home to Bieldside for the Dons score.

More significantly, Paul Lawrie harbours a dream to become the majority shareholder in Aberdeen Football Club, perhaps taking his place as chairman one day. Depending on his financial fortunes in world golf in the coming years, he has serious intentions in this direction, an intriguing prospect for everyone connected with Pittodrie. Already he has sanctioned his name to be used for whatever promotional purpose can benefit the club. It is a thought for the future.

In the modern manner, Aberdeen FC has its own website, attracting 36,000 unique visitors every month and regarded as one of the best in football. It was designed by Jeff Riley, boss of Imagica, and Dave Cormack, and covers everything from history and daily news to the manager's own section.

In these highly commercial days it is hard to believe that Aberdeen Football Club set out on its great adventures of the 1980s without as much as a shirt sponsor. How times have changed. The club was then run on a family-style basis, with directors Dick and Ian Donald and Chris Anderson dropping in around lunchtime to see that all was well.

As secretary, Ian Taggart ran the day-to-day affairs, with Barbara Cook as a vital cog, applying her good old Aberdonian common-sense to see that everything rolled along smoothly.

Apart from a few executive boxes at the back of the main stand there was very little income beyond the gate receipts on a matchday. But ticket sales were no longer enough. It was not until 1989, however, that the notion of developing outside revenue took root and David Johnston was appointed as the club's very first commercial executive.

Johnston grew up in Aberdeen and played for the junior Banks o' Dee but he was best known as a stalwart left-back for Dundee from 1968 until 1978, under the coaching of Jim McLean. His playing days over, he studied for a business degree and worked in the oilfield business around the world, from Aberdeen to Singapore and the United States, returning as general manager of his old club, Dundee.

Along with Jocky Scott and Drew Jarvie, David Johnston resigned when Angus Cook took over as chairman at Dens Park but later rejoined his former colleagues at Pittodrie, all three working under the managership of Alex Smith.

'It was getting harder to balance the books by ticket sales alone. Nowadays you have to look at all the possible ways of generating income,' says David Johnston, who still recalls wryly that the canny Dick Donald was not at all convinced his appointment was necessary. Dick was open to the persuasion of hard financial facts, however, and accepted the dawn of a new age.

That age would bring the full commercial benefits of sponsorship, corporate activities, a club shop and, most of all, the whole new world of television, with the Scottish Premier League at one time planning its own TV service. Johnston was the first of a whole series of appointments, all made in order to exploit every possibility. In the vast area of the Richard Donald Stand, large numbers of supporters now gather in time for a splendid lunch before taking their place in the comfort of executive boxes.

It is the modern way. The level of football finance has soared to such dizzy heights as to baffle the bulk of supporters, who feel less and less in touch with the reality of the game they once regarded as their own. But the bottom line remains the same: a club such as Aberdeen must seek to live within its means. In other words, the basic philosophy of Dick Donald has never been more relevant.

That harsh fact was driven home in April 2002 when the League's own television plan was scuppered by Rangers and Celtic, and a serious rift developed between the Old Firm and the other ten clubs, who threatened to break away.

The cash-cow of televised football had indeed dried up and the game faced perhaps its biggest financial crisis of all time. Motherwell FC became an early casualty and others would follow.

The brave little town of Airdrie ran into serious football trouble, pinning its hopes on a survival package presented by former Don Steve Archibald, who had become something of an entrepreneur. When that scheme came unstuck, Airdrie was on the point of losing its football altogether. Football survived in the town only because the club was given permission to buy out the ailing Clydebank FC. Clydebank had withstood the onslaught of Adolf Hitler in the Second World War but could not save its football club from the blitz of modern football economics. Thus Airdrie had a team for season 2002–03 while the Bankies, the club that had given us the genius of Davie Cooper, went out of business.

In the lead-up to the Dons' centenary, the gloom of uncertainty that engulfed so much of the national game was relieved by the refreshing World Cup of 2002, held in Japan and South Korea. It was a time for shocks, with holders France among the early casualties. They were followed out of the competition by fancied contenders including Argentina, Italy and Mexico. But with some of those departures went much cynicism and downright cheating, to be replaced by the refreshing innocence of the newer football nations, such as the United States, Senegal and, most of all, South Korea. A team from South Korea had never won a World-Cup match but on this occasion succeeded in reaching the semi-final. It was a reminder of what can be achieved when you combine skill with fair play and exuberance – and commit yourself to the belief that all things are possible.

63

TOWARDS A NEW CENTURY . . .

S o we reach the centenary of Aberdeen Football Club with a salute to that array of colourful human beings who have shaped the story in their own distinctive and cumulative way.

The year 2003 is one of celebration, with special football attractions, parades and functions, combining one hundred years of club history with the coincidence of another major milestone – the twentieth anniversary of that night in Gothenburg when the Dons of Pittodrie carried off the European Cup Winners' Cup.

There is one special weekend marked down for a gala occasion to celebrate the greatest memory of them all, including as many as possible of the people who have graced the Pittodrie story down the years and helped to secure and cement the loyalty between club and supporters that has made us the community we are.

The history of the club is dominated inevitably by the extraordinary feats of Alex Ferguson and his European heroes but the fact that there is more to the story than Gothenburg becomes clear in a centenary portrait which has been painted by well-known Aberdeen artist Dod Dow.

Dod called for a consensus of opinion on who to include and while such matters are always of a subjective nature, few could argue with the final choice of twenty-five. In the hearts of Aberdeen fans, the entire team from Gothenburg would find a place in that roll of honour. More objectively, however, they have to be weighed against other great talents from down the century. So Dod Dow's composite painting is of these memorable figures, all of whom have made a special mark on the club:

Dick Donald	Willie Cooper	Bobby Clark
Chris Anderson	George Hamilton	Zoltan Varga
Alex Ferguson	Archie Baird	Joe Harper
Teddy Scott	Tommy Pearson	Willie Miller
Donald Colman	Fred Martin	Alex McLeish
Alec Jackson	Archie Glen	Gordon Strachan
Benny Yorston	Graham Leggat	Jim Leighton
Willie Mills	Charlie Cooke	
Matt Armstrong	Martin Buchan	

Football is not the be-all and end-all of life but it stirs among its followers an intensity of feeling they seldom experience elsewhere. The Beautiful Game, as it is called, is as surely an art form to its devotees as the opera or the ballet or the orchestral performance is to other people.

Of course, in a bid for greater sophistication it sometimes becomes the slave of cerebral systems, producing the comic opera of half-crazed managers standing on the touchline, seeking to direct their players like puppets on a string. (Do they not instruct them in advance?) For most of the time, they are merely giving vent to their own nerves and frustrations, with players understanding very little of the contortions.

Whether a team has a flat back four or a flat-footed five matters less in the end if they have the guile to play with the spontaneity and the brilliance of individual skill which will take the opposition by surprise. Football is really a much simpler game than we try to make it.

But, through all its highs and lows, it grips us and holds us in its thrall for a lifetime, here in the North-east of Scotland as much as anywhere. And now, as the sun goes down on the first hundred years, we await the dawn of a new century in all its mystery, as ever with the eternal hope and optimism of the human spirit.

As generations rise and pass away there will be new structures and new ways, unimaginable even today when so much is already changing. It is hard to believe that there is already a whole generation of under twenty-fives who remember nothing of Gothenburg.

But they and their children, by then the inheritors of some futuristic stadium, will have been inescapably enlightened on the greatest moment in the history of Aberdeen Football Club. In fifty years from now they will still be told that there are legendary names from Gothenburg they must never forget.

These heroes will be recited then as now – Jim Leighton, superb in goal; Doug Rougvie, a large and glorious character; John McMaster, with skills so smooth and exquisite; Neale Cooper, the gladiator; Alex McLeish, one half of the greatest defensive partnership the club has ever known, along with his captain, Willie Miller, the most important player in the history of the Dons; Gordon Strachan, the play-making genius of the team; Neil Simpson, for strength and determination; Mark McGhee, combining skill and power; Eric Black, the clean-cut thoroughbred; Peter Weir, a tower of strength and creative skill on the left; along with John Hewitt, the Super Sub himself; and those two men who missed the final – Stuart Kennedy, as fine a full-back as the club has known, and Dougie Bell, with ball control to mesmerise.

Guided by the rising star of British football management, Alex Ferguson, these are immortal names of Pittodrie Park, itself an indelible part of Aberdeen's history, from which we could call across the wild North Sea and hark for an echo from Scandinavian shores.

There can be no apology for rounding off this centenary history with the sweet sound of Gothenburg, the city where the dream created by Alex Ferguson finally came true. Gothenburg has become a word established in the vocabulary of Aberdonians, meaning 'a high point of experience' or 'the greatest night of your life' or just 'pure magic!' We'll remember all that, even when the pale blue lights of some new stadium are shimmering in the night sky and an eerie silence has descended upon the ghosts of dear old Pittodrie.

CENTENARY FACTS AND FIGURES

ABERDEEN FOOTBALL CLUB
1903–2003

Honours

European Cup Winners' Cup: winners 1983
European Super Cup: winners 1983
Scottish League Champions: 1954–55, 1979–80, 1983–84, 1984–85
Runners-up: 1911, 1937, 1956, 1971, 1972, 1978, 1981, 1982, 1989, 1990, 1991, 1993, 1994
Scottish Cup winners: 1947, 1970, 1982, 1983, 1984, 1986, 1990
Scottish Cup finalists: 1937, 1953, 1954, 1959, 1967, 1978, 1993, 2000
Scottish League Cup winners: 1946, 1955 1976, 1985, 1989, 1995
Scottish League Cup finalists: 1947, 1979, 1980, 1987, 1988, 1992, 2000
Drybrough Cup winners: 1971, 1980

Directors at Centenary

Chairman: Stewart Milne
Vice-chairman: Ian R. Donald
Directors: Keith Wyness (Chief Executive), Gordon Buchan, Martin Gilbert, Hugh Little, Chris Gavin

Managers

Jimmy Philip 1903–24
Paddy Travers 1924–38
David Halliday 1938–55
David Shaw 1955–59
Tommy Pearson 1959–65
Eddie Turnbull 1965–71
Jimmy Bonthrone 1971–75
Ally MacLeod 1975–77
Billy McNeill 1977–78

Alex Ferguson 1978–86
Ian Porterfield 1986–88
Alex Smith (with Jocky Scott) 1988–92
Willie Miller 1992–95
Roy Aitken 1995–97
Alex Miller 1997–98
Paul Hegarty (caretaker) 1998–99
Ebbe Skovdahl 1999–

Payroll at Pittodrie

Chief Executive: Keith Wyness
PA to Chief Executive: Linda Macdonald

Team manager: Ebbe Skovdahl
Assistant team manager: Gardner Spiers
Football general manager: David Johnston
Under 18–21 manager: Drew Jarvie
Youth Development manager: Chic McLelland
Goalkeeping coach: Jim Leighton
Senior community coaches: Neil Simpson, James Crawford
Assistant coaches: Scott Anderson, Stuart Glennie
Physiotherapists: David Wyllie, John Sharp
Fitness coach: Stuart Hogg
Head groundsman: Paul Fiske
Kit managers: Teddy Scott, Jim Warrender
Kit assistant: Charles Keith
Football assistant: Steven Gunn
Community manager: Alexander Finnie
Community assistant: Duncan Dallas
Football administration coordinator: Patricia Ritchie
Club doctors: Dr Derek Gray, Dr Steven Wedderburn
Chief scout: John Kelman (based Motherwell)
Scouts: Peter Brain (Glasgow); Jim Conway (England); Ian Cumming
(Aberdeen); Jamie Doyle (Glasgow); Billy Kerr (Dundee); Joey Malone
(Ireland); Joseph McCarthy (N.E. England); John McMaster (Glasgow);
Vinnie Mochan (Glasgow /Lanarkshire); John Murphy (Ayrshire); Peter
Reid (Lanarkshire); Kenny Smith (Glasgow); Bob Stables (Aberdeen);
David Stewart (Aberdeen); Robert Weir (Glasgow)

Players: Russell Anderson, Roberto Bisconti, James Blanchard, Richard
Buckley, Alan Carella, Chris Clark, Eric Deloumeaux, Alexander
Diamond, Laurent D'Jaffo, Robert Duncan, Ryan Esson, Richard Foster,
Robbie Hedderman, David Hutton, Duncan Jones, Peter Kjaer, Michele
Lombardi, Jamie McAllister, Murray McCulloch, Philip McGuire, Calum
McHattie, Calum Mackenzie, Darren Mackie, Kevin McNaughton, Scott
Michie, Leon Mike, James Morgan, Scott Morrison, Scott Muirhead, Ross

O'Donoghue, Stephen Payne, Mark Peat, David Preece, Kevin Rutkiewicz, Kevin Souter, Stephen Tarditi, Ben Thornley, Fergus Tiernan, Murray Watson, Darren Young, Derek Young.

Company secretary: Roy Johnston
Sales/marketing manager: Ian Riddoch
Sales/marketing coordinator: Elaine Brainwood
Corporate/sponsorship manager: Harvey Smith
Promotions manager: Jim Whyte
Marketing manager: David Macdermid
Marketing assistant: Malcolm Panton
Business development managers: Alan Dinnet, Angela Gordon
Customer services manager: Peter Roy
Operations manager: John Morgan
Operations administrator: John Metcalfe
Press officer: Andrew Shinie
PR internet coordinator: Caroline Calder
Accountant: Jacqueline Watt
Accounts assistants: Faye Spence, Ann Fleming
Buying and merchandising manager: Aileen Davidson
Club shop supervisors: David Reid, Catriona Young
Club shop sales: Wendy McLeod, Debbie Nichols, Gloria Officer, Lorraine Stuart
Customer services supervisor: Judith Quinn
Customer services: Lilian Christie, Jodie Petrie, Dorothy Robertson, Coleen Scott, Terry McDermott, Lynn Swinton, Louise Killoh
Scratch card administrator: Lorraine Whyte
Dons treble chance administrative assistant: Sally Small
Promotions-sales reps: John Joiner, Sandy Logie
Community coordinator: Cerise Barclay
Club electrician: Ashley Ruddiman
General assistant: George Ingram
Receptionists: Brenda McCann, Alyson Rankin

Maintenance: Willie Cargill, Dick Harper, Charlie McKay, Stan Milne, Jim Park, Alan Scott, Harry Scott, Luigi Spoggi, Jim Summers, Bob Sutherland
Cleaners: Agnes Fiddes, Mabel Morrison

Records

First player capped for Scotland: Willie Lennie, 1908

Most capped player: Jim Leighton – 91 full caps

Most first-team appearances: Willie Miller – 923

All-time top scorer: Joe Harper – 199 goals

Top scorer in one season: Benny Yorston – 46 league and Cup goals in 1929–30

Top scorers in one game: Paddy Moore scored six against Falkirk, 1932; Alex
   Merrie scored six against Hibernian, 1930; Ian Rodger scored seven in
   reserve game v. Leith Athletic, 1952; Dod Ritchie scored seven in reserve
   game v. Aberdeen University; Ian McNeill scored seven in reserve game
   v. East Fife, 1950

   In that last game the Dons won 15–0. Apart from McNeill, Ian Rodger
   scored six and Joe O'Neil and Alan Boyd one each.

   A tricky ball player, McNeill's career in football touched seven
   decades, starting at Aberdeen in 1949 and taking in Leicester City,
   Brighton, Southend, Dover and Ross County as a player. He was still
   assistant to the manager of Wigan Athletic in 2001!

Record score: Aberdeen 13 Peterhead 0 (Scottish Cup, third round, 1923)

Record crowd at Dons game: 146,433 at Scottish Cup final v. Celtic in 1937
   (Biggest crowd ever to watch a club football match in Britain, a record
   unlikely ever to be equalled)

Record crowd at Pittodrie: 45,061 at Scottish Cup fourth-round tie with
   Hearts, 13 March 1954

Club's first game: 15 August 1903 v. Stenhousemuir in the old Northern League

Jerseys

Aberdeen wore white in 1903 and changed to black and gold in 1904. Red
jerseys were first worn on 18 March 1939. Numbered jerseys were first
worn on 16 November 1946.

Full International Matches Played at Pittodrie

3 February 1900   Scotland 5   Wales 2   Attendance: 12,000
                   (Hamilton 2, Bell,   (Parry, Butler)
                   Wilson, Smith)

The Scotland team included R.S. McColl of Queen's Park, later famous for
his chain of sweetie shops.

12 February 1921   Scotland 2   Wales 1   Attendance: 20,824
(Andy Wilson 2)   (Collier)

21 November 1935   Scotland 3   Wales 2   Attendance: 26,334
(Napier 2, Duncan) (Phillips, Astley)

The Scotland team included Aberdonian Dally Duncan of Derby County.

10 November 1938   Scotland 1   Ireland 1   Attendance: 21,878
(Jimmy Simpson)   (Peter Doherty)

10 November 1971   Scotland 1   Belgium 0   Attendance: 36,500
(John O'Hare)

European championship qualifier. Bobby Clark, Martin Buchan and Steve Murray were in the starting line-up. Willie Young was a late addition to squad but not used.

16 May 1990   Scotland 1   Egypt 3   Attendance: 23,000
(Ally McCoist)

Friendly. Stewart McKimmie, Alex McLeish and Jim Bett were in the starting line-up.

2 June 1993   Scotland 3   Estonia 1   Attendance: 14,300
(Nevin 2, McClair)

World Cup qualifier. Stephen Wright, Gary Smith, Brian Irvine and Scott Booth were in the original squad. Wright withdrew injured and was replaced by Stewart McKimmie on the bench. Irvine was in the starting line-up. Booth and McKimmie came on as second-half substitutes.

8 September 1993   Scotland 1   Switzerland 1   Attendance: 21,400
(John Collins)

Another World Cup qualifier. Brian Irvine, Stewart McKimmie, Gary Smith, Scott Booth and Eoin Jess were in the squad. Smith pulled out injured. McKimmie, Irvine and Booth were in the starting line-up. Jess substituted for Booth. Former Don Bryan Gunn of Norwich was in goal.

7 September 1997   Scotland 4   Belarus 1   Attendance: 20,160
(Gallacher 2, Hopkin 2)

World Cup qualifier. It was played on Sunday, a day later than planned because of Princess Diana's funeral on the Saturday. Jim Leighton and Billy Dodds were in the squad. Leighton was in the starting line-up and Dodds came on as a late substitute.

371

14 October 1998   Scotland 2   Faroe Isles 1   Attendance: 18,517
                   (Burley, Dodds)

European championship qualifier. Derek Whyte was the only Aberdeen player in the squad, on the bench but not used. By this time, Dodds was a Dundee United player.

17 April 2002   Scotland 1   Nigeria 2   Attendance: 20,465
                (Dailly)

World Cup warm-up friendly for Nigeria, due to play in England's section in Japan. Spirited performance by young, inexperienced Scottish team in which new coach Berti Vogts tried out seven newcomers, including Aberdeen's Kevin McNaughton who made a highly creditable debut. McNaughton went on to become the Players' Union choice as Young Player of the Year in 2002.

Aberdeen players who have earned international recognition while at Pittodrie and elsewhere

Russell Anderson
Under-21 – 13 caps
Estonia 1997, 1999, 2000; Austria 1997; Sweden 1997; Latvia 1998; Finland 1998; Belgium 1999; Germany 1999; Eire 1999; N. Ireland 1999; Czech Republic 1999; Bosnia 2000

Steve Archibald (Aberdeen 1979–80; Tottenham 1981–86)
Full internationals – 27 caps
Portugal 1980, 1982; N. Ireland 1980, 1981(2), 1982; Poland 1980; Hungary 1980; Sweden 1981; Israel 1981(2); England 1981, 1984, 1985; Spain 1982, 1985; Holland 1982; New Zealand 1982; Brazil 1982; Russia 1982; E. Germany 1983, 1984; Switzerland 1983; Belgium 1983; France 1984; Iceland 1985; W. Germany 1986
Under-21 (overage) – 5 caps
Belgium 1980; England 1980(2); W. Germany 1980; Denmark 1981

Matt Armstrong
Full internationals – 3 caps
N. Ireland 1936; Wales 1936; Germany 1936

Inter-League – 2 caps
English League 1937; Irish League 1937

Archie Baird
Full internationals – 1 cap
Belgium 1946

Doug Bell
Under-21 – 2 caps
Denmark 1981; Yugoslavia 1984 (overage)

Paul Bernard (Oldham 1992–95; Aberdeen 1995–96)
Full internationals – 2 caps
Japan 1995; Ecuador 1995

B internationals – 1 cap
Sweden 1996

Under-21 – 15 caps
Romania 1992; Denmark 1992; Sweden 1992; USA 1992; Switzerland 1993; Portugal 1993(2); Italy 1993, 1994; Malta 1993, 1994; France 1993; Bulgaria 1993; Mexico 1993; England 1993

Jim Bett (Rangers 1981–83; Lokeren 1983–85; Aberdeen 1985–90)
Full internationals – 26 caps
Holland 1982, 1986; Belgium 1983, 1984, 1987; Wales 1984, 1985, 1986; England 1984, 1985; France 1984, 1990; Yugoslavia 1985, 1989; Iceland 1985(2); Spain 1985(2); Australia 1986; Israel 1986; Hungary 1988; Norway 1990; Argentina 1990; Egypt 1990; Malta 1990; Costa Rica 1990

Under-21 – 7 caps
Sweden 1981, 1982; Denmark 1981, 1982; Italy 1982; England 1982(2)

Eric Black (Aberdeen 1983–86; Metz 1986–90)
Full internationals – 2 caps
Hungary 1988; Luxembourg 1988

B International – 1 cap
E. Germany 1990

Under-21 – 8 caps
E. Germany 1983; Switzerland 1983(2); Belgium 1983; Iceland 1985(2); Spain 1985(2)

Scott Booth (Aberdeen 1991–97; Borussia Dortmund 1997–99; Twente Enschede 1999–2002)

Full internationals – 21 caps
Germany 1993; Estonia 1993(2); Switzerland 1994, 1996; Malta 1994; Faroe Isles 1995; Russia 1995; Finland 1996, 1998; San Marino 1996; Australia 1996; USA 1996; Holland 1996; Denmark 1998; Colombia 1998; Morocco 1998; Poland 2001; Croatia 2002; Belgum 2002; Latvia 2002

B Internationals – 2 caps
Wales 1994; Denmark 1996

Under-21 – 14 caps
Romania 1991, 1992; Bulgaria 1991(2); Poland 1991; France 1991; USA 1991, 1992; Switzerland 1992; Denmark 1992; Sweden 1992; Portugal 1992, 1993; Malta 1993

Jamie Buchan
Under-21 – 9 caps
Sweden 1997; Latvia 1998; Finland 1998; Lithuania 1999; Estonia 1999; Belgium 1999; Czech Republic 1999; Germany 1999; Eire 1999

Martin Buchan (Aberdeen 1971–72; Manchester Utd 1973–79)
Full internationals (34 caps)
Portugal 1972, 1975, 1979; Belgium 1972; Wales 1972, 1974, 1978; Czechoslavakia 1972, 1977; Brazil 1972, 1974, 1977; Yugoslavia 1972, 1974; Denmark 1973(2), 1976; England 1973; N. Ireland 1974, 1978; W. Germany 1974; Norway 1974, 1979; E. Germany 1975, 1978; Spain 1975; Rumania 1976; Finland 1977; Chile 1977, Argentina 1977; Peru 1978; Iran 1978; Holland 1978; Austria 1979

Under-23 – 3 caps
Wales 1971, 1972; England 1972

Alex Cheyne
Full internationals – 3 caps
England 1929; France 1930(2)

Inter-League – 1 cap
Irish League 1930

Bobby Clark
Full internationals – 17 caps

Wales 1968, 1971, 1973; Holland 1968; N. Ireland 1970, 1971, 1973; Portugal 1971; England 1971,1972, 1973; Denmark 1971, 1973; Russia 1971; Belgium 1972; Czechoslovakia 1972; Brazil 1972

Under-23 – 2 caps
Wales 1967; England 1967

Under-21 (overage) – 3 caps
Czechoslovakia 1977; Wales 1977; Switzerland 1977

Inter-League – 1 cap
English League 1971

Chris Clark
Under-21 – 1 cap
Poland 2001

Donald Colman
Full internationals – 4 caps
England 1911; Wales 1911; N. Ireland 1911, 1913

Inter-League – 1 cap
Irish League 1911

Bobby Connor (Dundee 1980–86; Aberdeen 1987–91)
Full internationals – 4 caps
Holland 1986; Saudi Arabia 1988; England 1989; Romania 1991

B internationals – 1 cap
E. Germany 1990

Under-21 – 2 caps
Sweden 1981, 1982

Charlie Cooke (Aberdeen 1963–65; Dundee and Chelsea 1966–75)
Full internationals – 13 caps
Italy 1966; Wales 1966, 1969; Portugal 1966; Brazil 1966; England 1968; Hungary 1969; Austria 1969, 1970; Iceland 1969; Cyprus 1969; Belgium 1971; Spain 1975

Inter-League – 4 caps
Italian League 1963; League of Ireland 1963; English League 1965; Irish League 1966

Neale Cooper
Under-21 – 13 caps
Denmark 1982; England 1982(2); E. Germany 1983, 1984; Switzerland 1983(2); Belgium 1983, 1984; Yugoslavia 1984; Iceland 1985(2); Spain 1985

Willie Cooper
Inter-League – 2 caps
English League 1935, 1936

Andy Cowie
Inter-League – 1 cap
Irish League 1948

Michael Craig
Under-21 – 2 caps
Belarus 1998; Latvia 1998

Billy Dodds (Aberdeen 1995–98; Dundee Utd 1998–99; Rangers 2000–02)
Full internationals – 26 caps
Latvia 1997, 2001; Wales 1997; Belarus 1997, 1998; Estonia 1999, 2000; Faroe Isles 1999(2); Germany 1999; Czech Republic 1999; Bosnia 2000(2); Lithuania 2000; England 2000(2); France 2000; Holland 2000; Eire 2000; San Marino 2001(2); Australia 2001; Belgium 2001, 2002; Poland 2001; Croatia 2002
B internationals – 2 caps
N. Ireland 1995; Wales 1998

Ryan Esson
Under-21 – 6 caps
Lithuania 2000; N. Ireland 2000; Croatia 2001; Belgium 2001, 2002; Poland 2001

Jim Forrest (Rangers 1966–68; Aberdeen 1969–71)
Full internationals – 5 caps
Wales 1966; Italy 1966; Belgium 1971; Denmark 1971; Russia 1971

Stephen Glass (Aberdeen 1995–98; Newcastle 1999–2000)
Full internationals – 1 cap
Faroe Islands 1999

B internationals – 2 caps
Denmark 1996; Wales 1998

Under-21 – 10 caps
Mexico 1995; South Korea 1995; Brazil 1995; Greece 1996; Finland 1996; Hungary 1996; Spain 1996; Austria 1997(2); Estonia 1997

Archie Glen
Full internationals – 2 caps
England 1956; Ireland 1956

Inter-League – 7 caps
League of Ireland 1954, 1955, 1956; Irish League 1955, 1959; English League 1956; Danish League 1956

Arthur Graham (Aberdeen 1972–77; Leeds Utd 1978–81)
Full internationals – 11 caps
E. Germany 1978; Austria 1979, 1980; Norway 1979(2); Wales 1979, 1981; N. Ireland 1979; England 1979; Argentina 1979; Peru 1980
Under-23 – 4 caps
England 1975; Sweden 1975; Romania 1975; Denmark 1976
Inter-League – 1 cap
English League 1972

Bryan Gunn (Aberdeen 1983–86; Norwich 1987–96)
Full internationals – 6 caps
Egypt 1990; Estonia 1993(2); Switzerland 1994; Italy 1994; Holland 1994

B internationals – 4 caps
France 1987; Yugoslavia 1990; E. Germany 1990; Sweden 1996
Under-21 – 9 caps
E. Germany 1984; Yugoslavia 1984(2); W. Germany 1985; Iceland 1985(2); Spain 1985(2); France 1990 (overage)

George Hamilton
Full internationals – 5 caps

N. Ireland 1947; Austria 1951; Belgium 1951; Norway 1954(2)
Inter-League – 2 caps
English League 1947, 1951

Joe Harper (Aberdeen 1970–72 and 1977–78; Everton 1973–75; Hibs 1975–76)
Full internationals – 4 caps
Denmark 1973(2), 1976; Iran 1978
Under-23 – 2 caps
Wales 1970, 1971
Inter-League – 1 cap
Irish League 1970

Jim Hermiston
Inter-League – 1 cap
English League 1974

John Hewitt
Under-21 – 6 caps
Italy 1982; E. Germany 1983; Switzerland 1983(2); Belgium 1984; Yugoslavia 1984

Frank Hill
Full internationals – 3 caps
France 1930; Wales 1931; N. Ireland 1931
Inter-League – 1 cap
English League 1931

Jock Hutton (Aberdeen 1923–26; Blackburn 1927–28)
Full internationals – 10 caps
England 1923, 1926; Wales 1923, 1926, 1928; N. Ireland 1923, 1924, 1926, 1927, 1928
Inter-League – 4 caps
English League 1924, 1925; Irish League 1924, 1926

Brian Irvine
Full internationals – 9 caps

Romania 1991; Germany 1993; Estonia 1993(2); Switzerland 1994; Italy 1994; Malta 1994; Austria 1994; Holland 1994

Alec Jackson (Aberdeen 1924–25; Huddersfield 1925–30)
Full internationals – 17 caps
England 1925, 1926, 1928, 1929, 1930; Wales 1925, 1926, 1927, 1928, 1929, 1930; N. Ireland 1925, 1926, 1927, 1929, 1930; France 1930

Eoin Jess (Aberdeen 1990–96 and 1998–2001; Coventry 1996–97)
Full internationals – 18 caps
Italy 1993, 1994; Malta 1993; Switzerland 1994; Holland 1994(2); Austria 1994; Finland 1995; Sweden 1996; San Marino 1996; USA 1996; Colombia 1996; Denmark 1998; Czech Republic 1999(2); Germany 1999; Faroe Isles 1999

B internationals – 2 caps
Wales 1994; Denmark 1996

Under-21 – 14 caps
France 1990, 1991; Norway 1990; Romania 1991, 1992; Switzerland 1991, 1992; Bulgaria 1991(2); Poland 1991; USA 1991; Germany 1992(2); Sweden 1992

Stuart Kennedy (Falkirk 1973–76; Aberdeen 1977–82)
Full internationals – 8 caps
Bulgaria 1978; Wales 1978; England 1978; Peru 1978; Holland 1978; Austria 1979; Portugal 1979, 1982
Under-23 – 3 caps
England 1973; Wales 1973, 1975

Graham Leggat (Aberdeen 1954–58; Fulham 1959–60)
Full internationals – 18 caps
England 1956, 1959, 1960; N. Ireland 1958, 1959, 1960; Wales 1957, 1959, 1960; Hungary 1958, 1960; Poland 1958, 1960; Yugoslavia 1958; Paraguay 1958; Germany 1959; Holland 1959; Austria 1960
Inter-League – 5 caps
English League 1954, 1958; Irish League 1955, 1957, 1958

Jim Leighton (Aberdeen 1979–88 and 1997–99; Manchester Utd 1989–91; Hibs 1994–97)

Full internationals – 91 caps (44 shut-outs)

E. Germany 1983; Switzerland 1983(2); Belgium 1983, 1984, 1987, 1988; Wales 1983, 1984, 1985, 1986, 1997; England 1983, 1984, 1985, 1987, 1988, 1989; Canada 1983(2); Uruguay 1984, 1986; N. Ireland 1984; France 1984, 1989, 1990; Yugoslavia 1985, 1990; Iceland 1985(2); Spain 1985(2), 1988; E. Germany 1986; Australia 1986(2), 1996; Israel 1986; Denmark 1986, 1996, 1998; W. Germany 1986; Bulgaria 1987, 1988; Eire 1987(2); Luxembourg 1987, 1988; Hungary 1988; Saudi Arabia 1988; Malta 1988, 1997; Colombia 1988; Norway 1989, 1990, 1998; Cyprus 1989(2); Chile 1989; Argentina 1990; Malta 1990, 1994; Costa Rica 1990; Sweden 1990, 1996, 1997(2); Brazil 1990, 1998; Austria 1994, 1997; Holland 1994; Greece 1995, 1996; Russia 1995; San Marino 1995, 1996; Japan 1995; Ecuador 1995; Faroe Isles 1995; Finland 1996, 1998; USA 1996, 1998; Estonia 1997, 1999; Belarus 1997, 1998; Latvia 1998; Morocco 1998; Lithuania 1999

Under-21 – 3 caps

USA 1979; Italy (overage) 1982(2)

Willie Lennie

Full internationals – 2 caps

Wales 1908; Ireland 1908

Inter-League – 1 cap

Irish League 1911

Andy Love

Full internationals – 3 caps

Italy 1930; Austria 1930; Switzerland 1930

Inter-League –1 cap

Irish League 1930

Fred Martin

Full internationals – 6 caps

Norway 1964(2); Austria 1954; Uruguay 1954; Hungary 1955; England 1955

Inter-League – 2 caps
League of Ireland 1953; English League 1954

Joe Miller (Aberdeen 1986–87; Celtic 1988–90)
Under-21 – 7 caps
Eire 1987; Belgium 1988; England 1988; Norway 1989; Yugoslavia 1989;
France 1990; Norway 1990

Willie Miller
Full internationals – 65 caps (12 as captain)
Romania 1975, 1986; Bulgaria 1978, 1987; Belgium 1980, 1984; Wales
1980, 1981, 1983, 1984, 1985, 1986; England 1980, 1981, 1983, 1984,
1985, 1986, 1987, 1988; Poland 1980; Hungary 1980, 1988; Sweden
1981; Portugal 1981, 1982; Israel 1981, 1986; N. Ireland 1981(2), 1982;
Holland 1982, 1986; Brazil 1982, 1987; Russia 1982; E. Germany 1983,
1984, 1986; Switzerland 1983(2); Canada 1983(3); Uruguay 1984,
1986; France 1984; Yugoslavia 1985, 1989, 1990; Iceland 1985(2); Spain
1985(2), 1988; Australia 1986(2); Denmark 1986; W. Germany 1986
(50th cap); Luxembourg 1988; Saudi Arabia 1988; Malta 1988; Colombia
1988; Norway 1989, 1990
Under-23 – 9 caps
England 1974, 1975; Wales 1975, 1976; Sweden 1975; Denmark 1976;
Romania 1976; Holland 1976(2)
Under-21 (overage) – 2 caps
Switzerland 1978; Czechoslovakia 1978
Inter-League – 1 cap
English League 1976

Willie Mills
Full internationals – 3 caps
Wales 1936, 1937; Ireland 1937

Jimmy Mitchell
Inter-League – 1 cap
English League 1955

George Mulhall (Aberdeen 1960–63; Sunderland 1964–65)

Full internationals – 3 caps
Ireland 1960, 1963

Inter-League – 3 caps
League of Ireland 1960, 1962; Irish League 1960

Steve Murray (Dundee 1968–70; Aberdeen 1970–72)

Full internationals – 1 cap
Belgium 1972

Under-21 – 1 cap
England 1968

Ernie McGarr

Full internationals – 2 caps
Austria 1970; Eire 1970

Mark McGhee

Full internationals – 4 caps
Canada 1983(2); N. Ireland 1984; England 1984

Under-21 – 1 cap (overage)
Denmark 1981

Phil McGuire

Under-21 – 2 caps
Belgium 2002; Latvia 2002

Stewart McKimmie

Full internationals – 40 caps
England 1989, 1996; Chile 1989; Argentina 1990; Egypt 1990; Costa
Rica 1990; Brazil 1990; Romania 1991, 1992; Switzerland 1991,1992,
1994; Bulgaria 1991; San Marino 1991; N. Ireland 1992; Finland 1992,
1995, 1996; USA 1992; Canada 1992; Norway 1992; Holland 1992,
1994(2), 1996; Germany 1992; CIS 1992; Portugal 1993; Estonia 1993;
Italy 1994; Austria 1994; Faroe Isles 1995(2); Russia 1995(2); Greece
1995, 1996; Sweden 1996; Denmark 1996; Colombia 1996

B internationals – 1 cap
France 1987

Under-21 – 3 caps (overage)
W. Germany 1985; Iceland 1985(2)

Alex McLeish
Full internationals – 77 caps (8 as captain)
Portugal 1980; N. Ireland 1980, 1981(2), 1982, 1984; Wales 1980, 1983, 1984, 1985, 1986; England 1980, 1981, 1983, 1984, 1985, 1986, 1987, 1988, 1989; Poland 1980; Hungary 1980; Sweden 1981, 1982, 1990; Israel 1981(2); Spain 1982, 1985(2), 1988; Brazil 1982, 1987, 1990; Belgium 1983, 1984, 1987, 1988; Switzerland 1983, 1991; Canada 1983(3); Uruguay 1984; E. Germany 1984, 1986, 1990; France 1984, 1989 (60th cap), 1990; Yugoslavia 1985, 1989, 1990; Iceland 1985(2); Australia 1986(2); Holland 1986; Denmark 1986; Bulgaria 1988, 1991; Luxembourg 1988 (50th cap); Saudi Arabia 1988; Malta 1988, 1993; Colombia 1988; Norway 1989, 1990; Italy 1989; Cyprus 1989(2); Chile 1989; Argentina 1990; Egypt 1990; Costa Rica 1990; Romania 1991; Soviet Union 1991(75th cap)

B internationals – 1 cap
France 1987

Under-21 – 6 caps
Wales 1978; USA 1979; Belgium 1980; England 1980(2); Eire 1987 (overage)

Tommy McMillan
Under-23 – 2 caps
Wales 1967; England 1967

Kevin McNaughton
Full international – 1 cap
Nigeria 2002
Under-21 – 1 cap
Latvia 2002

Charlie Nicholas (Celtic 1981–83; Arsenal 1984–87; Aberdeen 1988–89)
Full internationals – 20 caps
Switzerland 1983; N. Ireland 1983; England 1983, 1986, 1987; Canada 1983(3); Belgium 1984; France 1984; Yugoslavia 1985; Iceland 1985;

Spain 1985; Wales 1985; Israel 1986; Romania 1986; Denmark 1986; Uruguay 1986; Bulgaria 1987; Cyprus 1989

B internationals – 1 cap
France 1987

Under-21 – 6 caps
Sweden 1981, 1982; E. Germany 1983; Switzerland 1983; Belgium 1983; Yugoslavia 1984

Ian Purdie
Under-23 – 1 cap
England 1975

Dave Robb
Full internationals – 5 caps
Portugal 1971; Wales 1971; England 1971; Denmark 1971; Russia 1971

Under-23 – 3 caps
France 1970; Wales 1970; England 1971

Inter-League – 3 caps
Irish League 1970; English League 1971, 1974

David Robertson (Aberdeen 1987–91; Rangers 1992–95)
Full internationals – 3 caps
N. Ireland 1992; Switzerland 1994; Holland 1994

B internationals – 2 caps
France 1987; Wales 1994

Under-21 – 7 caps
Eire 1987; England 1988(2); Norway 1989, 1990; Yugoslavia 1989, 1990

Andy Roddie
Under-21 – 5 caps
USA 1992; Portugal 1992, 1993; Switzerland 1993; Iceland 1993

Doug Rougvie
Full internationals – 1 cap
N. Ireland 1984

David Rowson
Under-21 – 4 caps
Latvia 1997; Estonia 1997; Sweden 1997(2)

Duncan Shearer
Full internationals – 7 caps
Austria 1994; Holland 1994; Finland 1995; Russia 1995; San Marino 1995; Faroe Isles 1995; Greece 1996
B internationals – 2 caps
Sweden 1996; Denmark 1996

Neil Simpson
Full internationals – 5 caps
N. Ireland 1983; Uruguay 1984; France 1984; England 1987, 1988
B internationals – 1 cap
France 1987
Under-21 – 11 caps
Italy 1982(2); England 1982; E. Germany 1983, 1984; Switzerland 1983(2); Belgium 1983, 1984; Yugoslavia 1984; Spain (overage) 1985

Dave Smith (Aberdeen 1961–66; Rangers 1967–69)
Full internationals – 2 caps
Holland 1966, 1968
Under-23 – 1 cap
England 1967
Inter-League – 4 caps
English League 1966, 1967, 1968, 1970

Gary Smith
Under-21 – 2 caps
Germany 1992(2)

Jimmy Smith (Aberdeen 1965–69; Newcastle 1970–74)
Full internationals – 4 caps
Holland 1968; W. Germany 1974; N. Ireland 1974; Wales 1974
Under-23 – 1 cap
England 1967

Billy Stark
Under-21 – 1 cap
Iceland (overage) 1985

Derek Stillie
Under-21 – 13 caps
Russia 1995(2);   San Marino 1995, 1996; Mexico 1995; South Korea 1995; Brazil 1995; Greece 1996; Finland 1996; Hungary 1996(2); Spain 1996; France 1996

Gordon Strachan (Aberdeen 1979–84; Manchester Utd 1985–92)
Full internationals – 50 caps
N. Ireland 1980, 1982, 1983, 1984, 1992; Wales 1980, 1983, 1986; England 1980, 1983, 1984, 1985; Poland 1980; Hungary 1980, 1987; Sweden 1981; Portugal 1981, 1982; Spain 1982, 1985; Holland 1982; New Zealand 1982; Brazil 1982; Russia 1982, 1991; E. Germany 1983, 1984; Switzerland 1983(2), 1992; Belgium 1983; Canada 1983(3); France 1984, 1989, 1990; Iceland 1985; Australia 1986; Romania 1986, 1992; Denmark 1986; W. Germany 1986; Uruguay 1986; Bulgaria 1987, 1991; Eire 1987(2); San Marino 1991; Finland 1992

Under-21 – 1 cap
Belgium (overage) 1980

Andy Watson
Under-21 – 4 caps
Sweden 1981; Denmark 1981, 1982; Italy 1982

Michael Watt
B internationals – 1 cap
Denmark 1996

Under-21 – 13 caps
Romania 1991, 1992; Switzerland 1991, 1992; Bulgaria 1991(2); Poland 1991; France 1991; USA 1991; Germany 1992(2); Sweden 1992(2)

Peter Weir (St Mirren 1980–81; Aberdeen 1982–84)
Full internationals – 6 caps
N. Ireland 1980, 1984; Wales 1980; Poland 1980; Hungary 1980; Switzerland 1983

Derek Whyte (Celtic 1987–92; Middlesbrough 1993–97; Aberdeen 1998–99)

Full internationals – 12 caps
Belgium 1988; Luxembourg 1988; Chile 1989; USA 1992, 1996; Portugal 1993; Italy 1993; Japan 1995; Ecuador 1995; Latvia 1997; Finland 1998; Germany 1999

B internationals – 4 caps
Yugoslavia 1990; E. Germany 1990; Sweden 1996; Denmark 1996

Under-21 – 9 caps
Eire 1987(2); Belgium 1987; England 1988(2); Norway 1989; Yugoslavia 1989, 1990; Norway 1990

Jim Whyte
Under-23 – 2 caps
Wales 1967; England 1967

Jimmy Wilson
Inter-League – 1 cap
English League 1967

Robbie Winters
Full internationals – 1 cap
Germany 1999

Bobby Wishart
Inter-League – 1 cap
Irish League 1955

Alex Wright
Inter-League – 1 cap
English League 1922

Paul Wright (Aberdeen 1987–90; Kilmarnock 1991–98)
B internationals – 2 caps
Wales 1998; Norway 1998
Under-21 – 3 caps
Yugoslavia 1989, 1990; France 1989

Stephen Wright
Full internationals – 2 caps
Germany 1993; Estonia 1993

B internationals – 2 caps
Wales 1994; N. Ireland 1995

Under-21 – 15 caps
Bulgaria 1991; Poland 1991; France 1991; USA 1991; Switzerland 1992, 1993; Germany 1992(2); Sweden 1992(2); Portugal 1993; Italy 1993, 1994; Malta 1993, 1994

Benny Yorston
Full internationals – 1 cap
N. Ireland 1931

Harry Yorston
Full internationals – 1 cap
Wales 1955

Inter-League – 1 cap
League of Ireland 1952

Darren Young
Under-21 – 5 caps
Estonia 1997; Sweden 1997; Latvia 1998; Czech Republic 1999; Germany 1999

Derek Young
Under-21 – 5 caps
Wales 2000; Croatia 2001, 2002; Belgium 2001; Poland 2001

Willie Young
Under-23 – 2 caps
Romania 1975; Denmark 1975

SUMMARY
Discounting youth caps, the above 87 players have made 1,108 representative appearances (not all of them while with Aberdeen). That total is made up of 718 full international, 32 B international, 35 Under-23, 269 Under-21, and 54 Inter-League appearances.

Index

Abercorn 73

Aberdeen xi–xii, 14–15, 41, 147, 173, 295

Aberdeen Asset Management 41, 52, 54, 55, 56, 58, 64

Aberdeen Football Club

formation of club xii, 69–71; Pittodrie Park opens 70–1; elected to Second Division 72; introduction of black and gold strip 73; wins first trophy, Qualifying Cup 74–5; elected to First Division 75; tops Scottish League for first time 86, 88; ladies first charged admission (1908) 86; first benefit cheque (1910) 87; first win at Ibrox (1910) 88; first home win v Rangers (1910) 88–9; first European tour (1911) 89; Colman invents dug-out (1931) 83; start being called the Dons 91; the 1931 corruption scandal 128–30; South African tours 124, 144–6; Canadian tour 196; North American tours 203–4, 243; Sutherland take-over bid thwarted (1959) 208–9; 1969 takeover bid thwarted 222–3; 1971 fire at ground 239; seventy-fifth anniversary (1978) ix, 258, 261; win European Cup Winners' Cup (1983) 277–94; voted best team in Europe (1983) 297, 303; win double of League Championship and Cup (1984) 299, 300; buy first £1 million player 28; proposed move to Kingswells xiv, 40–1, 43, 54, 59, 64; soccer academy and youth scheme 41, 43, 45, 347, 349 see also Pittodrie Park

Playing honours:

European Cup Winners' Cup (1983) xii, 15, 275, 276, 277–83, 285–94, 321, 331, 342, 343, 352

European Super Cup (1983) xiii, 297–8

Scottish League Championship winners: (1954–55) xii, 3, 155, 178, 192–7, 220, 266, 267; (1979–80) 265–6, 267–8, 270, 320; (1983–84) 298, 299; (1984–85) 300

Scottish League Championship runners-up: (1911) 89; (1956) 207; (1971) 239; (1978) 256–7, 259; (1981) 271; (1982) 277; (1989) 4; (1990) 4; (1991) 4, 5–6; (1993) 12, 23; (1994) 23

Scottish Cup winners: (1947) 3, 155, 165–71, 232, 275; (1970) 3, 224–31, 234, 238, 241, 275; (1982) 273–5, 320; (1983) 283–4, 296; (1984) 299, 339; (1986) 302–3; (1990) 4, 9, 21, 313

Scottish Cup finalists: (1937) 7, 84, 141–3, 170–1, 225; (1953) 3, 155, 178, 187–8; (1954) 3, 155, 178, 188, 190–1, 225, 250; (1959) 3, 178, 207–8; (1967) 214–15, 218–19, 225; (1978) 257; (1993) 12–13, 23; (2000) 36–8, 334

Scottish League Cup winners: (1946) xii, 155, 161–4, 171, 181; (1955) 3, 155, 178, 202–3; (1976) 3, 233, 234, 249–52; (1985) 301; (1989) 4, 312–13; (1995) 28, 29, 351

Scottish League Cup finalists: (1947) 155, 171; (1979) 264; (1980) 264; (1992) 12, 23; (2000) 34, 35–6

Drybrough Cup winners: (1971) 3, 242; (1980) 270

Aberdeen Football Club Supporters Trust 50–2, 54, 60, 61

Aberdeen Journal 72

Aberdeen Press and Journal 30–1, 50, 128, 129, 142, 202, 229, 252, 295, 318

Aberdeenshire Cup 71

Abtrust *see* Aberdeen Asset Management

AC Milan 45

Advocaat, Dick 46, 341

Airdrie 28, 161, 195, 244, 300, 347, 359

Aitken, Roy 12, 24, 26, 28, 29–30, 236, 299, 332, 351

Ajax 246

Akranes, Iceland 298, 303

Albion Rovers 73, 96, 345

Alford 17

Allan, Charlie 57

Allan, G. 103

Allan, J.K. 103

Allister, Jack 176, 188, 189, 191, 193, 194, 196, 200, 310

Alloa 345

Ancell, Bobby 149

Anderson, Chris 14, 15, 51, 53, 239–40, 241, 242, 245, 248, 249, 252, 281, 288, 293, 302, 305–8, 317, 319, 342, 358, 362

Anderson, George 93, 96, 97, 101, 149–50, 151, 172

Anderson, Russell 37, 45

Angus, Ian 300, 321

Ann, HRH The Princess Royal 14

Annbank United 174

Annfield Plain 186

Arbroath 71, 74, 80, 128, 135, 148, 166, 302

Archibald, Bobby 93, 96, 97

Archibald, Steve 257, 258, 263, 265, 266, 268, 359

Arges Pitesti, Rumania 273

Armstrong, Matt xiv, 107, 118, 121, 135, 136, 137, 139–40, 141, 142, 143, 144–5, 147, 148, 157, 240, 262, 362

Arnott, Roddy 354

Arsenal 71, 74, 112, 113, 129, 270, 310

Arthurlie 73

Association of AFC Supporters Clubs 354–5

Aston Villa 93, 98, 104, 125, 340

Atkinson, Ron 310

Auld, Bertie 214, 227, 228

Austria Vienna 271

Ayr United 36, 73, 161, 212–13, 248, 249, 254, 257, 301, 344

Bachman, Gunter 246

Baird, Archie xii, 15, 155, 157, 158–9, 160, 161, 162, 167, 168, 169, 172, 178, 183, 200, 229–30, 262, 353, 362

Baird, Hugh 208

Banks, Gordon 243

Banks o'Dee 101, 126, 190, 358

Barcelona 246

Barry Town 29

Bayern Munich 277, 278, 279–82

Beckenbauer, Franz 273

Beckham, David 31, 112

Belabed, Rachid 34, 37

Bell, Dougie 263, 276, 277, 283–4, 286, 300, 304, 321, 328, 330, 345, 363

Bellshill Athletic 95

Bellslea Park 134

Benburb 217, 233

Benfica 32–3

Bennett, Dave 211

Bennett, Gordon 52, 61–2

Benton, Willie 72

Bernard, Paul 28, 38

Best, George 16, 179, 309, 353

Bethlehem Steel, Pennsylvania 80, 109, 134

Bett, Jim 5, 9, 10, 22, 24, 296, 304, 326

Beveren, Belgium 298

Beynon, Jackie 135, 136, 140, 143, 144–5, 157

Birmingham City 345

Bisconti, Roberto 45

BK Copenhagen 9

Black, Eric 273, 276, 279, 280, 283, 289, 290, 294, 296, 299, 300, 301, 307, 321, 342–3, 351, 363

Black, Ian 160

Black, Jimmy 107, 125, 126, 129, 135

Blackburn Rovers 12, 112, 116, 118, 125, 126, 248

Blackpool 150, 186

Blackwell, Harry 101, 103, 105, 111, 124, 135

Blantyre Celtic 160
Blantyre Victoria 176
Bodie, Dr Walford 100
Boel, Henning 228, 230, 243
Bolton Wanderers 22, 104, 150, 237
Bonthrone, Jimmy 15, 182, 241–2, 244–5,
    248, 347, 350
Booth, Scott 9, 10
Bosman ruling 19
Bournemouth 350
Boyd, Alan 163–4
Bradford City 29, 87, 90, 149
Brady, Liam 236
Brechin City 164
Bremner, Billy 8, 161, 244
Bremner, Ian 354
Brewster, Dod 91, 92, 96–7, 125
Brighton 339
Bristol City 342
Britton, Cliff 150
Brondby, Denmark 29, 32, 33, 48, 59
Brooklyn Wanderers 80, 109, 134
Brown, Bobby 189
Brown, Craig 336
Brown, J. 200
Brownlee, Ken 208
Brownlie, Jimmy 99–100
Broxburn Athletic 79
Bruce, Bobby 111, 124–5
Bruce, Duff 111, 124
Bryceland, Tommy 208
Buchan, George 228, 242
Buchan, Gordon 15
Buchan, J. 102, 103
Buchan, Martin (father) 147, 160
Buchan, Martin (son) 3, 160–1, 220, 226,
    228, 229, 230, 238, 242, 243, 275,
    351, 362
Buckie Thistle 90, 160
Buckley, Paddy 121, 187, 188, 189, 191,
    195, 196–7, 200, 202, 203, 204,
    212, 267
Burkinshaw, Keith 29–30, 31
Burnley 128, 180
Busby, Matt 309, 324
Butcher, Terry 342–3

Cairns, Tommy 78
Calder, Bobby 105, 169, 214, 231, 232–5,
    237, 238, 334

Calder, David 105
Caldwell, David 189, 191, 194, 200, 202,
    208
Callander, Mrs Mabel 222
Cameron, Ian 312
Carabine, Jimmy 141
Cardiff City 125, 302
Carnoustie Panmure 177
Carswell, Jimmy 236, 237, 329
Celtic 3, 4, 21, 35–6, 37, 39, 46–7, 57,
    63, 75, 83, 85–6, 89, 91, 100, 106,
    138, 142–3, 157, 182, 190–1, 207,
    211, 212, 214, 217, 220, 225,
    226–8, 236, 239, 240, 242, 243,
    250–1, 255, 258, 263, 265, 267,
    271, 274, 275, 283–4, 296, 298,
    299, 300, 302, 312, 320, 323, 324,
    330, 339, 340, 344; consider joining
    English Premier League 19, 63, 64,
    332–3; Old Firm domination xii, 22,
    26, 33, 34, 42, 56, 64, 141, 248,
    303, 320, 324, 327, 332, 341, 349,
    359; in transfers 30, 32, 73, 90,
    105, 126, 131, 139, 232, 233, 238,
    244, 317, 342, 343, 345
Chapman, Herbert 113
Charles, John 176
Charlton Athletic 150
Charlton, Bobby 16, 309
Chelsea 8, 112, 114, 123, 131, 156, 176,
    216, 235, 310, 322, 338, 339
Cheyne, Alec 117, 119, 121–3, 124
Chisholm, Euan 354
Chrystal, George (Chrys) 176, 183, 184,
    287
Churchill, Winston 157, 161, 293, 327
CIS League Cup 35, 45
Clark, Bobby 3, 61, 214, 216–17, 218,
    221, 224, 227, 228, 229, 230, 238,
    243, 250–1, 252, 259, 264, 266,
    267, 271, 320, 329, 330, 335, 337,
    342, 347, 362
Clark, John 258, 259, 260
Clark, Steve 8
Clarke, John 70, 91
Clemence, Ray 271
Clunie, Jim 190, 191, 200, 202, 208, 210,
    350
Clyde 10, 72, 74, 75, 106, 144, 149, 157,
    192, 193, 216, 250, 254, 255, 257,

263, 267, 300, 345
Clydebank 224, 229, 359
Cole, Andy 31
Colgan, Nick 46
Colman, Donald xiv, as player 77, 80,
    81–2, 85, 86, 88, 89, 90, 91–2, 96,
    97, 98, 99, 104, 107, 118, 133; as
    trainer-coach 83–4, 101, 109, 117,
    126, 131, 137–8, 140, 141, 143,
    149, 240, 362
Cologne 299, 322
Colquhoun, John 8
Compton, Denis 150
Compton, Leslie 150
Connon, Jacky 96, 97, 101
Connor, Bobby 9, 10
Cook, Angus 358
Cook, Barbara 358
Cooke, Charlie xiv, 3, 178, 200, 211, 233,
    235, 281, 362
Cooper, Davie 359
Cooper, John 189–90
Cooper, Neale 274, 283–4, 289, 300, 321,
    337, 340, 345, 351, 363
Cooper, Neil 351
Cooper, Willie xiii, 97, 116, 118, 130, 131,
    133, 135, 139, 140, 142, 143, 155,
    160, 161, 166, 167, 170–1, 172,
    175, 181, 362
Cormack, Dave 52, 61, 357
Cosgrove, Mike 124
Coutts, Douglas 211
Cove Rangers 337, 339, 343
Coventry 28, 30, 342, 343, 351
Cowan, Jimmy 181–2, 346
Cowan, Steve 270, 300, 321
Cowdenbeath 74, 97, 125
Cowie, Andy xii, 148, 155, 160, 162, 173,
    181, 200
Craig, John 233–4
Craig, Tommy 26, 29, 233, 351
Craigmyle, Peter 121, 150
crowd trouble 86, 89–90, 97, 100, 185,
    205–6, 256, 356
Cruickshank, Johnny 160
Crum, Johnny 143
Cruyff, Johan 246
Crystal Palace 149, 177–8, 326, 335
Cullis, Stan 150
Cumming, Dave 135

Cummings, James (son) 54
Cummings, Jim (father) 52, 53–4, 57,
    58–60, 61
Cummings, Keith 54
Cunningham, Andy 112
Cunningham, Donald 83
Curran, John 178
Currer, Herbert 136
Cuthbertson, John 167, 168

Dadi, Eugene 63
Daily Express 266
Dalglish, Kenny 250, 271, 327, 336, 340
Dalry Thistle 334
Darkie the Pittodrie cat 190
Darwen 80, 98
Davidson, Bobby 228
Davidson, Duncan 264
Davidson, Norman 208, 212, 350
Davidson, Stewart 92, 97, 105, 106
Dawson, Jerry 150, 175, 296
Delaney, Jimmy 143, 182, 183
Deveronvale 224, 335
Devine, Joe 140
Dewar, Andrew 355
Dibble, Andy 5
Dick, John 235–6
Dickie, Percy 131, 181
di Stefano, Alfredo 290
Ditchburn, Ted 151
Dodds, Billy 22, 24, 25, 28
Dolan, Jim 30–1
Donald, Herbert 14
Donald, Ian 15–16, 20, 41, 51, 52, 59,
    281, 358
Donald, James 14, 171
Donald, James F. 14
Donald, Dick ix, 13, 14–15, 17, 48, 51,
    53, 117, 203, 207, 240, 253, 254,
    255, 260, 281, 293, 307, 317, 318,
    319, 322, 332, 358, 359, 362
Donald, Peter 14, 15
Doncaster Rovers 136
Donoghue, Steve 100
Donside Paper Mills 53
Douglas, Jack 354
Douglas, Rab 46–7
Dow, Andy 36, 38
Dow, Dod 361–2
Drain, Dinger 82

Drybrough Cup 3, 242, 270
Dryden, Jackie 149
Dumbarton 70, 82, 93, 101, 109, 157
Dumfries 195
Dunbar, John 229
Duncan, Bob 347
Duncan, Mrs Flora 222
Duncan, John 222
Duncan, Tom 76, 88, 96, 98
Dundalk 343
Dundee 9, 22, 28, 42, 73, 76, 90, 93, 94,
    105, 147, 149, 166, 172, 181, 207,
    211, 217, 218, 224, 226, 235, 238,
    249, 252, 258, 263, 265, 300, 302,
    327, 341, 347, 358
Dundee Courier 181
Dundee United 8, 10, 12, 21, 24, 25, 29,
    30, 42, 130, 148, 217, 218, 219,
    244, 250, 264, 265, 267, 277, 282,
    296, 301, 303, 312, 313
Dunfermline Athletic 15, 25, 160, 212,
    214, 215, 217, 232, 239, 312, 317,
    338, 340, 345, 263, 339
Dunlop, Frank xii, 140, 142, 143, 155,
    160, 161, 163, 166, 167, 169, 170,
    171, 172, 200, 217, 230, 241, 275
Dunn, Tim 106, 112
Duntocher Hibs 208
Durrant, Ian 337
Dyer, Alex 149, 161
Dynamo Berlin 301

East Fife 182, 213, 267
East Stirlingshire 73, 263, 317
Edgar, Johnny 74, 92
Edward, Jock 105, 124
Eisenhower, General Dwight 182-3
Elgin City 90, 140, 345, 350
Elizabeth, HRH The Queen Mother 327
Ekstrom, Johnny 303, 325
Emery, Don 28, 95, 178, 179-82, 183,
    201, 222-3, 240
Empire Exhibition Trophy 156
English, Sam 37, 83
Erskine, Knight 70
European Championship 42, 327
European Cup (Champions Cup) 201, 214,
    215, 225, 226, 270-1, 272-3, 297,
    298, 302, 303-4, 309, 324
European Cup Winners' Cup xiii, 5, 8, 13,

55, 215, 220, 239, 275, 276, 277,
    298, 318, 324, 327
European Super Cup 324, 327
Evening Express 57, 71, 72, 86, 92, 139,
    163, 176, 183, 193, 200, 205,
    286-7, 287-8, 338
Evening Gazette 72
Everton 83, 96, 116, 125, 150, 156, 204,
    242, 244, 250

FA Cup 9, 150, 180, 210, 248, 270, 299,
    310, 324, 326-7, 331, 335, 336,
    341
Fairgrieve, John 179, 180, 182
Falkirk 6, 25, 28, 36, 72, 75, 79, 88, 92,
    128, 164, 175, 224, 250, 263, 267,
    344, 350
Fallon, Sean 191
Falloon, Eddie 135-6, 140, 143, 144
Famagusta 5
fan power at Pittodrie 9-10, 50, 313, 355
Farquhar, Lord Provost Margaret 327
FC Twente 311
Ferencvaros 247
Ferguson, Alex 3-4, 5, 6, 16, 30, 32, 33,
    46, 47, 77, 263-4, 268, 272, 273,
    276, 277, 279, 281, 282, 283,
    296-7, 298, 299,301, 311, 317,
    318-23, 325-6, 337, 338, 339,
    342, 347, 350, 361, 362; early
    playing career 317, 344; at
    Dunfermline 217, 317; at Rangers
    317; managing East Stirling 317; at
    St Mirren 254, 261, 264, 310, 317,
    330, 334, 343, 345; appointed
    manager of Dons ix-x, 260, 262;
    wins League Championship 266,
    320; wins European Cup Winners'
    Cup 286, 288, 289, 293, 320-1,
    352, 363; takes over as Scotland
    manager 302, 309, 318; at
    Manchester United xiii, 9, 15, 31, 48,
    309-10, 318, 326-7, 335-6, 324,
    349; knighthood 325, 327, 325;
    Freedom of Aberdeen 327-8
Ferguson, Ian 8
Ferranti Thistle 57
Feyenoord 225
Finney, Tom 156
Finnie, Sandy 348

First World War 82, 93–4, 96
Fitzpatrick, Tony 263, 343–4
Flanagan, Paddy 77
Fleming, Ian 43, 347
Fletcher MP, Alex 270, 293
Forbes, Charles B. 51, 106, 134, 149,
    150–1, 222, 228, 240
Forbes, Jimmy 139, 191, 200, 287
Forfar 71, 98, 126
Forres Mechanics 90, 118
Forrest, Jim 226, 227, 228, 230, 238, 243
Forsyth, Matt 99–100, 103, 105, 106,
    107, 111, 118, 261
Fortuna Dusseldorf 318
France Football 297
Fraser, Bobby 135
Fulham 76, 196, 339
Fyfe, Isobel 354

Gala Fairydean 97
Gallacher, Hughie 110, 123
Gallacher, Tommy 181
Galloway, David 129
Garner, Willie 252, 258, 319
Gault, Jimmy 92
Gavin, Charlie 139
Gavin, Chris 50, 60–1, 355
Gemmell, Tommy 214, 227, 228
Giggs, Ryan 31, 112, 179
Gilbert, Martin 41, 52, 54, 55–60, 64
Gillhaus, Hans 4, 9, 10, 12, 311–12
Glasgow Maryhill 81, 82
Glasgow Perthshire 81, 99
Glass, Stephen 22, 25, 28
Glen, Archie 175–6, 189, 191, 193, 194,
    195, 196, 198, 200, 202, 203, 205,
    207, 208, 210–11, 262, 267, 352,
    362
Glennie, Bobby 258
Gold, Lex 19
Goldwyn, Sam 15
Gorbachev, Mikhail 327
Gordon, Jimmy 89
Gothenburg club 303–4, 325; Ullevi
    Stadium xiii, 285–9
Govan, Jock 167, 169
Graham, Arthur 3, 225, 228, 231, 233,
    234, 244, 245–6, 250, 252, 330
Grampian Television 252
Grampian Tourist Board 41

Grant, Brian 8, 9, 301
Grant, Walter 97, 101, 103, 105, 111
Gray, Duggie 150, 240
Greig, Andy 92, 94, 133
Greig, John 260, 320
Green, George 149
Greenock 211
Groningen 311
Grosert, Sandy 101
Gunn, Bryan 320, 321
Guntveit, Cato 34, 38, 63

Hagan, Jimmy 150
Hair, Ian 347
Halkett, Ecky 73, 74, 78, 85, 92
Hall, A. 103
Hall Russell's shipyard FC 53, 134, 135,
    147
Halliday, Billy 156, 174
Halliday, David 93, 149, 155, 156, 160,
    161, 172, 174, 175, 176, 177–8,
    181, 185, 186, 187, 193, 199, 350
Hamburg 273, 297–8, 299, 342
Hamilton Academicals 72, 87, 117, 141
Hamilton, George xii, 15, 151, 155–7,
    159, 160, 161, 163, 167, 168, 169,
    172, 174, 178, 183, 185, 186, 187,
    188, 189, 191, 200, 201, 230, 352,
    353, 362
Hannah, Bobby 77, 78, 92, 94, 96, 134
Hansen, Alan 271
Hansen, Ebbe see Skovdahl, Ebbe
Harkness, Jack 112, 122
Harper, Joe 121, 185, 206, 227, 228, 242,
    243, 244, 249, 250, 252, 257, 259,
    267–9, 330, 362
Harris, Tony 163–4, 166, 167, 168, 173,
    187, 188, 200, 222, 262
Harvey, Joe 149
Hateley, Mark 5, 13
Hather, Jackie 186, 187, 188, 189, 191,
    193, 195, 200–1, 202, 203, 208,
    210, 240, 262, 267
Hather, John 186
Hay, Bill 144
Hay, David 236
Hay, Hugh 179, 204, 350
Hayworth, Dr Alistair 354
Heart of Midlothian 25, 30, 45, 63, 64,
    86, 90, 101, 125, 135, 150, 157,

174, 179, 188, 254, 301, 302–3,
    308, 312, 313, 319, 345
Hegarty, Paul 30, 31, 33, 332, 351
Henderson, Roy 187
Hereford 257
Hermiston, Jim 228, 330, 347
Herrera, Helenio 214
Hertha Berlin 245, 246
Hetherstone, Peter 22
Hewitt, John 272, 273, 276, 277, 279,
    280, 282, 289, 291, 297, 300, 301,
    302, 321, 328, 337, 342, 343, 345,
    351, 363
Hewkins, Ken 193
Hibernian 23, 26, 30, 36, 42, 45–6, 64,
    90, 101, 106, 112, 150, 157, 165,
    167–9, 187, 188, 199, 201, 203,
    212, 213, 217, 218, 219, 241, 244,
    248, 249, 250, 264, 265, 275, 296,
    301, 302, 327, 341, 354
Highland League 90, 102, 118, 120, 131,
    139, 210, 329, 337, 342
Hill, Frank 107, 125–6, 128–30, 135
Hogg, Jimmy 350
Honved, Hungary 239
Hosie, Alex 354
Huddersfield Town 79, 113–14, 125, 138,
    149, 156, 353
Hughes, John 227, 228
Hull City 28, 345
Hume, Jock 77, 79–80, 82, 85, 88, 89, 92,
    96, 97, 98, 99, 100, 107, 109, 133,
    134
Huntly 105, 139, 339
Hutcheson, W. 103
Hutton, Jock 95, 96, 97, 99, 101, 102,
    103, 104, 105, 106, 107, 111, 112,
    116, 118, 125, 136, 171, 179, 189
Hutton, Mungo 93
Hynd, Roger 256

Inglis, John 22
Inter Cities Fairs Cup 220
Inter-City League 90
Inter Milan 214, 298
Inverness Caledonian 90
Inverness Caley-Thistle 34–5, 141
Inverness Citadel 90
Inverness Clachnacuddin 90
Inverness Thistle 90

Inverurie Locos 18, 79
Ipswich 21, 272–3
Irvine, Brian 313
Irvine, Willie 8
Irvine Meadow 155
Irwin, Denis 31

Jackson, Alec xiv, 80, 109–15, 118, 119,
    122–3, 125, 134, 136, 138, 235,
    246, 362
Jackson, Colin 264, 274
Jackson, Jimmy 105, 111, 113, 116, 125
Jackson, John 109
Jackson, Walter 109–11, 113, 116, 125,
    134
Jackson, W.K. (Stonewall) 111, 116–17,
    124, 131, 135, 261, 293
Jaffrey, Willie 76
James, Alec 112, 235
Jamieson, Will 130
Jarvie, Drew 9, 244, 249, 250, 252, 270,
    320, 330, 347, 358
Jess, Eoin 5, 9, 10, 28–9, 38
Johnsen, Ronny 31
Johnson, President Lyndon B. 219
Johnston, Dave 214
Johnston, David 358–9
Johnstone, Derek 264
Johnstone, George xii, 140, 142, 143, 146,
    155, 160, 161, 167–8, 172, 178,
    217
Johnstone, Jimmy 179, 214, 227, 228

Kanchelskis, Andre 37
Kane, Paul 6
Keane, Roy 319
Kelly, Archie 174
Kelly, George 350
Kelly, Pat 178
Kelman, John 236–7
Kennedy, Ray 271, 339
Kennedy, Stuart 250, 252, 259, 263, 266,
    273, 279, 286, 300, 320, 321, 328,
    344, 345, 350, 351, 363
Kerr, Jimmy 167, 168–9
Kettering Town 207
Kiddie, Alec A. xii, 160, 162, 163
Kilmarnock 8, 78, 94, 99, 109, 111, 126,
    210, 212, 214, 217, 224, 249, 274,
    337, 340, 346

Kilsyth Rangers 346, 347
King, Arthur 88, 92
Kiriakov, Ilian 29
Kjaer, Peter 45
Knox, Archie 309, 326, 350, 352
Kombouare, Tony 29
KR Reykjavik 220

Lang, Johnny 143
Largs Thistle 167
Latapy, Russell 36
Lauder, Harry 100, 112
Laudrup, Brian 33
Laudrup, Fenn 33
Laudrup, Michael 33
Law, Denis 16, 114, 222, 309, 353
Lawrence, John 232
Lawrie, Paul 64, 356–7
Lawton, Tommy 150
Lech Poznan, Poland 277
Leeds United 8, 101, 244, 310, 335, 351
Legia, Warsaw 5
Leggat, Graham 189, 190–1, 194–6, 200,
    202, 203–4, 212, 246, 267, 362
Leicester City 131, 199, 342, 343
Leighton, Jim 8, 29, 37–8, 271, 273, 276,
    279, 290, 298, 300, 311, 320,
    326–7, 334–6, 340, 346, 362, 363
Leiper, John 222
Leith Athletic 72
Lennie, Willie 76, 78, 79, 81, 85, 87, 88,
    89, 92, 93, 101, 107, 133
Lemon, Jonathan 354
Lennox, Bobby 214, 227, 228, 236
Lennox, Lord Provost Robert 229
Lewis, W. Luther 109, 110, 134
Liddell, Billy 160
Little, Billy 195, 217
Little, Hugh 41, 54, 55, 56, 57, 58, 59, 64
Liverpool 105, 116, 125, 126, 160,
    270–1, 272, 273, 310, 320, 321,
    324, 339, 351
Livingston 45, 47, 57, 63
Livingstone, Duggie 125
Llanelli 191
Lloyd, Marie 100
Lochgelly United 71
Lokeren, Belgium 304
Lornie, Jim 195–6, 202
Lossiemouth 139

Love, Andy 121, 124
Low, Henry 73, 74, 78, 79, 93
Low, Wilfie 85, 87, 92
Lowe, A. 74
Lowrie, Tommy 182–3
Luton Town 310, 336

McAllister, Jamie 37
McAllister, Gary 351, 343
McAuley, Willie 73, 74, 78, 79
McCall, Billy xii, 160, 161, 167, 172–3
McClelland, John 274, 296
McLuskey, Pat 244, 265
McCoist, Ally 5, 312
McColl, R.S. 72
McConnell, Jock 92
McDermid, Bob 116, 118, 121, 124, 135,
    138, 167, 169
McDermott, Terry 271
Macdonald, Alastair 142
Macdonald, Iain 355
McDonald, John 274, 296
McDonald, Mike 249
MacDonald, Alex 217
McDougall, Frank 48, 300
McDougall, Neil 354
Macfarlane, George 92
Mcfarlane, Ian 233, 350
Macfarlane, Rab 73, 74, 77, 78, 79, 85,
    86, 92
McGarr, Ernie 211, 224
McGarvey, Frank 263
McGhee, Mark 265, 266, 274, 276, 277,
    279, 283, 290, 291, 298, 299, 300,
    319, 320–1, 322, 340, 342, 345,
    352, 363
McGill, Charlie 117, 118, 133, 135, 140
McGinlay, Brian 6
McGraw, Allan 340
McGregor, Bob 154
McGrory, Jimmy 112, 143
McGuire, Phil 45, 347
McHale, Jock 111, 124, 126
McIlvanney, Hugh 288, 325
McIntosh, Angus 85, 88, 89, 92
McIver, Gordon 221–2
McKay, Derek 224–5, 227, 228, 229, 243
Mackay, John 76, 94, 96
Mackay, Hugh 18
McKenna, Pat xii, 160, 161, 167

McKenzie, Johnny 135, 140, 143
Mackie, Darren 45, 46–7, 347
Mackie, J. 73
McKimmie, Stewart 9, 10, 300
McLachlan, Bert 93, 96, 97, 101, 102, 103, 105, 107, 111, 125
McLaren, Hugh 107, 125, 126, 128–9, 131, 135
McLaughlin, Joe 167
McLean, Adam 126, 131
McLean, Jim 267, 358
McLean, Tommy 217, 310
McLelland, Chic 258, 347
McLeish, Alex 9, 10, 34,266, 274, 276, 280, 289, 290, 296, 300, 320, 328, 340, 343, 352, 362, 363; as Motherwell manager 22, 23, 341; as Hibs manager 45, 46, 59, 341; as Rangers manager 46, 59
MacLeod, Ally 3, 15, 248–52, 254, 259, 260, 263, 301, 307, 330, 335, 347, 350
McLeod, Angus 96
McLeod, Tommy 124
McMaster, John 43, 266, 271, 276, 279–80, 282, 290, 320, 321, 339–40, 351, 363
McMillan, Tommy 214, 217, 218, 220, 228, 238, 243
McNab, John 339
McNaughton, Kevin 45, 347
McNeil, Hector 162
McNeill, Billy 15, 214, 228, 236; as manager of Dons 254–5, 256–7, 258, 259, 260, 263, 307, 311, 320, 337, 340, 341, 350
McNeill, Ian 237, 350
McNicol, Duncan 71, 74, 78, 79
McNicol, G. 73, 74
McPhail, Bob 112, 138
McQueen, Tommy 300
McRobb, Andrew 17
McRobbie, A. 102, 103
McStay, Paul 299
McStay, Willie 112
Main, Davie 92, 133
Maley, Willie 139, 211
Manchester City 5, 45, 90
Manchester United xiii, 8, 9, 16, 31, 48, 112, 131, 176, 182, 220, 242, 243,
299, 309–10, 311, 319, 322–3, 324, 326–7, 335, 341, 343
Mandela, Nelson 327
Mann, Robbie 41
Martin, Fred 177–8, 181, 187, 188, 189, 191, 193, 194, 195, 198, 199, 200, 202, 203, 208, 211, 221, 262, 267, 362
Mason, Jimmy 141
Mason, Paul 4, 9, 10, 21, 311, 312, 313
Massie, Alec 135
Matthews, Stanley 14, 150, 179
Meadowbank 57
Melrose, Harry 214, 215, 217, 218
Metz 342
Michie, Scott 347
Middlesbrough 30, 71, 73, 79, 92, 97, 105, 125, 130, 135
Mike, Leon 45
Millar, David 216, 217
Miller, Alex 30–1, 33, 274, 332, 351
Miller, Denis 15
Miller, Joe 21, 25
Miller, Kenny 26
Miller, Willie: early years 329; ix, 4, 50, 135, 236, 252, 259, 266, 267, 275, 276, 290, 292, 293, 296, 298, 300, 301, 307, 312, 313, 317, 318, 319–20, 321, 322, 328, 329–33, 340, 341, 351, 352, 362, 363; as Dons manager 9–10,12, 21–3, 24, 29, 30, 310, 331–2, 341, 351, 356; Ferguson on Miller, as player 319, 329, as manager 331–2
Mills, Mick 272, 273
Mills, Willie xiv, 84, 107, 118, 135, 136, 137–9, 140, 143, 145, 147, 156, 157, 191, 200, 262, 362
Millwall 342
Milne, Baillie Alexander 73, 76, 78, 98
Milne, Hamish 17–18
Milne, Dr J. Ellis 96
Milne, Stewart 16, 17–20, 29–30, 39, 41, 42, 43, 50, 52, 53, 54, 56–9, 62, 79, 355
Milne, Vic 73, 97–8, 101, 103, 104, 107, 125
Milne, Willie 92
Milne, W. 103
Mitchell, Brian 300

Mitchell, Jimmy 176, 188, 189, 191, 194, 198, 200, 202, 203, 204
Mitchell, Moyra 222
Mitchell, Roger 19
Mitchell, Sir Thomas 162
Mitchell, William 149, 151, 164, 171, 172, 198–9, 200, 209, 222, 232
Moir, Alec 101, 105
Moir, Billy 150
Mollers-Neilsen, Tommy 48
Montreal All Stars 204
Montrose 71, 121, 130, 164, 302, 339, 347
Moore, Paddy 121, 140
Morrison, Bobby 292
Morrison, Reggie 200, 201, 350
Mortensen, Lief 217
Mortensen, Stan 150–1
Morton 75, 87, 88, 106, 134, 141, 143, 176, 181–2, 217, 242, 257, 276, 282, 313, 321, 330, 340, 342, 343, 346
Morton, Alan 93, 110, 111, 112, 113
Motherwell xii, 5, 22, 23, 25, 28, 75, 82, 95, 105, 113, 117, 187, 256, 273, 291, 337, 341, 342, 347, 359
Mugiemoss 101, 120, 131, 135, 240
Muir, Jimmy 82, 85
Muir, Malcolm 124
Munro, Dod 134
Munro, Francis 214, 218
Munro, John 96
Murdoch, Bobby 214, 227, 228
Murray, Alick 183
Murray, Bertie 74, 78, 85, 88, 92, 93, 96
Murray, C.P. 102
Murray, George 228, 244, 258, 329
Murray, Steve 226, 238
Mutch, Cody 79, 86, 88
Mutch, Sandy 221–2

Nairn County 342
Narey, Dave 30
Naughtie, Jim 288
Neilson, Charlie 94, 96
Neilson, J.H. 96
Nelson, Sarah 50
Newcastle United 4, 72, 93, 149, 172, 175, 186, 319, 321, 337, 342
Newell, Mike 31

Nichol, W.D. 87, 89
Nicholas, Charlie 4, 9, 310, 312
Nicholas, Peter 310
Nithsdale Wanderers 123, 125
Niven, George 188
North-Eastern League 155
Northern League 71, 72, 74
Northern Light, The 60, 355–6
Norwich 22
Nottingham Forest 335
Notts County 180, 258, 265

O'Donoghue, Ross 247
O'Farrell, Frank 243
Ogston, John 212, 217
O'Hagan, Charlie 79, 85, 87, 88, 93, 133
'Old Beach Ender' see Gavin, Chris
Oldham 6, 28
O'Neil, Joe 188–9, 190, 200, 350
Ontario All Stars 204
Orion 70, 76
Ormond, Willie 213, 254

Paatelainen, Mixu 12, 22
Palme, Olaf 303, 325
Paper Tiger 355
Parker, Bobby 179–80
Partick Thistle 24, 78, 88, 95, 166, 234, 257, 264, 266, 313, 345
Paterson, R. 200
Paton, Johnny 95, 105, 111
Pattillo, Johnny 147–8, 159, 161, 178, 200
Pearson, Tommy: as player, 126, 173, 175–6, 178–9, 183, 186, 246; as Dons manager 209, 210, 211, 212, 213, 235, 241, 346, 350, 362
Peebles Rovers 183
Pelé 288
Penman, Andy 217
Perry, Mark 36
Persson, Orjan 217
Peterhead 80, 102–3, 131, 140, 329
Petersen, Jens 214, 217, 218
Philip, George 77, 107, 120
Philip, Jimmy 7, 72, 76, 77–80, 82, 87, 95, 98, 101, 105, 106–7, 126
Philip, William 79, 98, 108, 116, 124
Pirie, Tom 125
Pittodrie Park xi, xiv, 40, 70–1; club buys

ground 74; developments 125, 133; during Second World War 148; floodlighting installed 212; ground fire 239; south-side roofing 270; Richard Donald Stand 13, 14, 17, 18, 40, 43, 333, 339, 359; first all-seated, all-covered stadium in Britain 14, 281
Plymouth Argyle 125, 149, 172
Port Seton Athletic 244
Portadown 345
Porteous, Ian 300
Porterfield, Ian 4, 8, 310–11, 322, 331, 340, 343, 350–1, 355
Porto 298–9
Portsmouth 105
Prentice, John 188
Preston North End 112, 116, 125
PSV Eindhoven 9, 311

Qualifying Cup 71, 74–5
Queen of the South 140, 156, 187, 267
Queen's Park 76, 93, 106, 112, 164, 176, 212, 215, 216, 221, 229, 317, 340
Queen's Park Rangers 186, 352

Rae, James 76
Raith Rovers 22, 73, 94, 97, 129, 149, 207, 212, 267, 310
Rangers 4, 5–6, 12–13, 21, 24, 34, 36–8, 45, 46, 47, 57, 78, 83, 86, 88–9, 89–90, 93, 100, 111, 138, 149, 150, 157, 161–3, 171, 187–8, 188–90, 207–8, 211, 238, 249, 255–7, 258, 260, 263, 267, 274–5, 296, 300, 310, 311, 312, 319–20, 323, 330, 337, 342, 346, 356; consider joining English Premier League 19, 63, 64, 332–3; Old Firm domination xii, 22, 26, 33, 34, 42, 56, 64, 141, 248, 303, 320, 324, 327, 332, 341, 349, 359; in transfers x, 8, 26–7, 30, 32, 76, 112, 116, 126, 155, 158, 175, 216, 217, 220, 226, 232, 304, 317, 340, 345
Rankin, Andy 101, 103, 105, 106, 125
Ravn, Jorgen 217
Reading 310, 340, 342
Real Madrid xiii, 15, 289, 290–1, 343
Real Zaragoza 220
Red Final, The 355

Reid, Alec 118
Reid, Gordon 355
Reilly, Laurie 213
Renfrew Juniors 235
Rennes, France 29
Renton 74, 81, 109
Reykjavik, Iceland 55
Richardson, Lee 12, 13, 22
Riddoch, Ian 64
Riley, Jeff 357
Ritchie, Andy 276
Ritchie, George 124
Ritchie, Steve 257, 258
Robb, Davie 228, 230, 238, 241, 242, 243, 249, 250–1, 252, 347
Robbie, John 151, 174, 222
Robertson, Arthur 101
Robertson, David 6, 9, 10, 12
Robertson, Gordon 354
Robertson, Henry 222
Robertson, Jimmy 73, 74, 78, 96, 97, 103
Robertson, John 93
Robertson, Mark 354
Robson, Bobby 272, 273
Robson, Bryan 319
Roddie, Andy 9
Rogan, Anton 313
Rooney, Benny 236
Ross, Alec 105
Ross, Eddie 240
Ross County 340
Rougvie, Doug 28, 264, 266, 276, 290, 299, 300, 320, 321, 322, 328, 338–9, 343, 345, 351, 363
Rowson, David 38
Russell, Billy 83, 94, 126
Russell, Dave 149
RWD Molenbeek, Belgium 255

St Bernard 72
St Clements 160, 185
St Johnstone 5, 22, 46, 71, 131, 148, 187, 200, 217, 218, 257, 301
St Mirren x, 8, 28, 30, 48, 187, 195–6, 200, 207, 208, 249, 254, 260, 261, 263, 264, 265, 270, 274, 282, 298, 299, 300, 302, 310–11, 312, 317, 318, 321, 330, 334, 343, 345, 347
Sangster, Dr Jock 93
Savill, Peter 62

Scanlon, Ian 258, 265, 266
Schmeichel, Peter 31, 33
Scholes, Paul 31
Scorgie, Johnny 92
Scotland v England 97, 104, 110, 112–13,
    121, 138, 140, 142, 150, 157, 159,
    181, 200, 236, 347
Scotland v Ireland 92, 104, 174
Scotland v Norway 4
Scotland v Wales 104
Scott, Jocky 4, 7, 9, 15, 77, 249, 252,
    330, 347, 355, 358
Scott, Susan 354
Scott, Teddy 31, 329, 332, 340, 348,
    349–52, 362
Scottish Alliance Cup 121
Scottish Daily Mail 179, 210
Scottish Enterprise (Grampian) 41
Scottish Executive 42
Scottish Football Assocation (SFA) 105–6,
    125, 170, 201, 244, 256, 342
Scottish Football League 72, 96
Scottish North-Eastern League 148–9
Scottish Premier League 19, 22, 39, 62,
    64, 241, 248–9, 358–9
Scunthorpe 101,290
Sealey, Les 326, 336
Second World War 114, 148–9, 151, 158,
    161
Servette, Switzerland 303
Sexton, Dave 343
Shankly, Bill 8, 235
Shankly, Bob 8, 235, 324, 353
Sharp, Willie 166
Shaw, Betty (Mrs Dick Donald) 16
Shaw, Davie 167, 188, 196; as manager
    199–200, 201, 203, 207, 245, 209,
    350
Shaw, Jock (Tiger) 162, 199
Shawfield 144
Shearer, Bobby 207–8
Shearer, Duncan 12, 25, 28
Sheffield United 150, 337
Sheffield Wednesday 149
Shewan, Ally 214, 217, 219, 346
Shinner, Bert 71
Shrewsbury 339, 345
Simpson, Billy 188
Simpson, J.J. 92
Simpson, Neil 4, 42, 276, 279, 283, 289,
    290, 297, 300, 321, 328, 346, 351,
    363
Simpson, Peter 75, 87, 134
Sion, Switzerland 276, 349
Skol League Cup 4, 12, 21, 310, 311,
    312–13
Skonto Riga, Latvia 23
Skovdahl, Ebbe 29, 32–4, 45, 47, 59, 63,
    64, 237, 332; his youth policy 39,
    45, 47–8
Sky Television 43, 56
Slavia Sofia, Bulgaria 220
Sleigh, George 91, 104
Slessor, G. 103
Smith, Alex (manager) 4, 6–7, 8–11, 15,
    21, 23, 50, 311, 313, 331, 343,
    347, 351, 355–6, 358
Smith, Alex 217
Smith, Billy 194, 200
Smith, Dave 3, 26, 214, 217, 218
Smith, Gary 6, 12, 29, 354
Smith, George 312
Smith, Gordon 150, 159, 167, 213
Smith, Jimmy 101, 103, 105, 106, 111,
    121
Smith, Jimmy ('Jinky') xiv, 3, 178, 217,
    218, 219, 233, 281, 351
Smith, Joe 233, 244, 252, 330
Smith, Steve 133–4, 135
Snelders, Theo 4–5, 9, 10, 311, 313
Solberg, Thomas 34, 35–6, 38
Souness, Graeme 33, 271, 296
Southampton 79, 160, 180, 210, 342
Soye, Jimmy 87, 88, 89, 92, 133
Spain, Richard 222
Spence, Stewart 16, 51
Spencer, Sam 124
Spiers, Gardner 48
Standard Liège 45, 220
Stanton, Pat 264
Stark, Billy 48, 263, 299, 300, 301, 302,
    344
Stavrum, Arild 34, 36, 38
Stead, Willie 79
Steadward, Jimmy 166
Steel, Billy 93
Stein, Colin 217
Stein, Jock 26, 191, 212, 214, 215, 217,
    222, 228, 233, 239, 258, 260, 263,
    288, 302, 317, 318, 320, 321, 324

Stenhousemuir 8, 24, 71
Stephen, John 50, 52
Stewart, Hal 217
Stewart, Jim 274
Stewart, W. 69
Stillie, Derek 31
Stirling Albion 8, 207, 249, 267, 301
Stoke City 219, 243
Storrie, Jim 214, 219
Strachan, Gordon ix, 29, 30, 31, 178, 200,
    258, 263, 264, 265, 266, 268, 270,
    271, 272, 273, 274, 276, 279, 283,
    289–90, 291, 297, 299, 300, 310,
    320, 321, 322, 326, 335, 339,
    341–2, 349, 351, 352, 362, 363
Strathclyde Juniors 158
Strauss, Billy 135, 136, 140, 141, 142,
    143, 144, 147, 148, 157, 161, 200,
    201
Struth, Bill 211, 240
Stuart, Alex 254
Sullivan, Dom 250, 252
Summer Cup 213
Sunday Mail 159, 252–3
Sunday Standard 277–9, 293–4
Sunderland 79, 81, 91, 93, 129, 130, 310,
    330–1
Sunnybank 350, 352
Supporters Direct 51
Sutherland, George 101
Sutherland, T. Scott 208–9
Swan, Harry 201
Swift, Frank 211
Swindon Town 12, 180–1
Symon, Scot 26

Taggart, Ian 358
Taylor, D. 93
Taylor, George xii, 160, 161, 162, 163,
    167, 172, 200
Taylor, Ian 238
Taylor, Lenny 337
Taylor, Tommy 176
Teddy Scott Trophy 31
televising football 19, 56, 63, 319, 358–9;
    collapse of ITV Digital 43–4
Temple, Bob 142, 143
Templeton, Bobby 72
Tiernan, Fergus 347
Tirana, Albania 277

Third Lanark 92, 93, 99, 105, 118, 141,
    161, 187, 248
Thomson, Johnny 37, 83
Thomson, Peter 162
Thomson, Scott 25
Thornton, Willie 190
Toner, Willie 210
Tontine Athletic 81
Torino 13
Toronto All-Scots 134
Tottenham Hotspur 30, 92, 151, 216, 245,
    268
Travers, Paddy: as player 87, 88, 89, 90,
    92, 93; as coach 101; as manager 7,
    83, 107–8, 109–10, 111, 113,
    117–18, 123, 124, 125, 126,
    128–9, 131, 135, 137, 138, 139,
    144, 145, 149, 157, 183, 211
Turnbull, Eddie: as player 167, 168, 212;
    as manager 213, 214, 215, 216,
    217, 218–19, 220, 221, 224, 225,
    229, 238, 241, 346, 347, 348, 350

UEFA Cup 9, 22, 29, 42, 47, 54, 63, 255,
    272
Ujpest Dosza, Hungary 298
Ullevi Stadium see Gothenburg

Vale of Leven 84, 116
Valgaeren, Joos 46
Valur, Iceland 13
van der Ark, Willem 10, 311
van der Ven, Peter 4, 5
Varga, Zoltan xiv, 4, 114, 178, 200,
    245–7, 281, 312, 330, 362
Victory International (Scotland v England)
    159, 200
Victoria United 80, 79
Vilnius, Lithuania 29
Vizard, Ted 104

Waddell, Andy 211
Waddell, Willie (ex-Strathclyde Juniors)
    150, 158, 188, 212, 214
Waddell, Willie (ex-Renfrew Juniors) 158,
    167, 172, 207
Waddington, Tom 243
Wagstaffe, Dave 219
Waldron, Ernie 149, 178, 254
Walker, Bobby 179

Walker, Joe 92, 133, 134
Walker, Nicky 29
Walker, Tommy 150
Wallace, Rod 37
Wallace, J. 200
Wallace, Jock 258, 260
Wallace, Willie 214, 228
Wark, John 272
Warnock, Dave 126, 139
Warrender, Jim 348
Washington Whips 219–20
Waterschei, Belgium 282–4, 286, 345
Watson, Andy 265, 266, 273, 337, 341
Watson, C.G. 96
Watson, Frank 178, 183–4
Watson, Fred 92, 96
Watson, Greg 9
Watson, Tom 81
Watt, Clarence 101
Watt, Dave 355
Watt, Michael 5, 9
Webster, Jack (Vancouver journalist) 204
Wee Alickie 183, 184, 193, 287
Weir, James 76
Weir, Peter 48, 263, 272–3, 276, 277,
    278, 283, 290, 291, 297, 298, 300,
    321, 343–4, 345, 351, 363
Welsh, Brian 21
Welsh, Don 150
West Ham 236, 336
Westwood MP, Joseph 169
Whyte, Alex 51
Whyte, Derek 30, 38, 45, 63
Whyte, Jim (father) 346
Whyte, Jim (Chalky) (son) 214, 217, 218,
    219, 346, 347, 348
Willem II club 311
Williams, Evan 55, 227
Williams, Stan xii, 121, 146, 155, 157–8,
    160, 161, 162, 163, 167, 168–9,
    172–4, 200, 230

Williamson, Billy 244, 252, 330
Willoughby, Alec 225, 238
Wilson, George 88, 92, 133
Wilson, Harold 113
Wilson, Jimmy 214, 217, 282, 348
Winchester, Ernie 217, 218–19
Windass, Dean 28
Winters, Robbie 25, 37, 46, 63, 356
Wilson, Robert 19
Wiseman, J.T. 102
Wishart, Bobby 195, 197, 200, 202, 208
Wolverhampton 150, 219, 342
Wood, Johnny 92
Woodburn, Willie 189
Woodthorpe, Colin 22
World Cup 191, 254, 259, 273, 302, 327,
    341, 359–60
Wright, Alec 93, 96, 97, 107, 125
Wright, Alex 101
Wright, Paul 352
Wright, Stephen 9, 26
Wyllie, Harry 76, 79
Wyllie, Jock 87, 88, 90, 92, 98, 133
Wyllie, W. 97
Wyness, Keith 62–3

Yorke, Dwight 31
Yorston, Benny xiv, 107, 119, 120–1, 124,
    128–30 136, 185, 362
Yorston, Harry 181, 183, 185–6, 188,
    189, 192–3, 195, 196, 200, 201,
    202, 203, 204, 205–6, 262, 267
Young, Alec 176, 188, 189, 191, 194,
    196, 200, 203, 204, 350, 352
Young, Darren 45, 347
Young, Derek 45, 347
Young, George 188
Young, Willie 233, 234, 244–5
Yule, Bobby 101

Zerouali, Hicham 34, 36, 38, 45, 46, 63